Developments in Local Government Finance

To Werner Pommerehne (1943–1994)

Developments in Local Government Finance

Theory and Policy

Edited by

Giancarlo Pola
Professor of Public Finance, University of Ferrara, Italy

George France
Senior Research Fellow, National Research Council, Italy

and

Rosella Levaggi
*Research Fellow, Institute of Economics and Finance,
University of Genoa, Italy*

Edward Elgar
Cheltenham, UK • Brookfield, US

Published by
Edward Elgar Publishing Limited
8 Lansdown Place
Cheltenham
Glos GL50 2HU
UK

Edward Elgar Publishing Company
Old Post Road
Brookfield
Vermont 05036
US

British Library Cataloguing in Publication Data
Developments in local government finance: theory and
  policy
  I. Finance, Public 2. Local government
  I. Pola, Giancarlo II. France, George III. Levaggi, Rosella
  336'.014

Library of Congress Cataloguing in Publication Data
Developments in local government finance: theory and policy / edited
  by Giancarlo Pola, George France, and Rosella Levaggi
    Papers presented at a seminar held in Ferrara, Italy, Sept. 1994
    Includes index.
    1. Local finance—Congresses. 2. Local government—Congresses.
  I. Pola, Giancarlo. II. France, George. III. Levaggi, Rosella,
  1962–   .
  HJ9105.D48   1996
  336'.014—dc20   95–42286
                                                                  CIP
ISBN 1 85898 377 0

Printed and bound in Great Britain by
Hartnolls Limited, Bodmin, Cornwall

Contents

Figures

Tables

List of Contributors

Glen Bramley	Heriot-Watt University, Edinburgh, UK.
Paul J. Chapman	UK Department of the Environment, London, UK.
Howard Chernick	Hunter College, CUNY, New York, USA.
Bernard Dafflon	University of Fribourg, Fribourg, Switzerland.
Alan Duncan	University of York, York, UK
Peter Else	Sheffield University Management School, Sheffield, UK.
Lars P. Feld	St. Gallen University, St. Gallen, Switzerland.
George France	National Research Council, Rome, Italy.
Guy Gilbert	University of Paris X ,Paris, France.
David King	University of Stirling, Stirling, UK.
Gebhard Kirchgässner	University of St.Gallen, St. Gallen, Switzerland.
Anthony J. Laramie	Merrimack College, North Andover, USA.
Rosella Levaggi	University of Genoa, Genoa, Italy.
Douglas Mair	Heriot-Watt University, Edinburgh, UK.
Werner Pommerehne †	University of Saarland, Saarbrücken, Germany and University of Zurich, Zurich, Switzerland.
Rémy Prud'homme	University of Paris XII, Paris, France.
Andrew Reschovsky	University of Wisconsin-Madison, Madison and US Department of the Treasury,Washington D.C., USA.
Yvon Rocaboy	University of Rennes, Rennes, France.
Peter Smith	University of York, York, UK
Stephen Smith	Institute for Fiscal Studies, London, UK.
Erich Thöni	University of Innsbruck, Innsbruck, Austria.

Acknowledgement

The editors thank all the contributors for their cooperation in the preparation of this book, in particular by providing their papers on diskette. Much additional work was needed, however, to harmonize the different contributions. In this the editors were greatly helped by the word processing skills of Marco Salgarelli and Nicola Simoni to whom they express their profound gratitude. The costs of the Ferrara seminar at which the papers were first presented were financed in part with contributions from the Italian Ministry of the University and Scientific Research and the Italian National Research Council.

Introduction

Problems of local government and local finance continue to be at the centre of the policy debate in most countries. This is the case both in federal countries and in those with relatively centralized systems of government. There is considerable heterogeneity among countries in terms of organization and financing of local government, in patterns of change and in priorities for reform, but a number of the problems being faced are remarkably similar. What is interesting is how economists from different national contexts can use quite different approaches to study similar issues.

In September 1994, 20 European and American researchers specializing in local government finance gathered together in Ferrara, an elegant renaissance city in northern Italy. The seminar was held in the suggestive surroundings of the late fifteenth-century Palazzo Giordani on the campus of the University of Ferrara. The majority of participants were British members of the Study Group on Local Government Economics who had generously agreed to break with tradition and move the venue of their periodic meeting from the United Kingdom to Italy. The editors, in particular Giancarlo Pola who organized the seminar, wish to thank them.

This book contains the papers presented at the Ferrara seminar, revised by the authors under the coordination of the editors. The individual papers will have their intrinsic interest for the contribution they make to the different subspecialisms of local government and finance. That apart, however, at first glance they may seem quite heterogeneous. A reading of them will reveal instead some important common aspects. One is the systematic use of theoretical concepts and principles in the analysis of policy issues. Another is the emphasis on institutions. What emerges in a striking way from the book is that arrangements for the intergovernmental distribution of responsibility for service provision and revenue-raising power are under continuous scholarly review. A leitmotiv of the collection of essays presented here is the importance *de facto* of 'localness' in government and the need therefore for real, as opposed to formal, devolution of power. Related to this, another recurrent theme is that local government must be accountable and hence a common interest for many authors is how to ensure this. The book is divided into four parts. Inevitably, not all will agree with how the papers have been allocated among these, particularly in the light of the comments just made. The criterion used by the editors has been to assign a paper on the basis of what they consider to be the central issue it addresses.

In the first part of the book, 'New Solutions to Old Problems', a number of rather traditional issues in local government are addressed using modern approaches. Thus, Bramley analyses the question of needs and demand for local services. His concern is with the factors determining local service usage by different income-level households. The database for his multivariate model is that produced by a recently completed field study on current living standards in Britain. The model, applied to three local services, is quite effective in distinguishing between demand, felt-need and rationing as determinants of service usage. The chapter provides interesting findings on the redistributive effects of expenditure for the three services studied. They confirm that local service expenditure is not systematically pro-poor, not even for the poorest households.

Duncan and Smith's chapter also considers the issue of needs. Its objective is to develop statistical methods for estimating 'necessary' expenditure levels for local services. To this end, the authors develop a model aimed at distinguishing as much as possible between the influence on expenditure of 'legitimate' factors (needs) and 'illegitimate' factors (so-called 'endowment effects'). It is clear that the latter cannot form part of a formula for determining the allocation of the central grant to local authorities. The model is applied to inpatient hospital services and local government expenditure. Duncan and Smith show how even quite sophisticated statistical techniques for estimating local spending needs can be disturbed by the presence of illegitimate factors.

The chapter by Chapman studies the issue of local government expenditure needs from yet another angle. The basis for allocating central funding for local government in the UK since 1990–91 has been the Standard Spending Assessments (SSAs). The chapter evaluates factor analysis as a technique for selecting social and economic deprivation measures for the SSAs, the criteria used in the selection process for the SSAs and the underlying methodology for the SSAs. Chapman suggests that statistical analysis played an important part in the recent review of deprivation measures used for the SSAs, but observes that this did not substitute entirely for the use of judgement in the selection of deprivation measures.

Part one concludes with the chapter of King which examines the issue – so far never really resolved in the literature – of the optimal size of local government. Britain is currently undergoing a drastic reform of the boundaries and competences of the two levels of subcentral government, the districts and the counties. The intention is wherever possible to merge these jurisdictions with a view to optimizing resource utilization. King suggests that the 'general' optimal size can be deduced from that for a number of key competences, for example education, social services, roads and policing. In the event that there is one optimal size for the key competences, this should be adopted for all remaining competences. King's chapter reaffirms the utility of the concept of marginalism – in this case in the study of the optimum size of local government – when he concludes that 'local authorities should be enlarged in size so long as the extra gains exceed the extra losses'.

The second part of the book, 'Applying Theory to the Real World', consists of four chapters. All involve attempts to submit theoretical models of local finance to empirical testing. The countries considered are France, Italy and the US. The '*taxe professionnelle*' is a key local tax in France. It is a business tax and its base is the rental value of the assets of a firm plus a certain proportion of its wage and salary bill. Just as with the '*Gewerbesteuer*' in Germany, it is the major revenue source of local government. This is so despite the fact that in the literature business taxes tend not to be considered 'good' local taxes. Prud'homme's chapter examines in detail the factors underlying the unexpected growth over time in the base of the *taxe professionnelle* in relation to GNP. The chapter also describes how the communes showed themselves ready to use their power to increase the rate of the tax. The combined increases in the base and rate of the *taxe professionnelle* have created what is considered to be an excessive tax burden for businesses. Indeed, the French government has felt compelled to intervene and assume part of the liability of firms for this tax.

France is also the context for the chapter by Gilbert and Rocaboy. Between 1982 and 1986, there was a major transfer of competences to the *communes* and *départements*. According to the authors, this devolution was quite rational although it was not accompanied by the radical reform of local finance which many observers felt was needed. Under the reform, each tier of French government was assigned a specific 'block of competences'; in only a limited number of cases was there to be sharing of competences. Gilbert and Rocaboy focus on the geographical variation in expenditure for welfare services which are a *département* competence. They build a model to explain this. On the basis of this, they conclude – going against the conventional wisdom – that the 'resource' factor is at least as important as the 'needs' factor in explaining geographical variation in welfare expenditure. If one *département* spends more for the welfare of its citizens than another *département*, it does so also because it is richer and not simply because it has more poor among its population.

Part II remains in the Mediterranean area with the chapter of Levaggi. This presents a model aimed at helping to explain the spending behaviour of Italian local communes and intercommunal variation in expenditure. As a result of organizational and fiscal reforms in the early 1990s, communes in Italy enjoy considerable discretion in managing their budgets. This came after a long period during which expenditure was financed by guaranteed central funding allocated mainly on the basis of the historical expenditure criterion. Central grants are no longer the major source of revenue for local governments. An important new property tax has been introduced which is administered directly by local governments. Starting from this situation, Levaggi designs a utility-maximizing model for local government based on the well-known concept of incremental budgeting. This model is tested using data for a sample of 93 communes in an attempt to predict how expenditure patterns change as a result of the availability of revenue from the new property tax. Subcentral revenue and expenditure have non-marginal macroeconomic effects, particularly in federal systems.

The chapter by Laramie and Mair examines the macroeconomic impact of state and local governments in the US using a model based on a Kaleckian macroeconomic theory of tax incidence. This considers both income distribution and fiscal incidence. It is assumed that the economy operates with a surplus of labour and equipment and that, therefore, the incidence of various taxes is determined by expenditure flows. Empirical estimates presented in the chapter suggest that the reaction to taxes is minimal, at least in the short run. In particular, the profits tax has no negative effect on net profits or household income. This leads the authors to suggest that the federal government should increase its use of the profits tax to finance grants to subcentral governments.

The third part of the book, 'Local Government and Local Policymaking: Autonomy and Constraints', contains contributions which suggest just how wide the field is in which local governments have or could have an important role in policymaking. Realistically, however, this role must be constrained. It is obvious that optimality in the provision of local services does not depend only on the jurisdictional size. The intrinsic efficiency of the governmental machinery in delivering a given level of service using the minimum quantity of resources is also important. In his chapter, Else argues that the production of local services can 'fail', remaining inside the efficiency frontier. This can occur when one or both of two conditions hold: the preferences of citizen-users for services differ from those of local government managers; there is information asymmetry favouring those who deliver the services rather than those who use them. Else suggests that perhaps the most effective way of increasing production efficiency is to continue to constrain the budgets of political decisionmakers. Responsibility for health care tends in many countries to be shared among different tiers of government. However, the particular nature of the service in question means that considerable autonomy on the expenditure side of the budget has to be given to the local level.

France's chapter asks if differences in health-care governance systems help to explain why a national health service seems to have performed less well in Italy than in the UK. A key difference here is the relatively weaker vertical line of control in the government of health in Italy. Subcentral government accountability in health will probably be strengthened with the recent transfer to the regions of significant responsibility for funding health care. However, France cautions that quasi-market reforms currently being introduced in the SSN could weaken the capacity of subcentral government to control health expenditure.

Thöni's chapter tackles quite a different question, namely the role of subnational governments in shaping European Union regional policy. Thöni argues that the introduction of a supranational level with competences for regional policy may have significant implications for intergovernmental relations. In particular, the freedom of action of subnational authorities in federal states risks being circumscribed. The author suggests that subnational governments should have a greater role in formulating European Union regional policies. This is warranted by their special knowledge and understanding of local conditions and by their key role in the implementation of Union regional policy. The role of subnational governments in Union policymaking should therefore be restored where there is a risk of its being downgraded (as, for example, in Germany) and strengthened where it is weak or even nonexistent (in unitary countries). Responsible management of the accounts of a local government is a golden rule which holds irrespective of the level of government at which policies are formulated. This is not mere rhetoric: the current literature contains normative and positive notions which justify greater fiscal discipline and greater control over local and intermediate government borrowing.

Dafflon's chapter considers this question with specific reference to the Swiss communes. These governments enjoy wide fiscal autonomy and, in line with the principle of subsidiarity, have a large number of competences. Dafflon observes that the budgeting behaviour of Swiss communes is generally responsible but argues that this is not spontaneous: budgetary discipline is imposed exogenously via appropriate constitutional rules. The author observes that limits on indebtedness by local government are seen as necessary for good government by much of the literature and by Swiss public opinion. Accountability is an attainable goal as long as the appropriate institutions and procedures are chosen and provided there is no fear of appearing 'out of fashion'.

The fourth and last part of the book, 'Fiscal Issues for Existing and Future Federations', deals with some of the problems resulting from the fact that subnational governments in federations may enjoy considerable freedom in the kind of tax systems they adopt. The federations considered are the United States, the European Union and Switzerland. The chapter by

Chernick and Reschovsky focuses on explaining differences in the progressivity of state and local income taxes in the United States. They develop a model based on the premise that fiscal interest groups play an important role in determining the degree of progressivity chosen by state and local governments. The more cohesive these interest groups are, the stronger their influence will tend to be. However, an important factor in explaining the underlying incidence pattern of state and local tax systems may be the extent to which citizens are economically mobile. This is because, the authors hypothesize, economic mobility weakens cohesion. The econometric results given in the chapter are generally consistent with the interest group model of tax choice but are inconclusive regarding the impact of income mobility.

With the chapter by Stephen Smith, attention moves from states which are already 'united' in a powerful and historically consolidated federation to a federation *in fieri*, one in the process of being created, as is the case with the European Union. The author asks if growing European integration will constrain the nature and level of local taxes used by member states and, if so, whether this will necessitate intervention by the supranational European government. Smith observes that, even more than in case of the United States, in the European Union we are faced with a basic tradeoff: there are potential benefits from diversity which justify instruments and policies tailored for the specific conditions of the individual member states; on the other hand, excessive differences between states generates efficiency costs, suggesting the need for harmonization (as in the case of local business taxation) or at the very least for coordination of policies for financing local government.

The chapter by Pommerehne, Kirchgässner and Feld suggests that useful lessons for the fiscal constitution of the European Union can also be drawn from the experience of other federations. The literature gives increasing importance to allocative inefficiencies of competing fiscal systems. These are often accompanied by negative distributive side-effects. Pommerehne, Kirchgässner and Feld investigate empirically the allocative and distributive properties of different fiscal systems co-existing within the Swiss Confederation. Fiscal competition seems to cause intercantonal mobility of high-income citizens. This takes place without causing breakdown in the supply of public goods or preventing some degree of income redistribution. The chapter may surprise somewhat when it suggests that in a future Europe the supranational level of government be financed via general and proportional taxes and progressive taxes be assigned to lower levels of government.

In Memoriam: Werner W. Pommerehne

Suddenly and totally unexpected, Werner W. Pommerehne died on 8 October 1994, of a heart attack, at his home in Sarreguemines, France. He was one of the few German economists engaged in Public Economics who are internationally known. After studying in Freiburg, Berlin and Basel he received his doctorate from the University of Konstanz and his habilitation from the University of Zürich. In 1986, he assumed a chair in Public Economics at the Free University of Berlin and since 1989 has held a chair at the University of Saarland. In addition, he was visiting professor at many other universities, for example, at Paris, Poitiers, Geneva and Vienna.

Werner Pommerehne was a political public economist. He was never interested in welfare considerations *per se*, which dominate large parts of modern public finance, but he always looked at the political institutions, which generate specific political and economic outcomes. In this respect, he was much closer to new institutional economics than to traditional public finance (see, for example, 1990). He investigated institutional arrangements at all governmental levels, be it federal, state, or local. In one of his earlier contributions (1978) he compared the different democratic systems of Swiss municipalities, which range from very pure direct democracies, where once a year the citizens come together in the 'Gemeindeversammlung' to decide about local public issues, to pure representative democracies where only the local parliaments decide without the possibility of referenda, including several mixed types with obligatory and/or mandatory referenda for certain issues. He was able to show not only that the median voter model works better the more direct a democracy is, but also that voter preferences are taken more into account. This reinforced his deep belief that elements of direct democracy should be included at all governmental levels.

He was an empirical public economist. He was rarely ever interested in theoretical models *per se*, but rather used such models to derive hypotheses about the performance of public institutions which he then tested employing econometric methods. The questions he was interested in were questions about how the real world works, not about the properties of theoretical models. He had a strong interest in different methods for the evaluation of preferences for public goods (1987), and he made a lot of comparative institutional analysis, be it, for example, about garbage collection in Swiss municipalities (1976), about federal structures (1977), about the development of public expenditure in federal states like Switzerland and

Germany (1988), or about the amount of redistribution in different countries (1979, 1993). In addition, he also used experiments to explore the behaviour of individuals and to check the propositions of economic theory (see, for example, 1981, 1982).

Local public finance was important to him for two different reasons. First, adhering to the principle of subsidiarity he was convinced that as many tasks as possible should be performed at the local level. This conviction was only secondarily based on welfare arguments *à la* Tiebout, that is on economic efficiency, but primarily on 'political efficiency': politicians can be better controlled the lower the level is on which a task is performed. Therefore, it has to be (empirically) analyzed which tasks can actually be performed on the local level (1991). Second, and not less important, he saw local communities as kinds of laboratories, where experiments with different political institutions could be performed. These were not only the questions of direct versus representative democracy, but also of public versus private production of public services (1976) or of private provision of public goods (1994).

The question of direct democracy is one of the subjects where he not only wrote major contributions but also was personally engaged. He hoped that his research could convince at least some people (in Germany and other European countries) of the advantages of a direct democratic system, which he had learned to know and to value in Switzerland. Another area was the analysis of drug markets, where he voted for a restricted liberalization. And, last but not least, his work as a director of the Europa Institut at the University of Saarland was intended to make the European Union more democratic and more federal. Thus, without violating scientific standards, Werner Pommerehne used his scientific potential to promote those political objectives of which he was convinced. In this sense, he was also a political economist.

There are several other research areas which should be mentioned like – not least – the economics of the arts, where he made important contributions (see, for example, 1989). As his voluminous list of publications shows, he was very cooperative: he wrote many of his papers with very different co-authors. In sum, European public economics has lost one of its most outstanding and productive members. However, what is worse, I personally – and many others, too – have lost a close friend.

Gebhard Kirchgässner

CITED WORKS BY WERNER W. POMMEREHNE

'Quantitative aspects of federalism: a study of six countries', in W.E. Oates (ed.), *The Political Economy of Fiscal Federalism*, Lexington/Toronto: DC Heath, 1977, pp. 275–355.

'Institutional approaches to public expenditure: empirical evidence from Swiss municipalities', *Journal of Public Economics*, **9** (1978), pp. 255–80.

'Postfisc income inequality: a comparison of the United States and West Germany', in J.R. Moroney (ed.), *Income Inequality: Trends and International Comparisons*, Lexington/Toronto: DC Heath, 1979, pp. 69–81. (Together with E. Smolensky and E. Dalrymple)

'Free riding and collective action: an experiment in public microeconomics', *Quarterly Journal of Economics*, **96** (1981), pp. 689–704. (Together with Friedrich Schneider)

'Economic theory of choice and the preference reversal phenomenon: a reexamination', *American Economic Review*, **72** (1982), pp. 569–74. (Together with Friedrich Schneider and Peter Zweifel).

Präferenzen für öffentliche Güter: Ansätze zu ihrer Erfassung, Mohr (Siebeck), Tübingen 1987.

'Government spending in federal systems: a comparison between Germany and Switzerland', in J.A. Lybeck and M Henrekson (eds), *Explaining the Growth of Government*, Amsterdam: North-Holland 1988, pp. 327–56. (Together with Gebhard Kirchgässner)

Muses and Markets: Explorations in the Economics of the Arts, Oxford: Blackwell, 1989, second edition 1990. (Together with Bruno S. Frey; translations into Italian, French, German, and Japanese)

'The empirical relevance of comparative institutional analysis', *European Economic Review*, **34** (1990), pp. 458–69.

'Fiscal interaction of central city and suburbs: the case of Zürich', *Urban Studies*, **28** (1991), pp. 783–801. (Together with Susanne Krebs)

'Tax harmonization and tax competition in the European Union: lessons from Switzerland', Paper presented at the ISPE Meeting, Linz, 19–21 August 1993. (Together with Gebhard Kirchgässner)

'Voluntary provision of a public good: results from a real world experiment', *Kyklos*, **47** (1994), pp. 505–18. (Together with Lars P. Feld and Albert Hart)

PART I

New Solutions to Old Problems

1. Who Uses Local Public Services? Need, Demand and Rationing in Action

Glen Bramley

1. INTRODUCTION

Local government represents a substantial part of the overall welfare state in Britain and elsewhere, and is particularly important in the provision of services in kind as opposed to cash benefits. Our knowledge of the distribution of such benefits in kind has been very patchy, but recent surveys including many carried out by MORI for individual authorities have provided a fuller picture (Bramley et al. 1989, Bramley 1990a, Bramley and Smart 1993). The central question motivating these studies has been whether local public services are an effective mechanism of redistribution in favour of the poor and disadvantaged or whether many of these services are in fact used more by the better off. Is the capture of welfare state services by middle-class interests (Le Grand 1982, Goodin and Le Grand, 1987) a particular feature of local government?

But while we may know more descriptively about patterns of service usage, the underlying reasons for these may be far from clear. For example, higher-income households may use a service more than lower-income households, but this need not necessarily imply a positive income elasticity of demand for the service; this outcome could reflect indirect causality (for example, the rich have more cars and better access) or more fortuitous correlations with other factors (for example, household type and size). It is helpful in untangling the causes both to bring direct knowledge of service provision to bear and also to adopt a multivariate modelling approach to the data available from surveys. In this way the relative influence of particular explanatory variables within a plausible set may be assessed empirically.

The economic demand perspective may be applied to the analysis, for example estimating such parameters as income or price elasticities. Such model estimates may be valuable for forecasting or for welfare evaluation purposes. However, this task can be complicated by the nature of the

3

measure of usage which may be discrete rather than continuous and which may in turn reflect the way in which the service is provided (that is, discrete packages). The measurement of price is also problematic since local public services are normally free or subsidized; measures of user cost may be more appropriate.

Welfare service provision is widely argued to be directed towards goals of meeting needs rather than simply responding to demands. Can or should we direct our analysis of service usage to answering questions about need and, if so, where does this leave demand? I argue here that we can do this, and in more than one way since there are different concepts of need to be considered. This analysis does not necessarily substitute for the economic analysis of the demand, but rather provides additional dimensions to our understanding.

'Need' is an ambiguous and contestable concept (Hill and Bramley 1986, Ch. 4). Following Bradshaw (1972), one approach is to take the individuals, own perceptions, their so-called 'felt needs'. Felt needs may differ from effective demands because of inadequate individual resources, lack of availability of the service, lack of awareness, deterrence and other reasons. The survey method is obviously an appropriate way of getting evidence on felt needs, with more intensive methods exploring the reasons for use/non-use more fully.

The most important alternative approach to need is the normative one, involving 'third party judgements' (Williams 1974), which tend in practice to be made by bureaucrats or professionals. These judgements often relate to standards, and can be particularly important for services which are explicitly rationed and targeted on the basis of need. Other approaches to need, or variations on this theme, are discussed in Bramley (1990b, Chs 3 and 7). One of these alternatives, involving externalities in the form of non-user demands for services, can also be explored using suitable survey data (Bramley and Smart 1993, Ch. 5), but goes beyond the scope of this chapter.

Where local services are subject both to demand-side influences (felt need or preferences, together with economic factors) and to supply-side rationing, some problems arise in interpreting the statistical explanatory models. These problems are similar to the identification problem with normal supply and demand systems. Essentially, some observations may be cases where outcomes are determined by demand, while others may be constrained by supply factors, either the availability of a service (based particularly on funding) or the rationing decisions of providers. If these cases cannot be distinguished, much uncertainty will attach to estimates of any usage model which will generally be a reduced form.

The situation is improved if the models can incorporate measures of supply, although this may not provide a complete solution. Services provided by local government typically do vary between localities in their availability,quality and cost, with these variations reflecting local policy and budgetary differences as well as any differences in production conditions. To incorporate such variables, it is necessary to link individual household survey data sets for the country as a whole, or wide areas, with data sets relating to local authorities and their areas, using some sort of locational coding as a link. This is not always easy because of requirements of confidentiality, definitions of services and the failure to define this requirement into many surveys in the past (Evandrou and Winter 1988).

Ideas about need at a more collective or area level play a considerable part in the allocation of grants or spending permissions, particularly in Britain. The main grant system for local government relies heavily, through the 'Standard Spending Assessment' (SSA) mechanism, on regression analysis of past expenditure variations at local authority area level. This represents perhaps yet another need concept, albeit rather an incoherent one (Bramley 1990b, Ch. 7). Most of the debate about SSAs tends to revolve around the adequacy of these models as predictors of expenditure (Audit Commission 1993). What an analysis based on survey evidence of usage and preferences can offer is an alternative, more independent perspective on need, which may suggest rather different indicators or weightings favouring different areas.

Another example of area needs affecting resource allocation is where evidence of concentrations of deprivation in small areas is used as a basis for directing particular programmes or financial support to those areas. Such approaches tend to imply an assumption that the experience and outcomes of deprivation are worse by virtue of the fact of being juxtaposed spatially with other people experiencing the same or other deprivations. An analysis of usage survey data linked to area characteristics can also provide some test of this assumption, in relation to local public services.

2. THE MODEL

2.1. The Survey Question

This chapter is based on the 1990 *Breadline Britain* survey, a special national survey of poverty and living standards carried out by MORI as the basis for a TV series, which updated a 1983 study (Gordon et al. 1995, Mack and Lansley 1986). The survey as a whole is a rich data source on aspects of poverty and is particularly interesting in the way it develops indices of deprivation based on the opinions of respondents at large about what goods households should expect to have in Britain today.

In this chapter, though, I focus on just one question in the survey: this gave respondents a list of eleven selected local services and asked whether they used each service or not. In fact, respondents were given six options, as follows:

u(1) use – adequate
u(2) use – inadequate
u(3) do not use – do not want to/not relevant
u(4) do not use – unavailable/unsuitable
u(5) do not use – cannot afford
u(6) do not know

The eleven services were divided into groups according to whether they were relevant to all adults, to families with children under five or of school age or chiefly relevant to pensioners or people with disabilities. As should be immediately apparent, this form of question provides some basis for distinguishing the concepts of demand, need and rationing as introduced above.

2.2. Demand and Supply

Figure 1.1 attempts to set these possibilities in a conventional supply and demand framework, at the level of the individual household. Normal downward sloping demand functions D_1, D_2, D_3 are shown, with higher demand (for example D_3) associated with demographic factors which make the service more relevant, preferences, and (presumably) higher income. The supply function to individual households is assumed to be a horizontal line corresponding to the sum of price P (if any) and user cost C_u. However, supply may be rationed, for example at the level Q_{SR1}, at which point the supply turns up vertically. Thus, case u(1) could be as illustrated where a demand curve cuts the supply (cost) schedule at less than the maximum ration; here demand is the constraint. However, for u(2) rationed supply is the constraint; the respondent says that although he or she uses the service it is inadequate (he or she would rather have more, taking quantity and quality together). It is interesting to note that this situation affects someone with a high potential demand for the service.

Case u(3) is shown at the origin, implying that the relevant demand schedule (D_0, not shown) goes through this point; we interpret 'not relevant' literally. u(4) does not use the service because it is not available; in their locality the supply schedule (Q_{SR0}) coincides with the vertical axis and they are 'rationed out'. Finally, we have u(5) who are not constrained by rationing, but rather by their ability to afford to use the service; their marginal value falls below $P+C_u$, probably because their income is low (if they placed very little value on the service, they would be more likely to fall into u(3)).

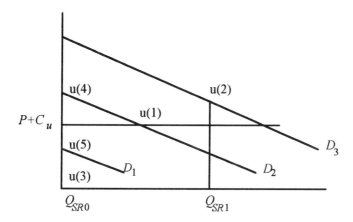

Figure 1.1   Price–demand relationship for rationed public service showing different possible survey responses

The analysis of Figure 1.1 assumes that continuously variable usage up to the rationing limit is possible. An alternative case of discrete packages modifies the analysis without fundamentally altering it for our purposes. This time consumers have to weigh up their total surpluses and costs rather than just look at the marginal values.

This diagram helps to show how misleading it could be to interpret the parameters of a model predicting usage in this situation with variable rationing. Some potentially high demanders are rationed out or constrained in how much they can have. With a data set of this form, the logical step forward is to concentrate on the cases which are demand-constrained when we attempt to fit a model for demand and discard the cases which are constrained by supply rationing (u(2) and u(4)). Thus the dependent variable for the demand model is the dichotomy u(1) (against u(3) or u(5)); 'use-adequate' against those who do not use it either because they do not see it as relevant or because they cannot afford it. More formally, the model derived using the logit transformation of this dichotomy is as follows:

$$\ln\{p(u(1))/[p(u(3)) + p(u(5))]\} = D\{Y, P, C_u, H, L, Z\} \qquad (1.1)$$

where Y is income, H is a vector of demographic attributes, L locational and Z social factors.

The logit transformation seems intuitively plausible for this kind of case, where one is explicitly modelling the odds of falling into one of two contrasting groups. The technique of logistic regression (alias logit) is one of the standard methods used to explain or predict a dichotomous dependent variable (Aldrich and Nelson 1984, Maddala 1988).

2.3. Need

What about 'felt need'? This would appear to be a much broader concept than effective demand. Anyone who uses the service must feel they need it (ignoring compulsion), however adequate or otherwise it is rated, while various non-user groups may also feel a need. In our scheme, all of the groups u(1), u(2), u(4) and u(5) could be said to exhibit felt need; only u(3) (do not use – do not want to/irrelevant) are not in need on this subjective basis. In Figure 1.1, any cases not at the origin count. The formal model becomes:

$$\ln\{[p(\mathrm{u}(1)) + p(\mathrm{u}(2)) + p(\mathrm{u}(4)) + p(\mathrm{u}(5))]/p(\mathrm{u}(3))\} = N\{H, L, Z\} \quad (1.2)$$

Notice here that income and price/user cost have been taken out of the model; this reflects one of the fundamental principles generally associated with the concept of need, that it should not depend on economic position. The remaining variables (demographic factors in particular) are essentially the same, although their relative weighting may turn out different. This model is fitted on the widest sample of cases, excluding only the 'do not knows'.

2.4. Rationing

Can we now complete the picture and model the rationing process? The way to do this is to take a different partial slice through the data, this time excluding the u(3) group who do not wish or need to use the service and concentrating on those whom rationing might affect. There are various ways the sample could be divided but for present purposes we take a broad definition of rationing: anyone in u(2), u(4) or u(5) is experiencing rationing (u(5) are included to reflect the fact that price or user cost may well reflect net expenditure and provision levels). The third formal model, for rationing, then becomes:

$$\ln\{p(\mathrm{u}(1))/[p(\mathrm{u}(2)) + p(\mathrm{u}(4)) + p(\mathrm{u}(5))]\} = R\{Y, H, L, Z, X\} \quad (1.3)$$

where X represents expenditure and provision levels of the service. Income is retained in the model to test for possible income-related rationing (for example, means tests). The coefficients on the *H* variables should reflect the rationing criteria applied by the service providers, consciously or unconsciously/indirectly, which may be contrasted with the weightings based on subjective need.

2.5. Services

The model is of fairly general applicability across services. It expects both demand-side influences and rationing effects, while allowing their relative importance to vary. Needs-based rationing is much more significant for some services than others, which may be more demand-led (Bramley and Le Grand 1992). In this chapter I apply the model to three different local services, which represent three points on the continuum from demand-led to needs-rationed. Sports centres (including swimming pools) are expected to be predominantly demand-led; home-help services for elderly or disabled people are expected to be predominantly needs-rationed; day care/nurseries for children under five are intermediate.

3. THE DATA

3.1. The Survey

It is clear that this model requires both individual household and linked locational (*L*) or local authority expenditure/provision data (*X*). A national survey which can allow such linkage is an appropriate basis for fitting the model.

The *Breadline* survey involved a national (Great Britain) quota sample from 80 sampling points with booster samples for certain potentially deprived urban areas. Adults were interviewed about their own attributes, situation and views, and in the process certain key information about the household was obtained. The total sample size was 1,831; however, the effective sample available after linkage to area data for England only excluding the booster and missing values is 896, while the subsamples to which the questions about child care and home help were addressed are 255 and 334 respectively.

3.2. Individual Explanatory Variables

A fairly wide range of individual and household attributes are available from the survey, as can be seen from the list of definitions in the appendix. The demographic group includes seven household-type indicators, number of children, two age indicators, sex, ethnicity, age and two disability/health indicators. Apart from NKIDS these are all dummy variables. The second group relates to socio-economic attributes and includes the continuous variable for equivalent household income (EQBREAD) and dummy variables for class groups, employment categories and other relevant factors like housing tenure, benefit recipient and car ownership. A composite measure of deprivation is also used, based on the *Breadline Britain* methodology of lack of 'essentials' as defined by a majority of recipients. Thus, we are not confined to a single measure of current income in assessing how well or badly off households are and relating this to service usage.

3.3. Area Level Variables

The postcodes of sampling point addresses were used to pinpoint the location of the 80 sampling points in terms of (1) local authority district and (2) type of Census enumeration district in terms of the ACORN classification system. A file of data at local authority level covering expenditure on the relevant services, and provision and pricing indicators where available, was compiled from various sources including CIPFA (1990), Department of Health (1992) and Society of County Treasurers (1992). So far as possible this refers to the same year (1990/91). This file is then linked to the survey micro data set.

The general influence of type of locality on access/user cost and rationing processes is tested for using one general indicator of rurality, the sparsity of population (persons per hectare) of the district. Two types of small area are singled out by dummy variables to test for the influence of small area concentrations of deprivation: ACORND (areas of older terraced housing) and ACORNG (areas of public housing with high deprivation).

Table 1.1 shows the full breakdown of responses to the usage question for the three services of special interest. Between a tenth and two-fifths of actual users rate the service as inadequate. Not using the service because of its inadequacy or unavailability is more significant for the child-care service, where most households (with children) feel a need. While the numbers excluded in this way from home-help service are small relative to the number receiving the service, they are not trivial. Relatively few in any case give 'cannot afford' as the reason for not using the service.

This reflects the fact that these are publicly provided services, either free or heavily subsidized. There is a worryingly high proportion of the elderly group coded as 'do not know' in response to this question. It is not clear why this should be so (interview fatigue?), but this does affect the analysis adversely, reducing the number of observations seriously in a case where there are precious few users anyway. For the purposes of this chapter, responses in this category ('do not know') for home help are treated as though they were coded u(3) ('do not use – do not want to/irrelevant').

Table 1.1 Detailed response to usage question for three selected services

Response	Sports facilities	Child care	Home help
u(1) Use – adequate	43.2	42.7	9.5
u(2) Use – inadequate	10.5	17.8	1.6
u(3) Do not use – do not want/irrelevant	39.5	23.5	42.7
u(4) Do not use– inadequate/unavailable	3.8	7.7	1.4
u(5) Do not use – cannot afford	1.3	0.6	0.8
u(6) Do not know	1.7	7.7	43.9
Base (=100%)	896	255	334

Broadly descriptive results for the distributional patterns of usage of all the services included in the *Breadline* study are reported by Bramley (1995 forthcoming) and comparable analyses for a number of local surveys may be found in Bramley and Smart (1993). In general, demand-led services in the leisure field, including sports, are used more by the better off. Services for children (like child care) are used slightly less by higher-income and higher-class groups but are still used more by non-deprived than by deprived households. Needs-rationed services for groups like the elderly and disabled (including home-care) and a few other services like buses and school meals are used more by lower-income and deprived groups.

4. MODEL RESULTS

As already noted, the technique used to fit the models is logistic regression, as implemented on the package SPSS. The Tables 1.2, 1.3, and 1.4 show, for each selected service, models for demand, felt need and rationing. The coefficients show the effect of each variable on the log-odds of demanding/needing/being non-rationed. Interpretation is aided by the fact that most variables are dummies. Asterisks indicate the degree of statistical significance of the individual coefficients. The rationing variable is expressed as non-rationed: rationed in order to aid comparison with the other variables.

The choice of explanatory variables is determined first by judgements as to their potential relevance in each service and by the general model framework set out in equations (1.1) to (1.3) in Section 2. The final models shown are based on stepwise selection.

4.1. Sports Facilities

Table 1.2 shows the model results for use of public sports and swimming pool facilities across the whole sample of households, since this is a service open to all. Demographic factors play a strong part in all models: younger adults, larger adult households and those with children use sports facilities more. Gender, ethnicity and disability do not have very strong or significant effects overall, although the tendency is for females, disabled and black/Asian ethnic groups to use these services less.

Adding socioeconomic factors to the usage model significantly improves the explanation. Broadly the pro-rich character of the service (suggested also in earlier studies by Veal 1982 and Gratton and Taylor 1985) is confirmed: usage rises with income and is lower for council tenants; deprived households use sports facilities less. One slight counterpoint to this theme is the positive association with past unemployment; some people who have experienced redundancy and unemployment constitute a distinct high-user group for sports centres.

What conclusions can we draw from the differences between the demand, need and rationing models? First, in relation to the demographic factors the demand and need models are generally rather similar. Two potentially disadvantaged groups, lone parents and the disabled, exhibit lower demand but show no difference in felt need. Families with school-age children and younger respondents show a stronger tendency to demand the service. Respondents over 75 do not feel so much need for this service. Second, comparing these models in relation to socioeconomic factors, it is clear that higher social class (and perhaps indirectly income) is associated with a greater felt need (preference) for using these facilities, as well as a greater effective demand. The pattern on deprivation is consistent with that for lone parents and the disabled; demand is reduced but felt need is the same for deprived households. Area characteristics do not feature in either of these models.

What about the effects of rationing? Sports facilities are not a service which is strongly targeted or rationed on the basis of needs assessments of individuals. Nevertheless, rationing effects may operate indirectly, via differential spending levels, patterns of provision of facilities, and how they are managed (for example which activities are encouraged).

Table 1.2 suggests that the rationing model does differ from the demand

and need models. The demographic effects are more neutral, as we would expect. Nevertheless, there is still some evidence of families with children and younger users being favoured.

Table 1.2   Logistic regression models for usage of sports facilities

	Demand	Felt need	Rationing	Usage
Constant	–3.29	–2.33	–0.25	–2.13
SEX	–	0.22*	–	–
MULTI	0.90**	0.69***	–	1.05**
LONPAR	– 0.77**	–	–	– 0.69*
KIDSUSA	0.69**	0.67***	–	0.83**
KIDSSA	1.32***	0.82***	–	1.43**
NKIDS	0.44***	0.45***	0.29***	0.32*
AGEYNG	1.02***	0.51***	0.43**	0.71**
AGE75	–	– 1.29***	–	– 1.44**
DISAB	– 0.36**	–	–	–
COUNCIL	– 0.52**	– 0.58***	–	– 0.61**
EQBREAD	0.0022***	–	–	0.0023**
BENEFIT	–	–	– 0.62***	–
CLASSAB	–	0.40**	–	–
CLASSC1	0.32*	–	–	–
PASTUNEM	0.59**	0.35**	0.39**	0.39*
DEPRIV	– 0.38*	–	– 0.47***	– 0.38*
CAR	0.44**	0.39***	–	–
RECRTN	–	–	ns	–
SPARS	–	–	– 0.77***	–
ACORND	–	–	0.94**	–
–2 Log Likelihood	824.1	1568.2	1005.6	996.9
Significance	97.8	98.9	98.9	99.0
Correct predictions %	74.0	73.9	73.5	72.0
Number of cases	759	1455	912	1480

Note: For each independent variable, the table shows the coefficient giving its effect on the log odds ratio (use:not use), with asterisks indicating level of statistical significance *=75%;**=90%; ***=95%; ****=99%; indicators of overall and incremental model performance are given at bottom.

The evidence does not suggest discrimination in favour of deprived groups, but rather the reverse, with negative signs on both DEPRIV and BENEFIT. Expenditure on the service (RECRTN) is not statistically significant but other area characteristics play some part, with residents of sparse areas being rationed out by poorer access to facilities.

In general, for sports facilities the modelling approach seems to work reasonably well, telling a plausible story about the overall patterns and yielding some interesting insights into the role of demand- and supply-side factors.

4.2. Day Care for Under-Fives

Table 1.3 shows the application of a similar set of models to local authority child-care services for children under five (primarily day nurseries and nursery education) to the restricted set of households potentially eligible to use these services. With the much smaller sample, the statistical significance of the models as a whole is poorer and fewer individual variables stand out as significant. Also partly for this reason, the demographic factors are less dominant in the overall explanation. Number of children and, in some of the models, health problems and younger respondents (parents) show significant positive associations with usage. These patterns seem to reflect demand-side rather than rationing decisions (needs-based rationing is more likely to operate in the day care provided by social services departments). There is surprisingly no consistent relationship with lone parenthood, while younger household heads and disability show non-significant positive associations with usage. For ethnic minority households the association is again negative but insignificant.

Socioeconomic variables are quite significant, with high-class (AB) households demanding and feeling the need for the service much less (presumably they use the private sector more, but possibly also have more voluntary stay-at-home mothers).

There is some negative income effect also on felt need. However, deprived households also record a lower need for the service (perhaps because here few mothers work). One type of neighbourhood, older terraced houses, shows a lower demand and felt need for the service; this may be because of stronger family ties and informal care arrangements prevalent in such areas. The pattern of rationing appears again to be significantly different. While no very clear demographic factors emerge, rationing seems to favour higher-income households, although it also helps those in the lowest social class and those with a history of unemployment. One provision variable (nursery education places) has a detectable effect on this measure.

Table 1.3   Logistic regression models for usage of child-care (nursery)
            facilities

	Demand	Felt need	Rationing	Usage
Constant	− 3.33	− 3.50	− 0.19	− 2.90
KIDSSA	–	–	–	–
NKIDS	0.85***	0.84***	–	0.67***
AGEYNG	–	0.84*	–	–
HEALTH	–	0.73*	–	0.61**
EQBREAD	–	− 0.80*	1.09**	–
CLASSAB	− 2.82***	− 1.98***	–	− 1.78***
CLASSDE	–	–	− 1.10***	–
PASTUNEM	–	–	− 1.13***	–
DEPRIV	–	− 0.96**	–	− 0.87***
GEXPCHPC	–	–	ns	− 0.0054*
FC1	–	–	ns	–
FC2	–	–	ns	–
PCTU5NE	–	–	0.042*	–
ACORND	− 1.63**	− 1.06*	1.68**	–
−2 Log Likelihood	149.1	179.0	188.5	305.0
Significance	83.9	96.1	97.6	97.9
Correct predictions %	74.8	80.0	70.7	71.1
Number of cases	147	200	157	263

Note: Interpretation as for Table 1.2.

Again, these results draw out the point that rationing processes may differ
markedly in their effects from the patterns of demand and felt need. The
model as reported is not very robust statistically and would benefit from
larger samples and closer attention to certain key explanatory factors,
particularly the labour force participation of mothers.

4.3. Home Help

The third service examined is the home-help (or home-care) service, the
most important of the domiciliary services provided by local authority social

service departments to frail elderly and and some other clients with physical disability. The analysis in Table 1.4 is performed on households over retirement age or with a disabled member. The service is generally rationed on the basis of some assessment of need although this is an area of local discretion and may be quite subjective. Charges are typically but not invariably levied, but usually with rebating for low income. Evandrou (1987) and Evandrou and Winter (1988) review evidence and issues in the rationing of this service.

Table 1.4   Logistic regression models for usage of home-help service

	Demand	Felt need	Rationing	Usage
Constant	–	4.82	– 2.13	– 2.98
SINGELD	–	–	–	1.05**
AGE75	–	–	4.49***	0.80*
DISAB	–	–	–	1.11***
HEALTH	–	–	– 2.78**	–
PASTUNEM	–	–	–	– 1.05*
CAR	–	– 2.35***	– 3.57***	– 0.99*
GEXPHHPC	–	–	ns	–
DE8	–	–	0.19*	–
GE7	–	–	ns	–
ACORND	–	–	2.81*	–
–2 Log Likelihood	–	76.3	46.3	204.8
Significance	–	–	–	99.9
Correct predictions %	–	92.6	96.4	88.0
Number of cases	62	190	140	255

Note: Interpretation as for Table 1.2.

It is to be expected and reassuring that the main systematic influences on usage are demographic. Elderly people living alone and households with someone having a disability are more likely to use the service and so also are the over-75s. These findings are consistent with earlier studies. Overall, the models are not particularly impressive predictors, as is shown by their inability to generate more correct predictions in a situation where only 10.3

per cent of the subgroup use the service. The underlying reason is partly that the *Breadline* survey (like other general-purpose surveys) does not go far enough into a detailed needs assessment for individuals based on their particular health and household circumstances. However, it may also reflect considerable local variation and subjectivity in the rationing process. In addition, as already noted, the large number of 'do not knows' is a further problem.

The sub-models are particularly affected by the attrition effects on numbers of cases. No meaningful model can be fitted for demand, and the only significant factor in the felt-need model is having a car. This factor also shows up in the rationing model; presumably elderly people with a car tend to be better off financially, more mobile and better able to access a range of other services which lessen their dependency on home care. The rationing process appears to favour the very elderly (over-75s) but rather surprisingly seems to disfavour those with health problems. There is a slight positive relationship with the indicators of charges income as a percentage of expenditure; this is consistent with one view in social services, that charges can be used positively to make the service available to more people.

It is interesting to compare results from this exercise, based on 1990 data, with Evandrou and Winter's analysis based on the 1980 General Household Survey (1988, p. 26). Fitting to our data a model closely comparable to theirs reveals some similar findings and some differences. The models concur in finding positive associations with disability, elderly living alone and the interaction of the two, and lack of a bath; and negative associations with home ownership and income. They differ in several respects, including: (1) the negative association with HEALTH in the *Breadline* model versus a positive association with moderate disability in the earlier study (these variables are not strictly comparable); (2) the positive association with DE8 (charge income as percentage of expenditure) versus the negative association with both pricing indicators in the earlier study; (3) the reversal of signs on the expenditure and hours variables. There may be substantive explanations for all of these differences in the way the service and its rationing has been changing over the recent period. For example, it may be more consciously targeted on people with more severe disability and the expense of those with moderate disability, with a consequential tendency to increase the intensity of service (hours per client); charges may have been used more positively by many authorities to generate revenue to support the service. While these tendencies provide a plausible story to account for the differences, caution is still in order because of the definitional differences which affect many of these variables.

4.4.   Local Expenditure Needs Assessment

Surveys such as that discussed in this chapter can provide an independent basis for exploring the need for local service provision and offering a critique of existing resource allocation methods. Particular forms of model based on individual attributes may be interpreted as a needs index, as for example in the case of the 'felt-need' models presented earlier. These results may suggest somewhat different indicators from those used in the official resource allocation process. For example, our model for sports facilities emphasized age factors, whereas these do not feature in the relevant SSA formula (although this does cover a wider block of services).

The model interpreted here as a rationing function may be helpful in this context in giving indications of how local service providers actually ration on the ground. Particular care is needed with this kind of interpretation, however, both to ensure that an adequate range of relevant individual variables are included and also to ensure that adequate account is taken of area-level and resource effects. The models illustrated above did attempt to do this, although not necessarily in a very adequate way.

In general, we would expect local authority expenditure on a particular service to have a positive relationship with the probability of using the service, and a negative association with the experience of constraints on usage or problems with a service. This assumes that extra expenditure, at the margin, contributes to the quality, range, delivery and accessibility of a service in such a way that more usage is encouraged and constraints on usage are overcome. This need not necessarily apply, for example where the service is strictly rationed and the expenditure affects quality rather than quantity or where the service is so well provided that the market is effectively saturated. Part of the motive for including local expenditure in the model is to see how this effect operates in different services. In the three examples looked at closely here, expenditure or provision variables did not feature strongly, even in the rationing models to which they logically belong.

A second motive is to see whether including this factor in the models alters the influence of any of the individual variables, such as income, class or deprivation. Are we to any degree confounding individual and area effects, who you are versus where you are? In general, standards of provision of local services are not uniform and variations in expenditure are a major if not the only cause of such differences. There may be systematic associations between where different income/class/deprivation groups live and the supply/quality of local services and, if so, this would mean that some confounding of the two effects is a real danger. In practice, in nearly all cases the inclusion of these extra area-level variables does not seriously alter the effects of the income, class and deprivation variables. Indeed, in the majority of cases the effect of the class/income/deprivation variables is slightly reinforced.

We have also explored in a limited way the influence of type of locality on facets of service usage. Sparsely populated rural areas may limit service usage and we would expect this to show up in demand or rationing models (as in the case of sports facilities). The ACORN neighbourhood type variables are rarely significant once allowance is made for the individual/household variables, although the areas of older terraced houses showed up as significant in the case of child care.

5. CONCLUSIONS

Although local government comprises a significant segment of the welfare state in Britain, to characterize its service provision activities as systematically pro-poor would be a considerable misrepresentation. As with other parts of the welfare state, the primary determinants of (re)distribution are demographic, skewed towards families and the old. Beyond this, the services provided by local government are diverse and the way they are targeted or rationed varies significantly, so we would not expect all to play a similar distributional role.

Nevertheless, the findings reported in this chapter and in other related work present a rather disappointing message, particularly in relation to the poorest households. The results are based primarily on an analysis of data from the *Breadline Britain* survey of 1990, but they echo and reinforce findings from earlier work using local surveys.

A threefold approach to modelling specific service usage at individual levels is sketched out, distinguishing demand, felt need and rationing. This approach, which relies on a particular form of question adopted in the *Breadline Britain* survey, provides one solution to the identification problem associated with systems where both demand-side and supply-rationing factors may be operating. The approach has been exemplified with respect to three services at different points on the continuum from universal demand-led to targeted and rationed services: sports facilities, child care and home helps. The results are plausible and encouraging, at least in part, but indicate that to be fully effective one needs large sample sizes and appropriate, perhaps more detailed, questions. More work is also needed on the link with area-level data on spending and needs assessments to enable this approach to provide an effective basis for evaluating and perhaps modifying these systems of resource allocation.

REFERENCES

Aldrich, J.H. and F.D. Nelson (1984), *Linear Probability, Logit and Probit Models*, Quantitative Applications in the Social Sciences Series, **45**. Newbury Park, Ca: Sage.

Audit Commission (1993), *Passing the Bucks: the Impact of Standard Spending Assessments on Economy, Efficiency and Effectiveness*, **1** and **2**, London: HMSO.

Bradshaw, J. (1972) 'The concept of social need', *New Society*, **30**, 30 March, 640/3.

Bramley, G. (1990a), 'The Demand for Local Government Services: Survey Evidence on Usage, Distribution and Externalities', *Local Government Studies*, November/December, 35–61.

Bramley, G. (1990b), *Equalization Grants and Local Expenditure Needs: The Price of Equality*, Aldershot: Avebury.

Bramley, G. (1995 forthcoming), 'Poverty and local government services', in D. Gordon et al. (eds), *Bread line in Britain in the 1990s*, London: Routledge.

Bramley, G., J. Le Grand and W. Low (1989), 'How far is the Poll Tax a Community Charge? The implications of service usage evidence', *Policy and Politics*, **17** (3), 187–205.

Bramley, G. and J. Le Grand (1992), *Who Uses Local Services? – Striving for Equity*, The Belgrave Papers, **4**, Luton: Local Government Management Board.

Bramley, G. and G. Smart (1993), *Who Benefits From Local Services? Comparative Evidence From Different Local Authorities*, Welfare State Programme Discussion Paper WSP/91, Suntory-Toyota International Centre for Economics and Related Disciplines, London: London School of Economics.

Cheshire County Council (1989), *The Use of County Council Services: 1 Distribution of Use*, Chester, Cheshire CC: Research and Intelligence Unit Paper Rand I/W3/GAH

CIPFA (1990), *Financial and General Statistics 1990–91*, Statistical Information Service SIS Ref 41.91, London: Chartered Institute of Public Finance and Accountancy.

Department of Health (1992) *Key Indicators of Local Authority Social Services 1990–91* London: Department of Health (SD3 Division).

Evandrou, M. (1987), *The Use of Domiciliary Services by the Elderly: A Survey*, Welfare State Programme Discussion Paper WSP/15, London: London School of Economics.

Evandrou, M. and D.Winter (1988), *The Distribution of Domiciliary and Primary Health Care in Britain: Preliminary Results on Modelling*

Resource Allocation in the Welfare State, Welfare State Programme Discussion Paper WSP/26, London: London School of Economics.

Goodin, R. and J. Le Grand (1987), *Not Only the Poor: the Middle Classes and the Welfare State*, London: Allen & Unwin.

Gordon, D., C. Pantazis, P.Townsend, G. Bramley and J.Bradshaw (1995), *Breadline Britain in the 1990s*, York: Joseph Rowntree Foundation.

Gratton, C. and P. Taylor (1985), *Sport and Recreation: an Economic Analysis*, London: E. & F.N. Spon.

Hill, M. and G. Bramley (1986) *Analysing Social Policy* Oxford: Blackwell

Le Grand, J. (1982), *The Strategy of Equality*, London: Allen & Unwin.

Mack, J. and S. Lansley (1986), *Poor Britain*, London: Penguin

Maddala, G.S. (1988), *Introduction to Econometrics*, New York and London: MacMillan.

Society of County Treasurers (1992), *Standard Spending Indicators 1992– 1993*, Kent: Kent CC on behalf of Society of County Treasurers, Society of Metropolitan Treasurers, and the Association of District Council Treasurers.

Veal, A.J. (1982), *Recreation in 1980: participation patterns in England and Wales*, Report to the Sports Council and the Countryside Commission, London: Polytechnic of North London.

Williams, A. (1974) 'Need as a demand concept (with special reference to health)', in A. Culyer (ed.) *Economic Problems and Social Goals* London: Martin Robertson.

APPENDIX 1A

Variable Definitions

Group 1: Demographic (survey-based, household level)

SINGELD	Single retired person household
COUPELD	Retired couple/two-person household
SING	Single adult under retirement age
LONPAR	Lone parent household (1 adult with children <16)
MULTI	Household with three or more adults
KIDSUSA	Couple with children under school age
KIDSSA	Couple with children, some/all of school age
NKIDS	Number of children
AGE75	Respondent aged 75+
AGEYNG	Respondent aged under 25
SEX	Male respondent
DISAB	Anyone in household with long-standing illness, disability or infirmity.
HEALTH	Health problem, on hospital waiting list, multiple GP consultations or hospital treatment.
ETHNIC	Black or Asian respondent

Group 2: Socioeconomic (survey-based, household level)

EQBREAD	Equivalent household income £ per week (equivalence scale as devised for *Breadline Britain* TV Series)
CLASSAB	Social Class of HOH professional/managerial
CLASSC1	Social class of HOH other non-manual
CLASSDE	Social class of HOH semi/unskilled manual
REBATE BENEFIT	Receiving Housing Benefit or rate/poll tax rebate
CAR	Household has one or more cars
FULLTIME	Respondent works full time
UNEMPLOY	Respondent unemployed
PASTUNEM	Respondent or partner unemployed in last year or at least two months in last ten years
COUNCIL	Council tenant
OWNHOME	Outright owner occupier

DEPRIV   Household lacks and cannot afford three or more 'essentials' as defined by majority of survey respondents

Group 3: Resource and Area Characteristics (area level)

3(a) Expenditure by service

Expenditure per head or per potential client in 1990/91, deflated by SSA London costs index. Sources: CIPFA (1991), *Financial and General Statistics*, revised estimate 1990/91 based on RER return, data supplied to author on disk; CIPFA (1992), *Local Government Comparative Statistics 1992*; Department of Health (1992), *Key Indicators of Local Authority Social Services* 1990/91.

RECRTN   Recreation (parks, sports, etc)
GEXPCHPC Gross expenditure childrens' personal social services per child
GEXPHHPC Gross expenditure home help service per elderly resident
FC1   LA day care places for under-fives per 10,000 aged 0–4
FC2   Independent day care places for under-fives per 10,000 aged 0–4
DE8   Home help fee income as % of gross expenditure
GE7   Home help hours per case per week
PCTU5NE   % of under-fives in nursery education

3(b) Standard Spending Assessments

SSA per head of total or relevant population, deflated by London costs index, for 1992/93 (SSAs for 1992/93 were very similar in most cases to 1990/91). Source: Society of County Treasurers (1992).

SSAPC23 SSA for 'other district services block' per head
SSANEPC SSA for education for under-fives, per resident 0–4
SSAPCC SSA for childrens' personal social services per child
SSAPED SSA for elderly domiciliary social services per elderly resident

3(c) Other area characteristics

ACORND   Enumeration district in ACORN cluster D, areas of older terraced housing
ACORNG   Enumeration district in ACORN cluster G, areas of council housing with higher levels of deprivation
SPARS   Sparsity of population in 1990, i.e. hectares per resident.

2. On the Use of Statistical Techniques to Infer Territorial Spending Needs

Alan Duncan and Peter Smith

1. INTRODUCTION

Most public expenditure is geographically specific. The central government therefore has to make a choice as to how to allocate its expenditures among geographical areas. Of course, this choice could be governed purely by political considerations, without reference to issues such as consistency or fairness. However, citizens, local governments and supranational organizations – such as the World Bank or the European Union – are increasingly insisting that central government expenditure is distributed according to some concept of equity. The pursuit of territorial equity is therefore very often an important objective of central government expenditure programmes. Thus, for example, the UK National Health Service has as a central objective the provision of equal access to health-care for those in equal need, regardless of where they live. In a similar vein, an important objective of central grants-in-aid to local governments is usually the pursuit of some sort of territorial equity (King 1984).

A variety of notions of equity exist, and they do not have the unambiguous connotation associated with the economic concepts of efficiency. For example, Mooney (1982) identifies seven different concepts of equity that could be applied to the allocation of health-care. However, central to most equity criteria is the idea that individuals or communities in equal need should be treated in an equal fashion. This principle therefore begs two fundamental questions: what is need and how is 'need' to be assessed?

We do not intend to dwell on what is meant by need. As Maslow (1943) elucidates, need is in practice usually a relative concept, and is also inevitably a subjective concept. Bramley (1990, Ch. 3) gives an extensive discussion and demonstrates the complexity and elusiveness of the concept of need. In particular, he points to the possible desirability of distinguishing between individual needs and collective needs. The focus of this chapter is territorial, and therefore collective, needs, but it should be borne in mind that for many services these may be no more than the sum of individual needs. For the purposes of this chapter we interpret territorial spending needs to be an assessment – in somebody's judgement – of the amount that a locality would spend if it were to adopt some standard set of policies and practices, taking into account the social and economic circumstances in the area. We take it for granted that the pursuit of equity is a central objective of most governments, and that – to that end – the case for measuring relative spending needs is given. Bebbington and Davies (1980a) give an extended discussion on this issue.

A variety of methods can be found which purport to measure spending need, ranging from the frankly judgemental to the impenetrably technical. Because of the essentially subjective nature of any needs-assessment procedure, it is rarely possible to secure consensus about how relative needs should be measured. However, in order to be seen to be impartial and consistent, governments are increasingly having recourse to statistical methods to infer relative spending needs. The purpose of this chapter is to draw attention to some important issues that arise when seeking to use statistical methods to such ends.

The next section discusses the rationale for using statistical techniques to infer spending needs, and points out some of the problems that arise. It is important that the measurement of needs is undertaken within a coherent model of supply and demand for public services. Section 3 therefore describes a theoretical framework for the measurement of spending needs in securing governmental equity objectives. Section 4 then discusses the consequences of this analysis for the empirical estimation of spending needs and the chapter ends with some policy implications.

2. RATIONALE FOR THE USE OF STATISTICAL TECHNIQUES

We have defined a locality's spending need as the amount of public expenditure a locality should incur if it were to adopt a standard set of policies and practices. The definition of what constitutes a standard set of services is problematic, and is discussed at length by Bramley (1990, Ch. 7). It could be defined in terms of inputs (amounts spent), in terms of processes (services provided), in terms of use, or in terms of outcomes. Moreover, it could be defined in terms of the impact on individuals or on communities. And the standard must presume some level of managerial efficiency in the delivery of services.

In general, because of measurement problems, it is infeasible to equalize on the basis of outcomes. In practice, because allocations must be made in financial terms it is usual eventually to express the standard level of service in terms of observable outputs. These in turn might be presented in terms of financial inputs – for example, as the costs of providing certain processes. Thus, in education most spending needs formulae are based on the assumption that the basic unit of need is the pupil, perhaps weighted for socioeconomic circumstances. The physical process is therefore the education of a pupil. This is converted into a financial allocation by applying a capitation rate, perhaps adjusted for different factor costs in different localities.

In principle, the resultant allocations should allow jurisdictions employing the standard mix of inputs, purchased at standard prices, and converted into education services with a standard level of efficiency, to deliver identical services to a given pupil. That is, because for a variety of reasons jurisdictions do not conform to standard practices, equalization must be on the basis of potential outcomes, rather than actual outcomes (Heald 1983, Ch. 10).

The use of statistical techniques to infer territorial spending needs according to this principle has become widespread in the UK. The most celebrated examples are the Standard Spending Assessments (SSAs) in local government, which are used by the central government as a basis for distributing grants-in-aid (Society of County Treasurers 1994), and the resource allocation formulae in the National Health Service (Mays and Bevan 1987).

The SSAs are developed by the central government, and a variety exist for different services. The SSA recognizes that in most circumstances needs are not directly measurable, and so they rely on the identification of a set of indicators of spending needs. A regression of actual expenditure in a set of local governments on these indicators then identifies the national average expenditure response to these needs indicators. The predicted value of expenditure emerging from the regression analysis for an individual territory then forms the basis for its spending needs assessment.

In the NHS, needs indicators have been developed by regressing measures of hospital inpatient utilization on a set of supply and socioeconomic variables (Royston et al. 1992). The unit of analysis was the electoral ward (population about 7,000). However, the resulting formula was used as a basis for allocating funds to much larger areas (Regional Health Authorities). Because – for the purposes of resource allocation – the supply determinants of utilization were considered illegitimate determinants of utilization, only the socioeconomic part of the regression equation was incorporated into the formula.

Nevertheless, although the use of statistical techniques to infer spending needs has become widespread, there is usually a lack of theoretical background to the work. Even authors who have thought deeply about the principles involved can find themselves eventually forced to develop a needs index using relatively crude regression methods on a set of readily available data (Bebbington and Davies 1980b). Indeed, less thoughtful researchers often resort to simple regressions of some output indicator on any explanatory variables they can find. They appear to believe that the high explanatory power of the regression in some sense justifies the use of the predictions that emerge as a basis for resource allocations.

One can of course argue that the use of statistical techniques is just expediency on the part of a government seeking to impart some respectability to the resource allocations it has to make. However, a more charitable interpretation is that, by using statistical methods, the central government is seeking to secure some reasonably impartial concept of fairness. This being the case, the reason for using regression methods to infer needs is that actual expenditure – which might be considered self-assessed spending need – is unacceptable in itself as an index of spending needs because localities will have different interpretations of appropriate levels of output. Therefore allocations based on self-assessments will treat localities inconsistently. In any case, if self-assessed need were to be used as a basis for allocating funds, then there would exist a dysfunctional incentive for localities to inflate their reported needs to secure a larger share of central government resources (Barrow 1986).

Regression analysis is a stochastic averaging device. Implicit in the use of regression analysis is therefore the notion that the average spending response to the chosen needs indicators is the appropriate basis for assessing spending needs. The averaging function implicit in regression analysis disposes of random fluctuations caused by differences in policies and efficiency between localities, which are captured in the error term.

Of course, if policies or efficiency are correlated with the needs indicators, then the regression equation will be biased. This was the reason the UK government temporarily abandoned regression analysis for local government spending needs assessments in 1981 (Bennett 1982). It believed that local governments with high degrees of social deprivation adopted spending policies which were higher than their needs indicators justified and that any regression based on actual spending would therefore inflate the apparent spending needs of these localities. This story illustrates that, although statistical methods may superficially appear to be value neutral, their use implies acceptance of a set of values which may or may not be acceptable to the organization undertaking the needs assessment.

It could, however, just as reasonably be argued that – for example – areas with low needs indicators have higher incomes than high-needs areas, and therefore demand higher levels of spending than their needs justify. Again, if this is the case, then any regression equation would lead to biased estimates of spending requirements. In general, it is impossible using statistical methods to distinguish variations in expenditure caused by variations in underlying needs from variations in expenditure caused by preference and efficiency variations, and the user of regression techniques must be aware of this potential limitation. If the analysis is undertaken at the level of the jurisdiction, this problem would appear to be entirely intractable. However, the use of lower-level data – perhaps relating to small areas or individuals – would appear to offer some prospect of reducing its importance.

The problem addressed in this chapter is as follows. Local territorial spending is readily found to be correlated with a large number of socioeconomic variables. Our thesis is that to the assessor of spending needs some of these correlations might reflect legitimate variations in spending in respect of the resource allocation problem, while others might reflect illegitimate variations. Recall that our definition of spending needs sought to measure the expenditure that localities would adopt if they pursued standard policies and practices. By legitimate variations in spending, we therefore mean variations in spending that are consistent with those policies and practices. Thus, in the health services example cited above, expenditure responses to variations in the health of populations were considered legitimate, while expenditure responses to hospital supply were considered illegitimate. In the local government sphere – where there is choice about local spending levels – we might consider expenditure responses to local incomes as illegitimate, and seek to exclude the income effect from any spending needs formula. By using the expression 'illegitimate', we do not imply that such influences on spending are illegal or undesirable. The expression simply implies that we do not wish our estimates of spending needs to reflect such factors.

We consider the illegitimate effects on local territorial spending to be caused by what we call territorial endowments. These are characteristics of areas which give rise to variations in output levels which are inconsistent with the standard policies assumed in the spending needs assessment process. Thus, for example, the endowments relevant to the NHS resource allocation problem might be the supply of NHS hospitals and general practitioners. These may give rise to variations in spending which should not be reflected in a spending needs formula. Similarly, in the local government field, endowments might be local income or central government grant. For most purposes, the central government would not wish a measure of spending needs to reflect the influences of these causes of spending variation, which are therefore – by our definition – illegitimate. In effect, this implies that our approach to measuring spending needs should assume not only standard policies and practices, but also standard endowments.

The problem that arises for the needs assessor is that – as noted above – it is rare to be able to measure needs directly. Instead, one must look for socioeconomic indicators that appear to be correlated with spending, with the inference that they are reflecting needs. And the above argument suggests that, to be legitimate, such needs indicators should be correlated with spending while being uncorrelated with endowments.

This issue has received surprisingly little attention in the literature. One exception is the NHS utilization study referred to earlier (Royston et al. 1992), which sought to accommodate endowment effects. It acknowledged that inpatient utilization may be a function of both needs and supply, and therefore developed an index of supply to incorporate into the utilization equation. However, the study methodology was subjected to severe criticism (Sheldon and Carr-Hill 1992). Furthermore, as we show later, the needs formula inferred from this analysis was faulty. Later work (Carr-Hill et al. 1994b) has sought to correct these shortcomings.

In their study of needs for personal social services among the elderly, Bebbington and Davies (1980b) sought to explain the number of elderly 'in need of care'. They recognized that 'the need judgement ought in principle to depend on the availability of [other social welfare] services'. However, in practice they were unable explicitly to accommodate this complication, even though the number of the elderly requiring care is likely to be strongly influenced by the availability of care facilities. They implicitly overcome this problem by confining their analysis to a single administrative area, thereby removing two important reasons for endowment variations – administrative policies and resource constraints.

Thus, in developing a spending needs formula based on observed public sector outputs it seems imperative to recognize the important role that endowment considerations may play in influencing output. In general, the endowment reflects the resources available to the locality. It is a trivial matter to develop mathematical models of local public goods which show that output is a function of needs and such resources. Yet most concepts of equity would insist that it should be only legitimate needs factors that are incorporated into any spending needs formula. The next section develops a model within which to consider both needs and endowment effects, as a prelude to examining the extent to which it may be possible to distinguish between them.

3. A SIMPLE MODEL OF DEMAND FOR LOCAL PUBLIC GOODS

The basic model put forward in this chapter is illustrated in Figure 2.1. Public sector outputs (Q) are the result of an interaction of population needs

(*N*) and the endowment of the area, perhaps expressed in terms of supply of public services (*S*). In this context, output should ideally be some measure of service provision, such as utilization. However, in practice, it may be measured by some proxy, such as expenditure. Endowment reflects the potential of the locality to produce outputs. It may reflect physical characteristics, or it may be measured by other proxies for local capacity to produce outputs. Endowment is considered to be influenced by three factors: legitimate needs (*N*), other exogenous factors unrelated to needs (*X*), and output (*Q*).

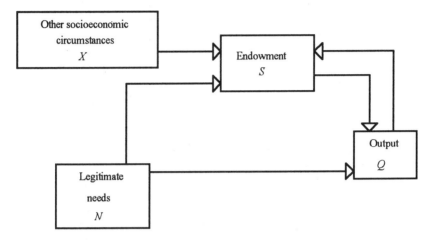

Figure 2.1   The simplified model of needs and output

The *X* variables are of crucial importance in what follows. They are social and economic factors which are correlated with local endowments relevant to the supply of public services, but which are not related to need. For example, in many countries, supply of high-technology health services has been concentrated in large conurbations. If these services stimulate additional output (as reflected, say, in inpatient episodes) compared with more rural areas, then there may be an observed positive relationship between urbanization and hospital utilization. But that relationship is the result of supply effects, and does not necessarily reflect population *needs*. If one wanted to use hospital utilization as the basis for building a model of health-care needs, it would therefore be necessary to disentangle the illegitimate (*X*) correlates of utilization from the legitimate (*N*).

Similarly, in most systems of local government, the central government distributes grants-in-aid to localities. In principle, of course, these grants might be purely related to legitimate needs. But it is more likely to be the case that they reflect spending needs only imperfectly. In practice, numerous circumstances conspire to contaminate the link between needs and such grants. For example, knowledge of the nature of spending needs may be imperfect; the data reflecting needs may be of poor quality or out of date; or the central government may have chosen not to distribute the grant purely on the basis of spending needs. Thus, if grants serve to stimulate expenditure, observed expenditure will to some extent be correlated with illegitimate factors X.

Equally, the feedback from outputs Q to endowments may be extremely important. For example, if health service utilization Q is low in an area, there may be pressure to increase provision of infrastructure S to satisfy unmet demand. Thus, it is quite plausible to posit a form of negative feedback from outputs to endowments in public sector services. This phenomenon is always likely to arise in situations where policymakers are concerned with issues relating to equity between jurisdictions (Smith 1992).

In practice, many of the effects in our model work with time lags. Thus, for example, because of delays in data collection, it is likely that spending needs at some time in the past are more important than current needs in influencing endowment. And it is likely that past output is more influential than current output in affecting endowment. Thus a full model may have a complex lag structure. However, for the purposes of this chapter, we assume that current needs are a fair proxy for past needs and that current output is a proxy for past output. Later work might refine this model.

In algebraic terms, the model has two components: an output equation

$$Q_i = f(N_i, S_i) \tag{2.1}$$

and a supply equation

$$S_i = g(N_i, X_i, Q_i) \tag{2.2}$$

where N is a vector of needs, S a vector of endowment variables, and X a vector of other (non-needs) socioeconomic data. Eliminating S from (2.1) and (2.2) gives rise to a reduced form equation for Q of the sort

$$Q_i = p(N_i, X_i) \tag{2.3}$$

which suggests that any indiscriminate empirical analysis of the relationship between output and socioeconomic circumstances is likely to reflect both legitimate (N) and illegitimate (X) causes of output Q.

If one is seeking to derive an index of spending needs based on observed outputs, the requirement is to identify a predicted level of outputs (a) that is sensitive to an area's legitimate spending needs, and (b) that assumes some standard level of service provision, given the area's needs. In principle, the process is as follows. First a standard level of endowment must be identified. That level of endowment $\overline{S}$ should reflect legitimate needs N, but not extraneous factors X, and is therefore of the form $\overline{S}_i = s(N_i)$. Then the standard level of *output*, given that standard level of endowment, is given by:

$$\overline{Q}_i = w(N_i, \overline{S}_i(N_i)) = q(N_i)$$

The needs index should therefore be based only on the N variables. The important analytic task is therefore first to identify the N variables. Then, if one believed that all the effects of the N variables were legitimate, output uncontaminated by illegitimate supply effects is given by the *truncated reduced form*

$$Q_i = q(N_i) \tag{2.4}$$

This equation reflects the impact of needs on output directly, and also to the extent that supply reflects those legitimate needs. However, it excludes the impact on Q of those parts of the illegitimate factors X which are not correlated with the legitimate factors N. If, for example, (2.1) is a linear functional form such as:

$$Q_i = \alpha + \sum_j \beta_j N_{ij} + \sum_k \gamma_k S_{ik} \tag{2.5}$$

then the coefficient on N_j in the *truncated* reduced form (2.4) will be equal to

$$\beta_j + \sum_k \gamma_k \partial S_k / \partial N_j$$

That is, the coefficient on N_j reflects legitimate needs factor j to the extent that it affects output directly through β_j and also to the extent that it is mediated through endowment via the expression

$$\sum_k \gamma_k \partial S_k / \partial N_j$$

In the context of Figure 2.1, this implies that the truncated reduced form (2.4) takes account not only of the direct impact of N on Q, but also of the correlation of N with S, and therefore of the impact of S on Q.

The user of statistical methods needs to decide whether to use the full correlation effect of needs indicators with output, or merely the partial (direct) effect. Assuming a linear functional form, all that is required to estimate the full effect of needs on output is to estimate an ordinary least squares regression of output on legitimate needs factors N. The coefficients on the N variables emerging from this analysis will then reflect the full impact of needs factors N on output. Assuming that current supply responses to legitimate needs are appropriate, no explicit consideration of supply is therefore required. It is noteworthy that, because it is a truncated reduced form, the regression equation will not exhibit the highest possible R^2. It will in general be possible to secure a better fit by indiscriminately adding additional X variables.

If only the partial effect of needs is considered relevant, then it is necessary to resort to the full equation (2.5), and to ignore in the resource allocation formula the part of the equation relating to endowments S.

Whether the full or partial approach is used is a matter of judgement. However, we would guess that – for most purposes – the full effect is required. The resulting formula will reflect endowments to the extent that they are correlated with legitimate needs, and this is likely to be consistent with the desire to capture the expenditure responses that would arise employing standard practices, and assuming standard endowments given the local levels of needs.

Unfortunately, in practice there is usually no a priori knowledge of what constitute legitimate needs variables. As a result, many empirical studies of spending needs first specify a list of potential indicators of needs. Then, using stepwise ordinary least squares regression techniques, those variables which are significant correlates of observed output are identified. If the list of potential indicators includes non-needs (X) variables, then such analysis is in effect yielding empirical estimates of equations of type (2). The regressions are therefore likely to be contaminated by endowment effects, and the usual requirement is for a 'pure' needs equation of type (2.4).

In general, therefore, even though there is no a priori knowledge of what might be legitimate N variables – some mechanism for distinguishing N variables from X variables must be found. It is not immediately obvious how this principle can be made operational. Studies of individual clients (for example, school pupils, hospital patients or social service clients) might yield useful insights into what are the legitimate determinants of needs among individuals, and it may be the case that these studies can indicate which needs variables should be used as legitimate determinants of territorial spending needs (Bebbington and Davies 1980b). However, it is not easy to design studies which eliminate endowment effects, even at the individual level. And such studies cannot give any guidance for communal services, such as police and fire.

In practice, it may therefore first be necessary explicitly to measure endowment in order to identify the correlates of endowment. This entails explicitly estimating the output and endowment equations (2.1) and (2.2) as a preliminary stage in identifying legitimate needs variables N, as a prelude to estimating the truncated reduced form (2.4). In order to do this it becomes necessary to find proxies for the relevant endowment variables S. The next section illustrates this process with examples from health services and local government in England.

4. TWO EXAMPLES

In this section we present, in the briefest outline, two case studies, which illustrate how the principles outlined above might be made operational. Fuller details can be found in the source documents.

4.1. Inpatient Hospital Services

The intention is to model demand for hospital inpatient services in the National Health Service (NHS), as described in detail by Carr-Hill et al. (1994b). As noted above, it is generally accepted that the supply of health-care facilities has a profound effect on utilization, either because limited availability constrains use or excess availability stimulates use. Utilization of NHS inpatient facilities is, therefore, presumed to depend on legitimate health-care needs variables N and health-care supply variables S, which are considered endowments. The nature of the N variables is unknown.

The year studied was 1990/91. Hospital services were then managed by 190 district health authorities, the budgets of which were set by the central government. Therefore, utilization at the district level is almost totally constrained. However, within districts, there may be differential responses to needs by the hospitals. Therefore, utilization was modelled at the small-area level (4,985 small areas with average population about 10,000, covering the whole of England). The form of the model was:

$$U_i = f(N_i, S_i)$$

where U is acute inpatient utilization standardized for age and sex (as measured by the ratio of actual costs to expected costs); N is a vector of health-care needs; and S is a vector of supply in small area i. The supply variables measured: the supply of NHS inpatient beds; the supply of general practitioners (primary care); the supply of private inpatient beds; and the supply of nursing and residential home places.

A rigorous and elaborate econometric modelling strategy was devised in which the supply variables were treated as endogenous (statistical tests confirmed endogeneity). However, the nature of the N variables was unknown. A set of 42 socioeconomic variables was therefore constructed, and used as instruments with which to model the supply variables. Moreover, the socioeconomic variables were also treated as potential needs variables. The intention was to develop a well-specified parsimonious model of utilization which incorporated the supply variables and which uncovered the most highly significant needs indicators. Eventually a model was developed using two stage least squares methods which contained the four supply variables and the following seven needs factors: density of population; mortality among those aged under 75; self-reported limiting long-standing illness among those aged under 75;unemployment; dependants (including children) living with a single carer; those in manual social classes; and those of pensionable age living alone. This is shown as the 'full' model in Table 2.1 (with standard errors in brackets).

Table 2.1   Full and truncated models, NHS acute inpatients' use

Variable	Full model	Truncated model
NHS inpatient supply	0.023 (0.050)	–
General practitioner supply	0.377 (0.081)	–
Nursing & residential homes supply	0.129 (0.067)	–
Private inpatient supply	0.121 (0.036)	–
Density of population	–0.037 (0.005)	–
% in manual social classes	0.073 (0.014)	–
% of elderly living alone	0.091 (0.024)	0.077 (0.013)
% of dependants with a single carer	0.058 (0.018)	0.044 (0.012)
% unemployed	0.047 (0.013)	0.029 (0.009)
Age-adjusted illness rate (under 75s)	0.109 (0.029)	0.253 (0.018)
Age-adjusted mortality rate (under 75s)	0.118 (0.021)	0.162 (0.013)

Source: Carr-Hill et al. (1994b).

Thus the purpose of this first stage of the modelling process was to develop a satisfactory model of utilization, and to uncover unambiguous needs variables, which explain utilization over and above supply. However, the requirement was to develop a measure which predicts the level of utilization that would arise in an area if it adopted national utilization rates in line with its health-care needs. Implicit in this definition is the assumption that the measure should be sensitive to an area's health-care needs, but dependent on its supply of health-care facilities only to the extent that they reflect legitimate needs. In this respect it is important to note that needs affect utilization in two ways: first, through their direct impact on utilization and second through their indirect influence on endowments (supply) which in turn influence utilization. Thus the analytic problem was to model utilization as a function of the needs variables that had been identified in the two stage least squares analysis.

This suggests that – once needs variables had been identified – the final stage of the analysis should be to carry out a regression of utilization on those needs variables only (that is, omitting the supply variables). In fact, because it was felt that there were additional effects of district health authority policies on utilization, this regression was carried out using the multilevel modelling methods developed in the education sector, rather than ordinary least squares methods (Paterson and Goldstein 1991). This is a further complication that lies outside the scope of this chapter. Moreover, two of the needs indicators were dropped because of their minor influence on the final equation. The chosen truncated model is shown as the final column of table 2.1. Formulae derived in this way are now being used as the basis for a national formula for the purposes of allocating over £18 billion of NHS resources annually (NHS Executive 1994).

4.2.   Local Government Expenditure

The biggest source of funds for English local governments is the central government grant-in-aid, paid to equalize for differences in territorial needs and taxable resources. In effect it accounts for over 80 per cent of all local government finance. A local government's grant is lump sum (fixed). The only other significant source of finance is the local property tax (the Council Tax). Therefore, all marginal spending must be met by the Council Tax. The intention of this study is to model the determinants of local spending (Duncan and Smith, 1994).

The basic model used assumes that the utility U of a representative voter in local authority i depends on the level of expenditure x_i adopted (a proxy for local services provided) and some measure of the level of local taxation t_i. Following standard modelling practice, it is assumed that U can be represented by the equation

$$U_i = \alpha_1 \ln(x_i - N_i) + \alpha_2 \ln(Y_i - t_i)$$

where N_i is a measure of legitimate expenditure needs in jurisdiction i, Y_i is income, and the parameters α_1 and α_2 are common across all jurisdictions. Throughout, all variables are measured in per capita terms.

The budget constraint of local authority i is given by $x_i = G_i + t_i$ where G_i is the per capita grant. Maximizing utility subject to the budget constraint yields the expenditure equation

$$x_i = \frac{\alpha_1 Y_i + \alpha_2 N_i + \alpha_1 G_1}{\alpha_1 + \alpha_2}$$

That is, per capita expenditure in authority i is a function of local income Y_i, legitimate needs N_i and central government grant G_i.

A further issue is that – in the year to be studied (1991–92) – the central government placed an upper limit (CAP_i) on the amount a local government could spend. This feature complicates the econometrics considerably, but does not materially affect the principles of the study method.

The units of analysis were the 296 non-metropolitan districts in England. A total of 16 socioeconomic variables were constructed from the 1991 Census of Population and other sources. Grant G was treated as endogenous. The intention was to find a satisfactory model of per capita expenditure (or desired expenditure among those districts spending at their upper limit) which included the grant G, income Y, and a small number of needs indicators. Using a censored regression with endogenous grant, very few of the socioeconomic variables displayed any statistical significance. The three exceptions were political control; the age-adjusted rate of limiting long-standing illness; and the proportion of 17 year olds not at school.

Interpreting these results is problematic. For most needs-assessment purposes, political control must be considered an illegitimate influence on spending. Furthermore, it may well be the case that spending needs are already captured in the grant G, so that the study methodology is inappropriate for identifying additional needs determinants of spending. But, if this is the case, then it is difficult to envisage any analytic procedure which can satisfactorily isolate needs effects. The usefulness of statistical analysis in these circumstances is likely to be limited. Nevertheless, the method has identified two variables – relating to long-term illness and early school-leaving – which do appear to have an impact on spending over and above any endowment effect, and which may therefore be considered legitimate needs indicators.

5. CONCLUSION

Many empirical studies of territorial spending needs have no theoretical framework and are based on inadequate statistical methods. The brief exposition here suggests the following issues must be considered before undertaking such studies:

- what is the purpose of the analysis? What are to be considered legitimate determinants of expenditure variations?
- To what extent is output currently constrained? Have any such constraints been properly modelled?
- What are the endowments which might affect spending? How are they to be captured?
- What are legitimate indicators of spending needs? How does their correlation with endowments influence the results?

The discussion suggests that, if current endowments are in any way contaminated by illegitimate factors, the modelling process may be very difficult, and may indeed be beyond the scope of existing methodology. Analysts must be forever vigilant about the limitations of their craft.

REFERENCES

Barrow, M.M. (1986), 'Central Grants to Local Governments: A Game Theoretic Approach', *Environment and Planning C: Government and Policy*, **4**, 155–64.

Bebbington, A.C. and B. Davies (1980a), 'Territorial Needs Indicators: A New Approach Part I', *Journal of Social Policy*, **9** (2), 145–68.

Bebbington, A.C. and B. Davies (1980b), 'Territorial Needs Indicators: A New Approach Part II', *Journal of Social Policy*, **9** (4), 433–62.

Bennett, R.J. (1982), *Central Grants to Local Governments*, Cambridge: Cambridge University Press.

Bramley, G. (1990), *Equalization Grants and Local Expenditure Needs*, Aldershot: Avebury.

Carr-Hill, R., G. Hardman, S. Martin, S. Peacock, T. Sheldon and P. Smith (1994a), *A Formula for Distributing NHS Revenues Based on Small Area Use of Hospital Beds*, York: Centre for Health Economics, University of York.

Carr-Hill, R.A., T.A. Sheldon, P. Smith, S. Martin, S. Peacock and G. Hardman (1994b), 'Allocating Resources to Health Authorities:

Development of Methods for Small Area Analysis of Use of Inpatient Services', *British Medical Journal*, **309,** 1046–49.

Duncan, A. and P. Smith (1994), *The Impact of Expenditure Limitation on Local Government Expenditure Choices*, York: Department of Economics, University of York.

Heald, D. (1983), *Public Expenditure*, Oxford: Martin Robinson.

King, D. (1984), *Fiscal Tiers: the Economics of Multi-Level Government*, London: Allen & Unwin.

Maslow, A. (1943), 'A Theory of Human Motivation', *Psychological Review*, **50**, 370– 96.

Mays, N. and G. Bevan (1987), *Resource Allocation in the Health Service*, Occasional Paper in Social Administration 81, London: Bedford Square Press.

Mooney, G (1982), *Equity in Health Care: Confronting the Confusion*. Discussion Paper No 11/82, Aberdeen: Health Economics Research Unit.

National Health Service Executive (1994), *NHS Resource Allocation*, Leeds: The Executive.

Paterson, L. and H. Goldstein (1991), 'New Statistical Methods for Analysing Social Structures: An Introduction to Multilevel Models', *British Educational Research Journal*, **17** (4), 387-93.

Royston, G.H.D., J.W. Hurst, E.G. Lister and P.A. Stewart (1992), 'Modelling the Use of Health Services by Populations of Small Areas to Inform the Allocation of Central Resources to Larger Regions', *Socioeconomic Planning Sciences*, **26** (3), 169-80.

Sheldon, T.A. and R.A. Carr-Hill (1992), 'Resource Allocation by Regression in the NHS: A Statistical Critique of the RAWP Review', *Journal of the Royal Statistical Society (Series A)*, **155** (3), 403–20.

Smith, P. (1992), 'Negative Political Feedback: An Examination of the Problem of Modelling Political Responses in Public Sector Effectiveness Auditing', *Accounting, Auditing and Accountability Journal*, **5** (1), 5–20.

Society of County Treasurers (1994), *Standard Spending Indicators, 1994– 95*, Stafford: Society of County Treasurers.

3. Judgement and Analysis: Developing Indexes of Economic and Social Deprivation for Local Authority Financing

Paul J. Chapman

1. INTRODUCTION

The methodology underlying the distribution of funding to local authorities in England has been based on a system of Standard Spending Assessments (SSAs) since 1990–91. This chapter is concerned with the measurement of deprivation factors and implications for the need to spend in local authorities. The chapter focuses on a number of SSA issues: factor analysis as a method for selecting deprivation measures for SSAs; the criteria which have been used in the selection process for the SSAs; and the underlying methodology for SSAs. The focus for illustrating these issues is the construction of the Other Services SSA formula in England for 1994–95.

SSAs are an assessment of the appropriate amount of revenue expenditure which would allow an authority to provide what is known as a 'standard level of service'. SSAs are a central part of public finance; they provide a basis for the distribution of local government support and are used as a benchmark for expenditure limitation. SSAs are primarily a basis for the distribution of central government support to local authorities. The SSA formulae are concerned with the distribution of resources; the overall funding available to authorities is a separate financial issue.

The total SSA represents broadly what central government estimates that local government should spend. The total SSA in 1994–95 was £42.7 billion (bn), or £37.8bn net of certain specific grants. SSAs are based on seven main service blocks. This chapter is concerned with the Other Services Block (OSB) which is one of these seven blocks. The OSB SSA was £7.7bn in 1994–95. This is divided into district- and county-level services, with £5.7bn allowed for district-level services (excluding interest receipts) in 1994–95.Certain limitations of the chapter should be noted. First, the analysis examines in detail the measurement of deprivation for the district-level Other Services SSA formula and is not concerned with the rest of the SSAs. Although this is only a small part of the SSA distribution mechanism, it illustrates the main issues involved in relating distribution to deprivation and indicates the basis for a part of the current SSA formula. Second, the focus is on the relationship between the costs of service provision and deprivation and not on measuring some abstract notion of deprivation. It has to be recognized that the measures of deprivation are ultimately used in an SSA formula and this might limit what would otherwise be possible. One simple matter is that it would not be desirable to have a very large number of indicators which would be inconsistent with the approach taken generally in SSAs, which is to avoid excessive complexity. Finally, any measurement of deprivation cannot be precise and one simple benchmark to evaluate the final results would have to be the plausibility of the new method compared with the equivalent approach which had been used to measure deprivation in the 1993–94 SSAs.

This chapter focuses on the review of the OSB SSA where an entirely new economic index was introduced along with a revised social index. The other changes in the OSB formula introduced in 1994–95 are not examined in detail.[1]

The chapter has three further main sections followed by conclusions. Section 2 considers some of the important methodology issues which are relevant to both SSAs and their relation to deprivation. Section 3 provides some further details about the structure of the OSB SSA and examines the problems identified with the previous formula. Section 4 sets out the structure of the analysis undertaken to derive the new formula, describing the factor analysis and defining the indexes derived from this factor analysis. Conclusions follow.

2. METHODOLOGY

2.1. Methodology Issues

The SSA methodology does not define a level of absolute need. SSAs are explained as 'providing for a standard level of service'. This essentially tautological explanation of SSAs means that there is no 'ideal base measure of need' to compare with the actual SSA. The SSAs are simply a distributional mechanism which estimates the needs of each authority compared with any other authority and divides the overall control total between authorities in proportion to their relative need. In following this conceptual framework, the measure of relative deprivation which is required need bear no relation with absolute need. Individual authorities could find their needs and resources moving in opposite directions. This possibility is important in assessing the outcome. The issue of whether an entirely different method of needs assessment would be better than this is not considered in this chapter.

The formula is a top-down approach. There is no direct estimate of the cost of particular services. The relative need of authorities is measured through indicators and amounts distributed are based on a given control total. This approach attaches great importance to the principle of 'fair shares' within overall resource constraints.[2]

SSAs are distributional formulae which are based on 'proxy' indicators which are used to indirectly measure variations in need. These indicators have to be related to factors which directly drive needs but they must also be outside the control of individual authorities. The proxies used should not to be confused with the provision of funding for the need for a particular service. For example, the housing benefit indicator is not used to specifically compensate authorities for costs associated with the provision of housing benefit; it is simply one of several indicators of economic deprivation.

SSAs are based on control totals which are then distributed among authorities on the basis of various indicators. For example, in OSB the district-level control total is divided between authorities on the basis of enhanced population. There are adjustments for economic and social factors, population density, population sparsity and area cost adjustment.

The most prominent technical issue concerning SSA methodology is the use of regression analysis. The current method seeks to base the SSA formulae on regressions of expenditure per head against indicators of need. An issue of increasing concern is whether the negative feedback from SSAs to expenditure invalidate these regressions. Hypothecation within the SSAs may exacerbate this problem if authorities feel bound to spend their service budgets equal to their SSA for a particular service. Where this occurs the variation in expenditure which drives the SSA formulae may become so weak and unrelated to need that the regressions provide no worthwhile information. It has been suggested that the system of local authority expenditure controls (the capping regime) has intensified this problem because authorities will be forced in the long run to spend at or near their SSA. This is certainly a long-run problem although it might be argued that the use of 1990–91 expenditure data was preferable to completely unconstrained expenditure data where systematic overspending might have distorted the data in a different way. This may be an issue for future reviews of SSAs.

The regressions used in SSAs are based on simple linear OLS estimation method. There is little account taken of more sophisticated diagnostics or non-linear specifications. Furthermore, the analysis does not systematically examine the residuals in detail. While this might be desirable in scientific experiments it might be difficult to apply to SSAs because it would involve more judgement – on specific technical issues on the choice of method, the interpretation of diagnostics and criteria for selecting outliers. For example, any residual analysis might suggest several alternative regression techniques to eliminate systematic variations in residuals.

It might seem inconsistent with this 'keep it simple' approach in SSA methodology to encounter the use of factor analysis in the development of composite indices of deprivation. However, one of the reasons for using a factor analysis is to limit, if not entirely exclude, judgement in choosing indicators of deprivation.

Indicators of need are often very highly correlated but it is also desirable for a distribution formula to reflect a range of factors because this reduces the possibility of an individual authority being unduly affected by a particular indicator which is not representative of its own situation. Otherwise the regression-based SSA would depend on some prior view of which indicators are the most important or a simple 'stepwise' approach in which 'goodness of fit' would determine the specification. In either of these cases the number of indicators which could be included would be limited where any significant multicollinearity is present. This is the main reason why a composite index approach is an attractive basis for reflecting deprivation in several SSA formulae. There is no clear theoretical basis for the selection of indicators for the OSB and the problem naturally lends itself to the use of composite indices; several indicators can be included without the statistical problems arising from a direct regression with separate indicators.

The purpose of the factor analysis is to limit the choice of indicators. Groups of indicators (referred to as factors) can be identified. From these groups we can identify representative subsets of indicators within groups. Having selected the indicators on this basis there is less scope in the regression stage to select or deselect any indicators purely on the basis of statistical fit or other arguments. The method limits the scope for judgement.

The choice of indicators in any SSA block must take account of a wide range of issues. One aspect of distribution is the range of indicators the authorities feel should be included. It is desirable to consider the inclusion of indicators where there is a widespread demand because it is desirable to satisfy as far as possible any common agreement by those affected by the choice of indicators. This choice is also governed by statistical criteria. For example, heavily skewed indicators are not as attractive as more normally distributed indicators; proportions based on a few observations are less attractive.

A fundamental issue in SSAs is the extent to which the formulae should aim to target need at a detailed or disaggregated level. In general, the SSA methodology adopts a highly aggregated view of needs provision. In the OSB SSA, over 30 very different services are grouped together and a single formula is applied across them all.[3]

The SSA methodology is based on the concept of a client group with an associated unit cost. The OSB client group is an aggregate of different client groups referred to as 'enhanced population'. Enhanced population consists of resident population with adjustments for commuters, overnight and day visitors. The unit costs of the client group are assumed to depend on indicators of need. Regression analysis is used to measure the basis for the precise costs of these indicators of need.

2.2. Measures of Deprivation Used in OSB

Until 1994–95 the OSB formula included an All Ages Social Index (AASI) to represent 'social' conditions. The AASI has been the subject of criticism in various studies.[4] The AASI included three housing-related indicators, an ethnicity indicator and a lone parent indicator. One of the main criticisms of the formula was that there was no allowance for economic factors especially unemployment. It was also felt that health-related indicators merited consideration. The absence of economic and health factors contrasted with the dominant role of housing factors.

One of the housing variables in the AASI was an indicator which reflected lack of facilities within households (lack of bath or inside WC). It was clear that this variable no longer served a useful purpose because only a small proportion of households now lacked these facilities. Even though housing indicators were well represented within the index it was also suggested that alternative housing indicators might be more effective.

Another criticism was that the deprivation ranking of authorities according to the AASI was implausible. Many authorities which were felt to be far from deprived had a very high ranking. This argument was difficult to evaluate because the index was not an index of deprivation as such, but an index measuring the need to provide certain services. Many of the problems can be traced to the emphasis on housing factors and the fact that other aspects of deprivation were not explicitly represented.

A further point about the AASI was that it consisted of census variables which could only be revised every decade following a new census. The new indexes, in particular the Economic Index, offer the possibility of more regular updating.

No changes were made compared with 1993–94 to the overall structure of the OSB SSA. In particular, the previous formula was based on an aggregation of service expenditure to provide for a single formula at the district level. One criticism of the OSB formula is that it covers a wide range of services and that it would be preferable to have a separate formula for each identifiable service.

Although disaggregation was considered, the simpler aggregate approach was preferred. The argument in favour of a more aggregated approach is that SSAs were constructed on the basis that the formulae should be understandable; a large number of separate formulae for each service would present a significant departure from this principle.

Finally, when the SSA outcomes in other services were examined it was clear that there was considerable dispersion. It was possible that this variation in SSAs might be reduced with a wider range of indicators although not all of the variation was due to the measurement of economic and social factors. However, many authorities appeared to have a very high SSA per head in the OSB SSA and most of these had very high values of deprivation measured by the AASI.

3. MEASURING SOCIAL AND ECONOMIC DEPRIVATION

Several selection criteria were applied to identify suitable deprivation indicators. First, any indicator had to be plausible as a measure of deprivation. This would be the case with any attempt to measure deprivation. Second, the final indexes would need to be relevant to the expenditure on the services provided. In practice, all the indicators which were finally selected for the indexes proved to be generally well related to expenditure. Third, any indicator had to have specific characteristics for SSA purposes; it needed to be available at the district level; it had to be robust at the authority level; and it had to be outside the control of authorities. Despite these constraints, it was still possible to include a wide range of potential indicators.

One approach to measuring deprivation would be to take existing measures of deprivation and apply these within the SSA formula. However, existing indexes were not developed for SSAs and this chapter does not present any direct comparisons of different indexes.[5] There are clear advantages in constructing indexes which are specific to the relevant deprivation factors. The revision of the SSA formula consisted of three stages:

1. a factor analysis was undertaken to inform the construction of deprivation indexes;

2. the selected indicators were standardized and then combined into composite indexes;
3. the weightings in the SSA formula on the indexes were based on a regression with unit costs as the dependent variable.

The analysis is based on the view that there will be groups of indicators which belong together; these groups represent an underlying influence. Whether or not this is the case would be confirmed by the factor analysis which is designed to identify these groups. The purpose of the factor analysis was to identify a set of indicators which represent a wider range of deprivation measures. It emerged in the analysis that the indicators which were selected could be combined into two groups. Composite indexes can be constructed from these identified groups of indicators (or subsets of them) and finally these composite indexes can be included as independent variables in a regression to explain unit costs.

There are specific advantages in this approach. First, the choice of indicators can be at least partially improved by the factor analysis. The alternative of a stepwise regression or any method using indicators separately would be impractical with so many (highly correlated) indicators. There are also some important advantages of using the composite indexes. First, several well-correlated variables can be included in the final regression analysis. Second, the robustness of the final SSA measures are increased by including several indicators of deprivation; it is much less likely that the SSA for any particular authority will be unduly affected by unrepresentative values of particular indicators. The approach reflected the recommendations by Bartholomew (1988).

The use of composite indexes poses several problems. The large number of indicators which were considered in the analysis meant that it was not practical to consider all the possible combinations of indicators within the indexes. It was also desirable to have a balance of different types of indicator. Finally, there was frequently a choice in selecting a specific definition of an indicator. For example, there were several possible measures of unemployment. These were all highly correlated and all were potentially suitable variables to reflect local labour market conditions.[6]

The data used in the factor analysis consisted of a wide range of economic, social and health-related variables; 65 variables were considered. The final analysis was based on a smaller 'core' data set of just 17 variables. The main stages of the factor analysis were:

1. computing the correlation matrix for all the variables;
2. extracting the principal components;
3. rotating the principal components;
4. identifying 'groups of variables'.

A brief explanation of each of these stages is provided below.

Variables which are poorly related at the initial stage of the analysis are unlikely to belong in the same index. Variables which are very highly correlated are equally unsuitable for inclusion for two reasons. First, adding highly correlated variables in an index will not add much further explanatory power to the final regression. Second, the inclusion of highly correlated variables may distort the factor coefficients on other variables.

The factor analysis was then applied to the core data set. To determine the composition of each index requires a particular method for factor extraction. This involves the computation of a set of coefficients or loadings for each factor. Each factor will have a set of coefficients which can be applied to all of the selected variables. The principal components method of factor analysis was used throughout.

The identified factors can be 'rotated' to identify sets of variables which are the most important for each of the factors. The factor rotation phase defines the variables within each index; each factor having a common theme such as social deprivation, economic status or housing conditions. The factor analysis rotation is a helpful but not essential aid to identifying the final indicators.

The main identified factors were the basis for choosing the indicators within each index. The exact index values were defined as the unweighted sum of the standardized values of each indicator. There are three advantages in using unweighted variables. First, normal updating would not require a new factor analysis. Second, an index using the sum of the unweighted variables is consistent with the aim of keeping SSAs simple. Third, an unweighted index would not depend on the choice of a particular factor analysis method.

A number of variables were removed from the analysis. The basis for the selection of the final set of variables used in the factor analysis was to reflect a wide variety of different deprivation factors. Many variables were too highly correlated with others in the data set and indicators with a correlation of above 0.9 were identified and one was selected.[7] Some variables were simply alternative definitions. For example, it was decided to omit from the further analysis all the census measures of unemployment. The census and DE measures of unemployment were all highly correlated with each other. The DE measures were preferred because they could be updated. The final list of variables included in the factor analysis is given in Appendix 3A. The final factor analysis output is given in Table 3.1.

Two factors were found to represent about 70 per cent of the total variation in the data. On the basis of this analysis two indexes were constructed; an index consisting of economic variables and an index consisting of social variables. The choice of the variables in the social index was betterdetermined by the analysis whereas the cut-off point for inclusion in the economic index was not as well defined.

Table 3.1   Factor analysis rotated factor matrix varimax method

	Factor 1	Factor 2
Rented accommodation	0.71245	0.45825
Purpose-built flats	0.43697	**0.78091**
Not self-contained or non-permanent accommodation	–0.23492	**0.63284**
Crowded accommodation	0.49591	**0.73052**
Without use of a car	0.85217	0.45012
Lower social class	0.76174	0.41484
Ethnicity	0.03117	**0.90141**
Unemployment	**0.88559**	0.27913
Births weighing more than 2,500 kg	0.65462	0.28936
Death rate for children	0.53937	0.10620
Years of lost life	0.88321	0.12686
Homelessness	0.46323	**0.71901**
Housing benefit cases	**0.82673**	0.41703
Standardized mortality ratio	**0.92206**	0.10387
Standardized morbidity ratio	0.93958	–0.02297
Lone-parent families	0.72187	0.57811
Ratio of long-term to total unemployment	**0.84921**	0.12451
Eigenvalue	9.89416	2.75212
% variation	58.2	16.2
Cumulative variation	–	74.4

Notes: Selected indicators in bold. Definitions in Appendix 3A.

The basis for choosing the indicators was to select indicators with the highest coefficient score from the factor analysis. There were three exceptions to this rule. 'Persons in households without a car' was excluded because it was decided that it might discriminate against rural areas where a car was more necessary than in urban areas. There were other variables with quite high coefficients in the factor analysis which did not have this problem. The 'mortality ratio' was chosen in preference to the 'morbidity ratio' and 'years of lost life' because the mortality ratio is a more commonly understood indicator and had been widely suggested as a potentially useful SSA indicator. The statistical results alone were not conclusive. Finally, it was decided that there should be five indicators in each index. This was judgemental, influenced by the choice of five indicators in the AASI which the new indexes would replace.

4. USING THE ECONOMIC AND SOCIAL INDEXES IN SSAS

The definitions of the economic and social indexes selected for the SSA formula were based on the factor analysis.

The Social Index is derived using:

- the proportion of households in purpose-built flats in residential buildings rented from local authorities, new towns or housing associations;
- the proportion of persons in accommodation which is not self-contained or non-permanent;
- the proportion of persons living at a density greater than one person per room;
- the proportion of persons in households born outside the UK, Republic of Ireland, the Old Commonwealth and the US;
- the number of households greater than one person accepted as homeless relative to the resident population.

The Economic Index contains the following series:

- total unemployment as a percentage of the total working population;
- the number of housing benefit cases as a proportion of population;
- the standardized mortality ratio for persons under 75 years of age;
- the proportion of persons in households containing lone-parent households with dependent children;
- the number of persons unemployed for more than one year divided by the total number of persons unemployed.

The choice of variables in the economic index was much less clear and a range of different variables emerged from the analysis. In particular, the health variables were found to belong in the Economic Index.

The Economic Index explained most of the variation in the original data. However, the relative importance of the two factors at this stage of the analysis must be distinguished from the final regression analysis for the OSB formula. Although some variables can be treated as alternatives (for example male and total unemployment rates) it is not possible to consider all the possible economic indexes for the regressions. In the regression analysis a number of options were considered. The output from the regressions showed that both Economic and Social Indexes were significant. The final regression output is shown in Table 3.2.

Table 3.2   Regression on unit expenditure

Variable	Coefficient	Statistic
Economic Index	2.162	6.828
Social Index	3.521	6.755
ED Density	0.282	3.044
Constant	83.320	–

Notes: Adjusted R^2 = 0.67. Number of observations = 361. Westminster and Kensington & Chelsea, City and Isles of Scilly were omitted as outliers. The City and Isles of Scilly have always been excluded from SSA regressions in all other services because they are so different in character from others. The two London authorities were omitted because the expenditure per head data for these authorities were clearly outliers and would have had undue leverage on the results. The dependent variable is based on total expenditure on all other services divided by 'enhanced population'. The latter is based on the numbers of residents in an authority plus weighted numbers of overnight visitors, day visitors and net commuter flows. The coefficients measure the 'unit cost' influence of each of the variables.

5. CONCLUSIONS

The new indexes have several major implications for the OSB SSA:

1. The introduction of economic factors, supported by the statistical analysis, is an important change in the district formula.
2. The factor analysis was useful in establishing the composition of the indexes. The lone-parent factor was found to belong in the economic index whereas it had been previously grouped with social factors. The health variables were found to be closely related with economic factors rather than with social factors.
3. The analysis suggested relatively minor changes in the measurement of social factors. There has been a relatively small change in the definition of the new social index compared with the previous social index (the AASI); three indicators are the same in the two indexes. Many of the criticisms of the AASI were arguably due to the lack of an adequate measure of economic deprivation rather than an inadequate measurement of social conditions.
4. The economic index, and to a lesser extent the new social index, can be anually updated. Any index fixed at a point in time is likely to become less relevant at least for some authorities experiencing rapid change. The possibility of reflecting change is an important option for future years.
5. It is clear that both judgement and statistical analysis played a part in

revising the approach to reflecting deprivation factors in the SSA formula. The factor analysis provided a statistical basis for refining but not excluding the use of judgement.

NOTES

1. Further details of the relevant work related to this chapter can be found in papers by the Department of the Environment (1993a) and (1993b).
2. An alternative would be a 'bottom-up' approach which attempted to estimate costs of particular services.
3. The type of service covered in the OSB district-level formula include concessionary fares, economic development, housing benefit, museums, planning and refuse collection. See the Local Government Finance Report (England) 1994/95 for further details.
4. See for example, Senior et al. (1992), The National Audit Office (1993) and Smith (1993).
5. One possible index which might have been used is the Index of Local Conditions. This includes several indicators which are also in the Economic and Social Indexes (see Department of the Environment 1994).
6. Exceptionally, the final specification of the Economic Index includes two measures of unemployment but one reflects the current rate of overall unemployment while the other reflects the extent to which an area has more or less long-term unemployment for a given degree of unemployment.
7. There was no precise statistical method for choosing which indicators to eliminate. One criteria was to eliminate indicators measuring the same aspect of deprivation such as unemployment. Another factor was to eliminate indicators which had a very low correlation with indicators which were finally selected.

REFERENCES

Bartholomew, R. (1988), *Measuring Social Disadvantage and Additional Education Needs, An Assessment of Methods Carried Out for the Department of the Environment,* Mimeo, London: London School of Economics.

Department of the Environment (1993a), *The Review of the All Ages Social Index and the Other Services Block Formula,* London: SWG:SSASG (93) (61).

Department of the Environment (1993b), *Further Analysis of the Other Services Block (Osb): Factor Analysis of the Proxy Indicators,* SWG:SSASG (93) (78).

Department of the Environment (1994), *Index of Local Conditions: An Analysis Based on 1991 Census Data.*

HMSO (1994), *Standard Spending Assessments,* London: Environment Committee, First Report

National Audit Office (1993), *Passing the Bucks,* London: National Audit Office.

Senior M, M. Powell, R. Knowles, K. Grime and R. Barker (1992), *Standard Spending Assessments, A Report for Wigan Metropolitan Borough Council,* Salford: Department of Geography, University of Salford,

Smith, P. (1993), *Measures of Social Needs in Standard Spending Assessments,* York: Centre for Health Economics, University of York.

APPENDIX 3A: VARIABLE DEFINITIONS

VAR01   Proportion of persons in accommodation rented from Local Authority/New Town or Housing Association
Source: 1991 Census

VAR02   Proportion of households in purpose-built flats in residential buildings rented from Local Authority/New Town or Housing Association
Source: 1991 Census

VAR03   Proportion of persons in accommodation which is not self-contained or which is non-permanent
Source: 1991 Census

VAR04   Proportion of persons living at a density of more than 1 person per room
Source: 1991 Census

VAR05   Proportion of persons in households without use of a car
Source: 1991 Census

VAR06   Proportion of residents in households with a head of household in the lower social classes
Source: 1991 Census

VAR07   Proportion of persons in households who were born outside the UK, Republic of Ireland, Old Commonwealth or US
Source: 1991 Census

VAR08   Number of persons unemployed as a proportion of the working population
Source: Employment Department

VAR09   Proportion of births weighing more than 2,500 g (average 1989–91)
Source: OPCS

VAR10   Death rate among children aged under one (average 1989–91)
Source: OPCS

VAR11   Years of life lost (average 1989–91)
Source: OPCS

VAR12   Priority needs households (more than one person) (average 1989–92) relative to mid-91 resident population
Source: Department of the Environment

VAR13   Housing benefit cases (including non-Income Support claimants) (average 1990–92) relative to mid-91 resident population
Source: Department of Social Security

VAR14   Standardized Mortality Ratio (average 1990–92, ages 0 to 74 years)
Source: OPCS

VAR15   Standardized Morbidity Ratio (age and sex, residents in households)
Source: 1991 Census (derived)
VAR16   Proportion of persons in households containing lone-parent families with dependent children
Source: 1991 Census
VAR17   Ratio of long-term to total unemployment
Source: Employment Department (derived)

4. A Model of Optimum Local Authority Size

David King

1. INTRODUCTION

The issue of optimum local authority size has been discussed by many economists (for example Tiebout 1961, Olson 1969, Tullock 1969, Oates 1972, Musgrave and Musgrave 1976, Breton and Scott 1978, and Atkinson and Stiglitz 1980). In an earlier work,[1] I built on this previous discussion to outline a model of optimum size. The principal purposes of this chapter are to formalize and develop that earlier model, and so highlight the key factors affecting optimum size. The developments of the earlier model include considering the implications of local authorities as enabling rather than producing bodies, that is of their being able to purchase services from private producers, so that even small authorities can secure all possible benefits of economies of scale in production if they purchase services from large enough private firms.

The scope for economists to make recommendations on local government structure is limited. In particular, the welfare gains and losses experienced by individual citizens from different structures will depend on their own preferences which will generally not be revealed. So economic analysis cannot hope to ascertain the exact optimum size. Nevertheless, economic analysis should at least indicate the main factors on which the optimum size depends.

The chapter is organized as follows. Section 2 discusses some basic issues concerned with local authority size, Section 3 presents the model, Section 4 presents three developments of the model, and Section 5 presents some conclusions.

2. ISSUES OF LOCAL AUTHORITY SIZE

This section considers four issues relating to the concept of optimum local authority size. The first is whether size should be measured by area or population. This chapter assumes that the relevant factor is population, as does all earlier theoretical work. Of course, a decision to have more populous authorities is equivalent to making them larger in terms of area, and vice versa, but it is supposed that welfare depends directly on population rather than area.

The second issue is how authorities of the appropriate populations could be created. This chapter adopts the normal procedure by assuming that the local authority boundaries are the variables, so that authority populations can be increased by widening the boundaries and having fewer authorities or vice versa. This procedure assumes there is no technological reason why the authorities providing any local service could not be increased or decreased in area and population. An alternative procedure is to assume that local authority boundaries are effectively fixed by technological factors. Thus the area covered by a television transmitter or a flood control scheme might not be alterable, so the only way to alter the population that benefits from the service is physically to move people in or out. Although there is an interesting literature on this approach,[2] it does not seem appropriate for most local authority services and is not explored further here.

The third issue arises from the fact that the model developed here indicates the main factors that determine the optimum population size for an individual local authority service. In practice, it might be found that there was a different optimum size for each local authority service. If so, there would be two policy options. One would be to establish for each local service a set or tier of authorities of the appropriate size, so that there would be many tiers of authorities. The other would be to establish a modest number of tiers and entrust each tier with a range of services for which it was close to, if not exactly, the optimum size. This issue is considered briefly in Subsection 4.3, but the model outlined here is concerned with the initial step of ascertaining the optimum size for a single particular function.

Finally, whatever population size emerged as optimal for a particular tier, it might not be practicable to make all authorities that size because of geographical boundaries, townships, ethnic, religious or cultural groups and so on. These very real problems are ignored here as the model focuses on the basic factors that should be taken into account in determining optimum size, but they would have to be considered in practice.

3. A MODEL OF OPTIMUM SIZE

Suppose a country with a total population of n has no local authorities at present. It contemplates introducing a tier of authorities to provide a single service. Each local authority would provide – but not necessarily produce – a single service for its residents, in accordance with the wishes of its median voter. Each authority would be given the same population size S. The boundaries of the authorities, and hence S, are variable, though S is necessarily constrained by $1 \le S \le n$. As there are at present no local authorities providing the service, any current provision of it must be provided by individual citizens for themselves. So the present situation is represented by regarding $S = 1$. The aim of the model is to show the key factors which determine the optimum value for S, that is S^*, which is the value which maximizes welfare for the citizens of the country as a whole.

The model ignores the problems of interpersonal comparisons of utility and social welfare functions by assuming that the aim is a simple one of maximizing the sum of individual utilities. It is assumed that all consumers have equal incomes and equal (constant) marginal utilities of income, so that consumer surplus gains and losses can be taken as measuring welfare gains and losses. It is also assumed that incomes and preferences are constant over time so that it is necessary to look only at the gains and losses in any particular year and see which size of authority results in the maximum net gain; the implications of relaxing this assumption are noted in Subsection 4.2.

Why might welfare rise if $S > 1$ and individual provision is replaced by group provision? There are three reasons. First, group provision may reduce the unit cost of the service concerned. Second, with individual provision, citizens will ignore the external effects of their provision on other citizens in their locality; these effects will be internalized with group provision. Third, with individual provision, citizens will ignore the external effects of their provision on citizens outside their locality; with local authority provision there may be scope for bargains between different authorities to help take account of these externalities.

Typically, the actual benefits from group provision will fall short of the hoped-for gains as there will be a shortfall, or loss, to set against the hoped-for gains. The reason that citizens' welfare will not increase by the amount they hope is that the quantities and qualities of the service that will be provided will now be decided by their local authorities, not by citizens themselves, and thus may differ from the quantities and qualities that the citizens desire. S^* is the size that secures the largest gap between the hoped-for gains and the losses. Thus S^* depends on the relationship between S and the hoped-for gains and losses. So each possible S must be examined to see which one produces the largest gap. This chapter focuses on the potential gains from a reduction in unit costs and the shortfall arising from the loss of individual control. The effects of internalizing externalities are considered briefly in Subsection 4.1, but a full discussion of them would require a separate chapter.

Subsection 3.1 examines the potential gains from a fall in costs. Subsections 3.2, 3.3 and 3.4 consider the shortfall and optimum size in three different circumstances. Subsection 3.2 assumes that preferences are homogeneous within areas and between areas; 3.3 assumes that preferences are heterogeneous within areas but that the distribution of preferences is homogeneous between areas; and 3.4 assumes that preferences are heterogeneous within areas and that the distribution of preferences is heterogeneous between areas.

3.1.   Costs and Authority Size

To understand the hoped-for gains from local authority provision, the relationship between authority size and service costs must be explored. The fall in unit costs as S rises from its initial value of 1 depends on the relationship between the total cost of a service, C, the level of service, indicated by the number of units consumed by each person, Q, and the number of people in each area, that is the size of area, S. It is assumed that this relationship is given by:

$$C = kQS^{\alpha} \qquad\qquad (4.1)$$

where $k > 0$ and $0 \leq \alpha \leq 1$. This relationship is similar to those discussed by Borcherding and Deacon (1972) and Bergstrom and Goodman (1973). It follows from (4.1) that the cost per person, C/S, is $kQS^{\alpha-1}$ or $kQ/S^{1-\alpha}$. The unit cost per person, C/QS, is given by $kS^{\alpha-1}$. This is also the average tax-price per person, P, and it can be re-expressed as:

$$P = k/S^{1-\alpha} \qquad\qquad (4.2)$$

Notice from (4.1) that if $\alpha = 1$, one of its extreme permitted values, then $C = kQS$. Here the cost per person, C/S, equals kQ, irrespective of authority size, and the unit cost per person, C/QS, is simply k. So in this case there are no gains from lower unit costs per person as individual provision is replaced by successively larger local authorities. If $\alpha = 0$, its other extreme permitted value, then $C = kQ$. This is the pure public goods case where costs depend only on the service level and are independent of population. Here the cost per person, C/S, is given by kQ/S, and the unit cost per person, C/QS, by k/S. So the unit cost per person falls proportionately as population rises.

Much of the local public finance literature assumes that local authorities provide pure public goods so that $\alpha = 0$. However, in the United Kingdom, it has been noted by Foster, Jackman and Perlman (1980) and the Local Government Commission (1993) that there is little evidence for economies of scale in local services and hence little evidence that $\alpha < 1$. This limited evidence may arise because unit costs level out at a size below that of most existing authorities. Nevertheless, this chapter will assume that $\alpha < 1$ since otherwise a major argument for group provision disappears.

The assumption that $\alpha < 1$ leads to three important inferences from the formula given in (4.2) for the tax-price, that is $P = k/S^{1-\alpha}$. First, if $\alpha < 1$, then P falls continuously as S rises. Second, the minimum possible P, P_m, occurs with the maximum possible S, that is with $S = n$, which effectively means with central government provision. Third, only one S corresponds to each P; this means that it is legitimate for the following subsections to proceed by first ascertaining the optimum tax-price, P^*, that is the tax-price which maximizes welfare, and then substituting P^* into the relationship $P = k/S^{1-\alpha}$ to ascertain the optimum size S^*. In short, $S^* = (k/P^*)^{1/(1-\alpha)}$.

3.2. Optimum Size with Homogeneous Preferences within and between Areas

In this subsection it is assumed that all citizens have identical preferences as well as identical incomes. These assumptions mean all citizens have identical demand curves for the service concerned. So if private provision prevailed, all citizens – facing the same market price – would provide equal quantities. This subsection also assumes that if local authorities are established, the citizens in each area will be provided with equal quantities of the service and will be asked to pay equal tax-prices for each unit that they consume. With each citizen consuming the same quantity of the service, equal tax-prices will arise if each citizen faces the same tax bill; with equal incomes, this will occur with either a poll tax or an income tax, and with equal preferences it will also be met with a sales tax or excise duties.

With falling unit costs, each citizen will hope to gain some consumer surplus, as illustrated in Figure 4.1. Following Oates (1972), it is assumed that all citizens have straight-line demand curves, and the figure shows the demand curve, DD, for an individual citizen for a service whose provision is currently secured by private citizens at a unit price of P_0. This citizen consumes Q_0 units (per year), as do all other citizens as they have identical demand curves. If local authorities of size S_1 are established, the unit cost – or unit tax-price – per citizen falls to P_1. Local taxes ensure that each citizen is confronted with this price. Each citizen now wants to consume Q_1 units and so hopes to become better off by the amount of consumer surplus in the shaded area between the prices line at P_0 and P_1. This gain should materialize, given the assumption that the median voter rule prevails, for each area's median voter, like all other citizens, has the situation depicted in

Figure 4.1, and thus wants the quantity Q_1 when the price is P_1.

To calculate the gain, suppose the citizens demand curve is given by $Q = a - bP$, subject to two constraints. The first is that $Q = 0$ if $a < bP$: in other words, at or above some choke price, P_c, where $P_c = a/b$, the consumer would demand zero rather than a negative quantity. The second is that $P_c > P_0$, so that the consumer is on $(a - bP)$ at P_0 and makes some purchases at that price. This second constraint simplifies the discussion but is not essential.

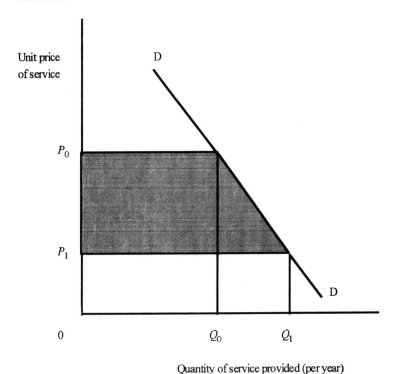

Figure 4.1 The demand for a local public service and the consumer surplus

The gain in consumer surplus from the fall in price to P_1 has two parts which are shown by the shaded rectangle and the shaded triangle on Figure 4.1. The first part is the gain from consuming Q_0 units at P_1 instead of P_0; its value is $Q_0(P_0 - P_1)$ or $(a - bP_0)(P_0 - P_1)$. The second part is the gain from consuming the extra $(Q_1 - Q_0)$ units at a price P_1 which is below their marginal benefit to the consumer; its value is $\frac{1}{2}(Q_1 - Q_0)(P_0 - P_1)$. Since

$(Q_1 - Q_0)$ equals $(a - bP_1) - (a - bP_0)$ or $b(P_0 - P_1)$, the second gain equals $\frac{1}{2}(b(P_0 - P_1)^2$. So the total gain is:

$$G = (a - bP_0)(P_0 - P_1) + \frac{1}{2}(b(P_0 - P_1)^2.$$

This can be re-expressed as:

$$G = aP_0 - aP_1 - bP_0^2 + \frac{1}{2}bP_1^2. \tag{4.3}$$

The result given in (4.3) can be generalized for any value of P, and it can be expressed as a sum to get the total gains, ΣG, for the entire population n, in a given year, so that:

$$\Sigma G = n(aP_0 - aP - \frac{1}{2}bP_0^2 + \frac{1}{2}bP^2). \tag{4.4}$$

where Σ here, and subsequently, is taken as $\sum_{i=1}^{n}$. It follows from (4.4) that:

$$\delta \Sigma G/dP = n(bP - a). \tag{4.5}$$

Equation (4.5) indicates that $\delta \Sigma G/dP$ is zero, so that ΣG is at a minimum, when $(bP - a) = 0$, which, given that $Q = a - bP$, occurs when the price equals P_c. ΣG will be negative at this point as a result of the assumption that $P_c > P_0$, since (4.4) shows that ΣG is zero if $P = P_0$ and is lower if $P > P_0$. ΣG rises as P falls, and it would reach $n(aP_0 - \Sigma bP_0^2)$ if P fell to zero. Thus the relationship between ΣG and P (when positive) is as shown by the curve G in the upper part of Figure 4.2; G becomes horizontal once P_c is reached since, at higher prices, consumers continue to consume nothing and hence lose no more consumer surplus. The lower part of Figure 4.2 shows G', or d $= \Sigma G/dP$, which, as noted, is zero at P_c and which falls as the price falls below P_c; G' becomes horizontal once P_c is reached since, as just noted, consumers lose no more surplus beyond that price. Finally, note that as ΣG rises as P falls, so ΣG is at a maximum when P is at P_m, that is when $S = n$. So if all citizens have identical preferences, $S^* = n$ and central government provision is called for.

3.3. Optimum Size with Heterogeneous Preferences within Areas but Homogeneous Preference Distributions between Areas

This subsection relaxes the assumption of uniform preferences. It assumes that within different areas of the country, people may have different preferences. However, it also assumes that the pattern of distributions is the

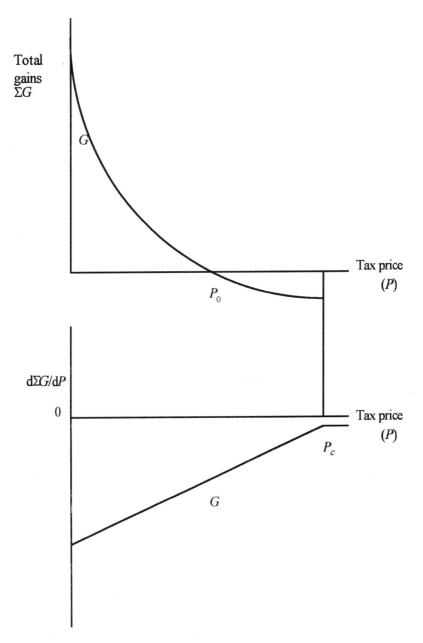

Figure 4.2 Total and marginal gains as a function of the tax-price

same in all areas of the country. An example of this would be where all citizens have one of only three demand patterns – 'high', 'medium', and 'low' – and where in every street the proportion of citizens in each category was the same. If the distribution was such that in every street the median voter had medium preferences, then these preferences would determine the level of provision in all authorities, no matter what size of authority was established, from street size upwards. Only with tiny authorities – such as single citizen ones – would citizens with high or low preferences have a chance of having their preferences met.

The scenario considered here is admittedly different from the scenario used in much of the local public economics literature which supposes that, while preferences may vary strongly between localities, they typically vary only a little within localities. This conventional scenario can be used to give some justification for local provision. In contrast, in the scenario examined in this subsection, it might seem there can be no point in local provision. For if the cost falls from group provision were never substantial, then it seems that individual provision would be best so that citizens could determine their own consumption levels. Conversely, if group provision offered substantial cost savings, then it seems that big groups would be best; for the medium preferences will prevail with all group sizes, and larger sizes of S – given, that $P = k/S^{1-\alpha}$ – offer a lower price. However, this subsection shows that there may still be a case for local authority provision.

With varying preferences, different citizens will have different demand curves. The curve for the ith individual is taken to be $Q = a_i - b_i P$ subject to two constraints. The first is that $Q = 0$ if $a_i < b_i P$: in other words, at or above some choke price which equals a_i/b_i, the consumer would demand zero rather than a negative quantity. The second is that $P_c > P_0$, so that the consumer is on $(a_i - b_i P)$ at P_0 and makes some purchases at that price. As before, this second constraint is not essential but simplifies the discussion.

If $S = 1$, each citizen will face some common price P_0 and will select the preferred quantity Q_0 – though these quantities will now vary between citizens. With group provision, and with authorities of population size S_1, each citizen will face a common new price P_1, and each citizen will desire a new quantity Q_1; again these quantities will differ between citizens.

Each citizen would hope that the group would select the quantity desired by that citizen. It is possible to calculate the gain in consumer surplus that each citizen would hope to secure, as shown in (4.3), allowing that for each citizen there will now be an individual a_i and b_i. So the total hoped-for gains for the tax-price P, corresponding to any particular size S, would be:

$$\Sigma G = \Sigma(a_i P_0 - a_i P - \tfrac{1}{2} b_i P_0^2 + \tfrac{1}{2}(b_i P^2).$$

Although this is now the sum of many different individual relationships, it will have the same general form as each of those relationships and so it will have the general form shown by G in Figure 4.2. ΣG will still equal zero if $P = P_0$, while if $P = 0$, ΣG would be given by $\Sigma G = \Sigma(a_i P_0 - \tfrac{1}{2} b_i P_0^2)$. Also,   d $\Sigma G/dP$ would be given by:

$$d\Sigma G/dP = \Sigma(b_i P - a_i). \qquad (4.6)$$

This clearly rises as P rises, as shown by G' in the lower part of Figure 4.2. And $d\Sigma G/dP$ will reach zero only at the price, P_c, which is now defined as the choke price for the consumer with the highest demand. S_0 once P_c is reached all citizens consume zero and further price rises would have no effect, so that G and G' are horizontal beyond this price.

In practice, group provision denies individual choices over quantities: each citizen must accept the group's, or rather the median voter's, choice. So few citizens will realize all their hoped-for consumer surplus gains. Thus it is necessary to consider the shortfalls – or losses – at each tax-price. The shortfalls will typically be different for each S; for each S results in its own P and hence in a different hoped-for Q for each consumer and, no doubt, in a different median voter decision over what the actual Q will be.

To examine the issue of losses, consider first citizen i who has the demand curve $Q_i = a_i - b_i P$. This citizen's losses depend on how far this demand curve diverges from the median voter's which is taken as $Q_m = a_m - b_m P$. Take a particular price, P_1, and suppose the quantity desired by i differs from the quantity selected by the median voter. As shown in Figure 4.3, the quantity could be greater or smaller depending on whether, at P_1, i's demand curve is to the left – as with D_i – or to the right – as with (D_i) – of the median voter's demand curve, D_m. In each case, the loss to i from having to consume at P_1 the quantity selected by the median voter, Q_{1m}, as opposed to i's preferred quantity, Q_{1i} – or (Q_{1i}) – is given by the shaded triangle.

The area of each shaded triangle is half the absolute value of the base, $(Q_{1i} - Q_{1m})$, times the absolute value of the height, which is $(1/b_i)$ times the base. So the loss, L, is:

$$L = (1/2b_i)(Q_{1i} - Q_{1m})^2 \qquad (4.7)$$

Now $(Q_{1i} - Q_{1m})$ is given by:

$$(Q_{1i} - Q_{1m}) = (a_i - a_m) - (b_i - b_m)P_1$$

which, taking A_i as $(a_i - a_m)$ and B_i as $(b_i - b_m)$, gives:

$$(Q_{1i} - Q_{1m}) = A_i - B_i P_1. \tag{4.8}$$

So (4.7) becomes:

$$L = (1/2b_i)(A_i - B_i P_1)^2.$$

A similar relationship holds at each price, so in general:

$$L = (1/2b_i)(A_i^2 - 2A_i B_i P + B_i^2 P^2). \tag{4.9}$$

It follows from (4.9) that:

$$dL/dP = (B_i/b_i)(B_i P - A_i).$$

This implies that, for i, the loss would be constant, that is independent of P, if $B_i = 0$, that is if i's demand curve had the same slope as the median voter's. Alternatively, if B_i is not zero, then dL/dP is zero – so the loss is at a minimum – when $(B_i P - A_i) = 0$. It follows from (4.8) that this occurs when $(Q_i - Q_m) = 0$, that is at the price when i's desired quantity equals the median voter's; and it follows from (4.7) that i's loss is zero at this price.

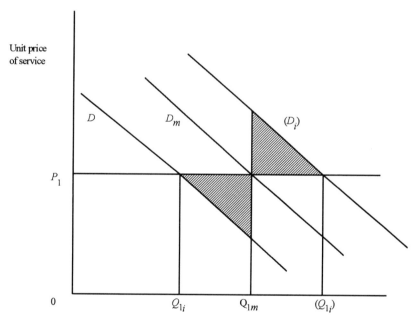

Figure 4.3   The optimum size of the service with varying preferences

Most citizens will have demand curves whose slopes differ from the slope of the median voter's demand curve. So, typically, B_i is not zero and i and the median voter have demand curves that intersect. The intersection may occur at a feasible price, that is at a price which could occur with a feasible value of S. The feasible range for P is given by $P_m \leq P \leq P_0$. This is because the minimum possible price is P_m, which occurs with the maximum possible authority size, $S = n$, that is with central provision, while the maximum possible price, P_0, occurs with the minimum possible S, namely $S = 1$, which occurs with individual provision. If the intersection occurs at a feasible price, then i's loss is zero at the S which results in that price, and it is positive with smaller or larger authority sizes.

However, the intersection may occur at a price below P_m, the price which would occur with central government provision, in which case i's loss is positive with the largest possible authority and increases as authority size falls and the tax-price rises. Alternatively, the intersection may occur at a price above P_0, in which case i's loss is positive with the smallest possible authority and increases as authority size rises and the tax-price falls.

The total loss for all citizens is derived from (4.9) as:

$$\Sigma L = \Sigma((1/2b_i)(A_i^2 - 2A_iB_iP + B_i^2P^2))$$

from which it follows that:

$$d\Sigma L/dP = \Sigma((B_i/b_i)(B_iP - A_i)). \qquad (4.10)$$

This shows that $d\Sigma L/dP$ is zero and independent of P, so that the total loss would be the same at each P, if every $B_i = 0$, that is if every individual's demand curve had the same slope as the median voter's. This is unlikely. What happens to $d\Sigma L/dP$ in other circumstances?

The answer is that $d\Sigma L/dP$ will be a linear function with a positive slope. This can be seen from $d^2\Sigma L/dP^2$, which is given by:

$$d^2\Sigma L/dP^2 = \Sigma(B_i^2/b_i)$$

and which gives the slope of $d\Sigma L/dP$. This slope is constant because each (B_i^2/b_i) is constant, and it is positive because each $B_i^2 > 0$ while each $b_i > 0$ provided no citizen regards the local service as a Giffen good. As $d\Sigma L/dP$ is a straight line with a positive slope, the curve relating ΣL to P will have a slope that constantly increases.

What is less certain is where the function between ΣL and P will be at a minimum. Using (4.8), (4.10) can be rewritten to show $d\Sigma L/dP$ at price P as:

$$d\Sigma L/dP = \Sigma((B_i/b_i)(Q_{m}P - Q_iP)).$$

This could have its minimum at any price. For instance, if there existed a single price where everyone wanted the same quantity, so that $(Q_{m}P - Q_iP)$ $= 0$ for all citizens, then $d\Sigma L/dP$ would be zero at that price – and indeed ΣL would be zero at that price.

In fact, it is much more likely that there is no single price where all citizens would want the same quantity. But there will still be some price where ΣL is a minimum, and this could in principle be at any price. For the present chapter, the chief interest is whether the minimum value of ΣL occurs with a price in the feasible range for P given by $P_m \leq P \leq P_0$.

As the minimum value of ΣL could occur at any price, it could occur at a price below, within, or above the feasible range. The upper part of Figure 4.4 illustrates these three possibilities. If the minimum ΣL occurred at a negative price, or a price below P_m, the relationship would be similar to that depicted by the curve L_x. If it occurred at a positive price between P_m and P_0, the relationship would be similar to that depicted by curve L_y. If it occurred at a price above P_0, the relationship would be similar to that depicted by curve L_z. The lower part of Figure 4.4 shows the corresponding curves for $d\Sigma L/dP$, or L', for the three L curves in the upper part.

Now $d\Sigma L/dP$ is at a minimum when the weighted sum of each citizen's $(Q_{m}P - Q_iP)$ – each of these differences is weighted by that citizen's (B_i/b_i) – is zero. So it is likely that if citizens' preferred quantities become more similar as P falls – that is as S rises – so that $\Sigma(Q_{m}P - Q_iP)$ gets smaller, then ΣL will tend to diminish as P falls, as with L_x. Conversely, if preferred quantities become more disparate as P falls and S rises, then it is likely that ΣL will tend to increase as P falls, as with L_z. And if preferred quantities are most similar at some intermediate P and S, then it is likely that ΣL will be at a minimum at some intermediate P, as with L_y.

To find the optimum authority size, it is necessary to look at the hoped-for gains less the losses as S increases or, equivalently, as P falls. The optimum tax-price occurs where there is the largest gap between ΣG and ΣL, that is where $d\Sigma G/dP$ equals $d\Sigma L/dP$, subject to two constraints, namely that P is in the feasible range $P_m \leq P \leq P_0$ and that the net gains exceed zero. If ΣL exceeds ΣG at each feasible price, it is better to have private provision, for with private provision $\Sigma L = \Sigma G = 0$. (Figure 4.4 shows $\Sigma L > 0$ when $P = P_0$ because it assumes each citizen must consume a medium amount of service no matter what the tax-price is; this does not in fact apply at P_0 when $S = 1$, but it does apply with every other S and P).

Subject to these two constraints, the optimum price, P^*, occurs where $d\Sigma G/dP = d\Sigma L/dP$ which, as (4.4) and (4.10) show, is where:

$$\Sigma(b_iP - a_i) = \Sigma((B_i/b_i)(B_iP - A_i))$$

which can be rearranged to give an expression for P^*, as:

$$P^* = (\Sigma a_ib_i - \Sigma A_iB_i)/(\Sigma b_i^2 - \Sigma B_i^2).$$

To find the optimum size, S^*, recall that $P = k/S^{1-\alpha}$. It follows that $P^* = k(S^*)^{\alpha-1}$, so:

$$k(S^*)^{\alpha-1} = (\Sigma a_ib_i - \Sigma A_iB_i)/(\Sigma b_i^2 - \Sigma B_i^2).$$

Inverting each side shows that:

$$(S^*)^{1-\alpha} = k(\Sigma b_i^2 - \Sigma B_i^2)/(\Sigma a_ib_i - \Sigma A_iB_i)$$

whence:

$$S^* = [k(\Sigma b_i^2 - \Sigma B_i^2)/(\Sigma a_ib_i - \Sigma A_iB_i)]^{1/(1-\alpha)} . \qquad (4.11)$$

subject, once again, to the two constraints noted in the last paragraph. Note that as there is a unique solution in terms of P, and as each possible P corresponds to only one possible size, so there is a unique solution for S.

In view of the constraints and the alternatives for the L and L' curves, it is useful to consider the possible outcomes. Suppose first that L takes the form given by L_x in Figure 4.4. Recalling the form of G, from Figure 4.2, it is clear that $d\Sigma G/dP$ cannot equal $d\Sigma L/dP$ in the feasible price range. The best policy is to have P_m, which means that $S^* = n$ and that there is central provision, provided only that $\Sigma G > \Sigma L$ at this price; if $\Sigma G < \Sigma L$, private provision is best, so that $S^* = 1$, while if $\Sigma G = \Sigma L$, it is a matter of indifference whether there is central or private provision.

Suppose, next, that L takes the form given by L_y or L_z in Figure 4.4. In either case it is possible for $d\Sigma G/dP$ to equal $d\Sigma L/dP$ in the feasible price range. If it does, and if $\Sigma G > \Sigma L$ at that point, then there is a case for local provision with authorities of the size that result in this optimum price. This situation is shown in Figure 4.5, using the solid L_y and L'_y curves to show a case where the minimum L occurs within the feasible price range, and the dashed L_z and L'_z curves to show a case where the minimum L occurs at a price in excess of P_0. For convenience, each case depicts the same optimum price P^*.

The possible outcomes shown in Figure 4.5 are, prima facie, surprising because the assumptions made include a homogeneous distribution of preferences between all areas. But local provision will still be optimal when

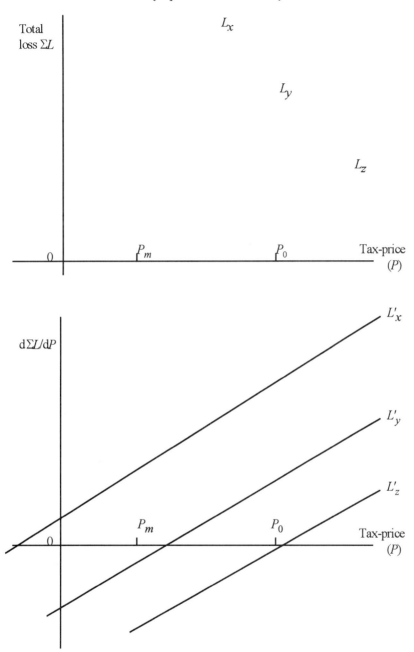

Figure 4.4 Gains and losses with heterogeneous preferences

prices below P^* create extra losses from lack of individual control over service levels that more than outweigh the extra gains arising from lower unit costs and tax-prices. The losses are reflected in the two L curves which both rise steeply as the price falls below P^*.

Incidentally, this reasoning also implies that with central government services, a fall in unit costs could result in a fall in welfare. This paradoxical result could arise if a majority of voters reacted by demanding more of the service, albeit valuing the extra at little more than the tax-price they have to pay, while a minority were coerced into paying for extra units that they value at far less than the tax-price they have to pay. Of course, if public service provision was always set at the welfare maximizing levels, these paradoxical results would not occur. The results come about simply because median voting does not, typically, lead to welfare maximizing results as noted, for example, by Bowen (1969) and Bergstrom (1979).

3.4. Optimum Size with Heterogeneous Preferences within Areas and Heterogeneous Preference Distributions between Areas

Subsection 3.3 showed that local provision may be optimal when preferences vary within localities, even if the distribution of preferences is homogeneous between all localities. The case for local provision is likely to be much stronger if preference distributions are heterogeneous between localities. This result can be demonstrated with a simple example. Suppose that some service is currently provided privately; and suppose all the citizens in the northern third of a country want a high level of service, all the citizens in the central third want a medium level of service, and all the citizens in the southern third want a low level of service. With care, this country could be split into three local authorities, with perhaps a substantial gain from lower unit costs and a zero loss from lack of individual control. Replacing such local provision by central provision may further reduce unit costs, but any resulting potential gains could be swamped by the losses resulting from everyone having to endure medium levels of service. In general terms, heterogeneous preferences are likely to result in L curves which slope downwards very steeply when S is high and P is low, and so the slopes of these curves may equal the slopes of the G curves at a high P and small S.

A further issue arises when the distributions of preferences are heterogeneous between areas. With local provision, the preferences of median median voters will vary so that different areas will have different levels of service and different tax rates. So citizens whose preferences are ill-met by their current areas may migrate to other areas. Such migration is likely to intensify the heterogeneity of preference patterns and further reduce the optimum size. Of course migrants may consider only their own welfare and ignore the external costs and benefits of any increases or

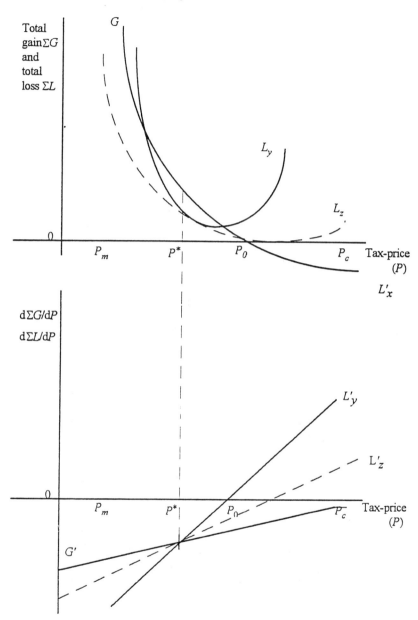

Figure 4.5   Gains and losses and the feasible price range

reductions in congestion that their moves cause. An exhaustive model of optimum size should – in principle – estimate the gains and losses from each possible size after allowing for any migration that will take place if that size is introduced. And allowance should also be made for all the direct costs and the net external costs and benefits of that migration.

4. SOME FURTHER ASPECTS OF THE MODEL

This section considers three further aspects of modelling optimum local authority size. Subsection 4.1 considers the question of group provision and the internalization of externalities. Subsection 4.2 considers the implications for optimum size of a change in incomes. And Subsection 4.3 considers the issue of multifunction authorities.

4.1. The Internalization of Externalities

It was explained in Section 3 that, aside from reducing unit costs, group provision could internalize some externalities. With private provision, the service – such as, say, street lighting – provided by each citizen may have external benefits, but these will typically be ignored when citizens decide how much service to provide. With group provision, the median voter will decide on the level of service by considering not only the direct benefits received from street lighting outside his or her own home, but also the benefits gained from lighting outside other people's homes. So there will be some improvements following the internalizing of intragroup externalities. Moreover, groups may be able to negotiate with each other to take account of some spillover effects between groups. A full examination of these effects of group provision would require a separate chapter, but the key point is that, as with the gains from cost falls, a distinction must be made between the hoped-for gains and the actual gains from internalizing externalities.

Suppose, for instance, that with individual provision all citizens ignore the external benefits of their provision. It is possible that each citizen would wish that many, even all, other citizens would provide more. With group provision, each citizen will hope to secure some gains through the internalization of externalities. These hoped-for gains could be added to the hoped-for gains from lower costs and so result in a higher G curve in Figure 4.5. Will these extra hoped-for gains increase or diminish as group size increases? There are two reasons why they might increase and there is one reason why they might fall.

One reason they might increase is that a larger group size should reduce the unit cost of local services and so increase the level of provision and hence the consumer surplus citizens get from increased provision elsewhere in their areas. The other reason is that with larger groups, more intercitizen externalities will become internalized within groups and hence should get taken into account.

The reason that the extra hoped-for gains might fall as group size increases is that the lower unit cost will encourage extra provision anyway, possibly to such an extent that individual citizens might no longer be concerned if externalities were not taken into account. To give an extreme example, suppose that large group sizes reduced the cost of street lighting so much that each group decided to floodlight every street, even without considering the effects that the lighting outside each home had on people other than the residents of that home. Here, if citizens were asked whether they would benefit from extra lighting outside other people's homes, they might all reply in the negative; so here no one would hope for gains through the internalization of externalities.

Note that any hoped-for gains from internalizing externalities will be only partially realized. Each citizen might hope for a certain amount of extra provision, but the actual amounts will be determined by median voters. In extreme cases, the shortfalls or losses could exceed the hoped-for gains. For instance, a small majority might choose to spend huge sums stimulating production, even though the consumer surplus they gained only slightly exceeded the tax-cost to them, while a large minority might be forced to pay large sums for this stimulus, sums which far exceeded any consumer surplus gains they obtained from it.

This brief analysis suggests that if the effects of internalizing externalities were allowed for in Figure 4.5, then both the G and L curves would shift upwards. But it would need a detailed empirical analysis to see how far their gradients changed, as reflected in the $d\Sigma G/dP$ and $d\Sigma L/dP$ curves, yet it is the intersection of these latter curves which determines the optimum size.

4.2. The Effects of Changes in Income

The analysis so far has considered the situation for a single year. The demand curves have been regarded as referring to quantities for a particular year, so the final hoped-for gains and losses relate to that year. Thus the analysis has indicated how the optimum size of authority could be determined for a single year.

As time passes, consumers' incomes and preferences alter, so their demand curves shift and the optimum local authority size alters. Assuming that incomes rise and that local authority services are normal goods, the demands for these services will typically rise over time. This rise will tend to raise the hoped-for consumer surplus gains that group provision might bring from lower costs. It may also raise the shortfalls that arise with group decisions, especially if the differences in the quantities that different citizens want increase. Thus it is not possible to say a priori whether the optimum size will increase or fall. The situation could be complicated by the fact that, as time passes, technology tends to improve, so that k in (4.1) may also fall. Equation (4.11) implies that a fall in k tends to reduce the optimum size.

This discussion implies that the optimum size of authorities is likely to change over time. Although structural change is costly, the appropriate response may be to have periodic reviews, and then determine the new size on the basis of which size will maximize the present value of the expected net gains – that is hoped-for gains net of shortfalls – for each year before the next review. It is interesting that the Local Government Commission sees its task as limited to equipping local authorities to meet the needs of the next 20–25 years.

4.3. Multifunction Local Authorities

The model presented here has assumed that local authorities provide a single service. In practice they provide many services. It would, in principle, be possible to ascertain the optimum authority size for each function and have one tier of authorities for each. Taken to extremes, this approach might mean separate tiers for crime protection advice, traffic police and criminal investigation police, and separate tiers for street lighting, road maintenance, verge maintenance and road cleaning.

This approach could lead to confusion in the minds of citizens. For example, which of the various road authorities should they contact if a tree fell across a road? Such confusion is likely to reduce accountability. Also, this approach would make it hard for related services – such as road maintenance and street cleaning – to be coordinated.

In these circumstances, it might be best to try to ascertain some idea of the optimum size for a few key functions – say education, social services, roads and police – and then see if they come reasonably close enough to entrust them to a single tier, or whether they might require two or three tiers. If there was a single tier for the key functions, this tier could probably handle all functions. If there were several tiers for the key functions, the remaining functions could be allocated between those tiers as seemed most judicious.

5. CONCLUSIONS

The main thrust of this chapter is to suggest that any estimate of the optimum size for a particular service requires a consideration of the gains and losses that come from changing authority sizes. A key gain which may accrue from increasing size is a fall in unit costs. A key loss is the loss of control by individuals of the quantity (and quality) of service that they will have. Local authorities should be enlarged in size so long as the extra gains exceed the extra losses. At the point where the extra gains just equal the extra losses is the optimum size.

NOTES

1. See King 1984;
2. See Olson 1969; Oates 1972; Musgrave and Musgrave 1976; Atkinson and Stiglitz 1980.

REFERENCES

Atkinson, A.B. and J.E. Stiglitz (1980), *Lectures on Public Economics*, London: McGraw-Hill.

Bergstrom, T.C. (1979), 'When Does Majority Rule Supply Public Goods Efficiently?', *Scandinavian Journal of Economics*, **81**, 216-26.

Bergstrom, T.C. and R.P. Goodman (1973), 'Private Demands for Public Goods', *American Economic Review*, **63**, 280-96.

Borcherding, T.E. and R.T. Deacon (1972), 'The Sources of Growth of Public Expenditures in the United States 1902-70', in: T.E. Borcherding, (ed.), *Budgets and Bureaucrats: the Sources of Government Growth,*, Durham, North Carolina: Duke University Press, 45-70.

Bowen, H. (1969), 'The Interpretation of Voting in the Allocation of Economic Resources', *Quarterly Journal of Economics* (1943), **58**, 27-48, Reprinted in: K. Arrow and T. Scitovsky (eds), *Readings in Welfare Economics*, London: Allen & Unwin, 115-32.

Breton, A.. and A.D. Scott (1978), *The Economic Constitution of Federal States*, Canberra: Australian National University.

Foster, C.D., R.A. Jackman and M. Perlman, (1980), *Local Government Finance in A Unitary State*, London: Allen & Unwin.

King, D.N. (1984), *Fiscal Tiers: the Economics of Multi-Level Government*, London: Allen & Unwin.

Local Government Commission for England (1993), *Local Government in Derbyshire: A Report to Local People*, London: Local Government Commission for England.

Musgrave, R.A. and P.B Musgrave (1976), *Public Finance in Theory and Practice, 2nd ed.*, Tokio:McGraw-Hill.

Oates, W.E. (1972), *Fiscal Federalism*, New York: Harcourt Brace Jovanovich.

Olson, M. (1969), 'The Principle of `Fiscal Equivalence': the Division of Responsibilities Among Different Levels of Government', *American Economic Review Papers and Proceedings*, **49**, 479-87.

Tiebout, C.M. (1961), 'An Economic Theory of Fiscal Decentralization', in National Bureau of Economic Research, (ed.), *Public Finances: Needs, Sources and Utilization*, Princeton NJ: Princeton University Press, 79-86.

Tullock, G. (1969), 'Federalism: Problems of Scale', *Public Choice*, **6** , 19-29.

PART   II

Applying Theory to the Real World

5. Impacts of Economic Change on a Local Business Tax Base: The Case of the French *'Taxe Professionnelle'*

Rémy Prud'homme*

1. INTRODUCTION

Business taxes, that is taxes paid by enterprises on their activity, profits, capital or wages, are said not to be good local taxes. A first argument is that businesses do not vote. In the theory of fiscal federalism, the main justification for local governments is that they make it possible for local people, through their votes, to get the mix of public goods and taxes that best suits their wants. This cannot be achieved with business taxes. This argument is not purely academic. Indeed, it led Mrs Thatcher's government to turn the British business property tax, a local tax, into a national tax.

A second argument, not unrelated to the first, is that business taxes are 'exportable'. Taxes paid by businesses are borne by consumers, capital owners and workers. When levied at the national level, they are mostly borne by nationals (although this is less and less true with the rapid globalization of economies). When levied at the local level, they are in the main not borne by locals, because most of the consumers, many of the capital owners, and sometimes even a number of workers, are not located in the local jurisdiction in question. The smaller local governments are, the truer this proposition is. A detailed study of the incidence of the French business tax in 40 communes of the Paris agglomeration (Martinez 1991) yielded export rates (the share of the tax borne outside the commune) ranging from 75 to 95 per cent. Exportability reduces accountability. It induces locally elected politicians to increase taxation, and the provision of public goods, beyond what is actually desired.

A third argument is that business taxation, particularly when assessed on business income, is volatile. What may be good at the national level, because

* The author is indebted to Sonia Guelton for the major part of the raw data utilized but remains responsible for any errors in how they are used and analysed.

of its counter-cyclical effects, is bad at the local level. Local governments cannot, and should not, be expected to contribute to counter-cyclical policies. In any case, they need stable sources of income.

A fourth argument is that local business taxation is unfair, in the sense that it usually leads to great interjurisdictional disparities in tax bases. This point is often overdone. All tax bases are unevenly distributed over space. But it is true that business-related tax bases are often more unevenly distributed than other tax bases. This is because business activity is usually more concentrated spatially than household income, or consumption or even property. Large industrial undertakings (such as nuclear power plants, for instance) in particular create tax base 'peaks' wherever they happen to be located. Furthermore, this distribution of business activities is often unrelated, when not inversely related, to the distribution of 'needs'. It used not to be so in the past, at least in France. Industry was predominantly found in suburbs inhabited by low-income people – by the people who worked in these industries. Low-income neighbourhoods were therefore high (business) tax base local governments. This elegant redistributive mechanism has unfortunately broken down. At least in developed countries, low income is now generated by low employment rather than by low wages. Low income areas tend to be areas without jobs, without businesses and without business tax bases.

In spite (or perhaps even because) of this, business taxes remain the most important component of local taxation in Germany and France. Not all Germans would agree with that statement since many consider the share of the federal personal income tax that accrues to local governments as a local tax. But if one defines local taxes as taxes the rate of which is decided by local governments, the *Gewerbersteuer*, a tax based on business income and capital, appears as the most important German local tax. In France, everybody agrees that the *taxe professionnelle*, a tax assessed on business capital and wage bills, is the most important French local tax. This is evident from Table 5.1.

There are three levels of subnational governments in France: communes (numbering 36,000), *départements* (numbering 100) and regions (numbering 22). All three levels levy the *taxe professionnelle*. In other words, the *taxe professionnelle* paid by a given enterprise is the tax paid to the commune where the enterprise is located (the tax base multiplied by the rate decided by that commune) plus the tax paid to the *département* in which the enterprise is located (the same tax base multiplied by the rate decided by the *département*), plus the tax paid to the region (the same tax base multiplied by the rate decided by the region).

Table 5.1 shows that the *taxe professionnelle* accounts for an important share of tax revenues of the three levels of government, particularly in the case of the most important level, communes, and a sizeable share of total resources (including grants, user fees and borrowing). The *taxe professionnelle* is also important relative to other French taxes, accounting for about 6 per cent of total French tax revenues (Table 5.2).

Table 5.1 Relative importance of the taxe professionnelle *for local government*

Tax revenues and resources, 1990	Percentage of total tax revenues	Percentage of total resources
For communes	38	14
For *départements*	28	15
For regions	27	15
For all local governments	33	14

Source: Ministère de l'Intérieur, *Les collectivités locales en chiffres*, La Documentation Française, Paris, 1993.

These data are given merely to provide an idea of the importance of the *taxe professionnelle* as a tax in general and as a local tax in particular and to show that as a tax it is not unimportant. Our concern here, however, is not with the yield of the tax, but with the evolution of the tax base over time. How does the base of a local business tax like the *taxe professionnelle* respond to economic change? How is it influenced by growth, by sectoral changes, by structural changes or by regional changes?

Table 5.2 Taxe professionnelle *and other French taxes, 1992*

Taxe professionnelle and other French taxes, 1992	(billions francs)
Value-added tax (TVA)	709
Personal income tax (IRPP)	318
Corporate income tax (IS)	163
Fuels tax (TIPP)	119
Local business tax (TP)	112
Stamps, registration dues, etc.	84
Other national taxes	188
Other local taxes	214
Total	1,887

Source: Ministère des Finances, *Notes Bleues* n°34.

Over the past decade or decades, the French economy (just as those of other industrialized countries) has undergone major changes. Four types of change are worth briefly noting here. First, the French GDP has grown at a relatively slow but constant rate of 1.4 per cent per year. This meant, for instance, a 25 per cent increase over the period 1980–90. Second, the sectoral distribution of GDP changed, with the share of industry declining rapidly. Third – and this may be more idiosyncratic – the relative importance of labour and capital in the production function was profoundly modified. By and large, the labour force did not expand whereas the stock of capital increased at a rate higher than the GDP growth rate. Fourth, the regional distribution of output also changed with the share of some regions, particularly the Paris region, increasing substantially.

In order to appreciate the impact of these changes upon the *taxe professionnelle* base, some understanding of the nature of this tax is necessary. The *taxe professionnelle* is assessed for, and paid by, each establishment (not enterprise) at the place where it is located. A multi-establishment enterprise, such as Pont-à-Mousson or Electricité de France, will pay the *taxe professionnelle* in and for each of its establishments. The rates are decided by local governments, but the tax is assessed and levied by the national tax administration (on behalf of local governments) in a uniform fashion throughout the territory.

2. DEFINITION OF THE TAX BASE

The tax base (B_i) can be presented as a function of the stock of capital (K_i), and of the wage bill (W_i), of the establishment :

$$B_i = \alpha^* K_i + \beta^* W_i \qquad (5.1)$$

with α and β nationally decided coefficients. The way K and α are estimated is rather complicated. A distinction is made between three categories of productive capital: land and non-industrial buildings, industrial buildings and equipment. Different estimation procedures, and different values of α, are used for each category. For the first two categories, α is taken to be equal to 8 or 9 per cent. For equipment, α is set equal to 16 or 12 per cent. The justification for these values is that the capital component of the tax base is supposed to be the 'rental value' of the capital used. On the whole, it seems that the capital component $\alpha^* K$ of the tax base as estimated is a reasonable approximation of the productive capital of businesses, at least at aggregated levels. The coefficient β is set equal to 18 per cent. This is a figure decided politically which at the time of the introduction of the tax in 1975 equalized the value of the capital component with that of the wage component, at the national level.[1] The tax to be paid in a given year t is assessed on wages and capital values of two years earlier, $t-2$. The full formula is therefore:

$$B_{i,t} = \alpha^* K_{i,t-2} + \beta^* W_{i,t-2}$$

This formula describes what is known as the 'gross base' of the tax. In practice, there are a number of abatements introduced over the years which are either general or specific to certain types of activities or investments. Taken together, they reduce the gross base by nearly 25 per cent. The gross base minus these abatements defines the 'net base' on which the tax is assessed. Because we are interested in the impact of economic change and not in the impact of tax law changes on the tax base, we will only use data (or estimates) for gross base.

For certain small businesses (professionals employing less than five persons), the tax base is equal to 10 per cent of sales. This 'sales element' of the tax base accounts for only about 3 per cent of the total tax base and will be ignored in most of what follows.

The French *taxe professionnelle* is therefore a hybrid creature. Because what is taxed is wages, not labour, it cannot be considered to be entirely a tax on production factors – unless one considers wages as a way to index labour. More interestingly perhaps, it is a tax assessed both on stocks (capital) and on flows (wages). It is a local tax, but it is a tax that has an impact on central government finances, in at least two ways. First, it is income tax deductible: an increase in the *taxe professionnelle* paid by an enterprise will reduce its taxable income and its income tax and, therefore, will be borne in part by central government. Second, central government has set a ceiling to the amount of the *taxe professionnelle* payable by an enterprise equal to 2.5 per cent of its value added; the difference between the tax paid by the enterprise and the tax received by the local government is paid by central government which now pays about 30 per cent of total tax revenues from the tax and is now the number one *taxe professionnelle* taxpayer.

3. GENERATION OF THE TAX BASE

The *taxe professionnelle* base is generated by economic activity. A convenient way to analyse the relationship of the tax base to economic activity, and its evolution, is to use generation coefficients. There are three types of such coefficients.

The first one is the general generation coefficient (g) which is the amount of tax base generated by one franc of value added ($g = B/Y$).

Coefficients of the second type could be called factors of production coefficients (g_j): they relate the tax base generated by each factor of production (B_j) to the amount of the same factor (F_j): $g_j = B_j/F_j$. More specifically, one can define a capital generation coefficient (g_k) which is the amount of tax base generated by one franc of capital $(g_k = B_k/K)$, a labour generation coefficient (g_l), the amount of tax base generated by one worker $(g_l = B_w/W)$ and, by an extension to the remuneration of factors, a wages generation coefficient (g_w), which is the amount of tax base generated by one franc of wages. It follows that the tax base can be defined as:

$$B = \Sigma_{jg_j}{}^*F_j$$

or more precisely, with B_r the small amount of tax base generated by sales:

$$B = g_k{}^*K + g_w{}^*W + B_r \qquad (5.2)$$

Coefficients of the third type are sector generation coefficients $(g_i = B_i/Y_i)$, defined as the amount of tax base (B_i) produced by the value-added in the same sector (Y_i). We can define therefore a secondary generation coefficient $(g_s = B_s/Y_s)$ which is the ratio of the tax base generated by the secondary sector (B_s) to the value added by the secondary sector (Y_s) and similarly a tertiary generation coefficient $(g_t = B_t/Y_t)$ which is the amount of tax base generated by one franc of value added in the tertiary sector. We therefore have:

$$B = \Sigma_i Y_i{}^*g_i \qquad (5.3)$$

There is a fourth type of coefficient, that which can be obtained $(g_{ij} = B_{ij}/F_{ji})$ by dividing the tax base generated by one factor in one sector (B_{ij}) by the value of this factor in this sector (F_{ji}). Thus, a capital–secondary generation coefficient $(g_{ks} = B_{ks}/K_s)$ will be the amount of tax base generated by one franc in the secondary sector.

The generation coefficients for 1984 are given in table 5.3.[2] The table underlines an important point: generation coefficients vary by sector. They are much higher (nearly 2.5 times) in industry than in the services. No finer breakdown is available. But it is likely that within each sector there are great differences in generation coefficients. There are two explanations for this: differences in exemption rates and differences in the production function, that is in the relative importance of labour and capital.

Exemption rates vary between the various sectors. In principle, all businesses are subject to the *taxe professionnelle*. But this rule has many exceptions which are important for the study of the impact of economic change on the tax base. Administrations, public institutions and non-profit organizations, are tax exempt. The same is true for agriculture, educational activities (even when these are purely commercial undertakings), newspapers and theatres and cinemas. A survey undertaken by the Ministry of Finance gives exemption rates (and their complement, coverage rates) by sector (Table 5.4). The table shows that nearly half of value added in France is not subject to the *taxe professionnelle*. The exemption rate is low for industry and commerce, but very high for agriculture and non-market services. Agriculture and non-market services are excluded from the analysis which follows.

Table 5.3   Generation coefficients by factor and by sector, 1984 (coefficients in francs)

Factor generation	Coefficients in francs
Capital (tax base/franc of capital)	0.028
Labour (tax base/worker)	7.518
Wages (tax base/franc of wages)	0.130
Sector generation coefficients (Tax base/franc o value added)	
Secondary sector (B_s/Y_s)	0.165
Tertiary sector (a) (B_t/Y_t)	0.064
General generation coefficient (B/Y)	0.119

Note: (a) excluding non-market services.

Differences in coverage rates are not the only explanation of variations in sector generation coefficients. The amount of tax base generated by one franc of value added subject to taxation – what could be called the 'true' generation coefficient – also varies from sector to sector. The data in Tables 5.3 and 5.4, taken together, suggest that true generation coefficients were in 1984 equal to 0.194 for the secondary sector compared to 0.121 for the tertiary sector. This is of course because the relative importance of capital utilized and wages paid per franc of value added varies between sectors.

4. TAX BASE INCREASE

Over the past decade, the *taxe professionnelle* base has increased fairly rapidly in real terms. Over the 1980–83 period, it increased at an average rate of 3.6 per cent. As suggested by equations (5.2) and (5.3), this increase can be explained by a number of factors: (a) changes in the total value added or GDP, (b) changes in the sectoral composition of GDP, combined with (c) changes in the sectoral generation coefficients, (d) changes in the relative importance of capital and wages, combined with (e) changes in the factor generation coefficients and (f) changes in factor productivity and by combinations of these factors. What is the relative contribution of these different factors?

Table 5.4   Exemption rates by sector, 1984

	Value added (billion francs)	Value added by taxed enterprises (billion francs)	Exemption rate (in percentage)	Coverage rate (in percentage)
Agriculture	175	6	96	4
Industry				
Manufacturing	1,097	985	10	90
Construction	242	156	36	67
Total, industry	1,339	1,141	15	85
Tertiary				
Saleable services				
Commerce & transportation	741	502	32	68
Renting	310	20	94	6
Finance & insurance	203	205	−1	101
Other market services	636	285	55	45
Total market services	1,890	1,018	47	53
Non-market services	750	7	99	1
Total tertiary	2,640	1,018	61	39
All sectors	4,155	2,165	48	52

Source: Ballayer 1988, p. 154.

The analysis was conducted for the 1980–90 period with regard to two sectors: the secondary sector (including construction) and the tertiary sector, excluding non-market services. The distribution of the tax base by sector (B_s, B_t) was not available. What was available was the distribution of the tax base by component $(B_w, B_k,$ and also $B_r)$, together with the capital and wages of each sector (K_s, K_t, W_s, W_t). Two assumptions were made: first, that the coverage rate by sector (c_s, c_t) known for 1984 remained constant over the period; second, that the coverage rates for a sector, for example

0.85 for the secondary sector, applied equally to capital and to wages (that is, 85 per cent of the capital of the secondary sector is subject to tax). With these (questionable) assumptions, tax base by sector was estimated as follows:

$$B_s = B_w^*(W_s^*c_s/(W_s^*c_s + W_t^*c_t)) + B_k^*(K_s^*c_s/(K_s^*c_s + K_t^*c_t))$$

$$B_t = B_w^*(K_t^*c_t/(K_s^*c_s + K_t^*c_t)) + B_k(K_s^*c_t/(K_s^*c_s + K_t^*c_t)) + R$$

Table 5.5 shows that the *taxe professionnelle* base increased by 96 billion francs or nearly 42 per cent over the decade studied. How can this increase be accounted for?

5. IMPACT OF GDP INCREASE

The increase of GDP, or more precisely value added by sectors that are not tax exempt which accounts for about 80 per cent of GDP, is a first explanation of why the tax base increased. Had everything else (that is the structure of GDP and the generation rates) remained constant, the 24 per cent growth in GDP would have led to a 24 per cent increase in the tax base. The change in GDP therefore explains about 58 per cent – only 58 per cent – of the tax base increase.

This suggests a 1.7 elasticity of the tax base relative to GDP. A more meaningful estimate obtained by regression analysis on yearly data for the 1980–93 period for the elasticity of the tax base relative to GDP is also 1.7. The base of the *taxe professionnelle* is therefore very elastic relative to GDP. Why is this so? Or, to put it another way, how can the remaining 42 percentage points of the tax base increase be explained?

6. IMPACT OF CHANGES IN THE SECTORAL COMPOSITION OF GDP

Table 5.5 gives the key figures utilized in the analysis. The table shows that the share of industry relative to services declined in the period studied. On the other hand, during the same period, the generation rates were consistently higher in industry (by 2 or 3 times) than in the service sector.

The combination of these two facts should have led to a decline in the tax base. One can calculate what the change in the tax base would have been had only the structure of GDP changed over the period (with total GDP and generation rates remaining constant).

Table 5.5 *Value added, tax bases and sector generation coefficients by sector, 1980–1990*

	1980	1990	Δ1980–90	Δ1980–90 (%)
Value added[a] (billion francs)				
Secondary (Y_s)	925	990	65	7.0
Tertiary[b] (Y_t)	1,074	1,490	416	38.7
Total[c] (Y)	1,999	2,480	481	24.1
Tax Bases (billion francs)				
Secondary (B_s)	159	195	35	27.1
Tertiary (B_t)	102	163	59	57.8
Total (B)	231	327	96	41.6
Generation coefficients				
Secondary (g_s)	0.172	0.197	0.025	14.5
Tertiary (g_t)	0.067	0.088	0.021	31.2
Total (g)	0.116	0.132	0.016	13.8

Notes: [a] In t–2, i.e. in 1978 for 1980 and in 1988 for 1990.
[b] Excluding non-market services, i.e. including only saleable services.
[c] Total value added, except for agriculture and non-market services.

Let M be this change and let subscript 1 stand for 1980 and subscript 2 for 1990:

$$M = \Sigma_i h_{i1}{}^* Y_{i1}{}^* (Y_{i2}/Y_2) - B_1$$

M, the impact of sectoral change upon the tax base is equal to –13 billion francs, or about –6 per cent of the 1980 tax base. This is only about 14 per cent of the total change in the tax base. The impact is negative, as expected, but it is less important than is commonly thought.

7. IMPACT OF CHANGES IN SECTORAL GENERATION COEFFICIENTS

Sectoral generation coefficients, that is the ratio of tax base to value added by sector, increased significantly both in the secondary sector and in the service sector, although they increased more (both in absolute and in relative terms) in the secondary sector. It is interesting to note that the total (or weighted average) generation rate increased by less than both its components – another illustration of the paradox of the whole and the part. This is explained by the fact that the relative importance of the service sector, the sector with the lower generation rate, increased during the period. The impact of these changes on the tax base can be calculated, all other things (total GDP and its sectoral composition) remaining constant. Let N be this change:

$$N = \Sigma_i g_{i2}{}^* Y_{i1} - B_1$$

N is equal to 45 billion francs which is a 19 per cent increase relative to the initial tax base and represents 45 per cent of the total tax base increase.

This impact can be broken down into two parts: the impact resulting from the change in the generation rate for the secondary sector (N_s) and the impact resulting from the change in the generation rate for the tertiary sector (N_t):

$$N_s = g_{s2}{}^* Y_{s1} + g_{t1}{}^* Y_{t1} - B_1$$

$$N_t = g_{s1}{}^* Y_{s1} + g_{t2}{}^* Y_{t1} - B_1$$

N_s is equal to 23 billion francs and N_t to 22 billion francs. Table 5.6 summarizes the above.

Table 5.6   First breakdown of tax base increase 1980–1990

	billion francs	in % of total increase	in % of 1980 base
Changes in:			
Value added (L)	56	58	24.1
Sectoral structure of value added (M)	–13	–14	–5.7
Generation rates (N)	45	47	19.4
in secondary sector	23	24	10.0
in tertiary sector	22	23	9.4
Residual	8	8	3.5
Total tax base increase	96	100	41.6

Source: Calculated as explained in the text with data from Table 5

The residual component, which is obtained by subtraction, is not an 'unexplained' source of tax base increase. It is merely the result of the combination of the other changes. The impact of each source is estimated, all other things equal. This means, for instance, that the impact of increased generation rates on the increase in value added is not taken into account. The residual reflects this second-order impact

8. IMPACT OF CHANGES IN THE STRUCTURE OF THE PRODUCTION FUNCTION

There is another approach that can be utilized to break down the increase in the tax base not explained by the GDP increase. It is related to the changes that occurred in the relative importance of labour and capital, or more precisely of wages and capital, in the French economy. Data on this question are given in Table 5.7.

Table 5.7   Value added, tax bases and generation coefficients by production factor, 1980–1990

	1980	1990	Δ	Δ/1980 (%
Value-added[a]				
Stock of capital (billion francs)	4,181	5,623	1,442	34.5
Capital remuneration (billion francs)	812	1,163	351	41.5
Labour (million workers)	15.2	14.7	−0.5	−3.1
Wages (billion francs)	801	877	76	9.5
Value-added[b] (billion francs)	1,999	2,480	481	24.1
Tax bases (billion francs)				
Capital component	118	190	72	61.1
Wages component	108	126	18	16.9
Sales component	5	9	4	80.0
Total tax base	231	327	96	41.6
Factor generation coefficients				
Capital (in francs)	0.028	0.034	0.006	21.4
Wages (in francs)	0.135	0.144	0.009	6.4
Total	0.116	0.132	0.016	13.8

Notes: [a] In *t*–2, i.e. in 1978 for 1980 and in 1988 for 1990.
           [b] Total value added, except for agriculture and non-market services.

It is possible to calculate the change in the tax base induced by the change in the relative importance of labour and capital, all other things equal. This is slightly more difficult than for sectoral changes. It is necessary first to estimate what wages, and remuneration of capital would have been in 1990 had the only change to have occurred been in the relative importance of capital and labour remuneration. It is then estimated what amount of capital this would have meant had the remuneration of capital remained unchanged. Finally, applying the 1980 factor generation coefficient to wages and capital and adding, it is calculated what the tax base would have been in that case: five billion francs more than in 1980. This is a measure of the tax base increase associated with the change in the structure of the production function.

9. IMPACT OF CHANGES IN FACTOR GENERATION COEFFICIENTS

It is simple to estimate what the tax base would have been in 1990 had the only changes recorded been in the value of the factor generation coefficients. This is equal to an increase of 24 billion francs due to the rise in the capital generation coefficient and 7 billion francs due to the increase in the wage generation coefficient. Table 5.8, an alternative to Table 5.6, gives the breakdown of the changes in the tax base which results.

Changes in the factor of production mix, that is in the relative importance of capital and labour, did not play much of a role. Here again, changes in generation coefficients explain an important part of the tax base increase.

Table 5.8   Alternative breakdown of tax base increase, 1980–1990

	billion francs	in % of total increase	in % of 1980 base
Tax base increase attributed to changes in:			
Value added (*L*)	56	58	24.1
Factors structure of value added	5	5	−2.1
Generation coefficients	31	32	13.4
for capital	24	25	10.4
for wages	7	7	3.0
Residual	4	4	1.7
Total tax base increase	96	100	41.6

Source: Calculated as explained in the text with data from Table 5.7

10.   IMPACT OF CHANGES IN PRODUCTIVITY

If the *taxe professionnelle* were a tax on factors of production, productivity improvements, all other things remaining equal, would lead to a decrease in generation coefficients and to a low (<1) elasticity of the tax base relative to GDP. The same quantity of factors would mean the same tax base. Productivity improvements would mean more value added. The ratio of tax base to value added would therefore decline. In the period considered, productivity increased, but tax base declined. How is this apparent contradiction to be explained?

The answer lies in the fact that the French *taxe professionnelle* is in fact not a tax on factors of production. It is a tax on one factor, that of capital, and on the remuneration of the other factor, that is wages. In order to understand the relationship between productivity changes and *taxe professionnelle* base changes, it is useful to look at the structure of productivity changes. This is given in Table 5.9.

Table 5.9   Partial and total productivity, 1980–1990

	1980	1990	Δ 80-90(%)
Partial productivity			
Labour: output/worker (in 1,000 francs)	131.5	168.7	+28.3
Capital: output/franc of capital (in francs)	0.478	0.4410	−7.7
Total productivity (output/equivalen worker, in 1000 francs)			
1990 capital converted at 1980 prices	64.9	69.5	+7.0
1990 capital converted at 1990 prices	64.9	72.7	+12.1

The total productivity increase hides two divergent trends: a rapid increase in labour productivity and a significant decline in capital productivity. How were these trends translated into *taxe professionnelle* base changes? The decline in capital productivity, all other things held constant, led to an increase in the tax base. Had the value added remained at its 1980 level, it would have required more capital and a consequent enlargement in the tax base of approximately 15 billion francs.

The labour productivity increase did not impinge directly upon the tax base.

What counts here is the wage bill which is a function of both labour force and labour costs. Had the value added remained at its 1980 level, it would have required less labour (−28 per cent) paid more (+13 per cent), that is a reduced wage bill (−19 per cent), which would have generated a smaller tax base (approximately 20 billion francs less). The decrease in the tax base induced by increases in labour productivity is cushioned by increases in unitary wages, but it is not eliminated. On balance, productivity increases did lead to a (modest) reduction in the tax base.

11. ANALYSIS OF CHANGES IN GENERATION COEFFICIENTS

The changes in both sector and factor generation coefficients − which are important − require explanation. They do not reflect modifications in the legislation (the data used are corrected for the few changes that did occur), but rather changes in the relation of tax base components to value added, and, beyond that, changes in the production function. A number of possible explanations or hypotheses exist.

First, increases in sectoral generation coefficients could result from intrasectoral changes in the composition of output. Within the secondary sector, but also within the tertiary sector, there are subsectors with different generation coefficients. This is because they have either different coverage rates or different true generation coefficients. It may be that the subsectors with the higher generation coefficients increased their relative importance in the period under study. This could explain increases in sectoral generation rates which are simply weighted averages of subsectoral rates. It is not possible to test this hypothesis, but there are no a priori reasons why it should be valid and it is extremely unlikely in any case that it could explain the sizeable increases recorded.

Second, changes in the capital generation coefficient could reflect changes in the structure of capital for both industry and services. Different types of capital are treated differently in the definition of the tax base. In particular, capital in equipment is more heavily taxed than capital in land or buildings: a franc of capital in equipment contributes more to the tax base than a franc of capital in land and building. The relative importance of equipment appears to have increased over the period studied. This must have increased the generation coefficient, all other things remaining equal.

Third, changes in both sectoral and factor generation coefficients could result from increases in coverage rates. The 1984 coverage rates − the share of value added by one sector that is subject to the tax − was taken to be constant throughout the period. It could have increased, either because of intrasectoral changes or because of an improvement in the tax collection effort. Unfortunately, there is no way – short of costly surveys – of verifying this hypothesis.

Table 5.10   Ratios of tax base components to value-added components, 1980–1990

	1980 (%)	1990 (%)	Δ 80 –90/80 (%)
Capital (B_k/P)	14.1	16.3	11.2
Labour (B_l/W)	13.5	14.4	6.7

Source: Calculated from Table 5.7.

A fourth hypothesis for the increase in sectoral coefficients is that in the definition of the tax base, capital is more heavily taxed than labour and that capital increased more rapidly than labour. The second part of this proposition is undoubtedly true.

This emerges clearly in Table 5.7. In the period examined and in the sectors considered (those that are not tax exempt), labour actually declined whereas the stock of capital increased by more than 34 per cent. The first part of the hypothesis, that capital is more heavily taxed than labour, is not as self-evident. The notion must first be given content. What is taxed under the *taxe professionnelle* is capital and the remuneration of labour, not labour. We can take the ratio of the capital component of the tax base to the remuneration of capital (B_k/P) and compare it with the ratio of the wage component of the tax base to the remuneration of labour (B_l/W). Table 5.10 gives these ratios for 1980 and 1990.

A franc of capital remuneration generated somewhat more (6.7 per cent) tax base than a franc of wages at the beginning of the period. This difference in factor generation coefficients may seem small, but, when coupled with the major increase in the relative importance of capital to labour remuneration, it explains a large share of the 45 billion franc increase in the tax base associated with the changes in generation rates. Let Q be the change in tax base induced by the shift in the relative importance of capital to labour remuneration, all other things held equal (that is total value added and factor generation coefficients), with g_l the generation rate for labour, g_k the generation coefficient for capital, and 1 and 2 the years 1980 and 1990 respectively:

$$Q = g_{l1}*(W_2/(W_2+P_2)*(W_1+P_1) + g_{k1}*(P_2/(W_2+P_2)*(W_1+P_1) - B_1$$

Q is equal to 30 billion francs. This is two-thirds of the tax base increase due to changes in sector generation coefficients and 31 per cent of the total increase in the tax base over the decade.

12.   CONCLUSIONS

The French *taxe professionnelle* has had, and still has, a very GDP-elastic tax base. It might have been expected to have a low (less than one) elasticity for two reasons. First, it relied more heavily on industry than on services and the share of industry relative to services declined sharply. Second, it is, at least in part, a tax levied on factors of production. This should be good for production (it does not discourage businesses from improving productivity), but it is bad for taxation (productivity increases mean less tax base per franc produced).

These two negative effects did to a certain extent materialize, contributing to a reduction in the tax base per unit of GDP. However, they were cushioned or more than offset by at least two other factors.

One is that the part of the tax base related to labour is assessed on wages and not on labour *per se*, that is on the remuneration of labour rather than on its quantity. Moreover, the remuneration of labour increased faster than the quantity of labour. The ratio of output to labour (productivity) increased rapidly, the ratio of output to wages increased more slowly, because real wages also increased during the period considered.

Another factor is that the tax base relied, and relies, somewhat more on capital than on labour or wages. Because the relative importance of capital increased very considerably during the period examined, this led to an increase in the amount of tax base generated per unit of output.These two factors do not, however, entirely explain the increase in the generation coefficients recorded. Additional factors may be intrasectoral changes or improvements in the coverage rate of the tax, but these remain unclear.

The net result is that the tax base increased very rapidly relative to GDP, as a matter of fact too rapidly. The burden of the tax on businesses became a problem, all the more so because tax rates were also increasing. The central government felt obliged to intervene in order to reduce this burden. The definition of the tax base was modified to that end, in other words, the legislation was changed (our analysis assumes instead that the legislation remains unchanged). Tax rebates were introduced. The government decided on a ceiling for the tax burden (relative to value added by each establishment); it pays the difference between the tax amount and the ceiling and has become the largest payer of this tax. In addition, disparities between local governments, or between types of enterprises, have increased in absolute terms even if they have not increased in relative terms and these have become more and more unpalatable. By now, the *taxe professionnelle* is one of the most heavily criticized taxes in France. It has fallen victim of its own success.

NOTES

1. To be more precise, β was initially equal to 20%, then reduced to 18% in 1983.
2. In what follows, all money figures are in constant 1980 francs; M stands for million and GF (giga francs) stands for billions.

REFERENCES

Ballayer, M. (1988) (Commission d'étude présidée par), *L'évolution de la Taxe Professionnelle*, Paris: La Documentation Française.

Guelton, S. (1994), *L'impact des mutations économiques sur l'évolution de l'assiette de la taxe professionnelle et sur sa répartition spatiale*, PhD Dissertation, Paris XII: IUP/Univ.

Martinez, P. (1991), 'Les exportation de taxe professionnelle des communes des Hauts-de-Seine', mimeo, Paris XII: L'oeil/IUP/Univ.

Pola, G. (1990), *La tassazione locale dell'attività produttiva: esperienze a confronto*, Bologna: Il Mulino.

6. Local Public Spending in France: The Case of Welfare Programmes at the *Département* Level

Guy Gilbert and Yvon Rocaboy

1. INTRODUCTION *

After several earlier attempts at reform, in part successful, important changes were introduced in France in the early 1980s regarding the distribution of powers, responsibilities and finance among the different tiers of government. A legislative package – 'Lois de Décentralisation and Lois de compétences' – was approved between 1982 and 1986 which was completed, in 1992, with the ATR Law ('Loi sur l'Administration Territoriale de la République').

Much has been written on the consequences of this 'process of decentralization' implemented in one of the most centralist countries in Europe (Gilbert and Delcamp (eds) 1993). Some authors have warned of the serious shortcomings of these new arrangements (inefficiency, waste, irresponsibility, corruption); others have instead stressed their merits (greater efficiency, accountability, flexibility and innovation in local public services). Only a few have hazarded to argue that the reforms have not had a decisive impact.

This reform was designed to transfer more powers, responsibilities and financial means to subcentral levels of government (currently 26 regions, created in 1982, 100 *'départements'*, 36,700 *'communes'*, 200 newly created *'communautés de communes'* and more than 18,000 special districts). There is no doubt that these objectives were achieved.

A key characteristic of the decentralization legislation is that it was concerned mainly with the transfer of responsibilities to lower governmental tiers. Although new fiscal resources were given to the regions, *département* and communes to finance the additional expenditure associated with the

---

* This article benefited from helpful comments by J. Lotz and W. Santagata. Remaining errors and omissions are ours.

redistribution of responsibilities, there was not the global reform of local taxation which was urgently needed at that time.

The redistribution of responsibilities was quite logical. Each level of government received a specific 'block of responsibilities'. In only a few cases was a responsibility allocated to more than one tier of government. The new arrangements apply only to 'compulsory' responsibilities (that is, those which a given level of government is obliged to perform). With 'voluntary' responsibilities, a local government is free to decide whether to perform them or not. This way of allocating responsibilities has the sweet smell of 'cartesianism' in line with long-established French administrative tradition. However, it has also the merit of lightening, discreetly, the fiscal burden of central government in at least two major areas: education, or more precisely the construction and maintenance of school buildings, which the central government neglected in the 1960s and 1970s; and social services, which seems to have become excessively burdensome for central government to finance on its own. Although earlier attempts at reform had been made – under the Barre government in the late 1970s – growth in welfare expenditure was very high at the beginning of the 1980s. This upward trend seemed ineluctable, the result of the pressure of 'social needs' and application of the rules introduced over decades of welfare state. From central government's standpoint, then, it seemed quite reasonable to try to distribute the burden more equally among the different tiers of government.

Unexpectedly, growth in welfare expenditure (an item transferred in the main to the *départements*, see Section 2) slowed down rapidly over the 1980s but picked up again at the beginning of the 1990s. How is this marked, and unpredicted, change in welfare expenditure to be interpreted? Is it due to a change, albeit unlikely, in voter preferences? Is it the result of an improvement in the productivity or efficiency of social services, now the responsibility of subcentral jurisdictions? Does it stem from a change, again unlikely, in 'social needs'? Or does it derive from the major changes in how social services were financed, which were introduced during the period in question?

To answer these questions it is first necessary to give a more detailed description of the institutional framework (Section 2). A theoretical model of welfare spending behaviour of *départements* is provided in Section 3. The empirical results are presented in Section 4. The chapter ends with some concluding remarks (Section 5).

2. THE MULTILEVEL INSTITUTIONAL STRUCTURE OF WELFARE PROGRAMMES

A clear distinction has to be made between compulsory welfare programmes (Aide Sociale Publique or Aide Sociale Légale – ASL) and voluntary welfare programmes. Lower tiers of government can use the latter to help needy individuals to supplement the assistance which they are obliged by law to guarantee to every individual meeting statutory eligibility requirements. To qualify for aid under compulsory programmes, individuals must satisfy eligibility requirements for age, disability and social or economic condition. But these only set minimum standards and lower tiers of government are free to provide additional aid to needy individuals. They may make supplementary cash transfers or in–kiñd assistance and can fix more generous eligibility standards. The official term for compulsory welfare programmes and voluntary programmes taken together is *'Action Sociale'*.

Before 1984, welfare programmes were basically the responsibility of the central level of government: part of this responsibility was delegated to lower tiers of government through a complicated system of co-financing and cross-subsidization. Since 1984, compulsory welfare programmes are the responsibility of the *départements* (legislation approved in 7 July 1983, 22 July 1983 and 1 January 1984). Central government continues to operate and monitor a limited number of welfare programmes (supplementing numerous and generous social security benefits).

The more important welfare programmes coming under the responsibility of the *départements* are:

1. free medical care for individuals with low income in the form of home aid and cash transfers (which account for 6 per cent of welfare expenditure of the *départements*);
2. aid for the elderly (mainly in-kind transfers such as housing, meals and home aid) (14 per cent);
3. aid for the disabled (subsidized housing, in-kind transfers) (25 per cent);
4. aid for childhood (cash or in-kind transfers) (36 per cent).

Central government still provides assistance under programmes of national scope (aid to the unemployed, the homeless, refugees) and sets minimum eligibility standards. It shares responsibility (and costs) with the *départements* for the RMI programme (providing a cash transfer to individuals with very low income which is linked to assistance (in-kind) aimed at improving the employability of the beneficiaries; central government finances the entire cost of the cash transfer provided under the RMI programme while 20 per cent of the in-kind transfer is financed by the *départements*). Since 1984, the *département* assembly (the Conseil Général) has the power, subject to certain legal restrictions, to decide the rules regarding age and income to be applied in determining eligibility for, and the amount per capita of, cash transfers. The Conseil Général may open or close institutions providing welfare and social services, and establish their operating procedures; it also sets levels of charges for social services delivered (for example, per diem charges for clients of social institutions), independently or in concert with central government. Before 1984, admission of patients to social institutions was essentially decided by the communes and *départements*. Where there was joint financing (communes + *départements* + central government), the say the centre had in admission decisions was in proportion to its financial contribution. At that time, the open-ended subsidy provided by central government to the *départements* for welfare programmes was on a matching basis: the average rate increased over time, reaching 60 per cent by the beginning of the 1980s.

The fiscal provisions contained in the decentralization legislation rest upon a simple principle. All additional expenditure responsibility transferred to the *départements* regarding compulsory welfare programmes is to be compensated for by central government. Compensation takes two forms. First, there is a transfer of taxes. A number of taxes, formerly levied at the central level, were ceded to the *départements* (motor vehicle registration fees and a tax on transactions in immovables). Second, the *départements* received a lump-sum grant, the DGD ('dotation globale de décentralisation') which is equal to the difference between the expenditure attributable to the transfer of responsibility less the value of the taxes ceded. Balance was in fact achieved in 1984 (Figure 6.1): had transfer of responsibility not taken place, central government would have had to meet 32.6 billion of the total of 52 billion francs spent on welfare and the *départements* 19.4 billion francs.

The rules governing subsidies for the local social sector are somewhat complicated in France. The *départements* receive two block grants from the centre: the DGF ('dotation globale de fonctionnement') and the DGD. Local governments (communes) contribute to the cost of welfare programme undertaken at the *département* level with an obligatory payment to the *départements* based on a uniform share of the *département* welfare expenditures. This share is fixed by the *département* assembly. This rather complicated mechanism is called the 'contingent communal d'aide sociale'. After 1984, the central government burden is 12.2 billion francs and that of the *départements* 39.8 billion francs. The additional 20.4 billion francs falling on the *départements* were fully compensated by the DGD (8.8 billion francs) and by the extra revenues from the vehicle tax (7.6 billion francs) and the tax on transactions in immovables (billion francs).

Since 1984, welfare expenditures explain nearly half of the current budgets of the *départements*. Revenues (taxes + DGD) received by the *départements* in compensation are general and not earmarked. The *département* assembly is free to set the rates of the two new taxes; consequently the tax rates differ from one *département* to another. The DGD and the main general-purpose grant (DGF) are adjusted upwards annually (up until now at a rate equal to the sum of the rate of inflation and two-thirds of the rate of growth of GNP (in volume)). This new set of fiscal rules has two important consequences: it increases the current budgets of the *départements*; and it creates further disparity in social expenditure among *départements*.

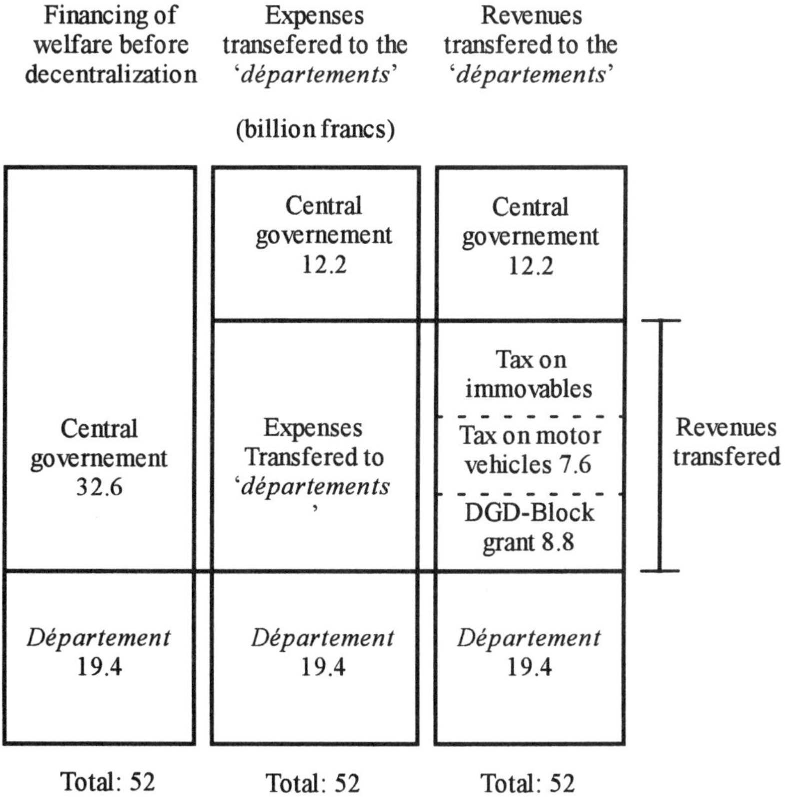

Financing of welfare before decentralization	Expenses transfered to the 'départements'	Revenues transfered to the 'départements'
	(billion francs)	

	Central governement 12.2	Central governement 12.2
Central governement 32.6	Expenses Transfered to 'départements'	Tax on immovables - - - - - - - Tax on motor vehicles 7.6 - - - - - - - DGD-Block grant 8.8	Revenues transfered
Département 19.4	Département 19.4	Département 19.4
Total: 52	Total: 52	Total: 52

Figure 6.1   The financing of decentralization, welfare budgets

Welfare expenditure at the *département* level before 1984 increased at an average rate of 1 to 2 per cent. It reached 42.5 billion francs in 1983, fell to

41.5 billion francs in 1984 and declined steadily after that date at an annual rate of 1 to 2 per cent (Figure 6.2). Over the same period, however, other current expenditure of *départements* grew at an accelerated pace (before 1984, the average annual rate of increase was roughly 1 to 2 per cent but after 1984 it was between 4 and 5 per cent). A form of substitution between welfare expenditure and other non-social expenditure probably occurred in the *département* current budgets.

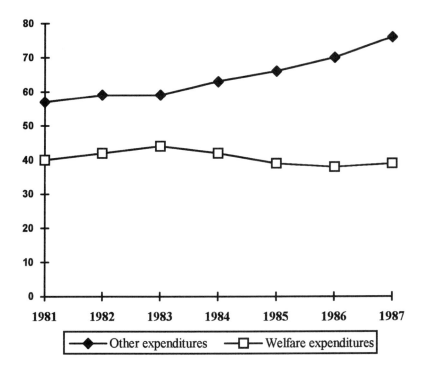

Source: Ministère des Affaires Sociales et de la Solidarité (SESI) et Direction Général des Collectivités Locales (DGCL).

Figure 6.2   Current budgets of the départements *(1981–1987) in constant 1987 billion francs*

This overall reduction in *département* welfare expenditure has had a direct effect on each of the main welfare programmes (aid for childhood – ASE; aid to the handicapped – ASPH; aid to the elderly – ASPA; medical care to the needy – AMG) (see Figure 6.3). A clear break in the trend can be observed about 1984. In addition, the disparities in social expenditure per capita among *départements* have increased: currently, there is an average range of 1 to 4 for each welfare programme.

If we wish to explain the basic roots of these trends in expenditure over time and to understand the reasons for the disparities in welfare expenditure among *départements*, we must go beyond a simple description of the institutions and aggregate data. Is it only a question of disparity in 'needs' as it is usually declared by official agencies (DGCL 1988)? Have disparities in resources played a role here? More precisely, have subsidization rules (open-ended versus closed-ended grants, matching versus lump-sum grants) played a part in determining the phenomenon examined here, as has often been argued (Bradford and Oates 1971)?

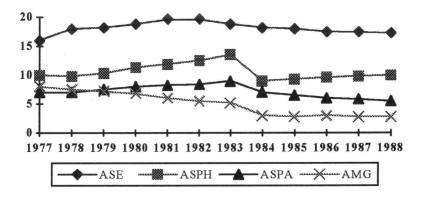

Source: Ministère des Affaires Sociales et de la Solidarité (SESI) et Direction Général des Collectivités Locales (DGCL).

Figure 6.3   Welfare expenditures (French départements*) (1977–1988) in constant 1988 billion francs*

3.   THE MODEL

We assume that each jurisdiction provides a quantity Q of social services. These services are earmarked for eligible beneficiaries, the 'assisted local population'. The services in question are quite heterogeneous. Some are labour-intensive (services provided under the form of in-kind services to individuals); others are capital or money-intensive or intensive in terms of current expenditure as in the case of other in-kind transfers or cash transfers directly provided to beneficiaries. Q represents the quantity of composite social good. This non-homogeneity will be translated by the relation

$$Q = l^\rho h^{1-\rho} z \qquad\qquad (6.1)$$

where l = number of local social workers
         h = number of assisted persons
         z = total social public service provided at the local level
         ρ = parameter describing the nature of the local service

If $\rho = 0$, then $Q = h.z$. This relation (identity) means that the number of social workers involved in the provision of social services has no influence on the quantity Q (this is the case of pure in-cash transfers). If $\rho = 1$, $Q = l.z$, labour is the unique input in the production function, the service provided to an individual depends only on the number of social workers, each of them assumed to be equally productive. Rho appears more or less to be an indicator of the nature (in-cash vs in-kind) of the composite social good.

The model assumes the existence of a decisive voter at the local level. Assuming the exogeneity of the number of local beneficiaries (no 'voting by foot') and the exogeneity of the number of social workers, the decisive voter determines the amount of local public services. His or her utility is assumed to depend on his or her private consumption level x_m, and on the level of local welfare programmes z provided to assisted persons in this jurisdiction.

Three arguments could be made to justify the inclusion of z in the utility function. The first rests on the usual altruistic hypothesis, the decisive voter being assumed to manifest some form of compassion towards disinherited persons in his or her jurisdiction. The second relates to the notion of 'comprehensive selfishness' as defined by Brennan (1973): the more the poor are 'too poor', the more the rich feel threatened in the 'peaceful enjoyment of his or her wealth'. In that sense, local welfare programmes are quite like a local public good (Pauly 1973). The third argument is the usual Rawlsian 'veil of ignorance'.

The utility of the decisive voter is assumed to depend positively on his or her private consumption x_m, and the level of social public services provided in his or her jurisdiction z.

$$U_m = U_m (x_m, z) \qquad\qquad (6.2)$$

where U_m is monotonically increasing in the two arguments, differentiable and strictly quasi-concave.

Welfare expenditure is financed jointly by contributions charged to the assisted population and by local public revenues. The assisted population contributes in a proportion α of the total cost of provision $C(Q)$. This parameter α is assumed to be exogenous.[1] The remaining share $(1-\alpha C)(Q) = E$ is financed out of local tax revenues and subsidies received from other levels of government. The decisive voter is assumed to be subject to fiscal illusion; he or she does not take into account the consequences for him or her of the increase in taxes levied at other levels of government as a consequence of an increase in the subsidies granted to his or her own jurisdiction.[2] The subsidies received at the local level are thus assumed to be exogenous.

There are two different types of subsidies received at the local level: a lump sum grant G, and a matching grant $S[(1-\alpha)C(Q)]$. Taxes are levied at a proportional rate t on a tax base B (assumed exogenous). Limited to welfare expenditure, the jurisdiction's budget constraint is :

$$(1-\alpha)C(Q) = tB + G + S[(1-\alpha)C(Q)] \qquad (6.3)$$

The budget constraint of the decisive voter is :

$$y_m = x_m + t \; b_m \qquad (6.4)$$

where y_m is the personal income of m, x_m, his or her consumption (price of consumption being assumed to be 1) and b_m his or her own tax base.

The local government maximizes (6.2) subject to constraints (6.1), (6.3) and (6.4). The first-order condition for optimality is:

$$\frac{\partial U_m/\partial z}{\partial U_m \partial x_m} = (1-\alpha)\left(\frac{l}{h}\right)^p \frac{h}{n}\left(1-\frac{\partial S}{\partial E}\right)\frac{\partial C}{\partial Q}\frac{b_m}{b} \qquad (6.5)$$

where n is the local population and $b = B/n$, the average tax base.

The partial derivative $(\partial S/\partial E)$ corresponds to the marginal rate of contribution to local welfare spending. Defining ρ as the elasticity of local social spending to the proportional subsidy $\sigma = (\partial S/\partial E)/(S/E)$ and $\tau = (S/E)$ the average rate of subsidy, the first-order condition could be rewritten:

$$\frac{\partial U_m/\partial z}{\partial U_m \partial x_m} = (1-\alpha)\left(\frac{l}{h}\right)^p \frac{h}{n}\left(1-\frac{\tau}{\sigma}\right)\frac{\partial C}{\partial Q}\frac{b_m}{b} \qquad (6.6)$$

Relation (6.6) gives the fiscal price (p_m) of the social public service for the decisive voter. It clearly depends on the average contribution rate and on the inverse of the elasticity of local spending to the matching grant $(-\tau/\sigma)$. A proportional subsidy leads to a price effect. Conversely, the lump-sum grant has no influence on the tax price. It only affects (positively) the quantity of services provided, just as an increase in the personal income of the decisive voter would do. The lump grant is thus equivalent to an increase in the resources of the decisive voter amounting at $g(b_m/b)$ where g is the per capita grant and (b_m/b) the tax share of the voter.[3] This leads finally to the usual demand function for local public services which combines private income, subsidies, and tax price. For jurisdiction i, the demand is:

$$z^i = f^i(y^i, p^i_m g^i, b^i_m / b^i) \tag{6.7}$$

4. EMPIRICAL ESTIMATES OF WELFARE EXPENDITURE AT THE LOCAL LEVEL

This section deals first with specification issues (Section 4.1) and with econometric estimates for a sample of French *départements* (Section 4.2).

4.1 Specification of the Equation

We assume that the demand function is of the constant-elasticity type.

$$\text{Log } z = \omega_0 + \omega_1 \text{Log } y_m + \omega_2 \text{Log } p_m + \omega_3 \text{Log}(g\, b_m / b) \tag{6.8}$$

where ω_1 is the income elasticity of local expenditure, ω_2 the price-elasticity, and ω_3 the elasticity with respect to lump-sum grants.

Using the expression of p_m from (6.6), the expression of z from (6.1) assuming in addition the marginal cost of production to be constant[4] we obtain per capita (per beneficiary) expenditure $(C(Q)/h)$

$$\text{Log}\frac{C(Q)}{h} = \omega_0 + \omega_1 \text{Log } y_m + \rho(\omega_2 + 1)\text{Log}\frac{l}{h}$$

$$+ \omega_2 \text{Log}\left[(1-\alpha)\frac{h}{n}\frac{b_m}{b} 1 - \frac{\tau}{\sigma}\right] + (\omega_2 + 1)\text{Log}\frac{\partial C}{\partial Q} + \omega_3 \text{Log} g \frac{b_m}{b} \tag{6.9}$$

and, after a number of calculations[5]

$$\text{Log}\frac{E}{h} = \omega_0 + \omega_1 \text{Log } y_m + \rho(\omega_2 + 1)\text{Log}\frac{l}{h} + \omega_2 \text{Log}\frac{h}{n} + (\omega_2 + \omega_3)\text{Log}\frac{b_m}{b}$$

$$+ (\omega_2 + 1)\text{Log}\frac{\partial C}{\partial Q} + (\omega_2 + 1)\text{Log}(1-\alpha) + \omega_3 \text{Log } g - \frac{\omega_2}{\sigma}\tau \quad \text{with } E = (1-\alpha)C(Q) \tag{6.10}$$

Equation (6.10) allows identification of the determinants of local welfare expenditure per beneficiary: personal income y_m, average number of social workers per beneficiary $(1/h)$, ratio of assisted persons to total population (h/n), tax share of the decisive voter (b_m/b), marginal cost of provision $(\partial C / \partial Q)$ (assumed to be constant), actual share of expenditure to be met by the local government $(1-\alpha)$, lump-sum grant per capita g, and average rate of matching grant (τ).

4.2 Econometric Estimates of Expenditure Behaviour

The model described above has been used for three welfare programmes at the *départements* level for 1989: the assistance for childhood programme ('Aide Sociale à l'Enfance' – ASE), the assistance for the elderly programme ('Aide Sociale aux Personnes Agée – ASPA), and the assistance for the handicapped programme ('Aide Sociale aux Personnes Handicapées – ASPH). Equation (6.10) has been used as specified above for ASE. Because of lack of data on the number of social workers employed by the ASPA and ASPH, for these two programmes a slightly different version of (6.10) has been used.

Equation (6.10) is over-identified because of linear restrictions on parameters. On the one hand, the sum of the elasticity of expenditure with respect to fiscal price and with respect to lump-sum grant must equal the estimated coefficient for the tax share variable (b_m/b).[6] On the other hand, the coefficient of the variable $(1-\alpha)$ which represents the 'actual rate of funding' must be linearly (and exclusively) dependent on the price-elasticity.

The non-linear least square adjustment procedure leads to quite satisfactory results for the ASE programme (Table 6.1). Differences in per capita expenditure among the *départements* on this programme is correctly explained $(R^2 = 0.828)$. Conversely, the results are far from satisfactory for expenditure for the handicapped and elderly persons: 40 per cent of the variance remains unexplained in the case of ASPH and 30 per cent in the case of ASPA. One of a number of possible explanations for these poor results is the difficulty of measuring precisely the number of social workers in the different sectors.

However, the estimates of the coefficients are significantly different from zero, and have the expected sign. The welfare programmes provided by the local public sector appear to be normal goods, as is usually the case in the econometric studies for developed countries. The first important difference with previous estimates for France is the high value obtained for the incomeelasticity (1.6 for aid to childhood, 2.5 for aid to the elderly as compared with the usual figure of 0.1 to 0.5[7]); these results appear much closer to the figures obtained for US jurisdictions (0.4 to 0.9) or Swiss jurisdictions (0.9 to 1.4).[8] If this preliminary result were to be confirmed, it would suggest that social expenditure at the *département* level is highly income-elastic. An increase of 1 per cent in average income per capita would lead, *ceteris paribus*, to an increase of 1.5 to 2.5 per cent in net per capita welfare expenditure. In other words, the welfare programmes would appear to be potentially redistributive.

Table 6.1 *Econometric estimates of the expenditure function (non-linear least square adjustment)*

Parameters	Childhood programme ASE	Aid to handicapped ASPH	Aid to elderly ASPA
Number of *départements*	71	77	73
Constant ω_n	−1.042	−1.368	−2.482
	(−3.03)	(0.40)	(−3.26)
Individual income elasticity ω_1	1.600	0.328	2.488
	(5.26)	(1.07)	(3.96)
(Tax) price elasticity ω_n	−0.445	−0.510	−0.483
	(−5.35)	(−7.45)	(−4.63)
Lump-sum grant elasticity ω_{λ}	0.303	0.452	0.886
	(3.76)	(5.29)	(4.76)
Matching grant elasticity σ	0.611	0.437	0.188
	(1.33)	(2.55)	(2.24)
Service parameters (ρ)	0.803	–	–
	(8.84)	–	–
R^2	0.828	0.569	0.684

Note: *t* ratio in parentheses.

Another important result is the (somewhat) low value of the fiscal price elasticity. Compared with the usual figure of −1 obtained by the previous studies already cited, estimated price-elasticity is about −0.5, a figure quite close to the estimates in US studies. Consequently, if the number of beneficiaries (which directly influences the fiscal price) increases, per capita welfare expenditure will reduce, but only to a small degree.

The effects of subsidies on the expenditure level are in line with economic theory. The signs of the coefficients with regard to lump-sum grants and to uniform (proportional) subsidies are positive and significant except for the case of proportional subsidies with assistance for childhood.

The elasticity of social expenditure to transfers is quite similar for assistance to the handicapped and for childhood regardless of the type of transfer involved (lump-sum or proportional). Conversely, the elasticity of expenditure to lump-sum grants is significantly higher than that to proportional grants in the case of transfers to the elderly. These results are in striking contrast with the usual textbook argument stating that the elasticity of expenditure to proportional grants must be higher than that to lump-sum grants. One explanation for this may be simply that proportional transfers are made by local governments and not the centre. The *départements* may be more careful in using financial resources coming from lower levels of government than in using those coming from higher levels of government even if the subsidies made by local governments take the form of matching grants. This again may be because fiscal illusion is more likely if the money comes from 'afar' (that is, central government) than if the money comes from 'nearby' (local jurisdictions). More precisely in France, there are strong political and individual links between members of the local assembly ('Conseil municipal') and mayor and those of the *département* assembly.

The values taken by the parameter r, relating to the nature of the welfare programme, are bounded to (0,1): if $\rho = 0$, the 'service' is a pure cash benefit; if it takes the value 1, the service provided is a pure in-kind benefit.[9] For childhood assistance, the estimated value for r differs significantly (student $t = -2.18$) from 1; $\rho = 0.803$. The childhood assistance programme by its very nature is much more similar to an in-kind benefit than to a cash benefit.

Summing up, the level of fiscal prices has little effect on social benefits provided to beneficiaries but these benefits are highly income-elastic. Allegorically speaking, this means that the poor are better off when they are only few in number and live in a wealthy jurisdiction than when they live in a poorer community along with many other poor.

4.3 Explaining Interjurisdictional Differences in Welfare Expenditure

In the debate in France on interjurisdictional differences in welfare expenditure, it is frequently stated that the very large differences in per capita social expenditure among *départements* are attributable to 'economic, social or demographic features' (Jacquet 1988). This a priori judgement is clearly unsatisfactory. Using the empirical results presented above (equation 6.10), it is possible to examine the reasons for such disparities in more depth.

The independent variables used in (6.10) can be classified in three categories: financial resources (individual income and public resources), financial needs and type of benefit provided by the jurisdictions.

The financial resources are composed of collective (*département*) fiscal resources and individual incomes and taxes. The former include subsidies granted to the *départements* by central government (DGF and DGD) and by local governments ('*contingent d'aide sociale*'). Individual incomes include personal income, the tax share and the matching rate (average rate of the matching grant). The only need-related variable is the (h/n) ratio number of beneficiaries/size of population: interpreting this ratio as a need-related variable is equivalent to assuming that the *départements* are 'neutral' vis-à-vis the socioeconomic environment, that is, they do not use this ratio in a discretionary way. The last category of variable, type of benefit, is simply the average number of social workers per beneficiary.

The contribution of each of these three categories of determinants to explaining variance in welfare expenditure per capita among *départements*, is measured as follows. The R_2 coefficient can be disaggregated as:

$$\sum_{i=1}^{n} \pi_i r_i (\sigma_i / \sigma) \tag{6.11}$$

with n: number of independent variables
π_i: regression coefficient of variable i on the dependent variable
r_i: partial correlation coefficient between variable i and the dependent variable
σ_i: standard deviation of the variable i
σ : standard deviation of the dependent variable.

Under some restrictions,[10] the contribution of the variable i Γ_i to the explanation of the dispersion of the dependent variable is approximately

$$\Gamma_i = \frac{\pi_i r(\sigma_i / \sigma)}{R^2} \tag{6.12}$$

After estimation of π_i, (6.12) gives the weight of each factor in explaining disparities in spending behaviour among jurisdictions. The results are presented in Table 6.2. On average, need-related factors and resource-related factors each explain half of total variance. Some comments are required in the case of the assistance for childhood programme. Because of the inclusion of the ratio (l/n) as an independent variable (the contribution of which the explanation of total variance amounts at 13 per cent), more than 25 per cent of total explained variance is concentrated under the personal income variable: the contributions of subsidies are thus rather limited (only 9 per cent for lump-sum grants and 4 per cent for proportional subsidies). The most important factor remains the needs factor which accounts for half of total explained variance.

Table 6.2 Sources of disparity in welfare expenditure at the
        département *level*

Variables	Childhood programme ASE		Aid to handicapped people ASPH		Aid to elderly people ASPA	
	Contribution of var. i to R^2	Γ_i in %	Contribution of var. i to R^2	Γ_i in %	Contribution of var. i to R^2	Γ_i in %
Resources	0.3151	38.10	0.2429	37.84	0.3435	55.05
Personal income (Y_m)	0.2097	25.35	−0.0065	−1.01	0.0410	6.57
Participation rate $(1-a)$	–	–	0.0473	7.37	0.1144	18.33
Tax share (b_m/b)	0.0003	0.04	0.0364	5.67	0.0976	15.64
Rate of prop. subsidy (t)	0.0325	3.93	0.0407	6.34	−0.0032	−0.51
Lump sum grant (g)	0.0726	8.77	0.1250	19.47	0.0937	15.02
Needs-related variables	0.4017	48.57	0.4000	62.30	0.2808	45.00
Beneficiary ratio (h/n)	0.4017	48.57	0.4000	62.30	0.2808	45.00
Type of programme	0.1102	13.32	–	–	–	–
Labour-intensity (l/h)	0.1102	13.32	–	–	–	–
R^2	0.827	100	0.642	100	0.624	100

Transfers to the elderly and the handicapped show some similarities. Two resource-related variables are of particuliar importance: average rate of the matching grant and lump-sum grants. Together they account for one-third of total explained variance and represent two-thirds of the contribution of resource-related variables to R^2. Need-related variables appear to be more important for the programme for the handicapped (62 per cent of total variance) than for that for the elderly (45 per cent). Partly this is because personal income and tax share contribute more to explained variance for the handicapped than to that for the elderly.

Although these results must be interpreted with caution, we may finally have some evidence to suggest that resource-related factors do play an important part in explaining disparities in welfare expenditure per capita among jurisdictions in France. If some *départements* spend more than others on welfare, this is not only because of higher needs. It is also because of greater availability of financial resources. The respective contribution of 'needs' and 'resources' to disparity is broadly equivalent. This result contrasts sharply with the conventional analysis which assigns a leading role to 'needs'. An early exception to this was Fréville (1966).

5. CONCLUDING REMARKS

Welfare-related expenditure is often considered to be the principal determinant of the increase in total expenditure by French *départements* over the period since the early 1980s. It is frequently held that the pressure of 'social needs' make this trend irreversible. An econometric analysis based on cross-sectional data of *départements* suggests, however, that the per capita level of social services provided at the *département* level depend on both need-related and resource-related factors (personal income, taxes and subsidies). The contribution of 'needs' and of 'resources' to explained variance in expenditure by *départements* on welfare is broadly equivalent. Moreover, the 'composite welfare good' appears quite similar to a normal good.

   If these results were to be confirmed, they would be in sharp contrast with the arguments customarily espoused by politicians and by the medical and social worker lobbies. The decentralization process which has involved a transfer of power to local governments since the early 1980s has in the end had no decisive influence on this situation.

NOTES

1. This assumption produces the same effects as a proportional subsidy on social expenditure.
2. If this assumption is quite debatable, the same is true for the assumption to the contrary, especially in the case of 'local jurisdictions' (see Gevres and Proost 1978).
3. Combining equations (6.2) and (6.4), we obtain $y_m + gb_m/b = X[((1-\alpha)C(Q) - S)/B]b_m$
4. In that case $C(Q)/Q = \partial C/\partial Q$ and $z = C(Q)/(l^p h^{1-p}(\partial C/\partial Q))$.
5. Using the approximation $\omega_2 Log(1-\tau/\sigma) \cong -(\omega_2/\sigma)\tau$ knowing that $0 < \tau/\sigma < 1$, and neglecting terms of Taylor's expansion equal and above 2.
6. Such a restriction could be interpreted in terms of fiscal illusion on the part of the decisive voter. Let us assume the spending function is of double-logarithmic form $z = \omega_0 y_m^{\omega_1} p_m^{\omega_2} (gb_m/b)^{\omega_3}$ which can be rewriten as $z = \omega_0 y_m^{\omega_1} (kb_m/b)^{\omega_2} (gb_m/b)^{\omega_3}$ with $p_m = kb_m/b$. Multiplying the fiscal price and per capita subsidies by an identical positive scalar, λ we obtain: $z = \omega_0 y_m^{\omega_1} (kb_m/b)^{\omega_2} (gb_m/b)^{\omega_3} \lambda^{\alpha_2+\omega_{23}}$. The $(\omega_2 + \omega_3)$ coefficient expresses the degree of homogeneity of the spending function with respect to both fiscal price and per capita subsidy. If $\omega_2 + \omega_3 = 0$, a proportional increase in fiscal price and per capita

subsidy will entail no modification in spending behaviour. In this case, the decisive voter is not subject to fiscal illusion.

7. See Guengant (1988). The figure of 0.1 to 0.5 for the income elasticity of demand for local public goods is probably partly due to the important role played by the tax-share in explaining consumer behaviour. The basic reason relates to the nature of the French local tax system. The tax-share levied on inhabitants varies very considerably between one jurisdiction. Another reason is that the main tax revenue source is a local tax on enterprises. As enterprises are concentrated only in a few communes, the ratio b_m/b varies widely and thus plays an important role in the econometric estimation.

8. International comparisons have to be used with care here. See Derycke and Gilbert (1988, Ch. 4) for a critical survey based on Swiss, Belgian, American and French studies. See also Inman (1979) and Pommerehne (1987).

9. Note that the estimation of r is impossible in the case that the (estimated) value for price-elasticity $\omega_2 = -1$.

10. Christ 1966, pp. 506–7.

REFERENCES

Bradford, D.F. and W.E. Oates (1971), 'Towards a predictive theory of intergovernmental grants', *American Economic Review, Papers and Proceedings*, **61**, 440–8.

Brennan, G. (1973), 'Pareto desirable redistribution. The non-altruistic dimension', *Public Choice*, **22**, 89–106.

Christ, K.F. (1966), *Econometrics Models and Methods*, New York: John Wiley.

Derycke, P.H. and G. Gilbert (1988), *Economie Publique Locale*, Paris: Economica.

DGCL (1988), 'Les dépenses d'aide sociale des Départements de 1984 à 1986, *Mission d'étude et de Statistiques*, Décembre 1988.

Freville, Y. (1966), Recherches statistiques sur l'économie des finances locales, Thése de Doctorat d'etat, Université De Rennes I.

Gevres, L. and S. Proost (1978), 'Some effects of taxation and collective goods in postwar America: a tentative appraisal', *Journal of Public Economics*, **9**, 115–37.

Gilbert, G. and A. Delcamp (eds). (1993), *La Décentralisation, Dix Ans Aprés*, Paris: LGDJ.

Guengant, A. (1988), 'L'influence des subventions sur la demande de services publics locaux', *Revue d'économie régionale et urbaine*, **2**, 231–48.

Inman, R.P. (1979), 'The fiscal performance of local governments : an interpretative review' in P. Mieszkowski and M. Straszheim (eds), *The Fiscal Performance of Local Governments : An Interpretative Review*, Baltimore: JHUP, 270–321.

Jacquet, J.C. (1988), 'Les conséquences de la décentralisation en matière d'aide sociale', Rapport du Conseil Économique et Social, *Journal Officiel*, 22 juillet 1988.

Pauly, M. (1973), 'Income Redistribution as a Local Public Good', *Journal of Public Economics*, **2**, 35–58.

Pommerehne, W.W. (1987), *Präferenzen Für Öffentliche Güter: Ansätze Zu Ihrer Erfassung*, Tübingen: Mohr (Siebeck).

7. Local Authorities' Expenditure Behaviour in Italy and Regional Differences

Rosella Levaggi[*]

1. INTRODUCTION

Local government in Italy has enjoyed mixed fortune over the past few years. After a period during which their fiscal autonomy was reduced to negligible proportions, Italian local authorities have once again the power to raise revenue through local taxes and to set expenditure level free from the *ex-ante* control from external audit organs such as the Comitato Regionale di Controllo (CORECO). The new independence on the expenditure side of the budget, coupled with the electoral reform introducing an adjusted majority principle, might have potentially beneficial effects on local government organization. However, the impact of the reform may differ quite widely regionally. Since 1978, grants-in-aid have followed rather different patterns;[1] this element, coupled with the practice of paying for local government current debts might have sensibly altered local government expenditure behaviour. This chapter will study communal councils' expenditure determination just after the introduction of ICIAP (a business tax) and before ICI (a property tax) were coming into the picture. The aim is to test whether, at this stage, expenditure determination presented any significant regional pattern which could also affect the response to the new season of local autonomy. The chapter is organized as follows: in Section 2 I summarize the main feature of local government finance in Italy with particular reference to the grant system; in Section 3 I present the theoretical model whose estimates are discussed in Section 4. In Section 5 I present the results of a simulation exercise aimed at forecasting the likely effects on expenditure deriving from the introduction of ICI and finally in Section 6 I present the conclusions of the analysis.

[*] I would like to thank Prof. Giancarlo Pola for gathering the dataset and for supplying information and comments on the Italian local government finance system.

2. THE REFORM

After the radical reform of 1974, local government in Italy had marginal
fiscal autonomy, so that up to 1988 virtually 90 per cent of the local budgets
were centrally financed. In 1989 local authorities gained a significant source
of local revenue with the introduction of ICIAP, the municipal tax on
businesses and the professions. The tax base is the surface occupied by non-
domestic buildings and the rate varies according to the sector of activity and
the classification of the area in which the firm is located.[2] As many of its
predecessors, despite its once and for all nature, the tax has continued in
existence and since 1990 ICIAP has been modulated according to the
income (or profit) of the taxpayer.[3]

In the period between 1974 and 1990, the main source of local
government finance was a grant from central government whose level had
not been homogeneous throughout Italy. The grant was, in fact, aimed at
equalizing local resources with a bias towards the councils in the south of
Italy which, for historical reasons, have always been poorer than the ones in
the north.

The equalizing grant was allocated using two criteria: the historical
criterion by which the grant was allocated on the basis of previous
expenditure and the criterion of objective parameters (introduced into Italian
law in 1981) by which the size of the grant was a function of objective
elements such as population, income per capita and so on. The ordinary
grant and the equalizing grants were destined to finance current
expenditure, but the first were distributed on the basis of historical
expenditure while the others adopted the second criterion.

The higher subsidies to councils in the south of Italy, coupled with the
questionable policy of paying for current debt has affected local government
spending behaviour in Italy and its accountability. Since only a marginal
part of total expenditure was financed at local level, it was possible to
increase expenditure without much dissent from local pressure groups.

The effect on the composition of local authorities' revenue of this
differential treatment for local authorities is quite dramatic as shown in
Table 7.1. On average, about 63 per cent of communal expenditure was
covered by grants in 1991, but while in the north the grant accounted for
only 54 per cent, in the south it covered about 75 per cent. Another
important revenue source is user charges and sale of services. In the north
they are about 7 per cent of total revenue, equally distributed betwen the two
sources; in the centre and in the south of Italy user charges represent only a
small fraction of total revenue.

The grant system was reformed in 1994, a year after the radical reform of
Italian local authorities, when ICI was introduced.[4] ICI is levied on owners

of domestic and non-domestic buildings, and development land, that is, it is a property tax. The tax base is the capital value, based on updated rateable values for buildings and the market value for development land. A number of exemptions are envisaged, and a reduction is applied to the owner's principal residence. ICI is levied at a rate between the *compulsory minimum* of 0.4 per cent and the ceiling of 0.65 per cent, which can be raised to 0.7 per cent under special circumstances. The 1993 yield corresponding to the minimum rate has been permanently deducted from the general central grant, after allowance for the revenue loss caused by the simultaneous abolition of INVIM (the tax on value increment of immovables). With the reform, local governments will have to rely increasingly on local resources.

Table 7.1   Local government revenue according to its source

	North	Centre	South	Average
Local taxation	24.93%	21.72%	17.12%	21.85%
of which:				
ICIAP	3.99%	3.65%	2.42%	3.46%
Refuse collection	8.14%	6.93%	6.81%	7.43%
Grants	56.31%	60.93%	74.45%	62.67%
Other sources	18.76%	17.35%	8.43%	15.48%
of which:				
User charges	3.10%	2.33%	1.12%	2.33%
Sale of services	3.84%	6.78%	2.54%	4.30%

Communes which previously received high subsidies can be expected to find it more difficult than others to adjust to the new situation once the reform is fully implemented, and they will be expected to raise about 55 per cent of their total expenditure from taxation and user charges. The shift from central to local money will mean that local administrators will have to be more accountable to their electorate than in the past, that is they will have to justify both levels of expenditure for different services and their increase. The next section explains some of these issues using a simple model of local government behaviour.

3. THEORETICAL FRAMEWORK

Any study of local variation in expenditure decisions requires a strong theoretical basis. To this end this section considers local authorities as rational social welfare maximizers; their behaviour reflects a trade-off between expenditure in local public goods and private consumption. If they behave according to a social welfare utility function which is separable into private and public goods consumption, the median voter objective function can be written as:

$$\text{MAX } w(\mathbf{x}, y) \tag{7.1}$$

where x is a vector of local expenditure per head in different services and y is a private composite commodity. If the central government was not distributing any grant, the local authority would raise all the money from local taxation; in Italy the main forms of finance will be represented by a property tax and a local business tax, therefore the budget constraint for local authority i can be written in terms of expenditure and fiscal capacity:

$$\sum_{i=1}^{n} q_i X_i + p_y Y = \bar{r}_P \text{ PTB} + \bar{r}_B \text{ BTB} \tag{7.2}$$

where X_i is the total amount spent in local public good i, Y is the total amount of the private good, PTB is the base for the property tax and BTB is the base for the business tax, q_i and p_y are prices. $\bar{r}_P$ and $\bar{r}_B$ are the maximum legal rate that can be applied to the property and the business base respectively. In the case of ICI, $\bar{r}_P$ is equal to 0.7 per cent while for the business tax a general ceiling is more difficult to define.[5] The distinction between property and business tax is necessary to derive the local budget constraint relevant to the median voter.[6] The process, described in Levaggi (1994), allows the budget constraint to be written as follows:

$$\sum_{i=1}^{n} q_i X_i + p_y Y = \bar{r}_P \text{ (MPTBT} - \text{(MPTB} - \text{APTB)} + \text{HPTB)} + \text{HBTC}$$

$$\text{HBTC} = \frac{\text{BTC}}{N} \qquad \text{APTD} = \frac{\text{PTBD}}{N} \qquad \text{HPTB} = \frac{\text{PTBB}}{N} \tag{7.3}$$

where x_i and y_i are amounts per head, N is the population of the local authority and MPTD is the tax base for the median voter, BTC is the revenue raised from the local business tax, PTBD and PTBB is the property tax paid by the domestic and the business sector respectively. It can be argued that the local decisionmakers are more interested in tax bills rather than tax rates. The budget constraint represented by equation (7.3) is now transformed in terms of maximum tax bill for the median voter; the tax bill is simply the tax base multiplied by the tax rate, hence:

$$\sum_{i=1}^{n} q_i X_i + p_y Y = \bar{t}_M \left(\frac{\text{APTD} + \text{HPTB}}{\text{APTD}} * \frac{\text{APTD}}{\text{MPTD}} \right) + \text{HBTC} \tag{7.4}$$

APTD/MPTD represents the contribution of the median voter with respect to the average voter. In the case of a poll tax with no rebates, for example, this term is equal to one, while in the case of a property tax it will vary according to the payment of the median voter relative to the contribution of the average voter.[7] Equation (7.4) shows that if local government decisionmakers use the tax bill paid by the median voter as one of their decision variables in setting expenditure, the property tax paid by the business sector, as well as the difference in contribution between the median and the average voter, is perceived as a matching grant.

Since central government finance in Italy is distributed as a lump sum, the budget constraint faced by a local authority is:

$$\sum_{i=1}^{n} q_i X_i + p_y = R$$

$$R = \bar{t}_M * d * h + HBTC \tag{7.5}$$

$$h = \frac{APTD}{MPTD} \qquad d = \frac{APTD + HPTB}{APTD}$$

where G is the lump-sum contribution from central government.

If a functional form for (7.1) is specified, a system of demand equation can be obtained maximizing the utility function subject to the relevant budget constraint. In this analysis a simple extension to the LES model has been used in which y is allowed to be non-separable from expenditure on local public services. The cost function is written as:

$$C(q,w,p_y) = a(q) + d(q)p_y + b(q)^{1-\theta_y} p_y^{\theta_y} w \tag{7.6}$$

$$a(q) = \sum_{i=1}^{n} q_i \alpha_i$$

$$b(q) = \prod_{i=1}^{n} q_i^{\beta_i} \qquad \sum_{i=1}^{n} \beta_i = 0$$

$$d(q) = d_y \prod_{i=1}^{n} q_i^{\delta_i} \qquad \sum_{i=1}^{n} \delta_i = 0$$

and the demand for public expenditure x_i can be written as:

$$q_i x_i = q_i \alpha_i + \delta_i d(q) p_y + (1 - \theta_y) \beta_i (R - a(q) - d(q)p_y)$$

$$p_y y = (1 - \theta_y) d(p) p_y + \theta_y (R - a(q) - d(q)p_y) \tag{7.7}$$

which is almost identical to the Linear Expenditure System apart from the 'non-separability terms' $\delta_i d(p)p_y$. α_i takes the form:

$$\alpha_i = \sum_{i=1}^{m} w_i vr_i \qquad\qquad i = 1,n \qquad\qquad (7.8)$$

where vr_i are needs indicators for each type of expenditure and w_i are the relative weights.

The strong evidence in favour of incremental budgeting behaviour presented in Levaggi (1994) resulted in adopting this model as a working hypothesis. The strong link between expenditure in previous years has been explained in the past using Wildavsky's theory of incremental budgeting and has been empirically tested by Elcock and Jordan. The theory of incremental budgeting is not completely satisfactory and recent studies have tried to explain links between expenditure in different years using other arguments. Borge et al. (1995), for example, explain incremental budgeting using a partial adjustment model with endogenous speed of adjustment. Once expenditure has reached an optimal level, it is quite difficult to move from it because of costs associated with changes and the pressure of interest groups. This approach is quite attractive, but it does not fully explain the observed tendency of expenditure to grow since it applies only to models in which taxation is not a choice variable.

A more appealing explanation is represented by the ratchet effect theory and a model based on this hypothesis is presented here. Although this model differs from those employed elsewhere, the essential ingredient of an incremental budgeting model is retained: a key determinant of the level of spending in any given fiscal year is the level of spending in the preceding fiscal year. The missing link between utility maximization and incremental budgeting is given by a variant of the ratchet effect theory. As its name suggests, in this model public expenditure reacts to expansionary policies by growing rapidly, but it does not respond to the same degree to policies aimed at cutting expenditure. In terms of the framework we have developed so far, the ratchet effect theory can be introduced by making further hypotheses on the determination of i through time.[8] At time 0, α_i is determined according to equation (7.8). In period 1, after the level of expenditure x_0 has been determined, the basic need indicator is updated as follows:

$$\alpha_{1,i} = \sum_{i=1}^{m} w_i vr_i + \phi(x_{i,0} - a_{i,0}) \qquad\qquad i = 1,n \qquad\qquad (7.9)$$

where ϕ is the grade by which the residents perceive past level of expenditure as needs. For a value of ϕ equal to one we have $\alpha_i = x_{i,0}$ It should be noted that, although local government's utility depends on the previous year's expenditure level, utility levels themselves are not related over time. An incremental model of the type described above is quite reasonable in the context of our estimation. In the first few years of application of the tax reform, communal councils will have to use past levels of expenditure as a benchmark and there will be strong pressure from interest groups and lobbies not to reduce the existing levels of expenditure for different services.

This is the basic framework in which local government expenditure behaviour will be analyzed. The theoretical model now needs to be translated into the budget constraint faced by local authorities in Italy and in the estimation of the parameters of the utility function.

4. ESTIMATION

Regional variations in local expenditure patterns have been analysed by studying current expenditure decisions for 93 district councils (*capoluoghi di provincia*) in Italy in 1991.[9] In that year the main sources of finance at local level were represented by local taxation (ICIAP, INVIM, refuse collection), user charges, the revenue from the sales of some specific services and block grant from central government.

In that year, local government fiscal autonomy was still marginal since only ICIAP and the tax on refuse collection were subject to discretionary application. Although local councils could set different levels of taxation for ICIAP, in this model – centred on the point of view of the median voter – this tax is a lump sum.

The revenue from the sale of services is represented by the user charges applied to most of the services offered by the council; the revenue from each service is used to define the implicit price for the expenditure to which it is referred, that is:

$$q_i = 1 - \frac{\text{revenue service } i}{\text{expenditure service } i} \qquad (7.10)$$

The revenue from refuse collection has not been considered as a user charge. The nature of the service offered, which covers domestic and industrial waste collection and road cleaning suggested that the revenue from this service should be considered – as in fact it is officially called – a local tax.

The budget constraint for local authorities in 1991 can then be written as:

$$\sum_{i=1}^{n} q_i X_i = R_{PR} + G + \text{HBTC} \qquad (7.11)$$

where R_{PR} is the revenue from other minor taxes.

The most important difference between equation (7.5) and equation (7.11) is represented by the exclusion of y from the budget constraint and by considering the budget constraint for the average rather than the median voter. The limited autonomy for what concerns domestic taxation means that local governments' budget constraint can be defined only in terms of current expenditure. This problem has important consequences for the simulation exercise we want to conduct in the next section and the only way to resolve it is to estimate a model in which expenditure on y is constrained to be zero.

The neoclassical theory of utility maximization subject to specific quantity restrictions can be used to derive the set of equations to be estimated, and in this chapter the approach developed by Blundell (1988) has been followed to obtain the rationed demand equation for good x_i and y

$$q_i x_i = q_i \alpha_i + \left[\beta_i + \frac{\theta_y / (1-\theta_y) \delta_i \, d(q) p_y}{y^* - d(p)} \right] (R - a(q) - d(q) p_y)$$

$$p_y y = p_y y^*$$

(7.12)

which is the familiar form proposed by Blundell (1988). These conditional or rationed demand equations highlight the way in which rationing on one good may influence the consumption decisions. First, there is the direct income effect $p_y y^*$ which is subtracted from total expenditure. Second, there is the effect on the marginal propensity to consume which alters β_i to the extent to which δ_i differs from zero. If $\delta_i = 0$, then separability would prevail and only the income effect would remain.

In the model being estimated here, y is constrained to be zero; this value can be obtained in the unrestricted version of the model if δ_y is zero and θ is one. If this is the case the demand equation represented by (7.6) becomes:

$$q_i x_i = q_i \alpha_i + \beta_i \, (R - a(q))$$

$$p_y y = 0$$

(7.13)

that is it collapses into an LES demand system. The rationed demand equation will be written as:

$$q_i x_i = q_i \alpha_i + \left[\beta_i + \frac{\theta_y}{(1 - \theta_y)} \delta_i \right] (R - a(q))$$

$$p_y y = 0$$

(7.14)

which implies that it is impossible to estimate δ_y.

As is usually the case in demand analysis, all equations in either the unrationed or rationed system contain the same explanatory variables. In addition, since both systems satisfy the usual adding up restrictions, we can delete one of the equations from the system without any loss of information.

Having presented the more technical details about the estimation procedure, let us now turn to the more important problem of determining the level of disaggregation to which the econometric model presented above will be applied.

Local services provided by communes in Italy are divided into three main categories:

- thirty 'institutional services' which are mainly represented by local public goods or mixed goods;
- twenty 'individual demand services' which are mainly merit goods;
- five 'productive services', a series of private goods which are produced by the local authorities.[10]

Productive services should represent a source of extra income for the communes which make them available. These services should be run on a profitable basis, and for this reason they are not explicitly considered in the model; we have simply included the difference between revenue and costs as a lump sum in equation (7.11).

The aggregation of the other services is quite important and needs to be studied carefully. As a first approximation, services have been divided into five categories corresponding to the main areas of local government activity, namely:

1. general administration;
2. local police;
3. education and culture;
4. housing;
5. social services;
6. street maintenance and street lighting;
7. economic development.

However, the fifth category is too heterogeneous and does not allow for the influence of interest groups on local government decisionmaking to be tested. For this reason, this category has to be divided into three groups:

5a. social care;
5b. refuse collection;
5c. other social services.

Closer inspection of the budget data shows that this classification is not satisfactory because of the abnormal behaviour of housing expenditure. In theory, this type of expenditure should represent the cost to provide shelter to low-income families. Local authorities in Italy can either provide this service through payment for private rented accommodation or by renting council houses. The two options clearly have quite different expenditure implications. In theory the use of the matching grant should solve some of the problems since this method allows only the part of expenditure which is not covered by user charges to be modelled; however, the direct operation of council houses causes other problems related to the mixture between current receipts and the income derived from the sale of council houses. For this reason, housing has been modelled as if it was a productive service.[11]

It is important to note that expenditure per capita is not uniformly distributed across Italy. Communes in the north spend an average of L. 1,322,000; this amount is reduced to L. 1,264,300 in the centre and to L. 1,113,900 in the south of Italy. Differences in expenditure could be partially explained by the different size of districts councils which are on average larger in the north than in the other two regions. However, the most plausible explanation is related to the number of services they provide and the analysis of expenditure shares shed more light on the possible causes for this difference.

Table 7.2   Shares of expenditure in the different services

Eqn n°.	1	2	3	5a	5b	5c	6	7
North	0.2637	0.0596	0.2332	0.1485	0.0944	0.0680	0.1063	0.0277
Centre	0.2800	0.0745	0.2013	0.0975	0.0898	0.0728	0.1544	0.0310
South	0.3483	0.0781	0.1449	0.1048	0.1368	0.0590	0.1123	0.0230

Table 7.2 shows that, while for services such as local police there is not much geographical variation in the share of total expenditure, for other services such as education the share of total expenditure in the north is twice as high as the corresponding amount in the south. This reflects the fact that in the south most schools are run by the state instead of local councils.

Finally, it is interesting to note the higher share for general services and refuse collection in the south. Both categories of service are labour-intensive and their relative weight could be explained by the practice of overstaffing local government in order to decrease unemployment in these depressed areas.

Equation (7.13) corresponding to the unconstrained model and equation (7.14), the corresponding constrained equation have been estimated using SHAZAM and the results are presented in Tables 7.3 to 7.5.

The models fit the data quite well as shown by the summary statistics presented in Tables 7.2 to 7.5. It should be noted that the Durbin–Watson statistic has a rather different interpretation in cross-section studies. The absence of serial correlation is to be interpreted as evidence that the model does not consistently over- or underestimate local authorities with relative high/low expenditure per head. Equations 7.6 and 7.7 present the lowest R^2, especially in the regression for the north and the centre.

The hypothesis of a nested utility function cannot be rejected for any model since θ is always significantly different from zero. In the north and the centre, the constraint on income plays a neutral effect on expenditure shares since all the δ_i are not significantly different from zero. In both cases, the model suggests that a binding budget constraint exists at the top level and that expenditure at the lower level is set according to consolidated rules within this constraint. This result confirms the findings by Borge et al. (1995) for Norway despite the use of a different approach. It is a quite different story for the councils in the south of Italy for which five out of eight coefficients for δ_i are significantly different from zero. The coefficients of the regression presented in Tables 7.3 to 7.5 can now be compared with the expenditure shares presented in Table 7.2 in order to get a picture of expenditure behaviour. For the north and centre, δ_i are not significantly different from zero, hence the comparison can be done using the coefficients for β in the constrained model. β represents the share of residual income which is allocated to each type of expenditure after the basic needs have been satisfied. If this coefficient is similar to the share, we can conclude that the incremental model is quite stable and that expenditure is probably allocated on the basis of a well-established top-down procedure. At the highest level, the increase in expenditure is decided on the basis of income available through grants-in-aid and taxation; the same increase is then applied to all the categories of expenditure. A large difference between β and the share can be interpreted in terms of an evolutionary process within the local authority. This could be because of the change in the composition of the political pressure group on the presence of strong competing lobbies pressuring for increases in expenditure. In this case, in fact, the presence of a binding budget constraint at the top level means that residual income is allocated on the basis of a bargaining process among the different parties. The introduction of local taxes could be an important factor in altering this equilibrium; the local taxpayers may want only certain types of expenditure in return for their payment and this might drastically alter the share of expenditure on different services. Although the coefficients of the regression presented in Table 7.3 and 7.4 are quite different, a comparative analysis also using Table 7.2 leads to the conclusion that the behaviour for marginal expenditure in the north and the centre is nowadays quite similar. The only difference is represented by education, whose share of total expenditure is decreasing in the north and increasing in the centre. This might be the result of different factors and one of the most important could be the different birth rate in the two areas.

The regression for the south presents some quite interesting features which are worth noting. The hypothesis of separability between private goods and public services cannot be rejected for most equations since δ_i is significantly different from zero. In standard microeconomic theory the difference between the parameters of the constrained and the unconstrained model can be interpreted as evidence of a binding constraint. In this model, because of the peculiar value of the constraint, the result can also be interpreted in terms of contrafactual models: one in which local contribution is almost negligible and the other in which issues such as local accountability play an important role.

Table 7.3   Estimation of local government behaviour in the north

	Unrestricted model	Restricted model		Goodness of fit	
Eqn. n°.	β_i	β_i	δ_i	DW	R^2
1	0.288	0.304	0.048	1.8454	0.913
	(9.458)	(2.219)	(0.135)		
2	0.050	0.047	−0.009	1.4199	0.886
	(7.752)	(1.630)	(0.114)		
3	0.142	0.141	−0.002	1.3663	0.944
	(6.359)	(1.423)	(0.009)		
5a	0.136	0.112	−0.073	2.3164	0.978
	(11.52)	(2.226)	(0.580)		
5b	0.087	0.088	0.001	1.5793	0.927
	(5.811)	(1.310)	(0.007)		
5c	0.072	0.092	0.061	1.9481	0.976
	(5.539)	(1.747)	(0.483)		
6	0.151	0.140	−0.036	1.6718	0.717
	(5.003)	(1.068)	(0.104)		
7	0.070	0.072	0.006	1.698	0.787
n = 41	= 0.2418 (1.7771)				

Note: The values in parentheses represent student's t statistics

Table 7.4   Estimation of local government behaviour in the centre

	Unrestricted model	Restricted model		Goodness of fit	
Eqn. n°.	β_i	β_i	δ_i	DW	R^2
1	0.337	0.339	0.006	1.860	0.918
	(4.465)	(2.690)	(0.119)		
2	0.054	0.057	0.001	1.336	0.874
	(4.334)	(2.353)	(0.020)		
3	0.160	0.155	−0.018	1.697	0.960
	(5.691)	(2.467)	(0.030)		
5a	0.112	0.117	0.013	2.219	0.908
	(2.865)	(2.281)	(0.016)		
5b	0.075	0.087	0.037	2.105	0.975
	(4.944)	(3.359)	(0.006)		
5c	0.082	0.085	0.007	1.933	0.944
	(2.235)	(2.153)	(0.037)		
6	0.108	0.121	0.042	2.122	0.795
	(2.952)	(2.286)	(0.168)		
7	0.072	0.038	−0.099	1.085	0.842
n = 26	= 0.2495 (2.1489)				

Note: The values in parentheses represent student's *t* statistics.

Bearing this in mind, it is interesting to compare both β for the constrained and the unconstrained model with the shares presented in Table 7.2. The behaviour of β in the constrained model shows that local authorities would increase the supply of labour-intensive services such as general services and refuse collection while there does not seem to be much return for the payment of taxation. The typical services for which businesses – the only taxpayers in our model – could have a return are transport and economic services. This is the result of the very small incidence of local government taxation on its total revenue; however, the model shows that local authorities in the south might face big problems in relation to local accountability and we might expect a big change in their expenditure behaviour after the introduction of ICI. As far as the other services are concerned, income seems to play a strong substitution role with expenditure

Applying Theory to the Real World

and it would seem that local government would choose to reduce some of the most important social services.

Finally, the magnitude of θ could be interpreted as a forecasting parameter in determining which councils should choose the highest rate of taxation. In this case, we should expect the northern districts to apply the lowest rate and the southern ones to apply the highest.

However, this prediction might be undermined by the problem of non-uniform rules to evaluate rateable value across Italy. In the next section the simulations and the problems arising from this exercise will be treated in greater detail.

Table 7.5   Estimation of local government behaviour in the south

Unrestricted model		Restricted model		Goodness of fit	
Eqn. n°.	β_i	β_i	δ_i	DW	R^2
1	0.488	0.518	0.171	1.885	0.932
	(8.096)	(4.694)	(0.450)		
2	0.069	0.034	–0.192	2.48	0.886
	(3.796)	(0.013)	(3.825)		
3	0.112	0.058	–0.299	2.552	0.886
	(2.956)	(0.753)	(2.608)		
5a	0.092	0.046	–0.256	1.941	0.949
	(4.229)	(0.091)	(3.368)		
5b	0.109	0.059	–0.276	2.611	0.921
	(4.1)	(1.141)	(3.009)		
5c	0.069	0.035	–0.191	1.879	0.874
	(2.161)	(0.342)	(2.155)		
6	0.057	0.151	0.517	2.192	0.958
	(2.021)	(6.053)	(2.314)		
7	0.000	0.095	0.527		
n = 26	= 0.1527 (5.5106)				

Note: The values in parentheses represent student's *t* statistics

5. SIMULATIONS

The estimates of the model presented in Section 2 can now be used to simulate the effect on expenditure of the introduction of a tax on the domestic sector, namely ICI. ICI is, as we have shown in Section 2, a property tax. The communes can set its level between 0.4 per cent and 0.7 per cent. In my model, using the data for the rates and the revenue produced in 1993 for the year 1994 I have simulated the likely effects on expenditure were this tax in force in 1991. It is necessary to first calculate the total fiscal capacity of the communes. To do so we can observe that the tax base can be obtained using rate and revenue as follows:

$$\text{Tax Base} = \frac{\text{Revenue}}{\text{Tax Rate}} \qquad (7.15)$$

After the introduction of ICI the grant-in-aid from central government has been reduced by the minimum revenue that must be raised using ICI.[12] The difference between the maximum amount that can be raised by ICI and the minimum can then be added to total income.

The simulation exercise presents a technical limitation; the particular level at which we had to restrict y makes it impossible to obtain an estimate for δ_y. This is quite an important problem since δ_y determines which part of the extra resources is used to provide local services and which part is allocated to private goods.

For this reason Tables 7.6 and 7.7 show some simulations using different values for δ_y. The prediction about θ is exact, in that local authorities in the south which had the lowest value have in fact chosen the highest rate. However, the south, in spite of having the highest ICI on average would have increased its expenditure by the lowest amount. This result depends on the way in which per capita rateable value is distributed. Rateable values in the south are quite low; Palermo with a population of about 700,000 has a rateable value very similar to Padua with 215,000 inhabitants.

The change in total expenditure will have different effects on the composition of expenditure according to the sign and importance of the estimated δ_i. Table 7.7 presents the changes in expenditure per head for each category. The simulations reported in Table 7.7 are obtained using the coefficients of the constrained model, even where δs were not significant. This allows comparison of the results for the first two models with the results obtained for the south; use of the parameters from the constrained model might produce a bias in the parameters, but since δ was very small the errors we might make are going to be almost irrelevant.

Table 7.6   Simulation of likely effects of the introduction of ICI on total expenditure of district councils

North			
Initial expenditure	1,322,700		ICI
$\delta_v = 0$	10.16%		0.00590
ICI raised in 1994		$\delta_v = 6096.19935$	0.00503
ICI 0.4%		$\delta_v = 133127.95034$	
Centre			
Initial expenditure	1,264,300		
$\delta_v = 0$	10.55%		0.00585
ICI raised in 1994	8.41%	$\delta_v = 30456.27818$	0.00544
ICI 0.4%		$\delta_v = 150460.04542$	
South			
Initial expenditure	1,113,900		
$\delta_v = 0$	7.02%		0.00611
ICI raised in 1994	3.80%	$\delta_v = 19080.30589$	0.00524
ICI 0.4%		$\delta_v = 41627.63741$	

Table 7.7 supports the conclusions of the analysis presented in the previous paragraph. For the centre and south the equilibrium in expenditure that has been reached suggests that the introduction of ICI will not produce large changes in local government behaviour. The situation is rather different in the south; increased local accountability might well mean that taxpayers are going to ask for an increase in the supply of the services they use most and we can expect a substantial change in the composition of their expenditure.

6. CONCLUSIONS

This chapter has presented the estimates of the behaviour of council expenditure in Italy in 1991. In that year, communes had limited freedom in setting their tax–expenditure ratio being free to set the level of ICIAP, a business tax. The aim of the work was to study regional expenditure variations at district level and to simulate the impact of ICI, the major source of revenue for local authorities in the foreseeable future, on local

Table 7.7 Composition of expenditure in simulation

North

Bench	0.348*	0.078	0.308	0.196	0.124	0.09	0.14	0.036
% increases in simulation								
$\delta_y = 0$	11.96%	10.50%	5.21%	4.77%	5.61%	17.01%	12.12%	46.37%
ici 1994	6.60%	6.84%	2.40%	1.24%	1.26%	10.68%	5.99%	34.15%
ici 0.4%	0.25%	2.42%	-0.93%	-2.92%	-3.88%	3.19%	-1.26%	19.68%

Centre

Bench	0.354	0.093	0.254	0.123	0.114	0.09	0.195	0.039
% increases in simulation								
$\delta_y = 0$	7.81%	5.16%	11.90%	11.50%	10.03	-1.87%	0.1729	27.36%
ici 1994	5.23%	3.51%	10.30%	8.39%	7.96%	-4.35%	15.62%	24.70%
ici=0.4%	-4.96%	-2.99%	3.82%	-1.16%	-0.18%	-14.13%	9.02%	14.22%

South

Bench	0.387*	0.087	0.161	0.117	0.152	0.065	0.125	0.025
% increases in simulation								
$\delta_y = 0$	7.40%	-3.65%	-0.73%	0.71%	4.77%	5.91%	13.73%	63.18%
ici 1994	2.60%	-5.08%	-2.03%	-0.71%	3.38%	3.98%	9.40%	49.87%
ici=0.4%	-3.06%	-6.77%	-3.58%	-2.32%	1.73%	1.70%	4.28%	34.14%

* in million of liras

131

spending patterns. Councils are assumed to set their expenditure according to the maximization of the utility function for the median voter. The limited autonomy enjoyed by councils and its novel reinstatement has created some important problems in the estimation process and did not allow for the full use of the model. In order to simulate the introduction of ICI, a domestic tax for which councils will have the choice of setting its level, a model in which private consumption was a decision variable needed to be estimated. In 1991 such a choice was not possible since local authorities did not have any fiscal autonomy. This problem has been partially solved by estimating a consumption demand set in which it is assumed that one of the commodities is quantity restricted. After 20 years with virtually no fiscal autonomy, local councils did not seem to have a clear idea of the level of service that needed to be provided; for this reason a utility-based incremental model has given quite satisfactory results in terms of goodness of fit. The utility-based incremental model presented here shows that a well-established incremental procedure determines expenditure levels and its share in the councils in the north and in the centre. For the south, this procedure has been undermined by the grant system that has been applied in the past. Local taxation in this region is almost negligible and this has created a vacuum in local accountability.

The simulation exercise performed shows that local councils will probably increase their expenditure if the tax base is increased. The rate of taxation will be increased most in the south, even though in this region expenditure would increase less than elsewhere. This result depends on a non-uniform evaluation of the rateable value across Italy. Finally, the simulation exercise shows that we might expect important shifts in expenditure within the local authority and that the councils in the south of Italy might have to face drastic policy changes in the face of the reinstated local accountability.

NOTES

1. See, for example, Galmarini (1987).
2. In certain respects ICIAP may be compared to the French *taxe professionnelle*, but its scale is considerably more modest (about ten times smaller).
3. Following a ruling of the Supreme Court on the supposed 'non-constitutional' character of the first version.
4. ICI had been anticipated in 1992 by the experimental National Tax on Immovables (ISI).
5. In practice the decision of how much Y to consume will be represented by a choice of r_P and r_B below the maximum legal ceiling. The definition of the budget constraint in terms of private and public goods rather than in terms of expenditure and taxation allows a more general approach and to avoid the problems that arise the definition of the utility function in terms of one good (the expenditure on local public goods and one bad (local taxation). See Barnett et al. (1992) for more details on this specific point.

6. An important distinction must be drawn here between the budget constraint for the median voter and the local budget that is relevant to the median voter. In the first case we would include all the sources of income for the median voter while in this case we only consider the local decisions that affect his on her budget.
7. In the extreme case in which the median voter is not a home-owner, it would be equal zero.
8. The model is explained at length in Levaggi (1994).
9. The complete set of districts in Italy in 1991 was of 95 councils. Our sample comprises 93 of them since data for Agrigento and Catania was not available.
10. A complete list of the services is reported in Appendix 1.
11. That is we have deleted housing from the list of expenditures while the difference between receipts and expenses from this service has been added to the profits derived from productive services.
12. That is 0.4 per cent multiplied by the tax base.

REFERENCES

Barnett, R.R., R. Levaggi and P.C. Smith (1992), 'Local authorities expenditure decisions: A maximum likelihood analysis of budget setting in the face of piecewise linear budget constraints', *Oxford Economics Papers*, **44** (1), 21–43

Blundell, R. (1988), 'Consumer behaviour: theory and empirical evidence - a survey', *Economic Journal*, **98**, 16–65

Borge, L.E., J. Rattsø and R. Sorensen (1995), 'Local government service production: the politics of allocative slugginess', *Public Choice,* **82** (1), 135–58

Elcock, H. and J. Jordan (1987), *Learning From Local Authority Budgeting* , Aldershot: Avebury

Galmarini, U. (1987), 'Il riequilibrio delle dotazioni finanziarie dei comuni: i risultati di otto anni di legislazione', *Economia Pubblica*, **17**, 234–43

Levaggi, R. (1991), 'An incremental flypaper model for english local government expenditure decisions', *Economia Internazionale*, **3** , 230–45.

Levaggi, R. (1994), 'Analyzing Italian local authorities expenditure behaviour: a tentative explantion', *Working Paper 3/94*, Genova: Istituto di Finanza

Wildawsky, A. (1975), *Budgeting - A Comparative Theory of Budgetary Processes*, Boston: Little Brown

APPENDIX 7A

List of Services Provided :

N.1
Secretariat
Information service (computing)
Technical support services
Birth and death register
Statistical services
Tax revenue Services

N.2
Local jail
Local judge
Local police

N.3
Infant schools run by the council
Infant schools run by the state
Primary schools
Secondary schools
Further education
School buses
School meals
Summer schools
Libraries
Theatres and museums
Art galleries

N.5a
Housing
Summer camps, spas, etc.
Nursing and sheltered homes
Nurseries
Canteens

N.5b
Sewage
Drains and depuration
Refuse collection

N.5c
Cemeteries and autopsy service
Funeral services
Parks and gardens
Zoos, botanical gardens
Sport facilities
Public baths and public toilets

N.6
Roads maint. (within the city centre)
Roads maint. (outside the city centre)
Street lighting

N.7
Bill posting and advertising
Hostels, holiday houses, camping sites
Slaughter houses
Markets and exhibitions, fairs
Parking
Sea huts
Ports
Transport of meat by lorries (refrigerated)
Auditoria, congress facilities

The Five Productive Services Are:
Water
Gas
Pharmacies
Electricity
Milk

8. The Short-Period Macroeconomic Incidence and Effects of State and Local Taxes

Anthony J. Laramie* and Douglas Mair

1. INTRODUCTION

Typically, in discussions of fiscal policy, the role of the federal government is emphasized and that of states and local governments is ignored. This tendency is not surprising. The fiscal policies of any one state or locality are likely to have only a marginal impact on the performance of the economy. However, to conclude that the fiscal policies of states and localities have no significant impact on the national economy is erroneous for a number of reasons. First, state and local government receipts and expenditures represent a significant share of *GDP* and, thus, affecting aggregate spending and economic growth. Second, the provision of government goods and services is performed primarily at the state and local level, and is likely to have both aggregate demand and aggregate supply effects (see the *Economic Report of The President*, February 1994). Third, the rise of 'new fiscal federalism' in the 1980s, the federal government budget impasse ('gridlock' and increased demand for government services have forced states and localities to expand their tax base and the scope of their activities. Finally, given the existence of national trends in state and local fiscal policies, these factors, in concert, have come to bear on the aggregate performance of the economy.

In this chapter, we present a Kaleckian macroeconomic theory of tax incidence. Kaleckian macroeconomic tax incidence can be distinguished from the neoclassical general equilibrium approach to tax incidence on two points: (1) in contrast to the neoclassical approach, macroeconomic foundations are present in the incidence of various taxes; and (2) neoclassical notions of market clearing and full employment are replaced with Kaleckian

* Laramie gratefully acknowledges the support of the Jerome Levy Economics Institute of Bard College, Triveni Kuchi for valuable library services and Xenda Laramie for editorial assistance.

institutional pricing and underemployment. Also, we stress that the incidence of state and local taxes on personal income, corporate profits, sales and property depends on institutional factors embodied in the federalist system of the US which causes the incidence of these taxes to be different from the incidence of similar taxes levied at the federal level.

In order to examine the incidence and effects of state and local taxation in the US, we present briefly the orthodox and Kaleckian views on the incidence and effects of taxation; we describe the incidence implications of the composition of state and local government budgets and the budget stance in the US during the 1980s and 1990s; and we consider the impact of federal grants-in-aid on the incidence of state and local taxes. Some empirical evidence is provided; and we explore some macroeconomic policy issues.

In the conclusion, we argue that, given state and local government debt and deficit limitations, state and local taxes have little or no impact on the level of post-tax corporate profits. Increasing other taxes, such as personal income taxes and indirect business taxes, has no impact on corporate profits either, but these taxes reduce household incomes. Since interstate rivalry limits expansion of state taxation of corporate profits, we argue that intergovernmental relations should expand. The federal government should increase the corporate profits tax and use the additional revenues to fund federal grants-in-aid.

2. THE ORTHODOX VIEWS ON THE INCIDENCE/EFFECTS OF STATE AND LOCAL TAXATION

The orthodox views on tax incidence are reflected in the neoclassical theories of income distribution (see Kotlikoff and Summers 1987). Whether taxes are levied on commodities, incomes or wealth (property), they ultimately affect the demand for and supply of factors and factor returns. A comparison of factor incomes before and after the imposition of a tax is used to determine the incidence of the tax. Within this family of models, the economic incidence of taxes may be less than, equal to or greater than the legal incidence, and this incidence is independent of who pays the tax, whether producer or consumer, or of which level of government the tax is paid to, whether federal, state or local.

The neoclassical models of tax incidence range from standard partial equilibrium to general equilibrium to dynamic and are all supported by a core set of assumptions; that is, market clearing and the marginal product theory of income distribution. Moreover, when considering the effects of taxation in a general equilibrium framework, factors of production are assumed to be in fixed supply and highly mobile and aggregate demand effects of tax changes are assumed to be nullified (Mieszkowski 1972). This dependence on the marginal productivity theory of income distribution means that neoclassical theory can consider only situations of continuous full employment and is, therefore, inappropriate to the study of the macroeconomic effects of taxation. In this chapter, we utilize Kalecki's degree of monopoly theory of income distribution. This theory is expressed in the relationship:

$$\omega = 1 \, / \, [1 + (k-1) \, (j+1)];$$

where ω is a manual labour's share of value added, k is the ratio of aggregate proceeds to aggregate prime costs (i.e. the markup) and j is the ratio of expenditures on raw materials to expenditures on manual labour. Changes in the degree of monopoly factors affect k and thus lead to changes in w. Reynolds (1984) has produced evidence in support of Kalecki's theory and this has been further confirmed in more recent work by Laramie, Mair, Miller and Reynolds (1994).

Following Kalecki (1971/1937), Asimakopulos and Burbidge (1974) and Laramie (1991), we drop the assumptions of perfect competition, market clearing and fixed factor supplies; we allow for aggregate demand effects by assuming a non-homogeneous marginal propensity to consume; we replace the marginal product theory of income distribution with Kalecki's degree of monopoly theory of income distribution; and we recognize that the long run is made up of and dependent upon what has happened in many short periods. As a consequence, many of the standard neoclassical conclusions are reversed. To consider these issues, we now present the Kaleckian theory of tax incidence in detail.

3. THE KALECKIAN THEORY OF TAX INCIDENCE

Kriesler (1989) argues that micro and macroeconomic foundations stand side by side in Kalecki's analysis of capitalist economies. These foundations are present in the analysis of tax incidence. At the macro level, aggregate spending flows determine the level of profits. At the micro level, the degree of monopoly determines the distribution of income. Tax policies can affect the aggregate flow of spending and profits, but pricing decisions, as reflected in business markups, determine the intra/interindustry and class distributions of income. Ultimately, the confluence of these factors, as we illustrate below, determines the short-period incidence of taxes, and this incidence, in so far as it impacts on business investment, generates a long-period effect. To consider this issue further, we develop a Kaleckian theory of tax incidence. We stress, in particular, the effects of taxation on the aggregate level of profits. We begin with a review of Kalecki's contribution.

3.1. Kalecki's Contribution

Kalecki (1971/1937) recognized that an important implication of the publication of Keynes's *General Theory* was that the theory of the incidence of taxation had to be rethought. In his 1971/1937 chapter he analysed the effects of commodity, income and capital taxes on employment and the determination and distribution of national income with capital equipment and money wages given. Kalecki's simplifying assumptions were: (1) a closed economic system with a surplus of all types of labour and equipment; (2) workers spend all they receive as wages or transfer payments; and (3) a balanced state budget with all state expenditure financed by taxation.

Kalecki begins by considering short-period equilibrium in an economy without taxation and state expenditure. He defines gross profit as the difference between the value of sales and prime costs. National income is the sum of gross profits and the wage bill. It can also be defined as the sum of total consumption (C) and investment (I). Since, by assumption, workers consume all they earn, total gross profit (P) must be equal to capitalists' consumption (Cc) plus investment (I). Thus:

$$P = Cc + I. \qquad (8.1)$$

If ($Cc + I$) changes, a shift of marginal revenue curves would take place and employment would be 'pushed' to the point at which P would be equal to the changed ($Cc + I$). On the assumption that workers do not save, total gross profit (P) is determined by the rate of investment (I)–which is equal to capitalists' savings–and by capitalists' propensity to consume.

Kalecki then makes two assumptions about the determinants of gross profits: (1) the rate of investment (I) does not change immediately in response to some exogenous change as it is the result of previous investment decisions which require a certain finite length of time for completion; and (2) capitalists' propensity to consume is insensitive to expectations of changes in income. From these assumptions, it follows that $P = Cc + I$ will only respond to exogenous changes with a certain, not very short, time lag.

Kalecki goes on to introduce state expenditure (G) into the system which pays for the salaries of officials or is disbursed as doles to the unemployed, disabled, etc. He considers the funding of G, first, from a constant rate *ad valorem* tax, *Tw*, on all kinds of wage goods. This tax constitutes a new type of prime cost.

National income now equals gross profits (P) plus wages (W) plus wage goods tax (Tw). Also, national income equals consumption (C) plus investment (I). Workers' wages (W) equal workers' consumption (Cw). Total taxes (Tw) equal state expenditure (G); is, officials' salaries plus doles which are spent on the consumption of wage goods (Cw). Thus, gross profits (P) are again capitalists' consumption plus investment. Thus, equation (8.1) also holds good for an economy with commodity taxation. There is no change in the level of national income as there is no stimulus to capitalists' consumption or to investment. There has simply been a change in the distribution of income as a consequence of a shift in purchasing power from workers and officials to those on the dole. The effect on national income of the taxation of capitalists' consumption of wage goods Kalecki assumes to be negligible, because of the small percentage of their income which is devoted to the consumption of wage goods.

Kalecki next introduces a tax on capitalists' income (Ti) levied at a constant percentage. This is not a prime cost but part of gross profits. Entrepreneurs continue to maximize the difference between sales and prime costs. Gross profit (P) is now equal to capitalists' consumption (Cc), investment (I) and income tax revenue (Ti). Thus:

$$P = (Cc + I) + Ti \tag{8.2}$$

and the part of P received by capitalists is ($Cc + I$).

Kalecki proceeds to consider what will happen if the income tax is raised, say, from 15 per cent to 25 per cent. Given his assumptions, nothing will happen to investment and capitalists' consumption in the immediate post-tax increase period. The immediate effect is a rise in gross profits because of the rise in Ti. Employment will be pushed to the point at which P increases by the amount of ΔTi. However, ΔTi must raise the rate of interest, r, otherwise the net reward for lending will fall. The rise in r will not diminish the willingness of lenders to lend but will exert downward pressure on capitalists' willingness to invest. However, this may not be the final result because in the first period of the new income tax regime, P increases by just the amount Δti. If capitalists expect future returns to increase by the same amount as present returns, this will be just enough to counter the depressive effect of ΔTi on the inducement to invest. If that is so, then ($Cc + I$) remains unchanged: $P = (Cc + I) + Ti$ (where $\Delta Ti > 0$) will rise as, too, will employment. The principal result from the introduction of income taxation will be a rise in Cw from the unemployed. This will raise both the output and price of consumption goods and reduce the real consumption of already employed workers which will be offset by ΔCw of newly employed workers.

Finally, Kalecki introduces capital taxation (Tc) levied initially at a uniform rate of, say, 2 per cent on all forms of owned capital. Again, capital taxation does not constitute a prime cost and gross profits can be written as:

$$P = (Cc + I) + Ti + Tc \tag{8.3}$$

The immediate effect of raising Tc is to leave I and Cc unchanged but employment rises as a response to the increase in P of the amount DTc. In this case, however, Tc does not reduce the net profitability of investment nor does it raise r. Unlike the income tax (Ti), Tc is not a cost of production in the long run and, therefore, does not affect the net profitability of investment. Whether or not a lender lends does not affect the amount of capital tax (Tc) he pays. Thus, the inducement to invest is not weakened by ΔTc if the expected returns were the same as before. As shown above, gross profits have increased by ΔTc which improves expectations of future returns and strengthens the inducement to invest. Investment (I) increases and this causes a further rise in P and in employment. Tc not only increases P by the amount of ΔTc but capitalists' after-tax income $(Cc + I)$ also increases significantly. The increase in $(Cc + I)$ via the real wage bill is higher than in the case of Ti because of the stronger rise in employment induced by Tc.

From this analysis, Kalecki concluded that capital taxation is the best way to stimulate business and reduce unemployment as it has all the merits of financing state expenditure by borrowing but is distinguished from borrowing by the advantage of the state not becoming indebted. Kalecki doubted whether any government would have the political will to introduce it on any significant scale.

3.2. Recent Improvements to Kalecki's Theory of Tax Incidence

In its original formulation as outlined above, Kalecki's theory suffers from certain limitations. First, Kalecki, and his subsequent extension by Asimakopulos and Burbidge (1974), are short-period equilibrium models in which it is implicitly assumed that prices are set in some unspecified way by price leaders and that the aggregate supply curve is perfectly elastic. Damania and Mair (1992) have rectified this deficiency of the Kaleckian short-period model by means of supergame analysis of non-competitive behaviour. By introducing informational uncertainty and a trigger-pricing strategy to punish deviant behaviour, Damania and Mair demonstrate how Kalecki's short-period model can be made dynamic in a way entirely consistent with Kalecki's expectations of the timing of price wars over the business cycle.

Next, Laramie and Mair (1994) have developed a dynamic Kaleckian model of tax incidence by integrating Kalecki's theory of tax incidence with his theory of the business cycle. This model demonstrates that by affecting the rate of depreciation of capital equipment and by altering the distribution of income between wages and profits, changes in the structure of taxation impact on both the amplitude of the business cycle and the trend rate of growth of the economy. Finally, the way in which taxation is integrated into Kalecki's theory of income distribution is demonstrated by Laramie (1991).

By following Kalecki, but allowing for taxes on wages, profits and wages shares of industry value added are given as:

$$\pi/Y = [(k-1)(1+j) - O/W]/[(k-1)(1+j) + 1]; \tag{8.4}$$

$$W/Y = (1 - t_w)/[(k-1)(1+j) + 1]; \tag{8.5}$$

where π = aggregate industry profits; Y = value added; k = average industry mark up; j = ratio of material costs to industry wage bill; O = industry overhead costs; W = industry wage bill; and t_w = the tax rate on the wage bill. As reflected in equations (8.4) and (8.5), assuming profits taxes are not part of prime costs, the distribution of income is affected directly through changes in the tax rate on the wage bill and indirectly through the impact of taxation on industry markups, k (see Mair and Laramie 1992; and Laramie and Mair 1993).

The macroeconomic implications of Kalecki's theory of income distribution are developed as follows. The post-tax wage and salary share of gross private sector income is defined as:

$$V/Y = \beta/Y + \alpha; \tag{8.6}$$

where V = wage and salary income; β = after–tax salaries (a part of overhead costs); α = wages' share of value added. Assuming that k and j represent economy-wide aggregates, the right-hand side of equation (8.5) is set equal to α. This term is used to derive the basic Kaleckian income multiplier $1/(1-\alpha)$, where the level of national income is given as:

$$Y = (\beta + \Pi)/(1 - \alpha) \tag{8.7}$$

where $\Pi = \pi + T$.[1]

National income is expressed as a function of expenditures by finding an expression for after-tax profits. If we define aggregate profits simply as corporate profits, like Levy and Levy (1983), then:

$$\pi = I + X + (G - Tn) + D - Sp - Z; \tag{8.8}$$

where π = post-tax gross corporate profits; I = gross private domestic investment less the inventory valuation adjustment; X = net foreign investment; Tn = net (of transfer payments) government receipts; G = government purchases; D = the sum of corporate net interest and dividends; Sp = personal savings; and Z = the sum of non-corporate consumption of fixed capital, wage accruals less disbursements, capital grants received by the US and the statistical discrepancy (see Laramie 1994a for the derivation). The sum of corporate profits and tax receipts can be written as:

$$\Pi = I + X + G + D - Sp - Z. \tag{8.9}$$

Substituting equation (8.9) into (8.7) yields:

$$Y = [\beta + I + X + G + D - Sp - Z]/(1 - \alpha). \tag{8.10}$$

If we assume that dividends and interest payments are fixed in the short period, i.e.:

$$D = Do; \tag{8.11}$$

and that personal savings is a linear function of the national income; i.e.:

$$Sp = Spo + s(Y); \tag{8.12}$$

then the expression for national income is given as:

$$Y = [\beta + I + X + G + Do - Spo - Z]/(1 - \alpha + s). \tag{8.10'}$$

From equation (8.12) it can be seen that taxation plays no explicit role in affecting the level of national income but that the structure of taxation can affect the distribution factors, α and β (since β is after-tax salaries, where pre-tax salaries are assumed to be fixed). We now use equations (8.8), (8.10) and (8.10') to consider the macroeconomic incidence and effects of state and local taxation.

4. THE MACROECONOMIC INCIDENCE AND EFFECTS OF STATE AND LOCAL TAXATION

Within the model outlined above, the incidence of taxation on profits is determined by two sets of effects (see Laramie 1994a): (1) a public sector effect which depends upon the government's budget stance; and (2) a private sector effect which depends upon: (a) the reaction of personal savings to the tax/budget stance; (b) the reaction of investment to the tax in the long period; and (c) the change in corporate markups with respect to the tax.[2] As implied, a dollar increase in taxes, holding other things constant, results in a dollar reduction in post–tax corporate profits, but this effect is mitigated depending upon the public and the private sector effects. If the government spends the tax receipts on final goods and services, the incidence of the profits tax on corporations is reduced depending upon the reaction of personal savings to the resultant change in aggregate income. Moreover, if corporations respond to a tax by altering markups, then the economic incidence of the tax may further vary from the legal incidence. These various effects impact on future investment, through their effect on profits, which may lead to cumulative incidence effects.

In determining the economic incidence of any tax, the relative strengths of these various effects must be considered. The government's budget stance is a policy decision and typically, at the national level, little can be said about it a priori. However, it is possible to indulge in some speculation about the relative strengths of the private sector effects. These are expected to be relatively weak. First, consider the behaviour of savings. If the marginal propensity to save is small, then a change in income, given a change in any tax, is likely to have a small impact on post-tax corporate profits. Second, the extent to which taxes impact on aggregate post-tax profits, via the degree to which taxes are shifted through changes in corporate markups, is diluted by a number of factors. For example, in considering the incidence of the corporate profits tax, Pechman (1987) stressed that businesses only know their tax liability *ex post*, and, therefore, the immediate shifting of the profits tax through markup changes is unlikely; also, interfirm rivalry may inhibit the degree to which the tax is shifted forwards or backwards.

These sentiments are also expressed by Sylos-Labini (1979) when he argues that non-direct costs may not be passed along because of 'interfirm' differences. However, Coutts, Godley and Nordhaus (1978), in analysing the relationship between profit margins and corporate taxes, with UK data, have suggested that little shifting occurs in the short period (a year or less), but that there is some full, or more than full, shifting, in the medium and long runs respectively. Even if full, or more than full, shifting is the outcome, then the extent to which such shifting impacts on the level of aggregate post-tax corporate profits depends upon: (1) the change in aggregate income with respect to the change in profit margins; and (2) the extent to which personal savings change with respect to the change in aggregate income. Again, if the marginal propensity to save is relatively small, the change in corporate profits with respect to a change in corporate markups is expected to be relatively small. With the private sector effects relatively insignificant, the incidence of the corporation income tax depends largely upon the government budget stance. The economic incidence of the profits tax is determined politically or institutionally by the way in which these are reflected in the government's budget stance.

4.1. The Macroeconomic Incidence of State and Local Taxation

To consider the incidence of state and local taxes on corporate profits, we re-examine equation (8.8) and consider the institutional/political factors that have determined the budget stances of state and local governments. Moreover, we reconsider some effects that develop in response to the state and local government budget stances.

To consider the incidence of state and local taxes on aggregate corporate profits, the state and local and federal government budget deficits are separated in equation (8.8); i.e.:

$$\Pi = I + X + (G - T)_f + (G - T)_{sl} + D - Sp - Z; \qquad (8.8')$$

where the subscripts f and sl represent respectively the federal and state and local governments. We separate out the state and local government budgets from the federal government for three reasons. First, the state and local governments have an independent authority to raise and spend tax receipts. Second, state and local governments do not have the authority to create money or the economic wherewithal to engage in chronic deficit financing. Finally, state and local governments have various forms of legal limitations on their borrowings (see Aronson and Hilley 1986).

We now argue that the following factors, as mitigated by private sector reactions, impact on the incidence of state and local taxes: (1) the structure of state and local government receipts; (2) the expenditure functions of state and local governments; (3) the budget stance as determined by state and local deficit and debt limitations; and (4) intergovernmental relations. Following a brief discussion of these issues, the factors that impact on the incidence of state and local taxation on corporate profits will be summarized, and we will argue that private sector reactions, because of the state and local government budget stance, are unlikely to mitigate the incidence impact of state and local taxes on corporate profits.[3]

4.2. The Structure of State and Local Government Receipts

To begin, we examine the impact of the structure of government receipts by assuming that tax receipts are simply held, not used, by the state and local governments. By doing so, we consider how the private sector responses to the structure of taxation alone affects corporate profits.[4]

In the US *National Income and Product Accounts*, state and local government receipts are divided into personal tax and non–tax receipts, corporate profits tax accruals, indirect business tax and non–tax accruals, contributions for social insurance and federal grants-in-aid. From 1980 through 1993:Q1, on average the composition of tax receipts was as follows: 17.8 per cent of receipts; personal tax and non-tax receipts; 3.6 per cent – corporate profits tax accruals; 50.8 per cent – indirect business tax and non-tax accruals; 8.2per cent – contributions for social insurance; and 19.6 per cent – federal grants-in-aid.[5] Holding other things constant (on the right-hand side of equation (8.8)), the change in state and local tax receipts is inversely related to corporate profits (dollar for dollar). The effect of taxation on corporate profits is mitigated by the extent to which personal savings changes, given a change in state and local tax receipts. To consider the impact of state and local taxes on personal savings, we consider the incidence of these taxes on household incomes.

Personal tax and non-tax receipts are broken up into personal income taxes, non-taxes and other taxes. On average during 1980 to 1993:Q1, the personal income tax is the largest of this category, accounting for 13.6 per cent of total receipts. On average, non-taxes and other taxes accounted for 1.9 per cent and 2.3 per cent of total receipts, respectively. In an attempt to measure the distribution of tax burdens, Pechman (1986) allocated personal income tax to individual taxpayers. We do the same and conclude, therefore, that the impact of this tax on personal savings, and, thus, on corporate profits, depends on the household marginal propensity to consume.

Indirect business tax and non-tax accruals are divided into sales taxes, property taxes and other. Indirect business tax and non-tax accruals account, on average, for about 51 per cent of state and local receipts from 1980 to 1993:Q1. On average, sales taxes make up 24.4 per cent of total receipts, property taxes 20.5 per cent and other 5.8 per cent.

Like Pechman, we assume that sales taxes are shifted on to consumption and we assume that consumption expenditures fall by the full amount of the tax and, therefore, that personal savings are unaffected by the tax.[6] We make the same assumption with regard to 'other' indirect business taxes.

Property taxes represent taxes paid on land and improvements and can be divided into taxes paid on business property and homeowners' property. The taxes paid on business and homeowners' property are respectively 53 per cent and 47 per cent of state and local property taxes.

The homeowners' property tax is assumed to fall completely on imputed rental services derived from home ownership (included in personal consumption expenditures), and, therefore, like the sales tax, reduces consumption and the imputed income (net of the tax) by the amount of the tax. Corporate profits decline by the amount of the tax, if the decline in net imputed income causes an equivalent decline (with no impact on personal savings) in the consumption of goods or services produced in the corporate sector.

The property taxes paid by businesses, corporate and non–corporate, fall on their respective incomes.[7] These taxes can affect personal savings by altering the distribution of income to households, which is affected in two ways: (1) through an income effect; and (2) through a markup shifting effect. The income effect arises when the tax reduces the income flows to households. For example, corporate businesses may reduce their dividends or owners of non corporate businesses have less personal disposable income following an increase in the property tax The markup shifting effect occurs when busines alter their mark ups in an attempt to shift the tax. A change in markup, see equation (8.5), alters the distribution of income and the flow of income to wage earners. Given wage earners' marginal propensities to save, the level of personal savings falls and the level of profits increases, *ceteris paribus*.

Over the period, contributions for social insurance represented, on average, 8.2 per cent of state and local government gross receipts. Since 1986:Q4, surpluses of contributions to social insurance have kept state and local governments out of deficit. Following Pechman, we treat contributions to social insurance as falling directly on compensation to employees. As a consequence, its impact on corporate profits depends on the marginal propensity to save out of compensation to employees.

4.3.   The Expenditure Functions of State and Local Governments

As indicated above, one of the factors that influences the incidence of state and local taxes on corporate profits is the reaction of the private sector to the government budget stance. The private sector reaction depends on what state and local governments do with their receipts. If state and local governments receipts are saved and paid for via declines in consumption expenditures, corporate profits decline by the full amount of tax receipts, regardless of the source of tax receipts. If receipts are used to finance expenditures, then the impact of taxation depends on how these expenditures flow into the corporate sector. Government purchases of goods from the corporate sector, for example, flow directly back into the corporate sector, and, therefore, offset the negative impact of taxes on corporate profits. Government purchases from the non corporate sector, ignoring the foreign sector, compensation to employees, government transfer payments and government interest payments are payments to households, and the flow of these expenditures back to the corporate sector depends upon households' marginal propensities to save.

The functions of state and local governments are summarized in state and local government budgets, the bulk of which are devoted to government purchases. On average, from 1980 to 1993:Q1, 88.3 per cent of expenditures were devoted to government purchases. Of this amount, 58.7 per cent and 29.7 per cent of total expenditures were devoted to compensation to employees and other government purchases respectively. Government transfer payments to persons, net interest paid to persons, dividends received by government and subsidies less current surplus to government enterprises averaged respectively 22.4 per cent, −7.1 per cent, 1 per cent and −2.6 per cent. These data suggest that at least, on average, 70.3 per cent (100 per cent less 29.7 per cent) of state and local government expenditures were distributed directly to households'. Moreover, this distribution appears to be on the increase. Beginning in 1990, the share of state and local government purchases of total expenditures, excluding compensation to government employees, started to decline while the share of transfer payments began to increase.

These data suggest that much of the incidence of state and local taxes on corporate profits depends on the relative impacts of taxes and expenditures on personal savings. The imposition of taxes reduces personal savings, whereas the spending of tax receipts increases personal savings. To determine the relative impacts of these, the state and local government budget stance and the relative marginal propensities to save (with respect to changes in various state and local tax receipts and expenditures) must be ascertained. We now consider the state and local government budget stance and the impact of intergovernmental relations. In the following section, we consider the relative marginal propensities to save.

4.4. The State and Local Government Budget Stance

As is well known, most states have some form of legal restrictions, constitutional or statutory, which limits budget deficits. According to Fisher (1988, p.430), in thirteen states the governor must submit or the legislature must pass balanced budgets; another thirty-six states are prohibited from carrying budget deficits into the next fiscal year and many states have debt limitations. The existence of these restrictions has accounted for the surplus in state and local government budgets. State and local government budgets have typically maintained a budget surplus during the 1980s. This surplus has ranged from about 6 per cent to 12 per cent of its gross receipts. In the 1990s, much of this surplus was eliminated. In 1992, the state and local budget surplus was only about 0.8 per cent of gross receipts. This surplus can be attributed to the surplus in the state and local social insurance fund.

The 'other' portion of the state and local government budget surplus was consistently negative from 1987 through the first quarter of 1993.

This government budget stance implies that the distribution of gross receipts to various uses (as reflected in expenditures) follows a pattern similar to the distribution of expenditures and that the impact of state and local taxes on corporate profits depends upon the redistributive effects of state and local government budgets and the resultant impact on personal savings.

4.5. Intergovernmental Relations

Governmental relations among the federal and state and local governments encompass many activities, ranging from federal government mandates, to the deductibility of state and local taxes, to exclusion from federal taxes of state and municipal bonds, to grants-in-aid. During the 1980s, two of the major changes in fiscal intergovernmental relations that occurred were: (1) the elimination of the deduction for sales taxes; and (2) consolidation and reduction in grants-in-aid to state and local governments. The elimination of the deduction for sales taxes appears to have had little impact. The ratio of sales taxes to total receipts or to tax receipts shows no significant trend since its elimination under the Tax Reform Act of 1986. In contrast, the reduction in federal grants-in-aid, as described above, has induced state and local governments to reduce their budget surpluses and to increase their reliance on income and property taxes in order to balance rising expenditures. Thus, in determining the incidence of state and local government taxes, we are particularly concerned with the impact of federal grants-in-aid to state and local governments.

Federal grants-in-aid affect the incidence of state and local taxes on corporate profits by altering the government and budget stance. If the federal government has a marginal propensity to spend greater than the state and local governments, then the transfer of tax revenues from the federal to the state and local governments reduces the aggregate propensity to spend out of tax receipts and, thus, alters the impact of taxes on aggregate profits.[8] Moreover, if state and local governments substitute federal grants-in-aid for other revenue sources, like personal and property tax receipts, the incidence of these taxes on corporate profits and other forms of income may be altered.

In 1981, President Reagan proposed a 'new' fiscal federalism. The purpose of this proposal was to make government more responsive and to reduce the federal government budget deficit (see Aronson and Hilley 1986, p. 30). The evidence from the 1980s suggest that the Reagan Administration did have some success as states and local governments became less dependent on federal grants-in-aid, reduced their surpluses, slowed the rate of increase in their expenditures and increased their reliance on other forms of taxation.

Beginning in 1990, federal grants-in-aid as a percent-age of state and local receipts have increased. As of 1993, grants-n-aid were about 20.5 per cent of state and local receipts as compared to the low of 17.3 per cent in 1987 (and remaining almost flat through 1989) and the high of 25 per cent in 1978.

If we assume that federal tax receipts and expenditures are insensitive to changes in federal grants-in-aid (see note 6), then federal grants-in-aid have reduced the incidence of state and local taxes on corporate profits. Federal grants-in-aid have allowed states 'and local governments' average propensity to spend out of tax receipts to exceed one.

4.6. Measuring the Short-Period Effect of State and Local Taxes on Corporate Profits

The difference between state and local government expenditures and tax receipts, made up largely of federal grants-in-aid, as mitigated by the net reactions of personal savings to state and local tax receipts and expenditures, determines the impact of state and local taxes on aggregate profits. To consider the incidence of state and local tax receipts on corporate profits, we consider the impact of selected state and local taxes receipts and expenditures on personal savings, and we estimate the average propensity to consume out of state and local government expenditures directly distributed to households.

To estimate the impact of selected state and local tax receipts on personal savings, a personal savings function was estimated. Personal savings is expressed as a function of different definitions of personal disposable income and itself, lagged one quarter. Each of the variables was expressed in current dollars.[9] The first definition of personal disposable income is the standard definition provided in the *National Income and Product Accounts.* The second definition is the first definition plus net state and local government transfer payments which are defined as the difference between the sum of compensation to employees and transfers to persons and the sum of personal tax receipts and social security contributions. The third definition is the first definition less government transfer payments, defined as compensation to government employees and transfers to persons. Using these various definitions, the regression results presented in Table 8.1 were derived.

As shown in Table 8.1, all the coefficients, except those on the lagged dependent variable, are not statistically different from zero. These estimates imply that personal savings, at least within one quarter, is insensitive to changes in state and local net transfer payments, state and local transfer payments and corporate and indirect business taxes. As a consequence, the

Applying Theory to The Real World

incidence of state and local taxes, at least in the short period (one quarter), is determined by the difference between government expenditures and tax receipts.

Table 8.1 The impact of selected state and local tax receipts on personal savings (billions of dollars) 1980:Q2 to 1993:Q1 (ordinary least square estimates)

Constant	Personal disposable income	Net transfer payments	Transfer payments	Corp. profit tax	Indirect business tax	Personal savings $(t-1)$
79.402	0.0129^2	–	–	–	–	0.545
(3.126)	(0.256)	–	–	–	–	(4.63)
Adj. $R^2 = 0.284$	SER = 28.18	F = 1.2	DW = 2.06	–	–	
113.83	-0.325^3	0.263	–	–	–	0.476
(3.196)	(−1.288)	(1.37)	–	–	–	(3.740)
Adj. $R^2 = 0.296$	SER = 27.94	F = 8.17	DW = 2.06	–	–	–
76.47	0.164	0.408	–	− 2.13	− 1.80	0.482
(1.71)	(1.35)	(1.54)	–	(− 1.17)	(− 1.46)	(3.82)
Adj. $R^2 = 0.318$	SER = 27.5	F = 5.58	DW = 1.96	–	–	–
73.06	0.163^4	–	0.330	−2.40	−1.79	0.499
(1.60)	(1.33)	–	(1.25)	(−1.31)	(−1.420)	(3.98)
Adj. $R^2 = 0.310$	SER = 27.6	F = 5.76	DW = 1.97	–	–	–

Notes:
1. Defined as the difference between the sum of state and local compensation to government employees and government transfers to persons and personal tax and non-tax receipts and contributions for social insurance.
2. Personal disposable income is defined as in the National *Income* and *Product* Accounts (NIPA).
3. Personal disposable income is defined as the NIPA definition plus state and local personal tax and non-tax receipts plus contributions for social insurance less compensation to government employees less transfers to persons.
4. Personal disposable income is defined as the NIPA definition less compensation to government employees less transfers to persons.

To test for the robustness of this result, we attempt to estimate the average propensities to consume out various incomes: private sector compensation to employees; property incomes (the sum of corporate profits, proprietors' income, non corporate net interest (corporate net interest is already included in corporate profits) and rental income); federal government expenditures distributed directly to households (government compensation to employees, government transfers to persons and net interest paid by government); and state and local government expenditures distributed directly to households. To estimate these propensities, we used a variant of Weintraub's (1979, 1981) consumption coefficient.[10] As such, consumption expenditures are equal to the consumption coefficient times the wage bill.

Here, we alter this equation by including a random shock term. Thus, consumption is written as:

$$C = a(V) + \varepsilon; \tag{8.13}$$

where C = consumption expenditures; a = the consumption coefficient; V = wage bill (including salaries) and ε = random shock term. Since consumption can be defined as the sum of consumption out of private sector compensation to employees, consumption out of property income, consumption out of federal government distributions to households and consumption out of state and local government distributions to households, equation (8.13) can be rewritten as:

$$c_v(V) + c_p(P') + c_f\ (FD) + c_{sl}(SD) = a(V) + \varepsilon; \tag{8.13'}$$

where c_i = the average propensity to consume out of pre-tax incomes, where $i = v, p, f$ and sl, and where P' = property income, FD = federal government direct distributions to households and SD = state and local direct distributions to households. By rearranging equation (8.13') and by dividing both sides of (8.13') by the wage bill, V, we derive:

$$a = c_y + c_p(P'/V) + c_f\ (FD/V) + c_{sl}(SD/V) + \varepsilon/V. \tag{8.14}$$

By estimating (8.14), we are able to obtain estimates of the various average propensities to consume (see Table 8.2).

As evidenced in Table 8.2, during the sample period all the estimates of the average propensities to consume were statistically different from zero, except the average propensity to consume out of property income. The estimates of the average propensities to consume out pre-tax private sector income, direct federal government expenditures to households and direct state and local government expenditures to households are 0.837, 0.610 and 1.511.

These estimates are remarkable for three reasons. First, the average propensity to consume out direct state and local government expenditures to households is greater than one. This result suggests that personal savings, at least in the short period, at best is unlikely to change with respect to direct state and local government expenditures to households. Second, the average propensity to spend out of direct federal government expenditures to households is significantly lower than one and it is less than the average propensity to spend out of private sector compensation to employees. If the average propensity to spend is inversely related to the level of income over income classes, this result suggests that direct federal government expenditures to households have provided significant aid to higher-income households. This result is not surprising in the light of the large increases in net interest payments made by the federal government. Third, these results suggest that the impact of federal deficit on corporate profits during the sample period has been mitigated by the relatively low average propensity to consume out direct federal government expenditures to households (in addition to the trade deficit).

Table 8.2 Estimates of the average propensities to consume: private sector compensation to employees; property income; federal government direct distributions to households and state and local direct government distributions to households (maximum likelihood iterative technique provided by TSP)

c_y	c_p	c_f	c_{sl}
0.837	0.688	0.610	1.511
(6.58)	(0.559)	(2.658)	(2.838)
Adjusted $R^2 = 0.971$	SER = 0.081	F = 568.909	DW = 1.80

4.7. The Macroeconomic Effects of State and Local Taxation

Now that the short-period incidence of state and local taxation has been considered, we can speculate as to some of the effects. As evidenced in equation (8.10'), state and local taxation impacts on national income through three variables: the post-tax salary bill, b; the wage share, a; and government purchases, G, *ceteris paribus*. By differentiating (8.10'), with respect to b, G and a, we derive:

$$dY/d\beta = 1/(1 - \alpha + s); \tag{8.16}$$
$$dY/dG = 1/(1 - \alpha + s); \tag{8.17}$$

$$dY/d\alpha = [\beta + I + X + G + Do - Spo - Z]/(1 - \alpha + s)^2. \tag{8.18}$$

These results indicate that increases in tax rates that reduce the post-tax salary bill or the wage share, have a negative impact on national income. In contrast, an increase in the profits tax, assuming the profits tax has noimpact on the wage share, will increase national income, if the profits tax is used to fund an increase in government purchases.

This result has an interesting application to the study of state and local government finance. The corporate profits tax represents state and local government's weakest revenue source. It averaged only 3.6 per cent of total receipts during the sample period. Individual states, becasuse of capital mobility and the pressures of local business and threats of exit, are constrained in their ability to use the profits tax to fund projects even though such taxes are likely to stimulate growth and have no aggregate incidence impact on corporate profits. Instead, state and local governments clearly choose inferior policies; policies that play income classes off against each other. An increase in indirect business taxes, household property or sales taxes, reduces household consumption, but if spent by state and local governments, has no impact on corporate profits. The net effect is that some households, like middle-or-lower income households who do not receive transfer payments or have major stakes in corporations, are made worse off while corporate profits are unaffected. Corporate profits and household incomes, on aggregate, could be unaffected if the corporate profits tax was used to fund state and local government purchases.

The inability of state and local governments to use the corporate profits tax suggests an added rationale for federal grants-in-aid. The federal government has much greater latitude and does not face the same constraints, even in a 'global' economy, as state and local governments in levying corporate profit taxes. The federal government could rectify the deficiency in public investment which the Clinton Administration has alluded to, by increasing the corporate profits tax and by applying these funds to federal grants-in-aid. The result would be more balanced economic growth.

5. CONCLUSION

Because of institutional and political factors, the macroeconomic effect and incidence of state and local taxes has been shown in this chapter to be remarkably different from the incidence of similar federal taxes on corporate profits. Because of statutory or constitutional requirements, state and local governments have deficit and debt limitations. The US federal government appears to have an *ad hoc* budget process with little apparent connection between the revenue and expenditure sides of the budget. These state and local fiscal constraints, coupled with federal grants-in-aid, cause the state and local governments' propensity to consume out of tax receipts to exceed one and, therefore, have a negligible to positive impact on corporate profits.

This conclusion is reinforced by estimates of the marginal propensities to save out of disposable income and state and local net transfer payments and by the average propensity to spend out of state and local government expenditures distributed directly to households. The marginal propensities to save are not statistically different from zero; households' average propensity to consume out of state and local compensation to employees, transfer payments and net interest payments is statistically different from zero and greater than one. State and local indirect business and corporate tax receipts are shown to have no impact on personal savings in the short period. These estimates suggest that the primary factor determining the short-period incidence of local and state taxes on profits is the state and local government budget stance.

This result poses an interesting public finance problem by suggesting that corporate state and local profits taxes are preferable to other forms of taxation, such as indirect business taxes, for example, which reduce the incomes of households while having no adverse effect on post-tax corporate profits. In contrast, the state and local corporate profits tax has no impact on post-tax corporate profits or on household income. Given that the profits tax is the least utilized form of taxation at the state and local level, we suggest that the federal government increases its reliance on the corporate profits tax to fund federal grants-in-aid and thereby reduce the deficiency in public investment.

NOTES

1.   We are ignoring post-tax proprietors' income, rental income and non corporate net interest.
2.   A third effect should be added to the list: a foreign effect. The foreign sectors reaction to the government budget stance is reflected in net foreign investment, X. As the history of the twin deficits has shown, the incidence of taxes on corporate profits also plays out through this channel.
3.   In this section, we make reference to data that we tabulated from *NIPA* of the US. The tables are available upon request and not provided here because ofspace limitations
4.   We will ignore any foreign effects as mentioned in note 2. Given the state and local government budget stance, aggregate foreign effects are expected to be minimal in response to aggregate state and local fiscal policies.
5.   As indicated above, the most remarkable changes in the composition of state tax receipts were: (1) increases in personal income tax share of total receipts; (2) increases in the property tax share of total receipts; and (3) a decrease in the federal grants-in-aid share of total receipts.
6.   The equilibrium level of personal savings is altered depending upon the government budget stance. If government uses the sales tax to purchases goods, then the sales tax has no impact on the equilibrium level of savings.
7.   A breakdown of the property tax between corporate and non corporate businesses was not available. Again, we are ignoring uses of the tax receipts.
8.   The federal budget process and government budget experience from the 1980s suggests that federal government receipts may have little relation to one another. If the federal government

budget process is totally *ad hoc*, where receipts have no bearing on expenditures and expenditures have no bearing on receipts, then the federal grants-in-aid increase the federal government budget deficit and increase the state and local government budget surplus (assuming that the state and local government marginal propensity to save is positive). The net effect of the grants-in-aid on the aggregate corporate profits is, thus, the sum of the resulting changes in the federal and state and local government budget surpluses.

9. Current dollars were used because the nominal profits are determined by nominal expenditure flows. Given these nominal expenditure flows, real profits are determined by a weighted average of fixed investment price index and consumption out of profits price index. The latter is unknown.

10. Weintraub defined the consumption coefficient as the ratio of consumption expenditures to the wage bill in order to eliminate the standard (Kalecki-Kaldor-Robinson) assumption that capitalists do not consume and workers do not save.

REFERENCES

Aronson, J.R. and J.L. Hilley (1986), *Financing State and Local Governments*, 4th Edition, Washington DC: The Brookings Institution.

Asimakopulos, A. and J.B. Burbidge, (1974), 'The short-period incidence of taxation', *Economic Journal*, **84**, 267–88.

Coutts, K., W. Godley and W. Nordhaus (1978), *Industrial Pricing in the United Kingdom*, Cambridge: Cambridge University Press.

Damania, D. and D. Mair (1992), 'The short period incidence of taxation revisited', *Cambridge Journal of Economics*, **16** (2), 195–206.

Economic Report of the President (1994), Washington, DC: United States Government Printing Office.

Fisher, R.C. (1988), *State and Local Public Finance*, Glenview, Illinois: Scott, Foresman & Company.

Kalecki, M. (1968), *Theory of Economic Dynamics*, New York: Monthly Review Press.

Kalecki, M. (1971/1937), 'A theory of commodity, income and capital taxation', *Economic Journal*, **47**, 444–50, reprinted in *Selected Essays on the Dynamics of a Capitalist Economy, 1933–1970*, Cambridge: Cambridge University Press.

Kotlikoff, L. and L. Summers (1987), 'Tax Incidence' in *Handbook on Public Economics, Vol 2*, A.J. Auerbach and M.J. Feldstein, (eds) Amsterdam: North Holland, 1043–92.

Kriesler, P. (1989), 'Methodological implications of Kalecki's microfoundations' in M. Sebastiani (ed) *Kalecki's Relevance Today*, London: MacMillan, 121–141.

Laramie, A.J. (1991), 'Taxation and Kalecki's distribution factors', *Journal of Post-Keynesian Economics*, **4**, 583–94.

Laramie, A.J. (1994a), 'The incidence of the corporate profits tax revisited: a post Keynesian approach', Working Paper No. 109 Jerome Levy Economics Institute

Laramie, A.J. and D. Mair (1993), 'The incidence of business rates: a post Keynesian approach', *Review of Political Economy*, **5** (1), 55–72.

Laramie, A.J. and D. Mair, (1994), 'Taxation and Kalecki's theory of the business cycle', *Cambridge Journal of Economics* (forthcoming).

Laramie, A.J., D. Mair, A.G. Miller and P.J. Reynolds (1994), 'Kalecki's degree of monopoly theory of income distribution: some new results', Department of Economics, Heriot-Watt University, mimeo.

Levy, S.J. and D.A. Levy (1983), *Profits and the Future of American Society*, New York: Harper & Row.

Mair, D. and A.J. Laramie (1992), 'The incidence of business rates on manufacturing industry', *Scottish Journal of Political Economy*, **39** (1), 76–94.

Mieszkowski, P.M. (1972), 'The property tax: an excise tax or a profits tax?', *Journal of Public Economics*, **1**, 73–96.

National Income and Product Accounts of the United States, 1949–1993, Statistical Tables, US Department of Commerce, Bureau of Economic Analysis.

Pechman, J.A. (1986), *The Rich, the Poor and the Taxes They Pay*, Boulder, Colorado: Westview Press.

Pechman, J.A. (1987), *Federal Tax Policy,* 5th ed., Washington, DC: The Brookings Institution.

Reynolds, P.J. (1984), 'An empirical analysis of the degree of monopoly theory of income distribution', *Bulletin of Economic Research*, **36** (1), 59–84.

Schwartz, T.R. and J.E. Peck (1990), 'The changing face of fiscal federalism', *Challenge*, **33**, 41–46.

Sylos-Labini, P. (1979), 'Industrial pricing in the United Kingdom', *Cambridge Journal of Economics*, **3**, 153–63. Reprinted in M.C. Sawyer (ed), *Post Keynesian Economics,* Aldershot: Edward Elgar

Weintraub, S. (1979), 'Generalizing Kalecki and simplifying macroeconomics', *Journal of Post Keynesian Economics*, **3**, 101–6.

Weintraub, S. (1981), 'An eclectic theory of income shares', *Journal of Post Keynesian Economics*, **4**, 10–24.

PART   III

Local Government and Local Policymaking:
Autonomy and Constraints

9. Changing Perceptions of the Role of Local Government with Particular Reference to the United Kingdom

Peter Else

1. INTRODUCTION

Over the past 15 years local government in the United Kingdom has been subject to an unprecedented series of measures by the central government aimed at changing its powers, the way it operates and the environment in which it works. As might be expected, these changes have been analysed and commented upon from a variety of disciplinary perspectives. The aim of this chapter is to offer more of an economic perspective, and it argues that many of the changes can be viewed as a response to the public sector equivalent of 'market failure' in the operation of local government (which for convenience will be referred to simply as 'LG failure'), and can be appraised from that point of view. Within that context one particular concern of the chapter is with the changes which have been directed towards separating the provision of services from the responsibility for financing them. This has involved a major shift in the perceived role of local government from that of a direct provider of services to more of an 'enabling' or contracting role, in which individual authorities negotiate with a variety of other producing organizations to supply the services required.[1]

In the following pages, Sections 2, 3 and 4 discuss the potential sources of LG failure suggested by the relevant economic theory and thus provide a basis for the discussion of some of the recent changes affecting local government in the UK. This discussion starts in Section 5, and is continued in Section 6 with an analysis of the effects of contracting out the provision of local services, based on the model of the behaviour of public sector organizations set out in Section 4. Section 7 offers some conclusions.

2. THE 'FISCAL FEDERALISM' APPROACH

The approach to the analysis of local government covered in this section is usually referred to as the 'fiscal federalism' approach because it has its origins in the North American fiscal federalism literature of the early 1970s (for example Oates 1972[2]). The starting point of this approach is that some public goods, that is goods which are characterized by non-excludability and non-rivalry in consumption, are local in the sense that they benefit individuals only within a limited geographical area. It is then argued that if preferences vary between localities, economic welfare can be improved if the provision of these local public goods reflects local preferences.

While the approach has been developed in terms of local public goods, it should be clear that similar arguments can be applied to any good or service with localized benefits supplied collectively, whether it possesses the full characteristics of public goods or not. Moreover, once decisionmaking on local public goods has been decentralized, under the fiscal federalism approach, the central government can be assigned its traditional neoclassical role of correcting for the 'market' failures arising from this decentralization. This could potentially involve intervention for allocative, distributive or macroeconomic reasons. The allocative reasons arise where the provision of local public sector goods and services has spillover effects on neighbouring jurisdictions and could lead to subsidization, where spillovers are beneficial, and taxation, in the opposite case. Distributive reasons for intervention could arise if it was felt that lack of resources, or higher costs, should not restrict the choice of quantities of local public sector goods and services in particular localities. The central government may also wish to encourage or discourage local spending for macroeconomic reasons.

This approach thus provides a basic efficiency argument for local government, but it also provides a starting point for the identification of the factors which might cause the system to fail to yield an efficient allocation of resources (that is, LG failure as defined above), in much the same way as the corresponding analysis of markets can be used to identify potential sources of 'market failure'.

In a representative democracy, the demand curve for local public sector goods is essentially the demand curve of the group in power in the relevant local jurisdiction, reflecting their preferences for the goods, constrained by the need to retain sufficient electoral support to remain in office. On the other hand, for an optimal supply of these goods, the marginal benefits to the community need to be equal to marginal cost, which, if we confine ourselves to local public goods for the moment, requires the sum of the marginal benefits accruing to individuals, reflected in the vertical aggregation of the demand curves for local public goods for all the individuals in the area, to be equal to the marginal cost of supplying them. In a direct democracy, in which decisions are taken through majority voting, the actual demand curve would reflect the preferences of the median voter, at least with single-peaked preferences and appropriate voting procedures. However, it is only under rather restrictive conditions that median voter preferences lead to an optimal supply of the public good in question. In formal terms, as is well known, an optimal supply of a public good is determined where $\Sigma MB_i = MC$, where MB_i is the marginal benefit for voter i ($i = 1... n$). The median voter's preferred quantity is where $MB_m = t_m$, where t_m is the marginal tax price to that voter. The latter will also be the optimal supply only if $\Sigma MB_i = nMB_m$ and $t_m = MC/n$ or, in other words, if the median voter is also the mean voter and he or she faces a tax price equal to MC/n.

This suggests straightaway two possible sources of LG failure. First of all, the tax price faced by the median voter for local public services may not be very closely related to their marginal social cost. Indeed in the UK, in the past when more than half of local tax revenue came from businesses rather than local residents, the latter's tax price was almost certainly less than marginal social cost. The local taxes in force and the form of central government grants to local authorities were potentially additional distorting factors.

Second the median voter will not be the mean voter unless the distribution of preferences is symmetrical about the mean. But whether that condition is satisfied or not, in a system of representative government dominated by political parties, ruling groups are often able to pursue policies which do not have the support of the median voter. Indeed under the electoral system operating in the UK, between 30 and 40 per cent of the popular vote is often sufficient to maintain power. Further, it is not uncommon for less than half of those eligible to vote in local elections. In addition, while it is a convenient simplification for some purposes to assume that local voters choose between parties offering some homogeneous 'local public service', in practice the composition of the bundles offered are also likely to affect choices. Moreover, votes cast in local government elections also appear to be influenced to a significant extent by the performance of the national government. What all this suggests is that, in practice, individual local administrations may have considerable monopoly power which, as utility-maximizing economic agents, they can be expected to exercise in accordance with their own individual preferences. Consequently they may provide a more or less than optimal supply of local public services, leading to allocative inefficiency. There could also be productive inefficiency in the absence of competitive pressures to seek the most efficient way of supplying services.

3. THE AGENCY APPROACH

In the fiscal federalism approach, the emphasis is on local government providing local public sector goods and services in response to local preferences, However, it can be argued that that particular approach is not entirely appropriate in the UK context because a substantial part of local government activities, such as, for example, in the areas of education and personal social services, which together account for some 45 per cent of local spending, is largely concerned with the local administration of policies determined by the central government. In this context, it can be argued that the more recently developed 'agency approach', as articulated in Hughes and Smith (1991), is likely to provide a more useful basis for analysis. This approach draws on the extensive literature on decentralization in firms (which is usefully reviewed in Radner 1986), but seems to have been first explicitly applied to local government in Helm and Smith (1987).

In its extreme form, the underlying assumption to this approach is that the function of local government is to provide services which need to be produced at the local level, on behalf of the central government. Local government is thus essentially an agent of the central government carrying out the latter's policies and there is a principal–agent relationship between them. Local management is economically desirable because of the lower costs of obtaining information at the local level about local circumstances and to exploit the advantages of control in smaller scale units. The use of an elected local government rather than branch offices of the central government can be justified on the grounds that it provides a more transparent channel for receiving and taking account of user reactions and dealing with local difficulties (via relatively well-known local councillors seeking publicity rather than faceless bureaucrats preferring secrecy) and also as a control mechanism to constrain local X-inefficiency. From both points of view, if one group of councillors does not perform adequately, they can be replaced at the next election by others who might do better. In its extreme form, under this approach preferences of local voters are irrelevant as far as overall allocative decisions are concerned. In voting in local elections, the electorate simply makes a judgement about the relative efficiencies of rival groups of managers in providing the services and allocating that provision between users. The fact that the decentralized structure may provide a number of similar agents introduces an opportunity for yardstick competition[3] and allows comparisons between the performance of different agents to inform the choices of local voters and facilitate monitoring by the central government principal.

An obvious problem with this approach is that in its pure form, it would require the depoliticization of local government to ensure that voters' choices were based only on their perceptions of the managerial competence of the contenders for office. As long as elections are fought by political parties, questions of local managerial efficiency are likely to be only one of a number of issues affecting voters' choices. Again, this provides scope for individual local authorities to pursue policies involving productive inefficiency. If, however, the quantities of services to be provided are determined by a higher-level authority, whether there is allocative inefficiency or not will depend on the latter's decision-making processes which, of course, may have its own source of 'failure'.

It might also be noted in passing that the requirements for tax efficiency in this approach seem to be less demanding than with the previous one because there would be no need for individual tax prices to be related to marginal cost. Basically all that would be required, to provide voters with an incentive to vote for a more efficient administration, would be a tax which increases with local expenditure and is big enough to be a matter of concern to them.

4. THE INFLUENCE OF LOCAL BUREAUCRACIES

We can now take into account the fact that, in providing local services, local government, in common with any other level of government, has to operate through the agency of a bureaucratic organization. In this section, therefore, we outline a relevant model of bureaucratic behaviour, derived from the public choice literature, with a view to identifying further possible sources of LG failure. Such models are traditionally set in a scenario in which an elected authority makes grants to a 'bureau', charged with the responsibility for providing some government service. In the present context, this bureau might be an operational department within a particular local authority.

This kind of situation in fact involves a typical principal/agent problem in that the principal is less well informed about the cost of providing the service than the agent. A well-established standard solution to such a problem[4] involves the agent being offered a contract providing him or her with incentives which are compatible with those of the principal. Thus, in the case of firms, their directors/managers (the agents in this case) may be offered profit-sharing contracts to induce them to operate in the profit-orientated interests of shareholders (principals). With public sector organizations it is more difficult to devise incentive-compatible contracts of this nature, because it is practically impossible to assign property rights in the benefits accruing to the community from particular activities to the managers responsible for their provision, particularly where they involve the supply of public goods. In the absence of such contracts, some of the older models of bureaucratic behaviour would still seem to be relevant. Moreover in this general context, the pioneering model of Niskanen (1971), still features prominently in the relevant literature, if only as a starting point to the discussion as, for example, in Dunleavy (1991).

Niskanen postulated that public sector bureau managers seek to maximize their budgets on the grounds that this would also help to maximize managerial rewards in terms of salary, job satisfaction, status and the like. In most cases, this involves maximizing the output of the service subject to a break-even constraint. In some cases, however, it was acknowledged that demand constraints might mean that the grant-making body would only be prepared to make negative payments for particular marginal units. In such cases, Niskanen argued that surplus funds would be used to support cost-increasing activities (that is productive inefficiency) rather than increased output. However, if, as that implies, it is the case that cost-increasing activities can increase managerial utility, it seems more satisfactory to assume that this could happen at any level of output. Hence, for present purposes we utilize the later more general model developed in Migue and Belanger (1974), in which the bureau managers' utility function is specified as

$$U = U(Q, D) \tag{9.1}$$

in which Q is the quantity of public service produced and D is what Migue and Belanger referred to as the 'fiscal residuum' but which can, perhaps more clearly, be identified, following Williamson, as 'discretionary expenditure'.[5] This discretionary expenditure is basically any expenditure over and above that necessary to produce the output efficiently. It could involve using more inputs than necessary, either as a deliberate choice or as a result of 'managerial slack' and it might also include other expenditure which enhances managerial utility, by providing emoluments above market levels or benefits in kind.

The resultant model is represented diagrammatically in Figure 9.1. In that diagram, the curve TB depicts the relationship between total benefits from the public sector good or service being supplied, as perceived by the grant giving body, and the quantity provided (Q). For the purposes of this section, it can be assumed that this curve also represents the benefits to the local community, although, as we have already seen, it may in practice only be a rather imperfect reflection. TC_0 is defined to show the relationship between the total cost of providing the service, when resources are used efficiently, and Q. This latter relationship is drawn in Figure 9.1 as a linear one for convenience, but the use of a non-linear function would not materially affect the analysis. From these two relationships, a net benefit curve (NB), showing the surplus of benefits over costs at each level of Q, can be derived by simple subtraction. A key assumption in both the Niskanen and the Migue and Belanger models is that, in the context of a situation in which negotiations relate to a total package and asymmetric information, particularly with respect to costs, bureau managers are able to act as perfect price discriminators and extract all the surplus from the grant-giving agency. This means, in terms of our diagram, that the bureau managers' choice set is defined by the net benefits curve.

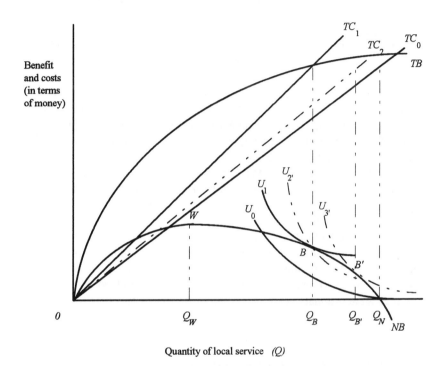

*Figure 9.1   Productive   versus   allocative   inefficiency   with   local
           bureaucrats*

In the case illustrated, the original Niskanen budget-maximizing bureau manager would seek a budget that would allow it to operate at N, and produce the maximum possible output consistent with breaking even (Q_N). This compares with the rather lower net benefit maximizing output of Q_W and hence would involve some degree of allocative efficiency.[6] However, if the utility function takes the more general form of equation (9.1) and can be represented in the usual way by a set of downward-sloping, convex-to-the-origin indifference curves like U_i $(i = 0,1...)$, the preferred position could now be anywhere on the downward-sloping section of NB. It would thus again involve some allocative inefficiency. Moreover, the preferred position could still be at N if the indifference curves were steeper than the net benefit curve in the vicinity of N, but that would be rather a limiting case. Of more general interest, therefore, is the kind of case illustrated in the diagram where, taking the indifference curves shown as solid lines, the preferred position is at B with an output of $Q_B < Q_N$ and discretionary expenditure of $Q_B B$, which thus raises costs above the productively efficient level. These additional costs displace the cost function in the diagram upwards to TC_1 intersecting TB at the preferred output.

In general, therefore, compared with the basic Niskanen model, a preferred position like B, implies that some allocative inefficiency is given up in exchange for productive inefficiency. Interestingly, however, it can be shown that, at least in crude aggregate consumer's surplus terms, it makes no difference to the welfare of the community as reflected in the total benefits curve. In a movement from N to B, the potential gain in consumer's surplus from more allocative efficiency is exactly offset by the losses arising from more productive inefficiency. Moreover, this result does not seem sensitive to the precise form of the underlying functions and applies whether they are linear or not.[7] Further, while it may be the case that bureau managers are not able to extract all the surplus benefits of the community (or their representatives), as long as they can extract a proportion of those benefits they will be faced with a choice set of similar form to that illustrated in Figure 9.1, with similar consequences. This analysis, of course, potentially applies to any situation in which production is through a 'bureau'. For the present purposes, however, its significance is that it identifies an additional source of LG failure to those considered in Sections 2 and 3 above.

5. THE CENTRAL GOVERNMENT'S RESPONSE

The preceding discussion suggests three questions to consider in an evaluation of the central government's attempts to deal with its perceptions of the shortcomings of local government in the UK. The first concerns the effect of the various changes on the relationship between local authorities' spending decisions and local preferences; a second is whether the various changes affecting the finance of local government confront local voters with the marginal social costs of the provision of local services. The third is whether the various measures directed at separating out the actual production of local services from the responsibility of procuring them can contribute to a reduction in the kinds of inefficiencies identified in the previous section. The first two, which relate to the potential 'failures' in the political decisionmaking process will be discussed in this section, while the third, relating to bureaucratic 'failures', is considered in Section 6.

As far as the first of these questions is concerned, one possible approach might be through a change in the electoral system to make it more difficult for entrenched party groups to retain power with minority electoral support and thus ensure that spending decisions become more responsive to local preferences. Replacement of the existing first-past-the-post system by some transferable voting system or proportional representation might be seen as one possible step in that direction, but that is not an option that appears to have been seriously considered by the UK government, partly no doubt because it might then be difficult for that government to resist pressure for parallel changes in the electoral system for general elections.

Instead the central government has taken steps, through restrictions on the spending and revenue-raising powers of local authorities, to restrict the discretion of local authorities in deciding on the quantities of local public services they provide. A particular aim of these restrictions has been to strengthen its control over public spending in general, but another has been to restrain the spending policies of what it has regarded as particularly high-spending local authorities and thereby to provide some protection for local taxpayers from the consequences of the decisions of their local councils. Some of the earlier measures imposed were perhaps not as effective as the government might have hoped,[8] but the effect of the various tax-rate capping measures applied in recent years has been to make it increasingly difficult for individual local authorities to spend more than their standard spending assessments (SSAs) which are meant to reflect the central government's view of what individual authorities need to spend to provide common service levels consistent with the central government's own public expenditure policies.[9] Moreover it has become apparent that, while these measures have been aimed at preventing 'overspending', there appears to have been a tendency for the expenditure of all authorities, whether they have historically been underspenders or overspenders relative to their SSA, to converge on their SSAs. The effects of these changes will be considered further in the next section, but one obvious consequence is that opportunities for individual voters to express a preference for more or less local public services with due regard for their implications for local tax levels, which is the basis of the fiscal federalism justification for local government, are disappearing. Indeed, given that the amount individual local authorities can spend on the provision of public services is largely determined by the formulae embodied in the SSA system, it is not clear that they reflect anybody's preferences.

Nevertheless, within the formula-driven total, local authorities have some freedom to allocate expenditure as they wish, subject to meeting certain centrally imposed statutory requirements. Local preferences could thus, in principle, be brought to bear in local elections on the way expenditure is distributed, particularly if different political parties propose different expenditure packages. However, such multidimensional choices might be difficult for individual voters to relate to, unless they had implications for something in which voters had a particular interest (for example the closure of a local library or school).[10] More plausibly, therefore, the emphasis of local party political debate might switch more to efficiency questions. This would be consistent to some extent with an 'agency' view of the role of local government, but other issues would still influence local choices and, in the absence of electoral reform, in many local authorities the competitive threat from potential alternative administrations would remain low.

Turning to the second question, the recent changes from a property-based local tax to a poll tax and the reversal back to a (differently constituted) property tax have been much debated, but from the point of view of this chapter the more significant changes have been the removal of the power of local government to levy taxes on local businesses and the replacement of central government grants varying with expenditure[11] by lump-sum grants. One consequence of these these measures is that, in aggregate terms at least, local voters now have to pay, through increased taxes, the full marginal cost of any expenditure above the SSA level. In principle, this should make them less willing to approve expenditure yielding low benefits in relation to costs and could thus contribute to an improvement in the allocative efficiency of local decisionmaking. However, there is no obvious incentive for local decisionmaking to take account of any external benefits from the expenditure. In addition, the fact that there are other constraints on the ability of local authorities to spend above their SSA level means that the precise relationship between local taxes and the marginal cost of local services is now of relatively little significance.

A provisional view, therefore, from the point of view of political decisionmaking is that it is not clear that the changes considered so far will do anything to improve allocative efficiency, but that they could have some, probably marginal, effect on productive efficiency.

6. THE IMPLICATIONS FOR BUREAUCRATIC BEHAVIOUR

In considering the third question identified in the previous section, relating more to potential bureaucratic 'failures', it is helpful to return to the model of bureaucratic behaviour outlined in Section 4. This model can also, as we shall see later, be used to shed further light on the effects of centrally imposed expenditure constraints on local government.

The measures to separate responsibility for production from that for procurement, which are the focus of our attention in this section, have taken several forms. The measure involving least change has been the devolution of managerial and financial responsibility to operating units. In terms of the model in Section 4, this means that the bureau is, to all intents and purposes, using the funds it receives from the elected body to buy the services it wishes to make available to the local community from a largely independent producer within the public sector. This change in the role of the bureau from producer to buyer is likely to make the bureau more interested in minimizing the cost of obtaining any given quantity of service. In terms of our model, it means that bureau managers have less responsibility for, and less interest in, the utility of the actual producers and would thus seek to reduce the latter's share of the 'fiscal residuum' appropriated in the form of productive inefficiency. For any given quantity of service, this would increase the funds available to finance productive inefficiency within the bureau itself, but with a utility function of traditional form this would reduce the marginal utility of productive inefficiency relative to the marginal utility of extra output. In terms of our diagrams, this would have the effect of making the bureaucrats' indifference curves steeper.

The effects of this can be seen by returning once more to Figure 9.1. If, in that diagram, the solid indifference curves can be taken to represent the bureau's utility function before devolution and the dashed lines the position after it, it can then be seen that the bureau's preferred position moves from B to B', involving more production of the local service and less discretionary expenditure. In other words, the prediction is for less productive inefficiency but more allocative efficiency. Given the fact that movements along the net benefits curve have no net effects on welfare, there would appear to be no overall net gains or losses to the community from this kind of devolution. On the supply side, bureau managers are better off,[12] by an amount depending on how successful they are in forcing producers to improve their productive efficiencies, but service producers are correspondingly worse off.

Bureau managers may be limited in their ability to enforce improvements in the productive efficiency of producers, particularly if the latter have some degree of monopoly power. But here the provisions for compulsory competitive tendering are relevant because clearly the more contestable the market for local services, the more difficult it would be for productively inefficient suppliers to survive. Moreover, a number of empirical studies have shown that productive efficiency gains have followed the introduction of competitive tendering.[13] In terms of Figure 9.1, any additional productive efficiency gains from this source will be reflected by a greater rotation of the bureau indifference curves in the vicinity of B and thus more substitution of allocative inefficiency for productive inefficiency. However, there are also two other possible effects which can be noted.

As part of the movement from B to B', the improvement in productive efficiency is also reflected in the downward shift of the operative total cost function from TC_1 to TC_2. TC_0, however, showing the relationship between costs and output when production is productively efficient will remain unchanged in the absence of any relevant technical change unless there is some consequent change in input prices. Now, in practice, competitive tendering has in a number of cases led to reduced labour costs because outside tenderers have not been bound by public sector wage agreements. This in turn has meant that workers in in-house organizations have also had to accept lower wages and conditions of service to have any chance of winning contracts. In terms of our diagrams this would be represented by a downward shift in TC_0. An additional consideration, however, is the fact that the substitution of market relationships between bureau managers and producers for administrative relationships will involve transactions costs for all parties, in that resources have to be devoted to seeking out market opportunities, formulating and monitoring contracts and the like. These transactions costs would have an offsetting effect on TC_0 in the diagrams.

Whether these additional transactions costs are sufficient to outweigh labour cost and other savings may vary from case to case. For the purposes of illustration, however, Figure 9.2 shows the case where there is a net reduction in costs shifting the total cost curve reflecting efficient production from TC_0 to the dashed curve $TC_{0'}$

With a reduction in total cost of producing any output, net benefits are correspondingly increased, shifting the net benefits curve to outwards to NB'. This allows bureau managers to increase allocative inefficiency or productive inefficiency or both, depending on their preferences. Figure 9.2, in which the bureau manager's preferred position is shown as moving from B' (corresponding to B' in Figure 9.1) to B'', illustrates a case where there is an increase in both.

Overall, however, in the situation illustrated there are again no resultant benefits to service users, because in our model all surplus benefits are expropriated by bureau managers. As already indicated, that is rather an extreme case and in practice for various reasons only a proportion of the surplus may be captured. Likewise some of the benefits of the reduced costs in Figure 9.2 might be passed on to users. However, even if they are, it need not represent an unambiguous improvement in community welfare. If labour costs fall, as a result of, for example, compulsory competitive tendering, and the gains are passed on to taxpayers, a substantial part of the gain to taxpayers is actually a transfer from suppliers of labour. The only real gain arises from any net benefits arising from increased output, which, on any plausible assumptions, are likely to be small in relation to the transfers involved. In contrast, transactions costs generally involve a real resource cost, in the sense that they involve the use of resources with alternative uses. In terms of the diagram, a small upward shift in the total cost curve as a result of transactions costs could be more than enough, when measured in crude consumer surplus terms, to outweigh the real gains from reduced labour costs. Of course, a redistribution of benefits from suppliers of labour to taxpayers may be considered a welfare improvement, at least by taxpayers. A redistribution to bureaucrats, however, might be considered less favourably.

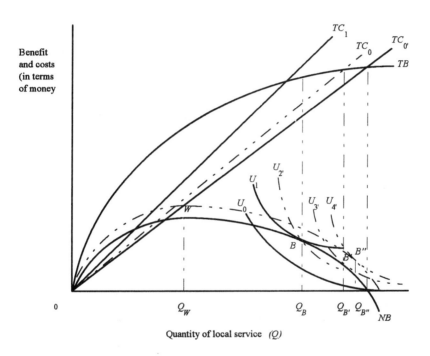

Figure 9.2 The case of the net reduction in costs of local services

Finally, turning again to the effects of expenditure restrictions, we can use our model to look at two particular aspects. The first is to consider the effect of the restrictions on overall local spending and the second the effect on individual local services. In both cases, the effect is to restrict political decision makers' demand for local services by limiting their ability to raise the finance for them. As far as the overall restriction on local spending is concerned, we can continue to use our basic diagram by considering a simplified situation in which local government supplies some homogeneous commodity, local services, the quantity of which is measured on the horizontal axis. In this situation, the effect of an expenditure ceiling is shown in Figure 9.3.

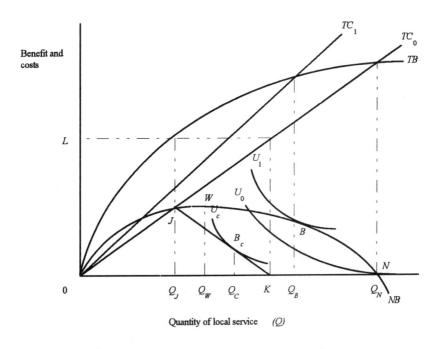

Figure 9.3   The effect of an expenditure ceiling on local bureaucrats

If the ceiling is set at L, the bureau's choice set is restricted to OJK,[14] where K represents the maximum output that can be financed by using the funds available for efficient production. If the constraint is binding, as in the case illustrated, it restricts the opportunity for bureau managers to enjoy the output of the service and discretionary expenditure. The case illustrated, where the new constrained optimum position is at B_c, shows a reduction in both output and discretionary expenditure compared with the original position at B, although there are other possibilities depending on preferences and the precise change in the choice set. The reduction in the output of local services suggested in the diagram implies a reduction in both allocative and productive inefficiency, but it would also be possible to have a situation in which there is more allocative inefficiency at B_c, if, as a result of the expenditure constraint, output is reduced sufficiently below the allocatively efficient level.

In a situation where total expenditure is restricted, but discretion is retained on its distribution between individual services, the effect of the overall budgetary contraint is to reduce the ability of the political decisionmakers to pay for individual services and thus to push their budget-constrained demand curve for any particular service to the left and the total benefit curve derived from it, reflecting their willingness to pay, downwards. The effect of this on the bureau's choice set is thus opposite to that illustrated in Figure 9.2, with the correspondingly opposite effects on the bureau's preferred position. Note, however, that the operative demand curve would no longer reflect the preferences of voters, even if it did before, and that again, there is still the possiblity that output is reduced below the allocatively efficient level. Subject to that proviso, however, our analysis suggests that expenditure constraints are more likely to be effective in dealing with bureaucratic failures than the kind of organizational changes favoured by the UK central government.

One further point can be made which is relevant to the analysis of any kind of expenditure constraint. Our rather simplified analysis ignores quality variables which could, in practice, be quite important in the sense that expenditure constraints will also reduce local authorities' willingness to pay for service quality.[15] Hence, it can be expected that they may also lead to some reduction in the quality of services offered, with, for example, dustbins emptied less frequently or increased class sizes in schools. It is here that another of the measures introduced by the government is relevant, the possibility of producing organizations 'opting out' of local control and obtaining funds from alternative public sources. This is is an option which is currently available to schools in the UK and one which is being actively promoted by the central government. This possibility imposes a constraint on local authorities' ability to cut expenditure in this particular area, because obviously the less generous local funding is, relative to the alternative, the greater the attractions of opting out. One effect of this, therefore, is to intensify the effects of expenditure constraints on services where there are no alternative sources of funds.

7. CONCLUSIONS

This chapter has identified two particular sources of local government 'failure' from the point of view of providing an optimal amount of local public services in a productively efficient way. The first arises from the discretion those in office may have, to exercise preferences which are divergent from the users of the services. This kind of 'failure' is likely to arise in any political system, but, in some areas of the UK, the electoral system and traditional party loyalties combine to reduce the contestability of the market for local political power. The second arises from the need to organize the supply of services through bureaucratic organizations which may seek to take advantage of information asymmetries to exercise their own preferences. Again, such 'failures' can arise at any level of government but a particular aim of this chapter has been to consider whether the various changes affecting local government imposed by the UK central government in recent years are likely to have had the effect of reducing their impact.

In this context, it has been suggested that, while the constraints on local governments' ability to finance expenditure above centrally prescribed limits might help to constrain the activities of any individual authorities with a tendency to oversupply local services relative to the preferences of local elections, it is doubtful whether the limits themselves, which are largely determined by SSA formulae, represent the preferences of any particular group. Hence the most that can be said about the effect of these measures on the allocative efficiency of local political decisionmaking is that it is indeterminate. They could, however, provide a stronger incentive for those in power to seek improvements in productive efficiency, partly because, with expenditure ceilings, that may be seen as the only way of financing an increase in local services, but also because, with reduced discretion on how much local authorities can spend, questions of efficiency are likely to become relatively more prominent in the local political agenda.

The 'failures' arising from bureaucratic provision were analysed using an explicit model in which bureau managers were assumed to maximize their utility subject to the constraints imposed by the demand for local services by political decisionmakers. A strong prediction of the particular model used was that separating the production of local services from the responsibility for procuring them would do little by itself to improve the overall efficiency of the system, although it should lead to improvements in productive efficiency. This was essentially because the model suggests that restructuring of this nature is unlikely to reduce the opportunities of bureau managers to pursue their own objectives; in fact it could increase them. In contrast, spending restrictions on local authorities would have the effect of restricting the effective demand for local services by restricting the budgets available to political decisionmakers. This in turn would restrict the opportunities for bureau managers to pursue their own objectives and, therefore, could be instrumental in reducing allocative and/or productive inefficiency, the precise effect depending on the latter's utility function.

Of course, the model from which these conclusions are drawn is a highly simplified one, particularly with respect to the number of variables it considers. Moreover, its assumption, that bureau managers are able to extract all the available surplus, makes it very much a limiting case. Obviously, however, there is scope for further study of these issues using less simplified models. The results also pose some interesting empirical questions. A number of empirical studies have identified cost reductions from contracting out and competitive tendering for local services. Whether the benefits of these cost reductions have been passed on to local taxpayers or not (as predicted in our model) would also seem to be a possible topic for empirical investigation.

NOTES

1. Parallel changes are also being introduced into other areas of government in the UK
2. More recent discussion of the approach can be found in King (1984), Helm and Smith (1987) and Hughes and Smith (1991).
3. This particular aspect of decentralization was emphasized in Salmon (1987)
4. See, for example, Rees (1985), Laffont (1989).
5. This is the term he used, in Williamson (1963) and elsewhere, for the corresponding expenditure in his 'expense preference' models of managerial firms.
6. It is easy to show that with linear demand and cost functions the 'Niskanan' bureaucrat produces twice the efficient output (see for example Brown and Jackson, (1990), pp. 200–202).
7. See the appendix for proof.
8. There is an extensive literature on the effects of these measures but a useful summary can be found in Travers (1986).
9. For further details see the chapters by Smith and Chapman in this book.
10. More technically, it is also the case that the voting process would be less likely to yield a unique order of preference even when individual preferences are single-peaked.
11. The relationship between the grant and expenditure became an increasingly complex one in the 1980s as the central government tried to introduce disincentives to higher spending.
12. They are also likely to be better off even if they remain at B because the benefits of discretionary expenditure are shared between fewer people. This is reflected in the labelling of the indifference curves in Figure 9.1.
13. See, for example, Szymanski and Wilkins (1993) and the references cited.
14. JK is drawn as a straight line because, with the linear total cost curve, each unit of discretionary expenditure given up allows the same increase in Q.
15. The quality of service offered may also be an argument in the bureau manager's utility function, which would be a further complicating factor.

REFERENCES

Brown, C.V. and I. Jackson (1990), *'Public Sector Economics'*, 4th Edition, Oxford: Blackwell.

Dunleavy, P. (1991), *Democracy, Bureaucracy and Public Choice*, Harvester Wheatsheaf.

Helm, D. and S. Smith (1987), 'The assessment, decentralization and the economics of local government', *Oxford Review of Economic Policy*, **3** (2), 1–21.

Hughes, G. (1987), 'Fiscal federalism in the UK', *Oxford Review of Economic Policy*, **3** (2), 1–23.

King, D.N. (1984), *Fiscal Tiers: The Economics of Multi-Level Government*, London: George Allen & Unwin.

Laffont, J.J. (1989), *The Economics of Uncertainty and Information*, Cambridge, MA: MIT Press.

Migue, J.l. and G. Belanger (1974), 'Toward a general theory of managerial discretion', *Public Choice*, **12**, 27–47.

Niskanen, W.A. (1971), *Bureaucracy and Representative Government*, New York: Aldine-Atherton.

Oates, W.E. (1972), *Fiscal Federalism*, New York: Harcourt Brace Jovanovich.

Radner, R. (1986), 'The internal economy of large firms', *Economic Journal*, **96** (Supplement), 1–22.

Rees, R. (1985), 'The theory of principal and agent', *Bulletin of Economic Research*, Part 1, 3–26, Part 2, 77–95.

Salmon, P. (1987), 'The logic of pressure groups and the structure of the public sector' in *Villa Colombella: Papers on Federalism*, Regensburg, pp. 55–86.

Szymanski, S. and S. Wilkins (1993), 'Cheap rubbish? Competitive tendering and contracting out in refuse collection 1981–1988', *Fiscal Studies*, **14** (3), 109–30.

Tiebout, C.M. (1956), 'A pure theory of local government expenditures', *Journal of Political Economy*, **64** (5), 416–24.

Travers, T. (1986), 'An honourable draw? Local versus central government in the 1970s and 1980s', *Public Money*, June , 48–52.

Williamson, O.E. (1963), 'Managerial discretion and business behavior', *American Economic Review*, **53**, 1032–57.

APPENDIX 9A

In Figure 9A.1, D is the demand curve for some public service and MC_1 is the marginal cost curve when production is efficient. As indicated these curves need not be linear. The 'Niskanen' output is that at which the total benefits from the public service, measured by the area under the demand curve to the right of relevant output, is equal to total cost, represented by the corresponding area under the marginal cost curve. In Figure 9A.1, when marginal costs are represented by MC_1, it is at Q_N, where the area ABC is equal to the area CEF. With less efficient production, the marginal cost curve might be MC_2 lying above MC_1, and in that case the output at which total cost is equal to total benefit is Q_D where the area $AGL = GHK$.

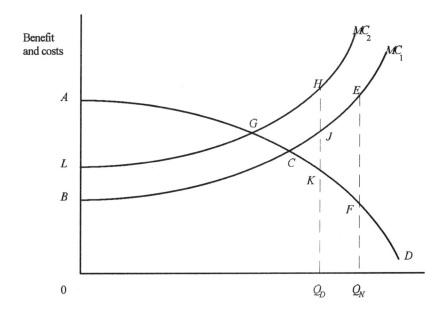

Figure 9A.1   Benefits, costs and demand for a public service

From Figure 9A.1, it should be clear that the area

$$ABC = AGL + BLGC,$$

while

$$CEF = GHK - GHJC + EFKJ.$$

Hence, since

$$ABC = CEF$$

$$AGL + BLGC = GHK - GHJC + EFKJ$$

and, since

$$AGL = GHK,$$

$$BLGC + GHJC = EFKJ.$$

The reduction in productive efficiency from the higher costs, represented by the left-hand side of this last equation is thus equal to the gain in allocative efficiency arising from the consequent reduction in output which is represented by the right-hand side.

10. Governance of Two National Health Services: Italy and the United Kingdom Compared

George France

1. INTRODUCTION

The British National Health Service (NHS) has been held up widely at the international level as a system which gives good value for money. 'Most observers acknowledge that the NHS generally, provides a high standard of care' (Le Grand 1993, p. 35); it is 'a successful institution' delivering a service relatively cheap to provide and administer (OECD 1992a, p. 121). Indeed it served as the model for the Italian national health service, the *Servizio Sanitario Nazionale* (SSN) created in 1978 (Ministero della Sanità 1979, pp. XVIII–XIX). The NHS came under criticism in the mid to late 1980s but it remained a highly popular and respected institution. The quasi-market reforms, proposed in the White Paper *Working for Patients* in 1989 and begun in 1990, were seen by their proponents as a way of improving an already good record, of getting even better value for money from the NHS. It has been quite a different story for the SSN. Under attack virtually since its creation, it has become increasingly unpopular and there is almost a consensus that the SSN has been providing poor value for money. The notoriety of the SSN is now international with the OECD describing it as 'a badly managed health care system' providing care of 'inadequate quality' (OECD 1992b, pp. 73, 86). The service is currently undergoing major reorganization on the basis of legislation introduced in 1992 and 1993.

We have, then, two national health services with apparently quite different fortunes. This chapter uses the British NHS as a reference model in an attempt to comprehend better why the 1978 design for the SSN ran into difficulty. This in turn may help in understanding whether the quasi-market reforms currently being introduced in Italy will improve the SSN's performance. The chapter focuses on the systems of governance of expenditure at the local level used by the two health services. 'Governance' includes the act of governing, the institutions, instruments and methods used for this and relations between governments and between government and citizens (OECD 1995). 'Governance capacity' refers to the performance of a national health service in attaining the three standard goals of a national health service: which are expenditure control, value for money and equity (McLachlan and Maynard 1982, p. 519).

The chapter begins by looking at some data on the governance capacity demonstrated by the two health services. It then considers the governance systems of the NHS and SSN in terms of three key aspects: vertical integration of the functions of finance and production of health-care; distribution of discretionary power among different levels of the health-care government; and market power of the national health service. This is followed by an examination of selected aspects of the reform of the SSN for their implications for the governance capacity of the service.

2. GOVERNANCE CAPACITY

2.1. Expenditure Control

In 1989 Italian per capita expenditure on health was greater than that of the UK ($1.050 in GDP purchasing power parities compared with $836). Italy was spending broadly what would have been expected given its per capita income; the UK spent considerably less than would have been predicted (Schieber et al. 1991, pp. 24, 26). Both countries can be considered to have held total public health spending relatively well under control. In 1980, public health expenditure in the UK was 5.2 per cent of GDP and was at broadly the same level in 1990. Italy's expenditure rose from 5.6 to 5.8 per cent over the same period and in the judgement of the OECD 'public health spending has grown more moderately than in other countries'. Between 1980 and 1990, the average annual rate of growth of real public health expenditure by persons covered relative to real GDP per capita was –1.1 per cent for the UK and –0.4 per cent for Italy (OECD 1992b, pp. 76–7). Using other measures, real public spending on health in the UK actually rose, the extent depending on the deflator used and on the category of care (Mayston 1990, Bloor and Maynard 1993).[1] The NHS, then, has a better record for expenditure containment but, all things considered, the SSN seems to have done reasonably well. Private health expenditure grew more rapidly over the 1980s in Italy as compared with most other major countries. Nevertheless, total health expenditure was judged 'not excessive' relative to other OECD countries at the beginning of the 1990s (OECD 1992b, p. 76).

2.2. Value for Money

The NHS and the SSN get quite different marks for how they have used resources. Blanket judgements are always suspect, however. Value for money is about the effectiveness, efficiency and economy with which resources are used. The problem with assessing the effectiveness of health services is that we can say very little that is definite about the role of health care in influencing health states or about the quality of care. Judged by standard health indicators like life expectancy and infant mortality, the NHS and the SSN seem to have performed similarly and to have quite adequate records compared with other countries (cf. Table 10.1). However, these indicators are influenced by a host of other factors. Perinatal mortality (a component of the avoidable mortality measure of the adequacy of health services) is instead considerably higher for Italy than for the UK. Italy, like other Western countries, has over time registered a substantial decline in avoidable deaths, but has always been, and still is, higher for many causes of avoidable death than the other countries, Britain included (Holland (ed.) 1988, CERFE 1992, p. 388). Much of the care provided by health services in any country is of unproven clinical effectiveness (Banta 1990; Maynard 1991) and even less is known about the cost effectiveness of alternative procedures (Drummond 1987). What is more, the information that we do possess on clinical and cost effectiveness seems to have a limited impact on doctors' decisions (Institute of Medicine 1985) or health policy (Drummond 1987).

It has been suggested that British doctors are more demanding regarding clinical effectiveness and more sensitive to cost considerations than, for example, their American counterparts (Jennett 1986, p. 117, Miller and Miller 1987) and, at least judging by the enthusiasm with which they adopt new medical technologies,[2] Italian doctors seem more similar to the latter.

The UK seems to be one of the countries where in recent years government has been active in sponsoring medical technology evaluation (Drummond 1992). By contrast, the Italian Ministry of Health has shown virtually no concrete interest in financing evaluative research (France 1994a).

A ten-country study of levels of satisfaction of patients with their health services conducted in the late 1980s found Britons and Italians among the least satisfied (Blendon et al. 1990), but a 1993 study of the European Union countries ranks Britons among the most satisfied with the quality of care and Italians among the least satisfied (Ferrera 1993)[3]. A 1992 survey of clinical and non-clinical quality of health services in Italy found quite large geographical disparities between north and south for technical (clinical) quality of hospital care; much greater differences were found for the treatment of patients by staff, comfort, food and hotel services in general. Interregional differences existed also for ambulatory care, but these were less marked (CERFE 1992). An indirect indicator of quality is nursing support: in 1987 there were 0.69 nurses per occupied bed in the NHS and 0.60 in the SSN (OECD 1990, p. 181). A common criticism of both national health services is lengthy waiting lists, but Italians seem to be better off here than Britons.[4] As we shall see, they also have much greater freedom in choosing providers.

Table 10.1   Selected indicators of health outcomes [1] and technical efficiency in health-care provision [2]

	UK	Italy	OECD
Infant mortality (per 1,000 live births)	9.0	9.1	8.2 [3]
Perinatal mortality (per 1,000 live births and late foetal deaths)	9.1	12.3	9.0 [3]
Life expectancy at birth for males (years)	72.4	72.7	72.1
Life expectancy at birth for females (years)	78.1	79.4	78.5
Life expectancy at 80 years for males (years)	6.4	6.2	6.3
Life expectancy at 80 years for females (years)	8.1	7.7	7.8
Average length of stay (days)			
– appendectomy	7.3	8.6	7.3
– normal delivery	3.5	6.3	5.1
Bed turnover [4]	36.8	23.7	24.7
Bed occupancy rate [5]	80.6	68.4	80.9

Notes:
1.   Schieber et al., 1991, p. 36, for 1988.
2.   OECD, 1992b, p. 88, end of 1980's.
3.   Excluding Turkey.
4.   Average number of cases treated per hospital bed.
5.   As percentage of available beds.

The NHS seems unambiguously superior as regards economy and technical efficiency, for example as judged by average length of hospital stay, intensity of utilization of beds and bed occupancy rates (cf. Table 10.1). According to the OECD (1992b, p. 89), administration costs for the SSN as a proportion of total public spending on health are more than double those for the NHS.[5] Other information reinforces this impression of a technically inefficient and wasteful SSN: very slow payment of suppliers' invoices (ISIS 1992), thereby generating extra costs for interest payments, and widespread irregular practices combined with inadequate or non-existent internal and external performance auditing systems (Ministero del Tesoro and Ministero della Sanità 1994, pp. 103–19). There is considerable geographical variation for these indicators with a clearcut tendency for the situation to worsen as we move from north to south. Wide geographical differences in technical efficiency are also reported in the UK, for example for average length of hospital stay and unit costs (Smee and Parsonage 1990). However, the history of the NHS in the 1980s has been characterized by ever intensifying activity aimed at increasing efficiency and this has produced results (Mayston 1990 pp. 75–7).

Also, then, for value for money the NHS seems overall to come out well ahead of the SSN. But this is not so for all indicators, and in any case the existence of wide geographical differences cautions against sweeping generalizations about the SSN.

2.3. Equity

It is really a case of the cupboard being almost bare when we get to looking for data to compare the two health services for equity. A definition of equity in health care sponsored by WHO is 'equal access to available care for equal need; equal utilization for equal need; equal quality of care for all' (Whitehead 1990, p. 11). It is not possible, however, to compare directly the UK and Italy on this basis.

Both national health services provide universal access to care which is supposed to be allocated on the basis of need. A cross-country study of equity (Wagstaff et al. 1989) found that both the UK and Italy exhibited greater inequality in the finance of health care compared with, for example, Holland, but the UK was less unequal than Italy; instead the UK was more unequal than Italy for the distribution of chronic ill-health across socioeconomic classes. Substantial class differences in ill-health still exist in Italy, however (Vicarelli 1993). Another study found that the allocation of NHS resources seemed close to meeting the criterion of 'equal treatment for equal need' and that the distribution of the financial burden was broadly in proportion to income (O'Donnell et al. 1993). Paci and Wagstaff (1993) found that overall the financing of the SSN was regressive, but another study places this conclusion in doubt (Belli 1993). The Paci and Wagstaff research was unable to reach any definite conclusions regarding the equity of health-care delivery but was inclined to the view that it was regressive; however, Mapelli (1994) suggests that the SSN may in fact be achieving its goal of meeting the needs of more disadvantaged households. In both countries there has been a reduction over time in regional inequalities in per capita health expenditure (Mapelli 1992, Mayston 1990), but considerable interregional differences have persisted in Italy (Garattini 1992). Substantial geographical differences are also found for availability of services, including expensive medical equipment (Agenzia Sanitaria Italiana 1994), with substantial flows of patients from southern to central and northern regions (Ministero della Sanità 1993).[6] Large geographical differences are recorded for waiting lists in the UK. These increased for the UK as a whole by almost 10 per cent between 1981 and 1988 with the increase being distributed rather unevenly geographically (Posnett 1993, p. 294). We saw above that there are considerable interregional differences in the quality of care in Italy.

Cross-country comparisons in a complex area like health care are difficult and frequently the safest course of action is to be inconclusive. This said, the collage of information considered above suggests that the NHS has demonstrated superior capacity in governance as compared with the SSN. This is particularly so for the value for money objective. The NHS has also done a better job in containing expenditure. With equity, the impression is that a patient's place of residence is less important in the UK than in Italy in determining the access he or she enjoys to care of standard quality.

3. THE BRITISH NATIONAL HEALTH SERVICE BEFORE THE REFORM

The NHS prior to the reforms introduced in 1990 had a number of characteristics which, taken together, may have given it a relatively strong capacity for governance of expenditure at the local level. The health service organization was highly integrated; discretionary power was concentrated at the central government level; and the NHS had strong monopoly and monopsony power.

3.1. Vertical Integration of Organization and Government

In industrial terms, the NHS was highly integrated in a vertical sense with a fusion of the finance and production functions. Excluding GPs, pharmacists and some other categories of doctors, virtually all health care financed by the SSN was produced in its own facilities operated by its own personnel. Vertical integration means that the purchaser (financer) of goods and services has the possibility to control directly the production behaviour of its suppliers: they are 'internal'. The degree to, and manner in which suppliers are integrated with financers (and regulators) of health care can have important consequences for conduct and performance (Evans 1981). The 'public integrated' model, of which the NHS was almost a polar case, contrasts with the 'public contract' and 'public reimbursement' models (OECD 1992a) where there is a clear split between the finance and the production roles and where providers are therefore 'external'.

By its nature, much of health care is produced and delivered locally, which means that detailed governance of the provision of this service must also be local. This creates a potential problem for a centrally funded NHS since it means that there is in practice a separation between the exercise of the finance function, that is the raising of revenues and their transfer to the local level, and the exercise of the production function. The benefits promised by vertical integration of a health-care organization are placed at risk. For these benefits to be actually obtained, the governance system must give the level of government which is responsible for raising the revenues to finance the service the power to control lower-level governments.

In the case of the NHS before the reform, a strong vertical line of control extended directly from the Department of Health, through the Regional Health Authority (RHA) and District Health Authority (DHA), down to the individual providers (hospitals and community health services). The governing bodies of the two tiers of authority were non-elected, with the chairman nominated by the Secretary of State for Health at his or her pleasure. Subcentral governments in health care in the UK, therefore, were little more than peripheral arms of the central government, delegated substantial decisionmaking autonomy but only because it suited the centre to do so. They were expected to apply centrally determined spending limits and policy directives (for example performances indicators, general management, the resource management initiative, cost improvement programmes, compulsory tendering) with very limited scope for discretion.

When decentralized decisionmaking was considered unnecessary or inopportune, the Department of Health used other methods, such as direct funding of prescribed drugs or the finance and administration of GP contracts through the Family Practitioner Committees which were territorially and financially completely separate from the DHAs. Elected local authorities right from the start had a limited role in the NHS and this diminished over time.[7]

3.2. Voluntary Integration of Doctors

In a formal sense, the vertical integration of the NHS was incomplete. GPs worked on a contractual rather than an employee basis, part of the compromise to get the NHS legislation approved in 1948. In the terminology used in this chapter, they were external providers posing potential control problems for the finance branch of the NHS. Moreover, while hospital doctors were employees they were only partially integrated in that they enjoyed strong 'property rights' over the use of health resources including, in the case of consultants, considerable freedom in setting the levels of their own work effort.[8] However, doctors were integrated 'informally' into the NHS. It is suggested (Day and Klein 1991 p. 44) that an 'implicit, unspoken concordat' existed between government and doctors whereby doctors were granted 'almost total clinical freedom' (Klein 1984, p. 87) in exchange for their recognition of the right by central government to fix the level of global health-care spending. There was a division of power: micro-allocation to doctors and macro-allocation to central government.

Quite apart from legitimizing its macro-allocative power, the pact suited central government, for doctors were not only prepared to use their micro-allocative power responsibly but were willing to administer the rationing process made necessary by the fact that supply was expenditure capped while health care was a free good at the point of consumption.[9] This reduced the political costs for central government of applying a tight budget constraint to the NHS.

3.3. Monopoly and Monopsony Power

A necessary condition for rationing to be possible – apart from the collaboration of doctors – is a public monopoly over health-care provision. This gives a national health service freedom to decide which services to provide or not to provide, where to provide them and in what volume. A public monopoly is possible even where there is a private health sector, but patients, if they wish to 'exit', must have to do so completely and pay out of their own pockets or with private health insurance.

The private health sector in the UK is relatively small and accounted for about 5 per cent of total health expenditure in 1987 with only 300 GPs in purely private practice (Rayner 1987 pp. 198, 201). Facilities were highly concentrated geographically and private health insurance was also concentrated geographically and directly correlated with socioeconomic class (Rayner 1986, pp. 16–17).[10] The private sector was important for a number of specialities – performing an estimated 25 per cent of all hip replacements and 20 per cent of heart disease surgery around 1988 (Bayliss 1988, p. 1458) – but patients had to 'exit' completely from the public service. The NHS was a largely closed market for the private sector.[11] This meant that the NHS providers did not have to compete with the private sector (for example in terms of the kind of clinical services available) in order to hold on to NHS patients.

The NHS also had potentially strong monopsony power over prices of factors (prescribed drugs, medical equipment and supplies, NHS staff and GPs, dentists and other contracted providers). Also here, the fact of a tight vertical line of control meant that this monopsony power was actually exploited by the Department of Health and the lower levels of the NHS government (Robinson 1988; Mayston 1990).

3.4. The Move to Reform

Towards the late 1980s, the government was facing mounting criticism from the public, the medical profession, NHS administrators and the parliamentary opposition for the supposedly parlous state of the NHS. Hospitals were cutting services and running deficits and representatives of the medical colleges were predicting 'imminent breakdown' (Griggs 1991, p. 421). The notion that the NHS was 'underfunded' had extensive support, but this was contested by the government which was supported in this view from health economists not noted for being tender with government health policy (Barr et al. 1988, Parkin 1989, Bevan 1989a, 1989b). Substantial differences in operating costs among facilities, already noted, and large small-area variations in medical practice (McPherson 1990; Smee and Parsonage 1990) suggested that what was needed was not more funds but changes in incentive systems to promote better utilization of resources. GPs were singled out for criticism by government for not taking adequate account of the expenditure implications of their prescribing decisions; their 'property rights' embodied in strong clinical freedom were, that is, being placed in question.

Neo-institutional economics would describe the NHS before the reform as a contractual form characterized by a high degree of vertical integration aimed at reducing the transaction costs associated with exchange ('external' transaction costs). However, the process of vertical integration is itself not costless. The literature is vague (cf., for example, Williamson, 1985) on 'internal' transaction costs associated with vertical integration. Over and above supervision, management and coordination costs, they can be considered to include the costs associated with the exercise of decisionmaking power which accompanies an increase in the size of an organization with centralized authority. They also include the costs stemming from so-called 'inappropriate' decisions aimed at self-aggrandizement of the decisionmakers. Finally, there are 'influence costs', that is costs caused, for example, by employees succeeding in inducing decisionmakers to take actions to their, the employees, advantage and the inefficiencies which result (Milgrom and Roberts 1990). The position of the advocates of NHS reform was not cast explicitly in terms of reducing internal transaction costs or of seeking a better balance between internal and external transaction costs, but the government's criticisms of the NHS could perhaps be interpreted in these terms (Bariletti and France 1994). A high degree of vertical integration was now being seen as a problem and no longer as a virtue.

4. THE ITALIAN SSN BEFORE THE REFORM

In the debate leading up to the reform of the Italian health-care system in 1978, the principal reference model was the British NHS. In fact Italy abandoned the continental model of health funds and opted for a national health service providing universal and comprehensive care free at the point of consumption and financed publicly and centrally from compulsory contributions and general taxation.[12] However, the similarity between the two national health services ended here. The SSN prior to the 1992 reforms differed quite considerably from the NHS in the degree to which it was vertically integrated, the power of the centre over lower levels of government and the extent of its monopoly and monopsony power and its capacity to exploit this.

4.1. Mix of Integration and Contract

The Italian public health care system has been highly integrated, but to a lesser degree than the NHS. In 1991, 20 per cent of total public current expenditure went to finance services supplied by 'external' providers, almost always on contract. The degree of integration varied considerably according to the sector: 77 per cent of all inpatient days financed by the SSN were provided in its own hospitals staffed by salaried personnel, but it owned less than a third of the facilities it used to provide ambulatory specialist and diagnostic care (Ministero della Sanità 1993) while the doctors staffing SSN ambulatory clinics have worked on contract. Also GPs and paediatricians working for the SSN have done so on a contractual basis. There have been considerable interregional differences in the degree of vertical integration of the service. In 1990, 53 per cent of all ambulatory facilities used by the SSN in the north-western regions were contracted compared with 80 per cent in the southern regions. In the central region of Lazio, 39 per cent of all patients' days financed by the SSN were delivered in contracted for-profit hospitals compared with 6.5 per cent in the north-eastern region of Veneto (Ministero della Sanità 1992).

There are costs and benefits associated with both integration and contract. We saw that, as an organization, the SSN seems to have been X-inefficient with high administrative costs and wasteful use of staff and capital. In addition, there seems to have been a problem of abuse of discretionary decisionmaking power, for example irregular hiring of staff and fraud and corruption. There were also influence costs (irregular promotion and payment of overtime and performance bonuses, failure to punish absenteeism) (Ministero del Tesoro and Ministero della Sanità 1994, pp. 109–19, Corte dei Conti 1994). Finally, collusion between SSN managers and staff, common to all large organizations with strong trade unions like the SSN, contributed to the creation of formal and informal property rights for the staff regarding their control over the amount and quality of effort they supplied. Doctors and non-medical employees have tended to have an important say in decisions on their mobility within and between facilities. Senior hospital doctors have had very strong property rights – *vis-à-vis* non-clinical managers – over how their own labour is used and over the management of human and physical capital employed within their departments. The duties and obligations of doctors have tended to be ill-defined and/or poorly enforced (for example, rules governing private practice by public doctors). All this suggests that the SSN, because of weak control over its 'internal' providers, has been obtaining a lower benefit than might have been expected from what is, notwithstanding its extended use of contract, still a high degree of vertical integration.

The fact that the SSN has made quite ample use of the market to meet its needs for health-care services, particularly in some regions, suggests that it also incurred quite substantial external transaction costs. These costs are relatively simple to list but difficult to quantify. They refer to the administration of contracts for 80,000 doctors, 800 independent hospitals, over 9,000 ambulatory specialist and diagnostic facilities and 180 dialysis centres. More specifically, they are associated with drawing up contracts, billing and paying services provided and monitoring and enforcement of respect for contractual conditions. In the first instance, they are borne by both the SSN and providers but in the end mainly fall on the SSN.[13]

The administrative cost of administering GP contracts may have been low given that GP remuneration is largely capitation based, but substantial for contracts with providers reimbursed on a fee for service basis. The costs associated with drawing up contracts and monitoring respect for their conditions were perhaps lower than might be expected, because of the adoption of standardized contracts for specific categories of suppliers generally with uniform tariffs and use of extremely simple contracts and because the regions and *unità sanitarie locali* (USLs) apparently did very little monitoring of their external suppliers. It is not clear if this was deliberate policy to economize on external transaction costs, but it probably means that the SSN lost some of the benefits supposedly associated with contracting, in particular that of encouraging providers to pay maximum attention to questions of cost and quality.[14] Elementary contracts are, by definition, incomplete contracts which, when there is little monitoring or regulation, leave ample scope for opportunistic behaviour by suppliers. This seems to have happened.[15]

Unlike in the UK, the power of central government to set overall limits on health spending seems not to have been accepted by Italian doctors, who nevertheless have managed to preserve a high degree of clinical autonomy. As a whole, doctors, and in particular GPs, have declined to get involved in the rationing process and a logical corollary to this is that the medical profession as a whole has shown no great enthusiasm for even the mildest schemes of peer review of the prescription and referral behaviour of individual doctors.

4.2. A Weak Vertical Line of Control

This combination of possibly high internal and external transaction costs, that is, a failure to exploit the benefits and minimize the limits of integration and contract, may in part reflect the weak vertical line of control from the centre (The Treasury and Ministry of Health) down to the lower levels of government in the health sector.

The Italian Constitution provides for a three-tier system of subcentral government: regions, provinces and local authorities (communes). The regions enjoy considerable independence in matters of internal administration and organization. They also have legislative power for the areas of responsibility assigned to them under the Constitution. The most important area for the regions is health care, which accounts for well over half their total expenditure. Law 833 of 1978, which set up the SSN, gave central government responsibility for deciding how much of public resources should be dedicated to health-care, for allocating this among the regions and for national health planning (specifying national health care goals and priorities and setting minimum levels to be guaranteed throughout the country. The regions were to plan and coordinate health services within their territory and to decide how funding was to be allocated to the third tier of government in health, the *unità sanitaria locale* (USL). The USL was a new single-purpose agency with the task of delivering health care at the local level. Law 833 granted a limited direct role to the communes.

The arrangements adopted for financing the reorganized health service were broadly the same as those being used at that time to finance other activities of subcentral governments, that is mainly central grants. The burden for finding the revenues to finance the service therefore fell almost entirely on the state. However, quite apart from the fact of decentralization of power contained in the Constitution, the peculiarly local character of health-care delivery referred to earlier meant that substantial power regarding spending necessarily rested with the regions and in particular with the USLs. This skewed distribution of revenue raising and spending powers might not have mattered that much, had resources available to the sector been more plentiful. Instead, from its very birth the SSN has had to operate under a tight budget constraint. And right from the start the state has had difficulty imposing its authority to set overall spending levels for the SSN.[16] The regions were required by law to cover the deficits run up by their USLs but this remained a dead letter, lacking as they did independent revenue sources.

Central government and the regions were in constant disagreement over the adequacy of central grants for health. The regions accused central government of deliberately underfunding the service and there was some truth in this (for example, when calculating expenditure needs, the Treasury and Ministry of Health did not always make full allowance for inflation or for new remuneration levels already negotiated with staff and providers but still to become executive (Ministero del Tesoro and Ministero della Sanità 1994, p. 7)). The central authorities held instead that the regions were making insufficient efforts to make the USLs contain their expenditure and improve their efficiency, and indeed the regions did tend to concentrate a great deal of their energies on lobbying for more funds from the centre. The administrative apparatuses of some regions were probably not up to adequately controlling their USLs[17] which, by intention or default, enjoyed ample leeway in how they used resources. This may have had quite negative implications for efficiency and, at times, quality of care. Regional governments have tended, like national governments, to be relatively unstable and weak. However, the failure of regions to keep the USLs under tight control was almost certainly also due to the fact that they did not have to find the moneys to finance the deficits of the USLs and could react to criticisms of poor service quality by blaming the state's parsimony.

Inevitably the outcome of the conflict between the state and regions was to hinge on who got control of the USL. In an attempt to 'manage' the budget constraint so as to minimize the tradeoff between expenditure control and efficiency and quality, the Ministry of Health, rather like the British Department of Health, tried to impose measures to improve the performance of the USLs. These concerned, for example, standards for staffing and for the utilization of health-care facilities, including expensive medical equipment and requirements for setting up statistical systems and for internal and external auditing. However, the regions jealously protected their sovereignty and indeed tried wherever possible to extend it. They frequently took their case to the Constitutional Court and health jurisprudence accumulated since 1978 has established that the USLs are the creatures of the regions.

Incapacity to exert any significant influence on how health resources were utilized induced the central authorities to rely on crude macro tools such as mandatory across-the-board reductions in the hospital bed stock, freezes on staff hiring, holding down both remuneration levels of employees and contracted providers and the prices of prescribable pharmaceuticals and, of course, deliberate underfunding. The state and the regions can perhaps be thought to have engaged in an informal bargaining process to determine final funding levels: the state set ceilings which it knew could not be respected; the regions deliberately overstated the spending needs of the USLs, and in any case allowed these to run up deficits in the knowledge that the Treasury would in the end provide additional funding. However, the regions and USLs had to work in a situation of cash illiquidity and extreme uncertainty regarding final funding levels and this probably meant that less was spent than would otherwise have been the case (France 1986). Perennial intergovernmental conflict and uncertainty regarding funding levels must certainly have had deleterious effects on micro-management of resources, exacerbating the tradeoff between expenditure control and value for money goals: intensified efforts to contain costs generated lower efficiency. The measures adopted by the centre to contain global expenditure were deleterious for maximization of performance in that they probably encouraged those administering the USLs and facilities to concentrate on day-to-day 'crisis management' instead of developing medium-term strategies aimed at squeezing more services out of the scarce resources available.

4.3 Monopoly and Monopsony Power and Its Use in the SSN

We saw that the NHS enjoyed a virtual monopoly in the delivery of publicly financed health care and the private sector in the UK was small. In contrast, in Italy the SSN has no monopoly over the delivery of publicly financed care and the private sector holds a substantial share of the overall health care market. Summing the revenues from the sale of health-care to the SSN and those coming from private patients, the private sector accounted in 1991 for between 35 and 40 per cent of total national expenditure on health care.[18]

During the lengthy political debate leading up to the 1978 reform, strong support was expressed for virtually complete vertical integration of health care (McCarthy 1992, pp. 77–8); only a public monopoly would ensure adequate health planning and expenditure control. However, the right to free enterprise contained in the Constitution prevented forced absorption of private health providers. As a result, the SSN owned insufficient capacity to meet total demand for care and had no choice but to contract with private for-profit hospitals and ambulatory facilities. Moreoever, major concessions had to be made to the medical and hospital lobbies in order to obtain parliamentary approval of the reform bill: contractual status, rather than direct management by the USL, for university and research hospitals; contractual, rather than employee status, for all except public hospital doctors and the right for the last to practice privately; freedom of choice of provider by patients and hence pluralism of provision.

According to Law 833 and government policy, the contracted for-profit sector was supposed to complement and integrate with the public sector (Quaranta 1985, Ch. 7). Since competition between private and public providers for SSN patients was not envisaged, mechanisms set up to regulate the public–private relationship took little account of this possibility. However, what happened in practice depended, at least in part, on the clinical 'product' involved (Repetto et al. 1994). The main arena for competition between public and private providers for SSN patients seems to have been base and middle level elective surgery, gynaecology and obstetrics and orthopaedics. The private sector until relatively recently competed by offering superior hotel amenities and shorter waiting times, but for some specialties competition seems to have become increasingly technology-based.

Competition has been made easier by the fact that patients enjoy wide freedom of choice of doctor or facility. With a GP prescription in hand, they can, at least in theory, choose between: publicly owned and operated facilities, contracted non-profit providers (for example, university teaching hospitals, research hospitals, ecclesiastical hospitals), contracted for-profit providers and, under certain circumstances, private providers without a SSN contract and foreign facilities. The boundaries of patient choice have been extended since 1978, pushed out by decisions of the Constitutional Court based on a liberal interpretation of article 32 of the Constitution which grants citizens a vaguely expressed right to health[19] and political concessions to the strong aversion of patients and doctors to waiting lists (France 1988, 1989).[20] In practice, there has been less freedom of choice than is allowed by law because of geographical variations in the public–private mix, and since independent hospitals cover a much smaller share of total supply in absolute terms and in general offer a narrower range of medical specialties than public hospitals. Patients seemed ready to exercise the freedom of choice available to them, with approximately 600,000 patients crossing regional frontiers for hospital care in 1991, 6.3 per cent of all hospital admissions (Ministero della Sanità 1993, p. 182) and an estimated 25,000 patients using medical facilities in other European Union countries in 1987 (Association Internationale de la Mutualité 1991, p. 142).[21]

The SSN has therefore had greater difficulty than the NHS in using waiting lists for rationing and hence in limiting availability of costly medical procedures, in many cases not fully tested for clinical and cost effectiveness. Private providers have every incentive to encourage SSN patients to 'exit' from the public sector by offering medical services which they cannot obtain at all or not within a 'reasonable' (the term used in the legislation) time from public providers. Private providers seem to have led the process of diffusion of advanced medical technologies like CT and MR scanners, ultrasonics and lithotripters (cf., for example, Dirindin and Vanara 1992, Vanara 1992). This has tended to frustrate attempts by central government and regions to rationalize the acquisition and utilization of medical technologies in the SSN. New technologies initially prevented by planning norms and budget constraints from entering the SSN directly by the public 'front door' eventually sneak in via the private 'side window' as the SSN comes under increasing pressure – including from its own doctors – to provide such services directly (France 1989).

Instead, the SSN has had substantial potential monopsony power. It is by far the greatest employer of health personnel and purchaser of pharmaceuticals, medical supplies and medical equipment. Frequently, USLs are the major single buyer of goods and services in their territory. The state has been prepared to wield this power in salary negotiations with medical and non-medical staff trade unions and with the organizations representing the GPs. It has also used it to keep average pharmaceutical prices among the lowest in Europe (OECD 1992b, p. 82). At the subcentral level, some regions have been involved in bulk purchasing of pharmaceuticals for hospitals, medical equipment and supplies. However, for the reasons already suggested, the regions and USLs have had a limited incentive in using their monopsony power to extract favourable conditions from suppliers[22] and the state has been able to do very little about it.

5. USE OF NON-ELECTED SINGLE-PURPOSE BODIES

One similarity between the two governance systems was that they created non-elected single-purpose agencies for the delivery of care at the local level instead of using existing elected local authorities. While economists may differ on the degree of publicness characterizing the good 'health care', most – at least in Europe – accept that it is a merit good, justifying some form of public financing. Some form of public intervention is also warranted by society's desire to guarantee access to minimum or uniform levels of care (albeit vaguely defined) to all citizens irrespective of income or geographical location. Standard public finance theory suggests that the local authority is not the appropriate level of government to pursue this distributional goal.

Moreover, the benefit principle is not considered appropriate for financing health care while the ability to pay principle is applicable only at a higher level of government because of the need to pool health risks. Finally, scale considerations may suggest that the 'right-sized' territory for the delivery of health care does not always coincide with existing local authority boundaries[23]

Young (1988, p. 26) observes that acceptance of multipurpose authorities implies granting discretion regarding tradeoffs – in response to local needs and concerns – both between alternative modes and levels of provision within a service area or between service areas. Refusal by the state to accept this means that the interest involved is considered too important to permit discretion. Health care in fact seems to have been seen as different from, for example, street lighting or garbage collection in that it is considered inappropriate for levels of provision to be decided through the local political process. Health care is, or should be, consumed only when necessary and, because of information asymmetry, decisions on what and how much care should be consumed are mainly delegated to doctors as agents of patients. In addition, the health-care competence consumes such a volume of resources that it would tend to dwarf the other activities of multi-purpose authorities.

In the UK, doctors have apparently always been strongly opposed to significant local authority involvement in the NHS (Klein 1989, p. 187); this hostility pre-dates the creation of the NHS. In contrast, in Italy an attempt was made for a number of years to fuse the health management function with that of participatory democracy by having the members of the governing bodies of the USLs nominated by the local authorities. Intended to represent and promote the interests of patients, these bodies in many USLs quickly became machines for dispensing political patronage, vote gathering and party financing. Members tended to be nominated for their party affiliation rather than for their technical competence; this made for a highly politicized and improvized decisionmaking process, mortifying and demoralizing medical, administrative and technical staff. Criticism of these arrangements mounted and led to their modification in 1986. Executive power moved to bodies composed of senior administrators and doctors. In 1991, the post of USL director-general was created, endowed with major powers and appointed by the region[24]. These changes have been paralleled by the use of new mechanisms to safeguard patient interests[25].

However, an important difference remains between the two systems. In the NHS, the non-elected single-purpose DHA responded to the RHA which was also a non-elected single-purpose body under the direct control of the Department of Health. In contrast, in Italy the USL was responsible to the region, an elected authority with wide discretionary power. The UK arrangements were internally more consistent compared to those in Italy which broke the accountability chain between centre and periphery and as a result created a problem of incompatability among the three goals which the SSN was supposed to be pursuing.

6. REFORM OF SSN

To summarize, a series of indicators suggest more than marginal differences in the performance of the UK and Italian national health services in the pre-reform period. Judged in terms of key characteristics, the systems of governance of the two services are also quite dissimilar. Those of the NHS appear internally more consistent; the key features in a sense mutually reinforce each other. It seems reasonable to suppose that the SSN's difficulties in controlling its internal and external suppliers and its lack of monopoly power have adversely affected its performance. It also seems plausible to conclude that the diffusion of discretionary power in the government of health care in Italy has crucially affected the service's governance capacity with respect to expenditure containment, value for money and equity.

Would things have been different had the regions been more cooperative and/or had the centre had more power to intervene directly to control the USLs? The state in Italy has not got a good reputation for delivering quality services efficiently to citizens (Hine 1993). The centre has had much more power to intervene directly in local government affairs than in health care, but it has not had an important influence on local government performance (Buglione and France 1990). It is doubtful in any case whether the Ministry of Health in Italy could have exercised a hands-on approach with subcentral governments anything like that used by the UK Department of Health, even if it had had the power to do so. The Ministry has not shone for its capacity to plan, coordinate and monitor the SSN and has been repeatedly criticized for its lack of adequately specialized personnel and for the dilatory way in which it built up its informatics capacity (Senato 1987, Camera dei Deputati 1986, 1988). The reorganization of the Ministry envisaged by Law 833 kept being postponed and the number of staff working in that division of the Ministry with most of the responsibility for planning, coordination and monitoring the SSN was less (6 per cent of total staff in service in 1987) than that in several other divisions effectively shorn of any real responsibility after the 1978 reform (Buglione and France 1990, p. 368).[26] It is possible that, had the Ministry had more discretionary power over the USLs, cases of excessively poor performance would have been avoided. There might also have been less heterogeneity geographically in service provision. However, the price for this might perhaps have been to block the more progressive and innovative regions, a tendency to move the SSN to the lowest common denominator.

The comparative analysis presented here may help in evaluating a priori quasi-market reforms to be completed by 1997. It is not the intention here to examine this reform in detail, but at least two aspects are worth noting: the regionalization of the financing of the SSN and the conscious introduction of competition into the provision of health care. With regard to health financing, the regions have tended until now to respond in a common fashion to the negative incentives contained in the skewed distribution among different governmental levels of revenue and spending powers and responsibilities described earlier. This being the case and given the various constitutional, political and practical constraints under which a national health service in Italy has to operate, the new finance arrangements introduced with the SSN reform seem to have a powerful logic and should make the Italian system more internally consistent.

The new health legislation essentially confirms the discretionary power over the expenditure side of the budget accumulated by the regions since 1978, but this is now matched by an extension of the powers and responsibilities of the regions on the revenue side. The state contribution to health care is fixed prospectively. The Ministry of Health sets a *'quota capitaria'* which supposedly is sufficient to guarantee so-called 'uniform levels of services' for any citizen in any part of the country, although it is not at all clear what the basis is for determining these levels. This *quota capitaria*, multiplied by the number of residents and adjusted for interregional mobility of patients, establishes the annual gross contribution a region is entitled to receive from the state for health care. Under the new legislation, compulsory health contributions (from employees, employers and self-employed) are assigned to the region of residence of the patient. Regions are also given the power to increase contribution rates within limits contained in national legislation. They can apply higher co-payments rates, again within specified limits, and can introduce co-payments for services so far completely exempt. They are allowed to use other non-tied revenues to finance health care. The net financial entitlement of the region for health care is calculated by subtracting revenues obtained from compulsory health care contributions at standard rates from the gross entitlement. The difference between what a region receives and what is actually spent has to be financed by the region.

The legislation providing for the 'uniform levels' implicitly recognizes that these will be arrived at on the basis of the funding assigned to the SSN, set through the political process and contained in the annual Budget Law. In other words, it is the funding that determines the levels and not vice versa. This being the case, the mechanism of the 'uniform levels' may merely be an attempt to camouflage the intention to break the hitherto close link between the level of state funding for health and that of total public health spending. The evident aim is to transfer explicitly to the regions the responsibility for deciding the total amount to be spent on health in their territory. The hope is presumably that this will induce them to assume responsibility both for deciding how this expenditure should be allocated among competing health needs (that is, rationing) and for ensuring that health-care resources are used with maximum efficiency (that is, tighten their grip on the USLs).

Providing, of course, that the centre has the political will to grant the regions no more than what they are entitled to under the new formula, the regionalization of health-care financing could reduce the tradeoff between the expenditure control and value for money goals, in that one way of improving the former is to improve efficiency and to attempt to concentrate financing on services of proven clinical effectiveness. But the risk is that this is achieved at the expense of the equity goal, expressed as access to uniform care of reasonable quality on the basis of need irrespective of income or place of residence. The most central government will probably be able to do in the immediate future is to make the net financial entitlement conditional on the fact that a region provides the main categories of health services and to monitor for anomalous situations where particularly important single clinical services are not made available. The new financing arrangements could therefore accelerate the transformation – already in course – of the SSN into 21 *Servizi sanitari regionali*. This carries with it the risk of consolidating and perhaps enlarging existing interregional differences in the comprehensiveness of coverage, reflecting differences in regional revenue bases, and in the degree to which regional governments are prepared to apply patient co-payments. When you fall sick, where you live in Italy may become even more important.

The new financing arrangements also imply that support has weakened in Italy for the notion that health care is different from other local goods and services. Discretion is now given to an elected multipurpose tier of government (the region) to decide on tradeoffs between health care and other service areas. Room for manoeuvre here is, of course, very limited if we consider only regional own-source revenues – 2.7 per cent of total revenues in 1991 – but a region would have somewhat more leeway if we allow for general grant revenues, 6.6 per cent of total revenues (Buglione 1994, p. 885). The question really becomes interesting, however, if, as seems possible with the push to federalism or to a strong version of regionalism currently in course in Italy, the centre cedes substantial tax authority to the regions or if there is major revenue sharing. The crucial question, therefore, is how to protect the principle of geographical equity.

Italy and the United Kingdom are trying to introduce competition into their national health services and the comparative analysis presented in this chapter may also offer some useful insights here. Both countries have adopted a model of administered competition or quasi-markets, but, as with the pre-reform situation, the similarity between the two national cases is only superficial. Judged in terms of the extent of control which government exercises over the health-care system, Italy seems to have opted for a 'weak' form of administered competition while the UK has chosen a relatively 'strong' version.

Under the new legislation (Legislative Decrees 502/1992 and 517/1993), the SSN remains publicly financed but the principle of 'contract' becomes predominant *vis-à-vis* that of 'integration'. The principle of 'money following the patient', once applicable only to private providers, is now extended to public providers. Patients and their GPs will enjoy virtually complete freedom of choice of provider. Any private provider will be able to treat an SSN patient provided it is accredited, that is, possesses certain requisites. After a period of transition, public hospitals and ambulatory facilities, but not GPs or paediatricians, will depend for most of their revenues on the 'sale' of services priced using tariffs fixed by the region on the basis of nationally set criteria. Major hospitals are hived off from the USLs and those hospitals which remain with the USL are given major decisionmaking autonomy. The reorganization provides for a major redistribution of property rights over how health-care resources are used, away from doctors to managers of USLs and of single facilities. The property rights of non-medical staff over their supply of effort are also curtailed. It remains to be seen if the SSN will be able to enforce this redistribution in property right holdings. On this will depend to an important degree whether the rise in transaction costs inevitably resulting from increased recourse to exchange will be compensated by an increase in the efficiency and effectiveness of public providers and by a streamlining of the SSN bureaucracy.[27]

If the reforms, at least as contained in the national legislation, are fully implemented, the region and the USL may have little control over what patients consume. Transactions in the new health markets will tend to be bilateral between patients and their GPs and other providers: that is, health markets are to be organized on the basis of spot contracts. GPs have very limited direct financial interest in limiting drug prescriptions and referrals, although the high patient co-payments for virtually all services except in-patient care introduced in recent years could influence their behaviour here. Hence the region and USL risk finding themselves in the role of passive third parties paying bills generated by decisions over which they have little or no control. Health markets are in fact being introduced in Italy accompanied by relatively few regulatory mechanisms. Public providers are obliged to balance their budget on an annual basis and are regulated regarding borrowing and access to investment capital. But no mechanisms are envisaged to guard against abuse of market power at the local level by single or small groups of providers (through local monopoly, mergers or collusion) although there are important provisions to protect patients with regard to quality of service. Few procedures are envisaged to control against the propensity for provider to faced with a fixed price to increase their income via volume increases. The reforms being implemented could therefore worsen rather than improve the capacity of the SSN to control health expenditure.

In contrast, competition is being introduced into the British NHS under tight central control, if anything even tighter than under the pre-1990 arrangements. The UK reform involves a major change in one key feature of the NHS governance system as it existed before 1990: there is substantial de-integration with the majority of suppliers becoming external and a net separation being made between purchasing and provision. DHAs are expected to concentrate on first establishing the health-care needs of residents and then negotiating contracts with suppliers considered to offer the best combination of price and quality. GPs meeting certain requisites are given independent budgets for purchasing core services for their patients from external suppliers. A key element of British health-care markets, and where they differ crucially from those currently being introduced in Italy, are the contracts between DHAs or GPs and suppliers. Patients continue to have quite limited freedom of choice of provider. Providers in the new health markets in Britain are constrained by a series of limits placed on their property rights to acquire and dispose of capital and labour, to decide the prices they pay for factors of production and to select the services they provide. In addition, a regulatory framework is being set up to oversee the evolution in market structures (cf. NHS Executive 1994). At first sight, however, considerable decisionmaking power is devolved to providers and in particular to non-clinical managers. However some see this as a 'masquerade': what seems devolution is really increased central planning control (Paton 1993, p. 105). There is a strategic devolution to non-clinical manager of responsibility for micro-decisions on resource use (for example, medical audit or contracting), but it is suggested that this aims at highlighting local accountability for resource use. According to this school of thought, there is no real devolution of power; greater autonomy is granted only as long as local managers' decisions remain in line with policy objectives and financial targets set by the centre (Hughes 1991, p. 95). Also, the new external providers (trusts) are tightly controlled. Their governing bodies are non-elective, with the chairman appointed by the Minister of

Health. Trusts and GP fundholders can lose their special status if they fail to respect the rules. Disobedient governing boards of the DHAs run the risk of dismissal. The RHAs have recently been abolished and replaced by Department of Health regional offices. According to the government: 'The overall effect of these changes will be to introduce for the first time a clear and effective chain of management command running from Districts .... to the Minister of Health' (UK Government 1989, p. 13).

7. CONCLUSIONS

Both reforms aim at reducing the tradeoff between the two goals of expenditure control and value for money. The UK reform is the less wide ranging of the two in that it concentrates on the introduction of elements of competition into the public health-care service. The Italian reform is two-pronged: over and above trying to promote competition among providers, it seeks to shift a major share of the responsibility for financing health care down to the regions. In the case of Britain, care is being taken to introduce competition in such a way as not to compromise central control over variables considered to be strategic for control of global expenditure. Despite this, some observers (Le Grand and Bartlett 1993, Glennerster and Le Grand 1994) consider that quasi-markets could in the medium term increase the demand for health care, making it more difficult to contain growth in health expenditure.

Increased regionalization of health-care financing in Italy, *ceteris paribus*, might reasonably be expected to encourage expenditure control and promote greater efficiency. However, the way in which competition is being introduced into the SSN risks hampering expenditure control, in particular because of the potentially explosive cocktail of a very high degree of freedom of patient choice, pluralism of provision and fixed prices for services. The description of the Italian reform in this chapter however, is based on a reading of the national legislation which will have to be implemented by the regions. Past experience suggests that during the implementation process the more active regions or those with more efficient administrative apparatuses (they are generally the same), will use their autonomy and exploit the numerous ambiguities contained in the national legislation to adopt 'stronger' versions of administered competition. Their intention here would be to assure the region and the USL an active role in the choice of providers and in determining what services are to be provided and in what volume. However, other regions, especially in the south, with inefficient administrative apparatuses may de facto adopt even weaker versions of administered competition than that envisaged by the national legislation.

NOTES

1. Franco (1992, pp. 110–11) doubts that reliable estimates of health expenditure trends in real terms can be calculated for Italy with currently available data.
2. In 1991, Italy had at least 69 lithotriptors compared with 15 in the UK (Kirchberger 1991, p. 8). In 1993, Italy had 101 MR scanners (Agenzia Sanitaria Italiana 1994), approximately ten times what was required, according to Ministry of Health standards.
3. Public opinion is probably heavily influenced by the kind of media coverage a health service gets. This was quite negative in the UK in the period leading up to the publication of *Working for Patients* (OECD 1992a, p. 120) when the opinion survey cited in the Blendon et al. article was conducted. The media has been critical of the SSN, particularly in the last few years.
4. Twenty-six per cent of Italian patients requesting hospitalization waited more than 15 days before being admitted with some waiting for more than 97 days (OECD 1992b, p. 86) and with an average wait of 10 days (ACLI 1991). In the UK, 27 per cent of patients waited more than a year or more for hospitalization with some waiting over two years and with an average wait of 5 weeks (OECD 1992a, p. 120). Waiting lists may not allow fully for deaths, cancellations and transfers of patients between individual hospital waiting lists.
5. It is not clear, however, just how these have been calculated.
6. Given that so little of health care is of proven clinical effectiveness, the question is how much these differences really matter for health states.
7. In 1982, when the Area Health Authorities were replaced by the District Health Authorities, representation of local authorities on the governing board was reduced from at least one-third of total membership to a quarter. After the health care reorganization of 1974, local authorities were supposed to be consulted but this was never important. Abolition of the Area Health Au-thorities meant the end of shared boundaries with local authorities (Klein 1989, pp. 131, 138).
8. A property right is 'a socially enforced right to select uses of an economic good' (Alchian 1987, p. 1031) including their own labour. Property rights are rarely completely specified or enforced and frequently are partial or shared with other persons.
9. The standard example used to demonstrate how British doctors are prepared to participate in the rationing process is renal dialysis (cf. Gill et al. 1991).
10. More than half of all beds were located in London and contiguous regions. The North East Thames Region had 46 private hospital beds per 1,000 inhabitants compared with 3 in the Northern region and 9 in Scotland and Wales (Rayner 1986, pp. 16–17).
11. In 1987 private hospitals earned £18 million from NHS business compared with total revenues of £542 million (Laing 1989, p. 822).
12. In 1991, 49 per cent of SSN expenditure was financed by compulsory health contributions, 44 per cent by general taxation and borrowing, 3 per cent with patient co-payments and the remainder from own-sources of the USLs and contributions by the regions.
13. External transaction costs also included the costs of pre-contractual disputes, in the form, for example, of temporary cessation of service by external providers in protest over delays in contract renewal and review of tariffs. This has occurred quite frequently.
14. For example, use of standard tariffs for a category of providers instead of negotiating tariffs with single providers may mean that they are set to cover average costs for the category and possibly the operating costs of the least efficient providers.
15. For example, unnecessarily long hospital stay (private hospitals are reimbursed on a per-diem basis); failure to respect volume ceilings contained in contracts for ambulatory care (reimbursed by fee for service); poor service quality in some areas like longstay; billing for services not provided; GPs accepting capitation payments for patients dead or transferred to other doctors.
16. Between 1980 and 1983, the aggregate deficit of the USLs averaged annually 11 per cent of the initial funding level set centrally, for 1984–86 it was between 4.5 and 6.4 per cent and for 1987–92 it was 12 per cent with a high point of 20 per cent in 1990 (Veronesi 1994, p. 179).
17. The majority of regions were set up only in 1970 and it took some time for them to build up their civil services.

18. The estimate of revenues from private sector sales to the SSN used here excludes services by GPs and other doctors on contract and sales of prescribed medicines through contracted pharmacists. The estimate is based on data from Ministero della Sanità (1993) and Ministero del Tesoro and Ministero del Bilancio (1994).
19. Health jurisprudence by adopting a basically medical vision of health has tended to transform the right to health into a right to health care.
20. SSN patients have a legal right to use private contracted facilities if public providers are unable to provide the care prescribed within four days; in certain circumstances they can also use private uncontracted facilities. Authorization can be obtained to use health facilities abroad if the SSN is unable to guarantee certain clinical procedures within Italy inside pre-established time limits.
21. A survey in Sheffield found that 74 per cent of patients were either not prepared to travel at all for health care or only for distances not exceeding 16 km (Pike 1992). Statistics are not published on the volume of NHS patients travelling to other European Union countries for medical care, but it is believed that they amount to no more than a few hundred. Mobility will of course also depend on proc edures used to authorize use of providers outside patients' home areas and these seem to be more severe in the UK as compared with Italy.
22. On the contrary, for example the practice of many USLs to settle suppliers' invoices well after the due date has meant them having to accept higher prices.
23. Italy has over 8.000 communes, most very small (hence the territory of many USLs contains a number of communes) and some large (hence cities contain more than one USL).
24. This post was quite similar to that of general manager introduced in the UK in the early 1980s after the Griffiths Report (Griffiths 1983).
25. In Sweden, however, health is governed by the county councils and three municipal councils. That is, there are elected health authorities with revenue raising capacity. These authorities also receive central funding but it is they who determine levels of expenditure. Their independence stems from their power to levy taxes and their legitimacy comes from local elections. Inter-council competition in the provision of services is reported. Health spending in Sweden is among the highest in the OECD area and there is apparently great concern about this (Ham et al. 1990, p. 23).
26. The consistent tendency to underestimate the expenditure needs of the USL may therefore not necessarily always have been deliberate policy but the result of weaknesses in the Ministry's statistical service and in its capacity to process and analyse data.
27. Cf. France ((ed.) 1994b) for a series of essays by Italian economists examining the SSN reform.

REFERENCES

ACLI (1991), *L'immagine sociale della sanità in Italia: utenti e operatori dei servizi a confronto*, Roma: ACLI.

Agenzia Sanitaria Italiana (1994), '*Alta specialità: come, dove e con quali apparecchiature*', *ASI Settimanale*, **2** (25), 20-49.

Alchian, A.A. (1987), '*Property rights*', in J. Eatwell (ed.), *The New Palgrave: A Dictionary of Economics*, **3**, London: Macmillan, 1031-34.

Association Internationale de la Mutualité (1991), *Cross Border Care Within the European Community*, Brussels: Commission of the European Communities, Directorate General V.

Banta, D. (1990), *Pushing the Limits: Technology Assessment in Health Care*, Inaugural Lecture at University of Limburg, Maastricht, 17 May 1990, mimeo

Bariletti, A. and G. France (1994), 'Riforme pro-concorrenziali per il settore sanitario ed economia dell'organizzazione', *Giornale Degli Economisti e Annali di Economia*, **52** (1–3), 51–80.

Barr, N. et al. (1988), 'Reform and the National Health Service', *Welfare State Programme Discussion Paper No. WSP/32*, Suntory-Toyota International Centre for Economics and Related Disciplines, London: London School of Economics .

Bayliss R.I.S. (1988), 'The National Health Service versus private and complementary medicine', *British Medical Journal*, **296** (21) 1457–59.

Belli, P. (1993), 'Effetti redistributivi del Servizio Sanitario Nazionale', in M. Pace (ed.), *Le dimensioni della disuguaglianza*, Bologna: Il Mulino, 424–37.

Bevan, G. (1989a), 'The Government's proposals for hospitals', in G. Bevan and M. Marinker, *Greening the White Paper*, London: Social Market Foundation, 18–26.

Bevan, G. (1989b), 'Reforming UK health care: internal markets or emergent planning', *Fiscal Studies*, **10**, 53–71.

Blendon, R.G. et al. (1990), 'Satisfaction with health systems in 10 countries', *Health Affairs*, **9** (2), 185–192.

Bloor, K. and A. Maynard (1993), *Expenditure on the NHS during and after the Thatcher Years: its Growth and Utilisation*, York: Centre for Health Economics, University of York.

Buglione, E. (1994), 'Struttura ed evoluzione della finanza regionale', in Cinsedo (ed.), *Il Rapporto sulle Regioni*, Milano: Franco Angeli, 835–901.

Buglione, E. and G. France (1990), *La promozione della funzionalità nelle istituzioni pubbliche: il caso del governo locale*, Milano: Giuffre'.

Camera dei Deputati (1986), *Decisione e relazione della Corte dei Conti sul Rendiconto Generale dello Stato per l'esercizio finanziario 1985, Vol II*, Roma: Instituto Poligrafico e Zecca Dello Stato.

Camera dei Deputati (1988), *Decisione e relazione della Corte dei Conti sul Rendiconto Generale dello Stato per l'esercizio finanziario 1987, Vol II*, Roma: Instituto Poligrafico e Zecca Dello Stato.

CERFE (1992), *Rapporto sullo stato dei diritti dei cittadini nel Servizio Sanitario Nazionale*, Roma: Il Pensiero Scientifico Editore.

Corte dei Conti (1994), *Giudizio sul Rendiconto Generale dello Stato per il 1993*, Roma: Corte dei Conti.

Day, P. and R. Klein (1991), 'Britain's health care experiment', *Health Affairs*, **10** (3), 39–59.

Dirindin, N. and F. Vanara (1992), 'La litotrissia (Eswl): analisi dei costi e implicazioni di politica sanitaria', *L'ospedale*, **64** (1–2), 11–16.

Drummond, M.D. (1987), 'Economic evaluation and the rational diffusion and use of technology', *Health Policy*, **7** (3) , 309–324.

Drummond, M.D. et. al. (1992), *Survey of Economic Appraisal of Health Technology in the EC: Preliminary Results*, York: Centre for Health Economics, University of York .

Evans, R.G. (1981), 'Incomplete vertical integration: the distinctive structure of the health care industry in J.V. Der Gaag, M. Perlman (eds.), *Health, Economics and Health Economics*, Amsterdam: North Holland, 329–54.

Ferrera, M. (1993), *EC Citizens and Social Protection*, Brussels: EC Commission.

France, G. (1986), 'Assistenza sanitaria e compatabilità macroeconomiche: ricerca di un equilibrio', in F. Fichera (ed.), *La politica di bilancio in condizioni di stress fiscale*, Milano: Franco Angeli, 318–75.

France, G. (1988), 'Emerging policies for controlling medical technology in Ital*y*', *International Journal of Technology Assessment in Health Care*, **4** (2), 207–27.

France, G. (1989), 'Il controllo delle tecnologie mediche alla luce della sentenza n. 992/1988 della Corte Costituzionale', *Nomos*, **3**, 1–24.

France, G. (1994a), 'Centralised versus decentralised funding of evaluative research: impact on medical technology policy in Italy', *Social Science in Medicine*, **38** (12), 1635–41.

France, G. (ed.) (1994b), *Concorrenza e Servizi Sanitari*, Roma: Istituto di Studi sulle Regioni, CNR.

Franco, D. (1992), *L'espansione della spesa pubblica in Italia*, Bologna: Il Mulino.

Garattini, L. (1992), *Italian Health Care Reform*, York: Centre for Health Economics, University of York.

Gill, D.G. et al. (1991), 'Health care provision and redistributive justice: end stage renal disease and the elderly in Britain and America', *Social Science and Medicine*, **32** (5), 565–77.

Glennerster, H. and J. Le Grand (1994), *The Development of Quasi-Markets in Welfare Provision*, Discussion Paper WSP/102, Suntory-Toyota International Centre for Economics and Related Disciplines, London: London School of Economics.

Griffiths, R. (1983), *Report of the NHS Management Inquiry*, London: Department of Health and Social Security.

Griggs, E. (1991), 'The politics of health care reform in Britain', *Political Quarterly*, **62** (4), 419–30.

Ham, C. et al. (1990), *Health Check: Health Care Reforms in an International Context*, London: King's Fund Institute.

Hine, D. (1993), *Governing Italy: The Politics of Bargained Pluralism*, Oxford: Clarendon Press.

Holland, W.W. (ed.) (1988), *European Community Atlas of Avoidable Death*, Oxford: Oxford University Press.

Hughes, D. (1991), 'The reorganisation of the National Health Service: the rhetoric and the reality of the internal market', *Modern Law Review*, **54**, 88–103.

Institute of Medicine (1985), *Assessing Medical Technologies*, Washington DC: National Academy Press.

ISIS (1992), *Anche nel '91, notevoli ritardi nei pagamenti delle forniture*, *ISIS*, 12–19.

Jennett, B. (1986), *High Technology Medicine: Benefits and Burdens*, Oxford: Oxford University Press.

Kirchberger, S. (1991), *The Diffusion of Two Technologies for Renal Stone Treatment Across Europe*, London: King's Fund Centre.

Klein, R. (1984), 'The politics of ideology vs. the reality of politics: the case of Britain's National Health Service in the 1980s', *Milbank Memorial Fund Quarterly/Health and Society*, **62** (1), 82–109.

Klein, R. (1989), *The Politics of the NHS*, London: Longman, 2nd ed..

Laing,W. (1989), 'The White Paper and the independent sector: scope for growth and restructuring', *British Medical Journal*, **298** (25), 821–3.

Le Grand, J. (1993), 'The Evaluation of health care system reforms', *Il Politico*, **58** (1–2), 31–53.

Le Grand, J. and W. Bartlett (1993) *Quasi-Markets and Social Policy*, Houndmills, Basingstoke: MacMillan.

Mapelli, V. (1992), 'L'allocation des ressources entre les régions dans le Service National de Santé en Italie', in E. Levy and A. Mizrahi (eds), *De l'analyse économique aux politiques de santé*, Actes De L'atelier 4, Paris, 16–18 December, 51–60.

Mapelli, V. (1994), *La domanda di servizi sanitari: un'indagine campionaria*, Roma: CNR Progetto Finalizzato sull'Organizzazione e sul Funzionamento della Pubblica Amministrazione.

Maynard, A. (1991), 'Developing the health care market', *Economic Journal*, **101**, 1277–86.

Mayston, D. (1990), 'NHS resourcing: a financial and economic analysis', in A.J. Culyer et al. (eds), *Competition in Health Care: Reforming the NHS*, London: MacMillan, 67–109.

McCarthy, M. (1992), *Evolution and Implementation of the Italian Health Service Reform of 1978*, London: Chadwick Press.

McLachlan, G. and A. Maynard (1982), 'The public/private mix in health care: the emerging lessons', in G. McLachlan and A. Maynard (eds), *The Public Private Mix for Health: the Relevance and Effects of Change*, London: Nuffield Provincial Hospitals Trust, 515–58.

McPherson, K. (1990), 'Why do variations occur?', in T.F. Andersen and G. Mooney (eds.), *The Challenges of Medical Practice Variation*, London: MacMillan.

Milgrom, P. and J. Roberts (1990), 'Bargaining costs, influence costs and the organisation of economic activity', in J.E. Alt and K.A. Shepsle (eds), *Perspectives on Positive Political Economy*, Cambridge: Cambridge University Press, 57–89.

Miller, F.H. and A.H. Miller (1986), 'The painful prescription: procrustean perspective', *New England Medical Journal*, **314**, 1383–85.

Ministero del Tesoro, Ministero del Bilancio (1994), *Relazione Generale sulla Situazione Economica del Paese (1993)*, Roma: Istituto Poligrafico e Zecca dello Stato.

Ministero del Tesoro, Ministero della Sanità (1994), *Relazione sulla Spesa Sanitaria negli Anni 1989–1992*, Roma: Centro Stampa, Sistema Informativo Sanitario.

Ministero della Sanità (1979), *Towards the National Health Service in Italy*, Roma: Ministero Della Sanita, Centro Studi .

Ministero della Sanità (1992), *Attività gestionali ed economiche delle USL - Anno 1990*, Roma: Ministero Della Sanità, Servizio Centrale della Programmazione Sanitaria.

Ministero della Sanità (1993), *Attività gestionali ed economiche delle USL - Anno 1991*, Roma: Ministero Della Sanità, Servizio Centrale della Programmazione Sanitaria.

NHS Executive (1994), *The Operation of the NHS Internal Market: Local Freedoms, National Responsibilities*, London: Department of Health.

O'Donnell, M. et al. (1993), 'United Kingdom', in E. Van Doorslaer et al. (eds), *Equity in the Finance and Delivery of Health Care: An International Perspective*, Oxford: Oxford University Press, 236–57.

OECD (1990), *Health Care Systems in Transition: The Search for Efficiency*, Paris: OECD.

OECD (1992a), *The Reform of Health Care: A Comparative Analysis of Seven OECD Countries*, Paris: OECD.

OECD (1992b), *OECD Economic Surveys - Italy*, Paris: OECD .

OECD (1995), *Governance in Transition. Public Management Reform in OECD Countries*, Paris: OECD, Public Management Service.

Paci P. and A. Wagstaff (1993), 'Italy', in E. Van Doorslaer et al. (eds), op. cit, 149–65.

Parkin, D. (1989), 'Comparing health service efficiency across countries', *Oxford Review of Economic Policy*, **5**, 75–88.

Paton, C. (1993), 'Devolution and centralism in the National Health Service', *Social Policy and Administration*, **27** (2) 83–108.

Posnett, J. (1993), 'The political economy of health care reform in the United Kingdom', in R.J. Arnould et al. (eds), *Competitive Approaches to Health Care Reform*, Washington DC: Urban Institute Press, 293–312

Quaranta, A. 1985, *Il Sistema di Assistenza Sanitaria*, Roma: Giuffrè.

Rayner, G. (1986), 'Private hospital treatment', in A. Harrison and J. Gretton (eds), *Health Care UK 1986*, Newbury: Policy Journals, 13–24.

Rayner, G. (1987), 'Lessons from America? commercialization and growth of private medicine in Britain,' *International Journal of Health Services*, **17** (2), 197–216.

Repetto, F. et al. (1994), 'Il mix pubblico-privato nell'assistenza ospedaliera in Regione Lombardia', *Epidemiologia e Prevenzione*, **18**, 35–48.

Robinson, R. (1988), *Efficiency and the NHS: A Case for Internal Markets*, IEA Health Unit Paper No. 2, London: IEA Health Unit

Schieber, G.J. et al. (1991), 'Health care systems in twenty-four Countries', *Health Affairs*, Fall, 23–38.

Senato (1987), *Decisione e relazione della Corte dei Conti sul Rendiconto Generale dello Stato per l'esercizio finanziario 1986, Vol II*, Roma: Istituto Poligrafico e Zecca dello Stato.

Smee, C. and M. Parsonage (1990), 'Reform of the United Kingdom National Health Service: an economic perspective' (paper presented at the Second World Congress on Health Economics, Zurich, September 1990 (cited in OECD, 1992a, p. 120)).

UK Government (1989), *Working for Patients*, London: HMSO.

Vanara, F. (1992), 'Convenzioni, rimborsi in forma indiretta e costi della litotrissia extracorporea', *Mecosan*, **1**(1), 39–45.

Veronesi, E. (1994), 'La questione finanziaria nell'evoluzione del Servizio Sanitario Nazionale 1980–1992', in G. France (ed.), *Concorrenza e Servizi Sanitari*, Roma: Istituto di Studi sulle Regioni-CNR.

Vicarelli, G. (1993), *L'equità nella salute* in M. Pace (ed.), *Le dimensioni della disuguaglianza*, Bologna: Il Mulino, 391–410.

Wagstaff, A. et al. (1989), 'Equity in the finance and delivery of health care: some tentative cross-country comparisons', *Oxford Review of Economic Policy*, **5** (1), 89–112.

Whitehead, M. (1990), *The Concepts and Principles of Equity and Health*, Copenhagen: World Health Organisation.

Williamson, O.E. (1987), *The Economic Institutions of Capitalism*, New York: Free Press.

Young, K. (1988), 'Local government in Britain: rationale, structure and finance', in S.J. Bailey and R. Paddison (eds), *The Reform of Local Government Finance in Britain*, London: Routledge, 6–24.

11. Local Autonomy and the European Union Structural Fund Transfers: The Special Case of Regional Policy

Erich Thöni[*]

1. INTRODUCTION

Power-shifting is one of the most important issues in the process of European integration which is a major hallmark of the second half of the twentieth century. An inherent characteristic of the European Union (EU) is that it subtracts power or sovereignty from member states which is then transferred to the EU as a supranational body. The EU takes over functions of the member states and, as a so-called supranational body, has a very significant impact on member states as entities and on their inhabitants. Since the establishment of the European Community many competences have been shifted to the supranational level. The Treaty of Rome declared that the EC was to promote harmonious development of economic activity, continuous and balanced expansion, increased stability, greater improvement in living standards and closer relations between member states (Art. 2 EEC Treaty). The Single European Act, in operation since 1 July 1987, was aimed at removing all non-tariff trade barriers in order to have a real, single market with free movement of capital, labour, services and goods in place by the end of 1992. This meant granting new competences to the EU or strengthening its existing ones. The Treaty on European Union, or the Maastricht Treaty as it is known, which became operative on 1 November 1993, provides the legal framework for a political union encompassing a common foreign and security policy as well as cooperation in the fields of justice and internal affairs and for an economic and monetary union (EMU). Once again the competences of the EU are expanded (EC Commission 1989a, p. 14).

As far as regional policy is concerned, Article 130a of the Single European Act stresses the importance of strengthening the economic and social cohesion in the EU. This provision lays down the basis for a regional

[*] The author thanks P. Brändle for his assistance.

policy at the EU level. The EU supports the achievement of the cohesion objective through the use of the Structural Funds and other financial instruments. Principal responsibility for the achievement of the cohesion objective still lies with the member states. However, since regional policy measures at Union level should interact in a synergetic way with national and/or subnational regional policies, coordination is indispensable. Moreover, other national economic policies have to be conducted and coordinated taking account of the cohesion goal (EC Commission 1990). This implies, among other things, that aid granted by the member states is strictly monitored (Thöni and Ciresa 1990) and for this reason the monitoring of national aid can be regarded as an important component of EU regional policy. This is because the volume of aid made available by national governments to the regions depends more on a country's resources than on actual needs judged in terms of regional disadvantage (EC Commission 1992, p. 39 and p. 48). Consequently, some authors hold that the contribution to cohesion achieved by competition policy (and particularly by the control of state aids to enterprises) is at least as significant as that made by the Structural Funds, albeit using different means (Marques 1990) The Maastricht Treaty reconfirms the objective of economic and social cohesion and reinforces it by setting up a Cohesion Fund to provide financial support to projects in the field of the environment and to trans-European networks in the area of transport infrastructure. All this modifies the competences and also, as a result, the autonomy of all levels of government.

The debate on the sharing of competences for regional policy more or less neglects the question of the impact of this sharing on subnational authorities, even though in any governmental system these have important competences in this area. In some governmental systems – especially federal ones – it is important that there are regional and local governmental levels below the national level both to secure acceptance of regional policy measures by the local population and to ensure that the measures taken are efficient.

Central governments can compensate in part for loss of legal competences by participating in the EU decisionmaking process, but subnational authorities have very limited room here. Responsibility for the administration of regional policies are usually not transferred to EU bodies, which instead perform mainly monitoring and evaluation functions (Burtscher 1990). The extent to which subnational authorities participate in the administration of EU regional policy depends very much on the national constitution of a member state. Centrally organized countries, in which local authorities have very limited powers, are usually very wary about proposals for more local autonomy in regional policy matters and stress the principle of national responsibility for questions involving national power-sharing. In countries with a federal structure, subnational authorities, for example the states (*Länder*) and local governments (*Gemeinden*) in Germany, are responsible for national regional policy measures and lose competences – and therefore autonomy – as a result of EU curtailment of national aid to regions and of agreements between the EU and the national authorities on development priorities. Differences in the national constitutions of EU member states create uncertainties both for the coordination between EU, national and subnational regional policies and for the relationship between these different governmental levels.

Questions of monitoring national aid through the EU are by and large not addressed in this chapter (Thöni and Ciresa 1990). Its aim is, first, to examine the actual role of subnational governments, especially local governments, in EU regional policy using Structural Fund procedures. EU regional policy comprises a wide range of activities including preparation of development plans, implementation of so-called Community Support Frameworks and auditing. An important issue in this regard is what activities are to be carried out at what level, that is, at the EU, member state, regional or at the local level, and whether there is a loss of autonomy at any of these levels. Second, the chapter analyses the impact of EU regional policy on subnational economic policy, including potential growth effects, and considers the question of monitoring of regional aid programmes implemented by national governments and of subnational authority budgets. This is accompanied by a brief examination of the case for increased subnational participation in EU regional policy. Third, the chapter considers the current tendency towards regionalization in a number of countries and its implications for subnational participation in EU regional policy which are aimed at compensating for 'losses in autonomy'. The chapter ends with some concluding remarks.

2. EU REGIONAL POLICY VIA STRUCTURAL FUND PROCEDURES

The two southern enlargements (Greece in 1981 and Portugal and Spain in 1986) clearly resulted in a widening of income disparities within the EU and increased political pressure on the EU to help in structural adjustment in exchange for the new members opening up their markets. In 1989, the reform of the Structural Funds led to a doubling of transfer payments available to eligible regions, reaching ECU 13 billion a year between 1988 and 1992. The three Structural Funds are the European Regional Development Fund (ERDF), the European Social Fund (ESF) and the European Agricultural Guidance and Guarantee Fund (EAGGF), Guidance Section. The risk that some member states or regions might lose out as a result of the thrust to economic and monetary union led the EU to expand its regional policy again in 1992. In the Union's budget for the period 1993–99, deliberated at the European Council in Edinburgh, the largest increases in expenditure envisaged are in the area of 'structural actions' which include transfers from the Cohesion Fund, the Structural Funds and other instruments. The resources available to be committed under the Structural Funds and other structural operations represent cumulatively about ECU 161 billion or, on an annual basis, about ECU 23 billion (in constant 1992 prices).[1]

2.1. Structural Fund Procedures

The principles and operational arrangements of the Structural Funds are laid down in five regulations which became effective on 1 January 1989 and which were amended in 1994.[2] The main principles underlying the Structural Fund procedures are concentration, partnership, programming, additionality and improved monitoring and evaluation (EC Cmmission 1989b and EC Commission 1993a).

1. EU structural action is concentrated on five priority objectives[3] and on those regions experiencing the greatest difficulties. For regional policy action, the objectives 1, 2 and 5b are of particular interest. Measures under objectives 3 and 4 are to be implemented Union-wide.
2. To ensure that EU structural operations complement or contribute to corresponding national operations, they are established in partnership, that is, in 'close consultations between the Commission, the member state concerned and the competent authorities and bodies ... including the economic and social partners, designated by the member state at the national, regional, local or other level, with all parties acting as partners in pursuit of a common goal. The partnership covers the preparation, financing, monitoring and assessment of operations. It is conducted in full compliance with the respective institutional, legal and financial powers of each of the partners.' The notion of partnership is not so well defined, but it has innovated working relations between central authorities and local authorities, as for example in Greece and Portugal. The concept underlying partnership is comparable with the German constitutional notion of *Bündnistreue*, which stresses co-responsibility and cooperation. The nature of partnership differs from member state to member state, depending upon the degree of centralization or decentralization. In Germany, for example, the partnership is more active compared to countries characterized by less subnational autonomy. Some central governments, for example in the United Kingdom and in

Greece, are more restive about decentralizing regional action.

3. The reform of the Structural Funds has brought about a shift from a project-based to a programme-based approach. The programming procedure consists of three phases: the preparation of development plans, the definition of Community Support Frameworks (CSFs) and the definition of the forms of assistance. Programming makes it possible to take a coherent overall medium-term view of operations and to establish a framework for the preparation of these operations. The potential drawback of an unduly rigid adherence to plans as conditions change is balanced by the advantages of consistency.

4. Another important principle is additionality. Additionality means that, for each objective, each member state must maintain its public structural or comparable expenditure over the entire territory concerned at at least the same level as in the previous programming period. Allowance is made for the macroeconomic conditions prevailing when funding is made and for a number of specific economic factors, namely privatization, an unusual level of public structural expenditure undertaken in the previous programming period and business cycles in the national economy. The main reason for the requirement of co-financing from national resources – a minimum of 25 per cent of the value of each project – is to ensure that Structural Fund transfers are not used by a member state to refinance national policies. Controlling for additionality is carried out during the implementation of the CSF. Up until now, it has been difficult in some cases to obtain the information necessary to exercise these controls and to determine whether the funds actually reach the decentralized regions; this is particularly the case for Italy and the United Kingdom (EC Commission 1993b).

The regulations stress the importance of knowing how EU money is spent and whether it has been spent in an effective way. Monitoring and evaluation are primarily the responsibility of member states. Development plans must include the main results of past operations assisted by the Structural Funds and specify quantified objectives for operations proposed. The effectiveness of monitoring and assessment of EU structural action is very dependent on the smooth functioning of the partnership arrangements. Problems here concern mainly the quantification of medium-term objectives by member states and coordination of evaluative methods used.

Operationally, the Structural Fund procedure can be divided into fourstages (EC Commission 1989b).

1. National authorities prepare a development plan in partnership with the regional and local authorities concerned. The development plans take

two forms. Regional development plans concern objective 1 (at NUTS 2 level) and objectives 2 and 5b (at NUTS 3 level). For objective 1, plans may cover the entire territory of a member state, thus going beyond the regional framework. National development plans concern objectives 3 and 4. Each plan covers a period of three or six years and is updated annually. The development plan includes an economic and social analysis of the region, area, sector or problem concerned and, in particular: a description of the current situation; a description of the appropriate strategy to achieve the objective in question; an assessment of the environmental situation and its expected evolution; and an indication of the use to be made of the resources.

Theoretically, local governments take part in the preparation of development plans, but in practice their role, especially in the case of local governments, is limited. Development plans have to be drawn up very quickly and at the local level experts are in general either too expensive or not available. In countries with local self-government this may lead to a loss of autonomy, causing a democratic deficit (Siemer 1993).

2. A CSF is negotiated on the basis of the development plan and is decided by the Commission and the member state. It gives the broad lines of the measures to be taken and provides the reference framework for applications for assistance to be submitted to the Commission by the member state. The CSF covers a period of three or six years and includes a statement of the priorities for action; a detailed financial plan; the procedures for monitoring and assessment; and procedures for verifying additionality. In general, local governments are in a weak position in the negotiation of the CSF since the partnership in most cases includes only representatives of the Commission and the national or regional authorities (e.g. the *Länder* in Germany). Local governments usually are not involved (Siemer 1993, p. 88).

3. The third stage is operational and involves the implementation of the CSFs through the use of the appropriate forms of assistance in cooperation among the Commission, the member state and/or the competent authorities designated by the latter. In the case of objectives 1, 2 and 5b, the CSF is implemented through operational programmes, individual applications for large-scale projects, global grants, and part-financing of national aid schemes. Operational programmes (OPs) are the predominant form of assistance. An OP is a series of consistent multi-annual measures covering 2 to 6 years. The CSF can be implemented via OPs in different fields, such as in industry, tourism, peripherality, rural development and human resources. The CSF is implemented at all levels, with the national department or ministry of

finance usually having responsibility for overall supervision. Usually an OP designates a government department (the lead department) responsible at the national level for implementation of the OP; all other bodies involved report to this department. The extent of local implementation of projects or programme measures depends to a great degree on the objective under which the region is eligible and on the existence of local administrations or agencies.

4. Finally, CSFs and the assistance granted under them are monitored and assessed jointly by the Commission and the member states and operations are then modified if necessary. OPs are monitored on an ongoing basis using relatively open and transparent procedures. The task of the OP monitoring committee is to oversee implementation at the single policy measures level. The usual arrangement is for implementing agencies' to report to the lead department which has responsibility for ensuring that the agencies monitoring arrangements are working and that the proper financial controls are being exercised. The activity of the monitoring committee should enable the Commission to make any necessary adjustments to the volume, conditions of assistance and schedule of payments at the request of the member state (Mulreany and Roycroft 1993).

To summarize, both subnational and local autonomy are strongly influenced by the Structural Fund procedures. In particular, the role of local governments is limited in practice. In countries with local self-determination this leads or may lead to a loss of local autonomy.

3. IMPACT OF EU REGIONAL POLICY ON LOCAL ECONOMIC POLICY

3.1. Definition of Regions

Before analysing the impacts of EU regional policy on local economic policy, it is worth defining the terms 'region' and 'local authority' more precisely. In the EU, regions are classified by the so-called Nomenclature of Territorial Units of Statistics (NUTS) which was established by the Statistical Office of the European Communities (Eurostat) in cooperation with the other departments of the Commission. The aim is to provide a single, uniform breakdown of territorial units for the collection and presentation of Community regional statistics. The NUTS nomenclature employs a three-level hierarchical classification of regions for each member state (NUTS 1 – NUTS 2 – NUTS 3). At present, it subdivides the territory of the EU into 71 regions at the NUTS 1 level, 183 regions at the NUTS 2 level and 1,044 regions at the NUTS 3 level (EC Commission 1991a).

The NUTS classification is based in part on, and therefore corresponds to, national administrative boundaries, and in part on 'artificial' planning regions. In Germany, for example, the 16 *Länder* are the executive entities at NUTS 1 level, the 40 *Regierungsbezirke* are the executive entity at NUTS 2 level and the 543 *kreise* at NUTS 3 level. Belgium, which is divided into 3 regions, 9 provinces and 43 *arrondissements* is organized in the same way in the NUTS nomenclature. Ireland is divided into 1 executive entity at NUTS 1 and 2 levels and into 9 planning regions at NUTS 3 level. It follows that the 'regional/local authorities' ('*Länder*' and/or '*Gemeinden*') are defined differently in the different member states and because the national administrative and/or planning region boundaries vary, they play different roles.

The practical importance of the NUTS classification stems from the fact that it forms the basis for the identification of regions eligible for EU assistance, especially for EU Structural Fund transfers. The principal indicators used by the Commission in assessing the social and economic situation and development of the regions are GDP per capita, GDP per person employed and the level of unemployment.[4]

As far as the determination of regions eligible for Structural Fund transfers is concerned, the responsible committees consist of representatives of the member states and are chaired by representatives of the Commission. Regional or local authorities are not involved in this selection of eligible regions (Siemer 1993, p. 72).

3.2. Impact on Local Economic Policy

The most obvious impact of EU regional policy on local economic policy is quite simply that more funds are available. The indicative financial plan which is published in each CSF shows the total amount of Community grants available. The economic impact of the Structural Fund transfers on the local economy obviously depends on what cause–effect relationships are assumed. The EU presumes that an increase in private and public investment enhances local growth. Regional backwardness is considered attributable, in general, to problems hindering long-term growth and, in particular, to low investment levels due to relatively low availability of credit in private financial markets for private capital, relatively poor public infrastructure and low levels of human capital. The working hypothesis is that increased local investment leads to higher income per capita, higher productivity and lower umemployment rates. On the one hand, public investments in, for example, physical infrastructure, education and training and R&D are aimed at improving supply-side conditions in less-developed regions. On the other hand, stimulation of productive investments in industry, crafts and services are directly geared towards increasing investment. A striking feature of the approach is the assumed complementarity between public and private investment. Public investment is said to have positive externalities on private investment and thus economic policy interventions are needed to reduce disparities in regional growth (EC Commission 1989c, p. 4 and Pereira 1992, p. 2). Analysis of this concept would take us too far from the main concerns of this chapter, but its similarity to the new endogenous growth theories (cf. the complementarity between public and private investment caused by the characteristics of public goods and positive externalities of public investment) is striking. In addition, the policy concept of the Structural Funds and their presumed impact seems open to criticism because of the very general and mechanistic manner in which it is proposed (Ridinger 1992, p. 137 and Brändle 1994 p. 205).

Another impact of EU regional policy on local economic policy is the constraint it imposes on local regional policy through its competition policy. In fact, EU intervention is not limited to setting priorities (such as basic infrastructure, human resources, productive investment and rural development) when deciding on the CSF within the partnership framework or to the monitoring and control functions described earlier. Under Articles 92 and 93 of the EEC Treaty, it also monitors national aid (Thöni and Ciresa 1990, p. 24). Although most national aid is covered by the so-called 'de-minimis clause' and is approved without additional investigation, the Commisssion has the final say regarding national subsidies (Thöni and Ciresa 1990, p. 109). This has led to a loss of autonomy for subnational authorities in regional policy matters, particularly in countries with federal constitutions. Obviously some constraints on national aid are necessary if the Structural Fund transfers are to be effective and to reinforce the cohesion objective. Without such control there would be a danger of a proliferation of subsidies. However, judged from a political and particularly legal point of view, the Commission can be criticized for going beyond its competences under Article 92 and curtailing the competences of subnational authorities in the area of regional policy with the consent of national authorities but without that of local or regional authorities (Streinz 1994, p. 194 and Thöni 1994b, p. 169). To avoid potential conflict within the member state, it is therefore necessary to establish responsibility for specific aid programmes either at national level and/or at subnational level and to coordinate single regional policy measures (Thöni 1994b, p. 170).

Last, but not least, there is the question of the impact of EU regional policy on the fiscal policy of member states and their subnational authorities.

According to the additionality principle, member states are required to match an increase in Structural Fund allocations with at least an equivalent increase in the volume of structural aid.[5] This is to prevent the Structural Funds being used merely to replace national aid. It follows that increases in EU Structural Fund transfers imply an increased burden for public budgets of recipient countries. Correspondingly, if the emphasis of Structural Funds shifts from productive investment to public investment projects requiring high coefficients of public matching funds (e.g. infrastructure, human capital formation), this involves an increase in domestic public co-financing requirements and may strain the public budget.

The 'negative' budgetary impacts of Structural Fund transfers can be considered against the backdrop of the Maastricht Treaty convergence objective that a general government budget deficit should remain less than 3 per cent of GDP. The potential conflict between control of public expenditure to meet budgetary convergence criteria and national public spending required to take advantage of Structural Funds has led the principal recipient countries, such as Spain and Greece, to call for relaxation of the additionality principle. The EC Commission has agreed that domestic budget deficits exceeding the Maastricht maximum may be acceptable provided such deficits are attributable to increased investment in public capital formation rather than to higher current expenditure, for example for civil service pay; it is also prepared to relax the additionality principle in cases of serious budget deficit.[6]

The term 'national public co-financing', however, may conceal cost sharing among different adminstrations in the member states – that is between state, regional and local levels – and therefore also the fact that the additionality principle may be putting serious strain on local budgets. The Maastricht debt convergence can also be relevant in this context. The public debt criteria may cause 'national' conflicts since debt-financed co-financing could create crowding-out problems among the different national (government) levels. The financial plans contained in the CSFs provide a breakdown of how the financial burden is shared between Community grants, national public expenditures and private sector financing. National public expenditures are in turn broken up into central, regional and local contributions. Germany, Portugal, Italy and Greece are examples here.

The financial plan in the CSF for the five new German *Bundesländer* and Eastern Berlin for 1991–93 provides for total expenditures of ECU 14,126.6 million with 21.24 per cent financed by Community grants, 32.36 per cent by national administrations and 46.4 per cent by private funding. The states (*Länder*) bear the brunt of the contribution of national administrations with 27.4 per cent of total CSF expenditure; however, the share of local governments (*Gemeinden*) is very large, nearly 5 per cent of total CSF expenditures or ECU 700.4 million. The striking feature of the German CSF is that it is subnational administrations and not the federal government (*Bund*) which fund the national public expenditure required (EC Commission 1991b).

How costs are shared among the EU, the national public administrations and the private sector is quite different for Portugal. Under the CSF for 1989–93, for objective 1 regions, the proportion of total CSF expenditures met by Community grants amounts to 39.89 per cent, national public financing contributes 36.05 per cent and 24.06 per cent comes from private financing. Central government finances 20.84 per cent of total CSF expenditures, regional and local authorities finance 8.51 per cent, and public and other companies finance 6.69 per cent (EC Commission 1991b).

In the Italian CSF for 1989–93 for objective 1 regions, the EU contribution equals 47.5 per cent of total CSF expenditures, the national public contribution is 40.58 per cent and the private sector contribution is 11.92 per cent. The lion's share of the national public contribution falls on central government, 19.66 per cent of total CSF expenditure, while the regions' share amounts to 17.53 per cent (EC Commission 1991b).

With the Greek CSF for 1989–93 for objective 1 regions, Community grants explain 50.15 per cent of total CSF expenditure; there is a national public financing contribution of 40.46 per cent and a private financing contribution of 9.39 per cent. The Greek CSF does not break down national public funding, but the bulk seems to come from central government with a negligible regional contribution (EC Commission 1991b).

How the burden of financing CSF national public funding is distributed between the national level and subnational levels varies widely among the different member states. In Germany, subnational governments, that is the *Länder* and the *Gemeinden*, bear the totality of national public funding, whereas in Greece it is quite the reverse. Consequently, the EU regional policy has or may have important impacts on subnational economic policy, especially on the instrumental regional and local (public) finances. This is particularly important in countries which are highly decentralized, where this stands or can stand for (again) a loss of subnational, especially local autonomy.

Therefore, the rationale for more subnational participation as a substitute should be briefly analysed.

4. RATIONALE FOR DECENTRALIZATION OR LOCAL PARTICIPATION

4.1. Criteria for the Assignment of Economic Functions

The term 'general government' is used to cover all levels of government, namely the supranational authorities, the central or federal authorities at national level, the regional or intermediate level, and finally the local authorities or lowest level of government (Owens and Norregaard 1991). As noted, the relationship among different levels of government varies widely from country to country.

This is also the case in regional policy. Over and above historical factors, there were, and are, economic considerations bearing on how the allocation, distribution and stabilization functions of public economic policy are assigned to different levels of government. According to Musgrave, there is an a priori case for multiple jurisdictions caused by the spatial characteristics of public goods (Musgrave and Musgrave 1984, p. 507). The central government presumably assumes prime responsibility for economic stability, for an equitable distribution of income and for the provision of public goods from which all members of society benefit. In contrast the basic role of local government is the provision of public goods and services with spatial limitation, so that output is tailored to the particular tastes and circumstances of individual jurisdictions (Oates 1972 and Musgrave 1984). But, traditional 'fiscal federalism' theory – with its efficiency criteria which include economies of scale, spatial (geographical) externalities and individual preferences – gives only a rough indication of how functions should be assigned among different levels of government and neglects interjurisdictional relations and decision processes.

The exclusive assignment of economic functions to specific levels of government may not always make sense however; for example, local government participation in the administration of redistributive or local stabilization programmes may improve the effectiveness of government action. There are additional criteria for deciding on the degree to which economic functions should be centralized or decentralized. For instance, according to the principle of subsidiarity, competences should be granted by the lower to the higher level of government only if the former can no longer exercise them adequately. Another is so-called correspondence which emphasizes the identity of beneficiaries, payers and decisionmakers. The thrust of the correspondence criterion is that a mismatch may lead to inefficiencies: powerful beneficiaries cause an oversupply of public goods and powerful payers strive to cut expenditure. There should be a match between those who receive the benefits of collective goods and those who pay for them, that is, there should be 'fiscal equivalence' (Olson 1969).

In contrast to the output-oriented criteria of the 'economic theory of fiscal federalism' just discussed, process-oriented criteria take account of aspects of the decision process and political behaviour (Thöni 1986 and Dafflon 1989). Breton and Scott, for example, consider organization costs, namely signalling and mobility costs on the part of voters and administration costs and coordination costs on the part of politicians. Government functions are assigned to different jurisdictional levels on the assumption that the constituent assembly seeks to minimize total organization costs of the public sector (Breton and Scott 1978 and Thöni 1986). These 'process-oriented' criteria are at least as important as 'output-oriented' criteria.

Judged in terms of these two categories of criteria for decentralizing or centralizing economic functions, subnational participation in regional policy seems to have three important merits: first, local knowledge and experience is important for the design of particular regional policy programmes for specific geographical areas; second, local participation allows for greater diversity and experimentation in the use of policy instruments, thus helping policymakers to determine which policies are likely to be the most effective (cf. Hayek's characterization of competition as a process of discovery); and third, local participation increases the accountability of policymakers.[7]

4.2. Local Participation in EU Regional Policy

It is commonly agreed, then, that participation of subnational authorities in planning, in decisionmaking processes and in monitoring and evaluation of Structural Fund transfers is indispensable. This is reflected by the article in the Structural Fund regulations which deals with partnership. This article stipulates that EU regional policy is to be pursued in close consultation among the Commission, the member state concerned, subnational authorities and the economic and social partners. The extent to which subnational authorities should be involved is, however, in dispute. Partnership obviously leads to some degree of decentralization which is, at one and the same time, deemed to be very modest as seen from the German point of view and judged too far-reaching by other member states. For instance, the UK shrinks from the notion of local autonomy in major political matters. 'Partnership' can perhaps be thought of as a compromise among EU countries which opens the way to federalism (Schmidhuber 1989).

The role of subnational authorities has also been strengthened by the subsidiarity principle (Thöni 1994a). Article 3b of the EEC Treaty states that the Community shall act within the limits of the powers conferred upon it by the Treaty and of the objectives assigned to it therein. In areas which do not fall within its exclusive competence, the Community shall take action, in accordance with the principle of subsidiarity, only if and in so far as the objectives of the proposed action cannot be sufficiently achieved by the member states and can therefore, by reason of the scale or effects of the proposed action, be better achieved by the Community. Any action by the Community shall not go beyond necessity to achieve the objectives of the Treaty. There are different interpretations. Denmark, Great Britain and Greece – all unitary states – see subsidiarity as operating in a context where the national level retains the possibility to intervene and control. In contrast, federal Germany interprets subsidiarity with reference to all governmental levels. It may, moreover, be difficult to determine just to what extent it is necessary for the Community to take action, in particular given the doubtful amenability of the subsidiarity principle to judicial review (Thöni 1994a, p. 81). For the Community, how power is shared within a member state is a national affair. In Germany, for example, it is shared between the national government (the *Bund*) and the *Länder*, with the *Gemeinden* being left some room for self-government. Seen in these terms, it would make sense that the EU level of government should concentrate on establishing the principles for regional policy action, leaving implementation and administration functions to the member states. At the same time, however, it is necessary to create an institutional framework which involves subnational authorities in the determination of EU regional policy at the Union level as well as at the national level. The embodiment of local self-government in European primary law would seem to be an essential prerequisite here and should therefore be an objective of local governments (Siemer 1994, p. 67).

5. TENDENCIES FOR DECENTRALIZATION IN THE EU

The current trend towards regionalization in the European Union is, not surprisingly, welcomed by the subnational authorities. In general, regionalization refers to the process of dividing the national territory into smaller subnational units.

At the EU level, attempts are being made to strengthen subnational participation in EU regional policy. The European Commission advocates substantial local involvement in the formulation, implementation and monitoring of regional programmes. In 1988, an Advisory Committee of Regional and Local Authorities was established. This is supposed to pronounce on regional development and on the local and regional impact of relevant EU policies. The committee consists of 42 members who are elected representatives at the local or regional level in their own countries. This committee constitutes a direct link between the Commission and regional and local authorities.[8] The European Parliament, also in 1988, agreed upon a European Charter of Local Self-government, which defines and asserts the principles of local self-government.[9] The signatories of the Charter declare that local authorities are a main foundation of any democratic system; that the right of citizens to participate in the conduct of public affairs can most directly be exercised at the local level; and that the safeguarding and reinforcement of local self-government in the different European countries is an important contribution to the construction of Europe. Steps taken to reach these objectives include the recognition of the principle of local self-government in national legislation, the right of the local authorities to exercise the functions for which they have responsibility, availability of financial resources and the election of local representatives.

At the member country level, subnational participation in the formulation, implementation and monitoring of EU regional policy depends on the national constitution and countries differ widely as regards the extent of centralization or decentralization envisaged (Klepsch and Scleicher 1993). Structural Fund transfers are conditional grants for specific priorities or programmes. The recipient country has to match the funds, that is it has to provide a certain amount of national funding for each ECU received from the Structural Funds. Within member states, particularly those with federal systems, the balancing between the distribution of planning and decisionmaking functions, on the one hand, and the respective burden among the levels of government, on the other, plays a crucial role. The importance of the principle of fiscal equivalence is evidenced by the burden sharing involved by the co-financing requirement. The higher the contribution made by subnational authorities, the greater their influence on regional policy within the member state. Obviously, the degree to which there is centralization or decentralization influences the relationship between central government and local authorities. Perhaps of particular importance in this respect are different objectives at different jurisdictional and administrative levels caused by specific bounded interests (Thöni 1986, p. 117). At times, Structural Fund transfers, once granted, immediately lose their EU label and get used for purposes different from what they were originally intended. However, it is undeniable that local involvement in the planning and implementation of the CSF is in practice useful in the case of policies geared towards improving regional development. There has recently also been a tendency within a number of member states to strengthen subnational authorities. This process of regionalization is likely to improve the prospects of local authorities for attaining self-government. Ultimately, of course, it is the member state itself that determines the degree of subnational involvement, but tendencies such as increased horizontal cooperation between regions may also contribute to strengthening subnational government, especially local authorities, *vis-à-vis* the national authorities.

6. CONCLUSIONS

EU regional policy is a mixture of transfer payments to disadvantaged regions and control of national subsidies. The case for regional policies at the EU level requires first, that regional policies within the member states be coordinated in order to avoid wasteful overlapping and proliferation of national aid; and second, that regional policies be coordinated with other EU policies. From a political point of view, EU regional policy is necessary to enhance integration and to compensate regions that may be losing out in the integration process. Obviously, the introduction of a supranational level that has competences in the field of regional policy has a major impact. In federal states, the autonomy of subnational authorities (*Länder* and *Gemeinden*) in regional policy has been reduced. The Structural Fund procedures are concentrated on the relationship between the Commission and national governments. This means that subnational authorities, despite the fact that relations are based on the partnership principle, do not have a great deal of influence. Nevertheless, the additionality principle, the conditions attached to the use of Structural Fund transfers and the control of subsidies result in a loss of local autonomy which calls for increased participation of subnational authorities in EU regional policy. Arguments in favour of such participation include the value of local knowledge and experience in pursuing regional policies, greater diversity and experimentation in the use of policy instruments and greater involvement and accountability of policymakers. These advantages of subnational participation seem to be increasingly recognized, as borne out by the tendency towards regionalization in a number of member states and by endeavours to strengthen local participation at the EU level. For federal countries, increased participation by subnational authorities is made necessary by the fact that, given that such countries are already decentralized, there are limits on how far the loss of autonomy in regional policy caused by EU intervention can be compensated for internally. With unitary countries, the acceleration in regionalization which is likely to occur in the future should result in a strengthening of local participation at the EU level.

NOTES

1. See European Council in Edinburgh, 11-12 December, 1992, Conclusions of the Presidency, Part C (Delors II-Package).
2. See Council Regulations (EEC) No 2080/93, No 2081/93, No 2082/93, No 2083/93, No 2084/93 and No 2085/93.
3. Objective 1: promoting the development and structural adjustment of the regions whose development is lagging behind. Objective 2: converting the regions, frontier regions or parts of regions (including employment areas and urban communities) seriously affected by industrial decline. Objective 3: combating long-term unemployment and facilitating the integration into working life of young people and of persons exposed to exclusion from the labour market. Objective 4: facilitating the adaptation of workers of either sex to industrial changes and to changes in production systems. Objective 5: promoting rural development by: speeding up the adjustment of agricultural structures in the framework of the reform on the common agricultural policy; facilitating the development and structural adjustment of rural areas. Objective 5a has been extended to include transfers to regions facing adjustment problems in fishery industries. To this end, the Financial Instrument for Fisheries Guidance (FIFG) has been created.
4. Compare 10: The regions eligible under Objective 1 are the most important as they receive about two thirds of the whole Structural Fund transfers. The four cohesion countries (Greece, Portugal, Ireland, Spain) will receive about ECU 85 billion, namely ECU 70 billion from the Structural Funds and additional ECU 15.15 billion from the Cohesion Fund for the period 1994–1999. The new list of eligible regions, which has been agreed upon last year, also includes Merseyside in Northern England, the Highland regions and the Islands of Scotland, Hainaut in Southern Belgium, Cantabria in Spain, Flevoland in the Netherlands, the *arrondissements* of Avesnes, Douai and Valenciennes in France and the 5 new Bundesländer and Eastern Berlin as new Objective 1-regions. See EC-Commission (1993), Community Structural Funds 1994-1999, op. cit., p. 13.
5. See Article 9 of the coordinating Regulation No.2082/93.
6. Presentation on 'Convergence Programmes' by Mr. Mervyn Jones, DG II-A, May 18, 1993.
7. See Breton and Scott (1978), p. 111, Thöni (1986), p. 100. and Armstrong and Taylor (1985), pp. 252 and 266; also Galeotti et al..
8. See Official Journal 1988, No L 247, p. 23.
9. See Official Journal 1988, No C 326, p. 296.

REFERENCES

Armstrong, H. and J. Taylor (1985), *Regional Economics and Policy*, Oxford: Philip Allan.

Brändle, P.H. (1994), *Economic Evaluation of the EU Structural Fund Transfers,* Innsbruck.

Breton, A. and A. Scott (1978), *The Economic Constitution of the Federal State*, Canberra: Australian National University.

Burtscher, W. (1990), *EG-Beitritt und Föderalismus*, Innsbruck.

Dafflon, B. (1989), 'The assignment of functions to local governments: from theory to practice', *Working Paper No. 149*, Fribourg: University of Fribourg.

EC Commission (1989a), *Report on Economic and Monetary Union in the European Community* ('Delors Report').

EC Commission (1989b), *Guide to the Reform of the Community's Structural Funds*, Document, Brussels.

EC Commission (1989c), 'Orientations pour la politique régionale de la communauté (Objectifs 1 et 2)', *Doc. C (89) 287 final*, Brussels.

EC Commission (1989d), *Community Support Framework for Portugal, Objective 1, 1989–1993*, Brussels.

EC Commission (1989e), *Community Support Framework for Italy, Objective 1, 1989–1993*, Brussels.

EC Commission (1989f), *Community Support Framework for Greece, Objective 1, 1989–1993*, Brussels.

EC Commission (1990), 'Economic and social cohesion in the community', in *European Economy*, **46**.

EC Commission (1991a), *The Regions in the 1990s. Fourth Periodic Report on the Social and Economic Situation and Development of the Regions in the Community*, Brussels.

EC Commission (1991b), *Community Support Framework for the Areas of Eastern Berlin, Mecklenburg-Vorpommern, Brandenburg, Sachsen-Anhalt, Thüringen and Sachsen, Objective 1, 1991–1993*, Brussels.

EC Commission (1992), *Dritter Bericht über staatliche Beihilfen in der Europäischen Gemeinschaft im verarbeitenden Gewerbe und in einigen weiteren Sektoren*, Dokument, Brussels.

EC Commission (1993a), *Community Structural Funds 1994–1999*, Revised regulations and comments, Brussels.

EC Commission (1993b), *Third Annual Report on the Reform of the Structural Funds*, Document, Brussels.

Galeotti, F. E. Thöni and D. King (eds) (1992), *Local Government Economics in Theory and Practice*, London: Routledge.

Klepsch, E. and U. Schleicher (1993), 'Europa der Regionen – die Position des Europäischen Parlament', in F.L. Knemeyer (ed.), *Europa der Regionen – Europa der Kommunen*, Baden-Baden: Nomos.

Marques, A. (1990), 'Community competition policy and economic and social cohesion', *Regional Studies*, **26**.

Mulreany, M. and J. Roycroft (1993), 'The EC structural and cohesion funds', *Administration*, **41** (2).

Musgrave, R.A. and P.B. Musgrave (1984), *Public Finance in Theory and Practice*, New York: McGraw-Hill.

Oates, W. (1972), 'An economic approach to federalism', in S.H. Baker and C.S. Elliott (eds) (1990), *Readings in Public Sector Economics*, Lexington, MA: Heath.

Olson, M. (1969), 'The principle of "fiscal equivalence": the division of responsibilities among different levels of government', *American Economic Review, Papers and Proceedings*, **5**.

Owens, J. and J. Norregaard (1991), 'The role of lower levels of government: the experience of selected OECD countries', in: J. Owens and G. Panella (eds), *Local Government: An International Perspective*, Amsterdam: North-Holland.

Pereira, A.M. (1992), *Contributions for the Debate on the Future of Structural Fund Transfers in the EC*, Report to DG XVI, Brussels, 2.

Ridinger, R. (1992), 'Wirtschaftlicher und sozialer Zusammenhalt in der EG', *Europa-Archiv*, **47** (5).

Schmidhuber, P.M. (1989), 'Die Bedeutung der Europäischen Gemeinschaften für die Kommunen', in F.L. Knemeyer (ed.), *Die Europäische Charta der kommunalen Selbstverwaltung*, Baden-Baden: Nomos.

Siemer, S. (1993), *Die kommunale Wirtschaftsförderung und Die Regionalpolitik der Europäischen Gemeinschaften*, Carl Heymanns Verlag.

Streinz, R. (1994), 'Die Finanzhilfen der Deutschen Bundesländer', in H. Schäffer (ed.), *Wirtschaftsrecht und Europaische Regionen*, Berlin: Duncker & Humboldt.

Thöni, E. (1986), *Politökonomische Theorie des Föderalismus*, Baden-Baden: Nomos.

Thöni, E. (1994a), 'The Consequences of Subsidiarity in the Maastricht Treaty for Fiscal Federalism', in S. Urban (ed.), *Europe's Economic Future*, Wiesbaden: Gabler.

Thöni, E. (1994b), 'Spielräume der Förderungspolitik der Bundesländer (Insbes. Am Beispiel Tirols)', in H. Schäffer (ed.), *Wirtschaftsrecht und Europäische Regionen*, Berlin: Duncker & Humboldt.

Thöni, E. M. Ciresa, (1990), *Österreich und das Beihilfenaufsichtsrecht der EG*, Wien: Signum Verlag.

12. The Requirement of a Balanced Local Budget: Theory and Evidence from the Swiss Experience

Bernard Dafflon

1. INTRODUCTION*

The requirement to maintain an annual balanced budget is a key factor in ensuring fiscal accountability and budgetary discipline at the level of local government in Switzerland. Along with borrowing, it is subject to state (cantonal) control. Excessive budget deficits should be avoided for several reasons which are explained in Section 3. In practice, the judgement whether a deficit is excessive is open to debate: sometimes it is related to the sustainability of the fiscal position of individual local governments, sometimes it is evaluated in relation to an overall assessment of the economic situation and development (Thalmann 1992). Despite these definitional shortcomings, the golden rule of public finance – that public borrowing shall not exceed investment expenditure – is widely applied in existing federations and appears the most satisfactory from an analytical point of view (Dafflon 1994a, pp. 56–72). Complementing this rule, other criteria, such as deficit and debt to GNP ratios (at the national or cantonal level) or interest and amortization payments in proportion to fiscal revenues (at the local level) might prove helpful. This is not mere rhetoric. The majority of contributors in the fields of fiscal federalism and public choice economics present arguments, both normative and positive, which advocate fiscal and budgetary discipline and justify some form of control over government borrowing at the intermediate and local levels.

This chapter investigates why and how the balanced budget requirement is met at the local level in Switzerland. Since the fiscal structure of direct democracy in Switzerland is not as well known as that of other federal systems it will be described in Section 2. Section 3 presents some theoretical

* The author thanks J. Hall (Institute for Fiscal Studies, London), W. Pommerehne (†), and P.A. Watts (Institute of Local Government Studies, University of Birmingham) for their comments.

arguments which underpin the requirement for (current) balanced budget and restrictive borrowing practice at the local level. Section 4 describes the possible constitutional routes which may be used to implement effective cantonal control over both budget deficits and debt limitation in the communes. Section 5 concludes the chapter.

2. FISCAL AND RELEVANT POLITICAL STRUCTURES IN SWITZERLAND[1]

2.1. Public Expenditures

Responsibility for the majority of the budget items is shared, to some degree, by the three layers of government: (1) the commune, at the local level, (2) the cantons, at the intermediate level and (3) the Confederation, at the national level. Obviously, the Swiss Confederation has almost sole responsibility for services such as national defence and foreign affairs. But others, like education, culture, sports and recreation, health, environment, transportation and roads, generally remain the responsibility of the cantons and the communes. If we look at which of the two government tiers is the bigger spender for specific budget items,[2] the communes spend more for: culture sports and recreation (60 per cent), environment (59 per cent), administration (46 per cent), zoning and land planning (45 per cent), and forestry (43 per cent). The cantons lead for: law and justice (72 per cent), police (62 per cent), education (55 per cent), health (60 per cent). The fundamental principle in the distribution of tasks between the different levels of government is subsidiarity (Blöchliger and Frey 1993, p. 228). Competences are vested at the local level and can be transferred to a higher (intercommunal or cantonal) level only if the lower level is unable to provide a service 'efficiently'. The same principle determines the distribution of tasks between the cantonal and federal levels. A transfer of competence from the cantons to the federal government must be contained in a constitutional law approved with a majority vote by the population and by the cantons. Opinions diverge about which 'efficiency' criteria are appropriate for the organization (and the reorganization) of functions among the three layers of government.[3]

The de facto allocation of expenditure functions and of policy-making within the communes, the cantons and the Confederation does not obey simple rules that ensure neatness and smoothness. Instead, there is a rather elaborate system of checks and balances aimed at limiting horizontal and vertical coercion; as a result, the budgets of the different levels of government have become increasingly intertwined.[4]

2.2. Public Revenues

The main characteristics of the fiscal – financial system are the following.

1. Each level of government and each government within a given tier has direct access to at least two major revenue sources. Direct access is important in order to maintain financial autonomy.
2. For the cantons and the communes, taxation of individual income and wealth and of corporate business profits and capital ('direct taxation') is the major source of revenue (49 and 51 per cent).
3. In the Confederation, direct taxation (which is joint taxation with the cantons and the communes) is also important (41 per cent), but (exclusive) taxation on consumption and expenditure is even more important (52 per cent).
4. For the communes, the revenues from public property (6 per cent) and from sales and indemnities (23 per cent) including user charges, are also important revenue sources.
5. The cantons and the communes rely only to a limited degree on transfer payments. In 1991, the cantons received only 23 per cent of their revenue from the Confederation (16 per cent in the form of conditional grants and 7 per cent from revenue-sharing), and the communes only 17 per cent from the cantons (14 per cent conditional grants and 3 per cent revenue-sharing).

Tax sovereignty (the power of a government to decide which taxes to levy and how to organize taxation) lies primarily in the cantons and secondarily in the Confederation to the extent that is contained in the federal Constitution. This requires 27 laws (26 cantonal and one federal) for each tax system, with obvious problems of coordination and harmonization. Local governments have partial fiscal sovereignty in that they can choose between direct taxation and user charges and fees where appropriate. They have only limited flexibility with taxes since they must apply cantonal tax legislation and have only the power to set the annual coefficient of taxation as a percentage of cantonal taxes.

The objectives of fiscal sovereignty and fiscal flexibility are to enable each level of government and each government within a tier, to finance its own budget independently and according to its own criteria. This includes the capacity to finance expenditures for minimum standard (merit) goods and services set by a higher level of government (the so-called 'agency' role of local government), as well as for public services in response to the preferences of their own electorate, plus the power to choose between taxation and user charges and fees (the 'choice' role). As already observed, both fiscal sovereignty and fiscal flexibility imply direct access to numerous revenue sources and low dependence on transfer payments. This is quite the opposite of many representative democracies, where lower tiers of government depend almost exclusively on federal (cantonal) transfers.

2.3. Budget Responsibility

Cantonal and local governments enjoy fairly extensive but not unlimited fiscal autonomy. Two rules generally hold, one for the cantons as regards their own financial laws, and one for the communes in their jurisdiction. The first requires a more or less balanced (current) budget for providing goods and services. Swiss financial regulation makes it quite difficult for most local and cantonal governments to run or to accumulate deficits in their (current) budgets. If a large budget deficit were to occur, taxes would have to be increased. If local authorities do not follow this rule, a cantonal government can decide, independently of the commune, to raise the annual coefficient of taxation. The second rule concerns borrowing. In most cantons, public borrowing is allowed only to finance investment expenditure and then only if the local and/or cantonal government has the financial capacity to pay for the interest and amortization of the debt out of its current budget. Amortization rates are fixed according to the type of investment and the period of time over which the capital asset financed produces a stream of services. These two quite strict requirements are an expression of the principle of accountability or budgetary responsibility. They must be weighed against financial autonomy and access to revenue sources. On the one hand, cantonal and local governments have considerable independence in deciding the volume of public goods and services they provide, and have their own tax capacity. On the other hand, it is expected that these governments act in a responsible way and finance public services – in response to the demands of their electorate or in their role of agent for higher government levels – without excessive recourse to borrowing.

The Swiss political system also has some special characteristics which reinforce responsibility in budgeting.

1. Constitutional guarantees – the Swiss federal system emphasizes the sovereignty of subcentral jurisdictions, that is the cantons and local communities. This sovereignty is derived from the (federal and cantonal) constitutions, which contain not only the functions and competences of each government level, but also their right to levy taxes. The federal government has only those rights which the Constitution assigns to it. Constitutional amendments require the consent of both a majority of the voters and a majority of cantons. The allocation of

competences and revenue sources is therefore guaranteed for each level of government. Although the procedures for constitutional amendment are time-consuming and complex, each voter/taxpayer in a canton or commune is in a position to compare the costs and benefits of the public activity under consideration and to vote for the amount of public expenditure either in a direct vote or in a referendum.

2. Direct democracy – direct participatory democracy in the communes is provided for under most cantonal constitutions. Citizens may thus take part in the decision making process on all important political and economic issues (current budget, investment projects, tax coefficients, user–charge regulation, sale or purchase of local public property, membership in special purpose districts for joint production of public facilities, merging of communes).

3. Popular initiative and referendum – when democracy is representative, which is the case in a large majority of the cantons and in large cities, voters express their preferences on political and economic issues mainly via referenda; these may be held several times a year. Along with popular initiatives, the referendum is tantamount to an opposition party for local governments since usually all important public decisions are subject to voter approval. At the local level, the issues which are most frequently dealt with via the popular initiative or referendum procedure are: investment projects, taxation, user-charge regulation, property sales, association with and merging of communes.

4. Audit competences – the communal assembly of citizens, or the communal 'parliament' where it exists, elects a finance committee for the duration of the political term. The committee has not only audit competences, but also the power to investigate financial matters without prior warning. If necessary, it may lodge complaints against individual members of the local authorities for misuse of public funds.

Obviously these institutions of the federal system do not have the sole purpose of promoting (economic) efficiency in expenditure and taxation. The more direct and democratic the institutions are, the better is their general capacity to strengthen the system of checks and balances, by both dividing and sharing political decision-making power. They give citizens/voters/taxpayers multiple access to government, increase their capacity to control the budgets and reduce political and bureaucratic leeway in rent-seeking behaviour. In Hirschman's terminology, they not only have power of 'exit' (Tiebout-style mobility), but have also the option of 'voice'. The result has been that growth of government activity has been significantly lower than in representative democracies (Pommerehne and Schneider 1978), size of government is limited (Pommerehne 1978) and public expenditure is driven by the demand side (Kirchgässner and Pommerehne 1990).

Notwithstanding these institutions, almost all cantons have introduced additional regulations for budgetary procedures and public borrowing at the local level. The reasons for this are discussed in the following section in the context of fiscal federalism and public choice literature.

3. SOME THEORETICAL ARGUMENTS

In fiscal federalism, subsidiarity raises important questions of principle about the link between taxation and representation. In Switzerland, the a priori rule is that the government[5] which is responsible for expenditure decisions should be responsible for raising the revenue to fund them and should have control over, and responsibility for, revenue sources adequate to enable it to do so. Responsibility has two facets, within and between governments. Within (local) government, it corresponds to the duty to equate tax revenues and outlays and not to promise public services without taxes: it is 'a requirement of truth in packaging and labelling' as Tollison and Wagner (1987, p. 376) put it. Between governments, it is the obligation to coordinate vertically the allocation of functions and revenue sources so that, where responsibility is divided and shared, there is a commensurate division and sharing of the power to tax. The design of the federal constitution should not create vertical fiscal imbalance. This has been interpreted as a requirement for a (current) balanced budget, derived from the argument that the three 'circles' of voters, consumers of public services and taxpayers should coincide[6]. Extended to encompass the temporal dimension, this coincidence justifies the rule of pay-as-you-use finance (Musgrave 1959, pp. 562–63): in this case, over a succession of time periods consumers of public services are simultaneously the taxpayers. This rule provides some insight into what 'optimality' represents in the case of local debt limitation.[7]

The balanced budget requirement limits itself to saying that a government must be explicit about the uses to which it plans to commit resources: when it announces spending decisions, it must indicate how the resources to finance these will be obtained. However, there can be a choice as to whether this balance is achieved through taxation or borrowing. With taxation, it is impossible to increase government's utilization of resources in period $t0$ without reducing the utilization of resources by citizens in the same period $t0$. With borrowing, it is future taxpayers who bear the relevant financial burden, but this burden is not assigned at the time of borrowing. It is determined when debt is amortized or refinanced – at some time in the future. The issue is whether there should be explicit (constitutional) contraints on (local) budget and deficit-financing. In Switzerland, opponents argue that such constitutional limitation would impede local governments' ability to supply 'essential' public services.[8] Yet, strong support exists among citizens for the imposition (reinforcement or preservation) of some form of constitutional limitation on government exercise of budgetary powers.[9] The following arguments apply.

3.1. The 'Allocation Only' Argument

The first argument is that the appropriate fiscal role for local jurisdictions is to be found (almost exclusively) in the allocation branch. A commune cannot engage in aggressive redistributive policy for two reasons. First, the communes do not control the global progressivity of the tax system, which is decided by the cantons and the Confederation: management of the social security system is reserved to the central level. Second, interjurisdictional competition, increasing homogeneity in preferences for local public goods, and mobility (especially between neighbouring communes in urban agglomerations) reduce the distributional choices left to them.[10] In addition, the mandate for macroeconomic demand management is located at the central level. This means that local governments must conduct their fiscal affairs under a more restrictive budget constraint than higher levels. This restriction is implemented in the form of a current balanced budget requirement. Borrowing is restricted to the amount of projected outlays for investment items in the capital budget.

3.2. Pay-as-you-use Finance

Pay-as-you-use finance requires that the loan for any capital project should be paid off over its lifespan in such a way that the proportion of the total interest and repayment costs due in any one year equals the proportion of the project's total benefit enjoyed in that year. Strictly observed, this rule precludes the use of a current budget surplus as a source of finance for capital projects. Capital projects should be exclusively loan financed. In practice, the rule is often asymmetric. While it is true that loans can only be used to finance capital projects, the reverse does not hold; capital projects can be financed through loan and current budget surpluses or a combination of both (Dafflon 1994a, p. 157). Respect for this rule should avoid excessive debt and meet criteria of equity and efficiency.

The equity argument suggests that, during the current period of revenue use, taxpayers should not bear the full cost of public projects that promise to yield benefits over a sequence of time periods. Debt service and amortization payments raised by taxes in subsequent periods are a necessary part of the intertemporal fiscal exchange implied by the decision to finance a capital project (Buchanan 1987, p. 363).

Efficiency arguments are discussed by Wagner (1970) and King[11] (1984, pp. 277–83). Two of them are found in the current debate in Switzerland. First, a greater number of residents will support budget increases on any issue if they can shift part of the burden onto outsiders instead of bearing the full cost themselves. Debt finance, without pay-as-you-use *quid pro quo*, offers this possibility. Failure to discount future tax payments to service and amortize the debt entirely or anything less than the full capitalization in the domestic property values of the future tax liability related to loan finance, are two examples. The argument is that if the median voter expects to reside in a community for ten years, for instance, he or she would rationally prefer a 20-year amortization period to a 10-year period. Although the median voter might support debt finance under a 20-year amortization period if he or she expects to live in the community for only up to 10 years or to leave the community in 10 years' time, he or she might reject the debt issue if he or she had to live in the community the entire 20 years, or similarly, if the amortization period were only ten years. The real cost of the service is underestimated and this leads to overspending. If perfect matching of taxes and benefits through time seems weak, excessive debt finance could result unless external constraints are placed upon local borrowing decisions. The second argument is that liability for public debt is social and not personal. Thus no individual really bothers about excess public debt. Liability could be made personal only through a lump-sum assignment of liability for debt amortization and with the assignment becoming part of the taxpayer's estate in case of mobility or death. Alternatively, debt decisions are capitalized into property values when the tax base to finance debt service and amortization rests exclusively on properties (Wagner 1987 p. 209). Since neither of these two situations exists at the local level in Switzerland, the alternative is to restrict deficit-financing.

3.3. Rent-seeking

In the public choice approach, collective decisions emerge from the complex interactions of citizens, politicians, interest groups and bureaucrats. Common to all actors is the behavioural postulate that they pursue their own goals rather than social welfare. The particular insight of the rent-seeking literature is that the existence of rent, or the opportunity to create it in the political process, will induce rent-seekers to expend resources, at the limit to the full value of the rent perceived to be available, in order to entrap it. This will be easier with a soft budget constraint (taxation and borrowing) than with a hard budget constraint (taxation only). Without constitutional barriers, governments have the propensity to operate in the red, to generate budget deficits in response to demand pressures from voters and special interest groups (Buchanan, Rowley and Tollison 1987, p. 3). Consider the fact that groups which are organized around a shared interest are able to communicate their demands through the political process with much more clarity than can groups with varied and diffuse interests. The logic of action is almost identical for all 'special' government programmes. It is founded on the argument that the expenditure is too costly when financed only by the smaller group of beneficiaries, whereas it is a minute amount of taxation for each of the universe of taxpayers. In addition, special programmes are often qualified with positive externalities of some sort so that objections are not raised over the abandoning of benefit taxation for general revenue sources. In other words, the political value of the benefits which are provided by a special interest spending programme will be disproportionate relative to the political cost of paying for that programme if the necessary taxes are spread widely over the general taxbase. Extended to several special programmes, this logic leads to a situation similar to the prisoners' dilemma: what is rational for each individual group of rent-seekers worsens the overall welfare position of all groups and adversely affects the budget. The conjecture is that a relationship exists between the fiscal outcome of the political decisionmaking process and the status of the budget constraint. It is the possibility of budget deficits that provides politicians with the most significative part of their fiscal flexibility. Under a soft budget constraint (taxes and borrowing), political decision makers can be expected to give in more easily to the demands of interest groups and bureaucrats as only part of the tax bill has to be presented to the voters/taxpayers. Public programmes are then perceived to be underpriced to the extent that the economic agents are myopic and do not fully discount their future tax liabilities resulting from present deficit-spending (Moesen 1993, p. 174).

Consider three once-and-for-all redistributive programmes A, B and C, proposed by three distinct interest groups which benefit only certain groups of the citizens/voters – different for each programme – but which would be paid by all out of general revenue sources. General revenue sources can be taxes or borrowing. The question is: is the financing of redistributive programmes (A, B or C to be selected) by public borrowing adequate? Suppose further that with a hard budget constraint (taxes only), only two programmes could be implemented. The debate is closed-ended. The objective of one group can be realized only to the detriment of another: more expenditure for A means less for B or C. The budgetary procedure must balance the benefits of programme A with the (opportunity) costs of not having B or C. Similarly B must be weighed against A and C, C against A and B. Interest groups will have to defend their programmes; comparative costs and benefits will be made explicit. This procedure, it is argued, is efficient in the sense that only the two programmes with the largest cost–benefit difference when all costs are taken into account will be selected. With a soft budget constraint (taxes and borrowing), the financial situation is open-ended. No public debate is needed but logrolling becomes central: A consents to vote as B wishes in return for B's agreement to vote for his or her programme; the same will be agreed between A and C and between C and B. No group has to defend its programme by making explicit the benefits or arguing against inconvenience and costs that would have been pointed out by opponent groups in the closed-ended situation. There is no competition for scarce financial resources. The three programmes will be implemented, and financed with a tax – debt mix which is suboptimal.

Faced with the choice between a hard or a soft budget constraint, it is unlikely that individual local governments will choose the former in an outburst of public-spirited altruism. Moreover, in a system of competing local goverments, a commune which chooses more restrictive budget rules will place itself at a disadvantage when other communes are choosing the soft constraint. As for interest groups, local governments are caught in something approaching the prisoners' dilemma. The solution is for the nature of the budget constraint to be specified by law or by the constitution and its application controlled by a higher level of government, the canton for their communes.

3.4. The Cost of Debt Service and Liability

Since Swiss local governments cannot borrow from the Central Bank and cannot create money, deficits must be financed on the capital market. The questions of the cost of debt service, the liability of local governments and the attitudes of lenders regarding the risk that local communities will default are raised to justify debt limitations from three other points of view.

3.4.1. The cost of debt service
The general view, both in theory and practice, that debt service should be paid out of current tax revenues, has caused concern about the borrowing capacity of local government. This concern is illustrated by the fact that debt service is sometimes computed as a proportion of the total budget or as a proportion of total own revenues of a commune. In Switzerland, it is considered a danger signal when debt service exceeds 10 per cent of total tax revenues (Dafflon 1994a, p. 195). Thus, even when pay-as-you-use finance serves to justify local public indebtness, some kind of debt limits are required. The argument stems from practical experience. During macro-

economic difficulty and depression, some local governments found themselves committed to carrying debt service charges beyond their capacity. Since local governments could not repudiate their debt and could not be exposed to the legal remedies of private bankruptcy proceedings, the cantons had to step in, first to find *ad hoc* solutions[12] and second to curb further extravagance by imposing limitations on local borrowing levels.

3.4.2. Liability for debt

So long as the rate of increase in interest-bearing public debt does not exceed the rate of economic growth, interest charges on the public debt as a proportion of total product will decrease. It is sometimes argued that in this situation there is no need to amortize (reimburse) debt (Thalmann 1992, p. 285). But what happens if the reverse is true? Interest charges as a share of total budgetary outlays increase; at some point, the annual interest charge equals and then exceeds the annual deficit. Once this critical threshold is passed, the simple economics of default comes into play.

The usual argument is that lenders will react on the market before this point is reached. The principal safeguard that a municipality will not engage in excessive borrowing is the unwillingness of the capital market to lend to a commune which already has a high level of debt, except at prohibitively high interest rates that deter further borrowing. This is discussed in Breton (1977, pp. 22–3). The possibility that a local community could go bankrupt, or more precisely that prospective lenders could believe that a local government might find itself having to meet payments in excess of the revenues which its taxing powers allow, will mean that the cost of money to the local community will rise as more bonds are sold. To provide services in amounts equal to those supplied by other local governments implies higher costs either because interest payments will be higher or because current taxes have to be raised or both. This suggests that an optimal financial structure exists and also that residents move between communities in search of their most preferred finance structure.

If this reasoning is correct, attitudes of lenders towards the risk of local government default can be thought to represent a form of automatic regulation. But regulation by the market will be effective only if bankruptcy of a local government (or debt default or explicit debt repudiation by a local government) is possible. The institutional setting determines the feasibility of the solution described above. To illustrate this point, consider the status of local governments in most Swiss cantons. First, tax flexibility is often constrained by upper limits on tax coefficients. It follows that when the highest possible coefficients for local taxes are already in force, local taxpayers know that even with excessive borrowing they will not pay higher taxes tomorrow to pay for debt service. Nor, if further borrowing is possible, will they have to suffer cuts in public expenditure and services. Additional borrowing will not be discouraged by the capital market if lenders know that local governments cannot repudiate their debt and cannot undergo bankruptcy proceedings; the canton will eventually repay the debt and hence there is no reason either to restrict credit or to apply a risk premium.[13] With local tax limits and ultimate cantonal liability for debt, communes have no reason to refrain from deficit spending. The principal safeguard that local governments do not engage in excessive borrowing must come from other constitutional rules such as the balanced (current) budget principle and debt limitation. Obviously, the cantons have an interest in the implementation of such rules.

3.4.3. Crowding out

A third reason which has justified cantonal interference regarding local public debt is the crowding-out effect: when the public sector draws on the pool of resources available for investment, private investment is crowded out. There are two arguments here. The first one is traditional and not specific to local borrowing: when government increases its demand for credit, the interest rate must go up. Private investment becomes more expensive and less is undertaken. The second argument refers to the geographical segmentation of the capital market. Debt-financing at the local level results in liabilities which are largely external to the locality but 'internal' to the cantons: the predominant source of credit for the communes and the cantons are the commercial banks and insurance companies situated in the canton.[14] With tight monetary policy, competition for the credit resources available in the cantons exists not only between private and public borrowers, but also between local and cantonal governments. Of course, the capital market is not limited to individual cantons. But the evidence is that with limited credit facilities at their disposal, local and cantonal banks, and to some extent the regional branches of larger nationwide banks, have given priority to 'internal' private or public borrowers and have been reluctant to respond to 'external' demands for credit, thus introducing a *de facto* segmented capital market. Cantonal legal limitations on local debt were introduced to reduce the crowding-out effect; but they also had the positive effect – generally not envisaged in the legislation – of reducing competition for credit between the two levels of government – cantons and communes – to the advantage of the former.[15]

4. IMPLEMENTATION

In Switzerland, the constitutional (or legal) constraints on public budgets and borrowing vary according to the tier of government in question. Since responsibility for deciding and implementing these regulations is cantonal, they also vary from one canton to another, both for the canton itself and for its communes. In general, the rules applied to the communes by a canton are more restrictive than those for the canton itself.

4.1. Possible Constitutional Routes

Possible solutions are given in Figure 12.1. Solution (1) corresponds to the absence of any constraint. The other solutions present increasingly tighter constraints from left to right, with solution 6 involving the strictes rules. The final position of the communes in one particular canton depends on the answers to the following six questions.

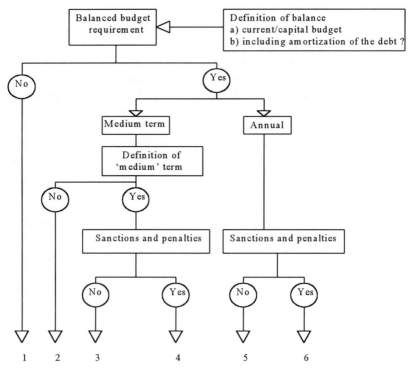

Figure 12.1 Possible constitutional (legal) constraints for balanced budget

1.   Is a balanced budget required?

2. In the affirmative, the rules must define the extent to which balance is required: the total (current + capital) budget or the current budget only? With a current balanced budget requirement, local governments can legitimately borrow to finance genuine capital investments. Taxpayers during the immediate period of revenue are not charged for the full costs of public projects that promise to yield benefits over a sequence of time periods. The intergenerational equity problem can be solved with appropriate rules for amortization.

3. Is amortization of the debt included in the outlays of the current budget (which must be balanced)? If it is, taxpayers–beneficiaries in periods following the debt issue-are faced with contractually committed interest and amortization charges that are offset by income- or utility-yielding public assets. The life of the capital public investment, thus the period of amortization, should be measured in terms not of physical duration but of economic usefulness.

4. If the rule of a balanced budget is constitutionally or legally fixed, is it an immediate or a medium-term requirement? That is, should each successive annual (current) budget be balanced, or is balance required on average for a sequence of time periods? The rule of annual balance produces a tighter constraint and leaves no intertemporal budget flexibility to smooth out irregular current outlays and revenues.[16] If balance is required on average for a number of annual current budgets, it introduces more flexibility in budget policies, but it also weakens budget discipline and opens the door to political discretion and interest group strategies. Hence the importance of the next question.

5. In the case of a medium-term balance requirement, is the 'medium term' adequately specified? The beginning of the sequence of time periods and the number of periods involved must be made explicit. Ideally, these should correspond to terms of office. If, instead, the political time horizon and that for the balanced budget do not coincide, asymmetry introduces a premium for the former and debt illusion on deficits in current budgets. The budgetary trap due to this difference in timing is illustrated in Figure 12.2.

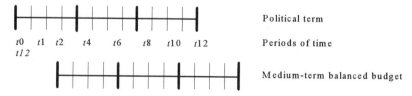

Political term

$t0$ $t1$ $t2$ $t4$ $t6$ $t8$ $t10$ $t12$ Periods of time
$t12$

Medium-term balanced budget

Figure 12.2 Asymmetry in political term and medium-term balanced budgets

Consider that the political term is 4 years, beginning in $t1$ in Figure 12.2. Suppose the periods over which the current budgets must balance on average are also 4 years long but do not coincide ($t2$ $t6$). What will happen? Simple public choice concepts, such as the proclivity of politicians to spend and their reluctance to increase taxes in order to remain in favour with their constituency, explain the prevalence of budget deficits with this asymmetry (of time periods and of behaviour). Politicians will overspend in years $t3$ and $t4$, incurring budget deficits and leaving their successors to restore balance. But the medium-term balanced budgets must be obtained by the end of year $t6$, in other words by the end of the first two years of the new political term. Why should newly-elected politicians promote a tight budgetary policy to free tax revenues to repay debt caused by past current deficits? And if they obey the rule, why should they not recapture political benefits by overspending even more in years $t7$ and $t8$, leaving their followers to re-equilibrate, and so on. Who will decide how much overspending in years $t7$ and $t8$, is 'too much'? Such behaviour is all the more likely if either the length of the 'medium-term' or the beginning of the period (the two conditions are not cumulative), are not explicitly defined.[17] Without legally binding definitions, the requirement for balance in a sequence of current budgets is an empty concept.

6. The final question concerns the sanctions and penalties when the requirement of a balanced budget or limits on local indebtedness are not respected. The public choice argument is that political sanctions for deficit spending and excessive debt, or political rewards for budgetary discipline, are unlikely at election times and are in any case insufficient because of the time lag between annual budgets and periodical elections. Sanctions must apply immediately. The standard penalty is that if a current budget deficit occurs, local expenditures must be cut and/or taxation increased. If local authorities do not respect this rule, the cantonal government can override the commune and raise the annual coefficient of taxation. On occasions, communal investment and debt financing may also have to be authorized by a special cantonal decree. In this case, the cantons may require pay-as-you-use finance and monitor its application, that is, require coincidence between the residual value of investments and the net amount of indebtedness (or the equivalence between book amortization and the effective annual repayment of debt) (Dafflon 1994a, pp. 185–90). The pay-as-you-use rule has not been respected if net debt is higher than the residual value of investments. A canton may defer authorization until the overdue amortization is paid; in the meantime, new investment financed by further borrowing would be barred.

Solutions 1, 2, 3 and 5 in Figure 12.1 can be grouped together since they make a balanced budget requirement redundant. The requirement of medium-term balance in the current budget allows a wide range of possible budget policies where there is no explicit definition of the beginning and the duration of the period (solution 2) or where there are no penalties for failing to take adequate steps to eliminate chronic deficit spending (solution 3). This does does not mean that balanced budgets are never achieved, but only that, since there is no obligation and no constitutional guarantees, equilibrium is rather a rare event. Budgetary discipline without constraints is highly vulnerable. Nor does this mean that unconstrained solutions attach more weight to Keynesian demand-management policies. Fiscal constitutions without a balanced budget requirement never subject local governments to stabilization policies which would be decided at higher levels of government (this could be a particular case of solution 4).

4.2. Evidence From One Canton

In Switzerland, the budget policies of local governments are represented in almost equal proportion by solutions 3, 4 and 6. In the Canton of Fribourg, for example, solution 6 applies. This was introduced in 1981 on the basis of two rules: first, the classical insight that public budgets should be balanced, revisited by Buchanan (1958, 1967) for the current budget and debt limitation; and second, pay-as-you-use finance (Musgrave 1959) for the capital budget, investment, and debt finance. These rules seem to a large extent to have restored budgetary discipline and led to moderation in local public borrowing (cf. Tables 12.1 and 12.2). Communes in the Canton of Fribourg were obliged to introduce the new regulations within a period of three years (1982–84). In the years following that period, the balanced budget requirement was respected overall, chronic imbalance and deficit finance became increasingly rare and excessive borrowing[18] was brought under control (Dafflon 1989).

From 1985 to 1990, local government finance in the Canton of Fribourg was characterized by a net positive outcome for the current budget. The year 1991 was the first one with an overall negative outcome. This was partly explained by the fact that Switzerland entered the current recession in late 1990, that is, before most other European countries (OECD 1993, p. 9). The financial situation of certain communes deteriorated as a result,[19] as is evident in Table 12.2 from the number of individual communes running deficits in 1991 (Table 12.2).This table also shows that under the new rules, the number of communes with a current budget deficit decreased steadily between 1981 and 1990. Excessive borrowing is also seen to have diminished between 1979 and 1988, but to have begun to rise again somewhat from 1989. There are two plausible reasons for this divergence: the decisionmaking process for capital investment and a change in the legislation on the communes introduced in 1990.

Table 12.1 Global budgets of the communes in the Canton of Fribourg

in million SFr.	1985	1986	1987	1988	1989	1990	1991
Current budget:							
−revenues	468.2	495.5	533.7	593.2	649.6	721.7	706.0
−outlays	454.6	483.6	534.8	580.1	639.6	714.0	712.3
result	13.6	13.9	8.9	13.1	10.0	7.7	−6.3
capital budget							
−revenues	60.8	53.9	62.9	96.4	98.5	90.0	100.0
−outlays	155.6	161.9	157.5	195.6	214.4	257.5	245.4
result	−94.8	−108.0	−94.6	−99.2	−115.9	−167.5	−145.4
Total	−81.2	−94.1	−85.7	−86.1	−105.9	−159.8	−151.7

Sources: 1985–1988: Dafflon 1989; 1989–1991: Annuaire Statistique du Canton de Fribourg, Etat de Fribourg.

Table 12.2 Number of communes with current budget deficit and excess borrowing

Year	N	current budget deficit	excess borrowing
1979	265	n.a.	75
1980	265	n.a.	54
1985	259	49	45
1986	259	47	28
1987	259	42	27
1988	259	21	28
1989	258	32	35
1990	258	20	45
1991	255	46	59
1992	254	n.p.	52

Sources: As for Table 12.1 Excess borrowing: Department of Communes, Canton of Fribourg.
Key: N number of communes (see note 13); n.a. not available; n.p. not yet published.

Because of a time lag between political decisions on capital investment, when works are effectively begun and when the first payments are made, most investment projects implemented at the beginning of the 1990s were decided during the more optimistic (if not euphoric) late 1980s. With recession, current budget revenues diminished, which created financial difficulties for some local governments leading them to suspend debt amortization. At the same time, the legislation regulating the communes was modified, relaxing cantonal supervision over local public investment and debt financing. Prior to 1990, each new investment project and borrowing had to be authorized by the cantonal authorities. The canton would control the financial situation of a commune before work on a project began and could defer local decisions on investment and borrowing if these seemed to endanger future respect for the balanced budget requirement or the pay-as-you-use rule. Local authorities, in the light of the improvements achieved over the 1979–88 period, considered this form of supervision to be unduly restrictive, administratively complex and costly and therefore to be simplified. They also felt that cantonal supervision of investment of all communes was a breach of autonomy in a situation when only some communes (and in decreasing number) merited such precautionary treatment. Under pressure from the communes, the law was changed in 1990 and cantonal supervision was limited to controlling debt limits. This means that capital outlays are no longer controlled as a matter of routine, but only if and when the debt limit of a commune is reached.[20] This change in the legislation was naive in the sense that it necessitates an *a posteriori* control of local investment and debt finance. Local government could behave strategically. Even if the values for financial indicators for a commune prior to its taking a particular investment do not call for cantonal supervision, if that investment means that the debt limit will be exceeded, the commune should in any case request cantonal authorization before beginning the project. Naturally, the authorization would be given only after the necessary measures to guarantee current budget balance were taken and provided the commune had not assumed excessive debt. A commune lacking the capacity to finance its demand is induced to ignore the authorization procedure. Examination of the accounts of the commune by the canton in the process of supervising respect for debt limits will reveal the true state of affairs, but only after the event. The canton at this point will require the commune to take corrective measures. These will have priority over all other budgetary or fiscal policies; there is an implicit threat of sanctions. In other words, the amendment of the law has transformed a 'precautionary policy' into a 'punitive policy'.

A third datum contained in Table 12.2 is the reduction between 1979 and 1992 of the number of communes in the Canton of Fribourg: for financial reasons, eleven local jurisdictions have been merged with neighbouring communes. The balanced budget requirement, coupled with debt control and dissuasive penalties against strategic behaviour, will no doubt increase the number of mergers in the near future.[21]

5. CONCLUSION

The purpose of this chapter has been to explain the role of balanced budget constraints and debt limitation for local government in Switzerland. Since the communes have a fairly high degree of autonomy to decide the amount of public goods and services they provide, by virtue of the principle of subsidiarity, and also have direct access to taxation and other own revenue sources, it might reasonably be expected that communal authorities would act in a responsible way. However, the evidence suggests that responsible budget behaviour does not come spontaneously. It requires a discipline imposed using constitutional rules. Four arguments, widely accepted in the public debate in Switzerland are proposed for justification. First, since the communes have principally allocative functions and virtually no responsibility for macroeconomic management, local deficit spending is not appropriate. Second, debt finance should be accepted for public investment only on a pay-as-you-use basis which permits temporal coincidence of benefits and costs (costs cannot be left implicit) and promotes intergenerational equity. Third, a balanced budget constraint discourages rent-seeking behaviour. Finally, limited indebtedness is also a question of (local) government solvency and image on the capital market. Implementation of a balanced budget requirement and debt limitation can take a number of routes. Care must be taken in choosing from among these solutions and to the organization of institutionalized controls at the cantonal level because both influence the results. From the recent example of the communes in the Canton of Fribourg, albeit a limited one, it is tempting to conclude that by choosing the appropriate procedures and institutions, budgetary discipline of the communes can be achieved. These rules are perhaps old-fashioned and may not qualify as 'new issues in local government finance' unless revisited. But in my opinion, they have much to recommend them and remain the best medicine for fiscal myopia.

NOTES

1. This section is based on the work of Blöchliger and Frey (1993), Schneider (1993), Dafflon (1994b).
2. Figures refer to 1991. 'Finances publiques en Suisse, 1991', Administration fédérale des finances, Berne, 1994.
3. Walsh (1993, pp. 32–5) summarizes the normative arguments. Wiseman (1989) argues that efficiency criteria must be related to the capability of strengthening political checks and balances through appropriate procedures and not to tax-and-expenditures outcomes as such.

4. There is continual dispute in the Swiss cantons about the effective extent of autonomy in local public expenditures, first and foremost because no single measure of independence is appropriate (Wolman 1990) so that the cantons and the communes have divergent claims. A second difficulty in measuring a decentralization concept is that the fiscal-financial relations between local and cantonal governments vary from one canton to another according to particular cantonal constitutions. My own calculation for a sample of communes in the Canton of Fribourg are based on the proportion of total outlays of the current budgets that the communes must spend for functions and services which are fixed by the canton (or the Confederation). This proportion varies between 30 and 50 per cent according to the population size of the commune. It is about 30 per cent for the larger communes with 2,000 inhabitants or more; and about 50 per cent for municipalities with 500 inhabitants, with variations that are approximatively proportional between these sizes. The percentage increases and becomes rapidly extreme for communes with less than 500 inhabitants, so that one might question what autonomy remains. Furthermore, these percentages are probably underestimated because they do not take into account debt service of investments which are required by federal or cantonal laws, as for example in environmental policies.

5. Either in the form of direct democracy (communal assembly of citizens) or in representative democracy (communal elected parliament).

6. The theoretical counterpart is Olson's equivalence principle (1969) for the design of subcentral juridictions.

7. For a discussion on pay-as-you-use finance and optimality in local debt limitation, see Aronson (1971), Wagner (1970), Hand and Mitchell (1971), Aronson and Maxwell (1967), Rolph (1967).

8. But the adjective 'essential' often relates to rent-seeking behaviour of interest groups.

9. For example: Buomberger and Schwab (1993), L'Huillier (1992), Wittmann (1992).

10. For a discussion of the theoretical support of these old arguments and recent evidence, see Walsh (1993, pp. 37–9 and 51–6). For a detailed and more nuanced account of the Swiss situation, see Blöchliger and Frey (1993, pp. 226–8).

11. Wagner's arguments and the discussion stimulated by it are summarized in King (1984, pp. 277–83).

12. Between 1977 and 1993, in the Canton of Fribourg, the cantonal government reimbursed the debt of 14 communes on condition that they merged with neighbouring larger communes. In these cases, the merging of a small commune with a larger one is the public counterpart of private bankruptcy.

13. The argument is that although the bankruptcy of a commune is technically possible, it is politically unacceptable. See note 12 above. Another example may be given. In 1984, the Canton of Fribourg enacted a new law on hospitals. One of the reasons for this law was the financial situation of the district hospitals, managed by local governments organized in associations. In order to eliminate excessive debt, the law compelled the communes to refund their share of the total debt of the hospital district to which they belong. But, at the same time, *ad hoc* legislation was passed so that the canton could distribute grants to the communes unable to pay their share without going into the red despite maximum tax coefficients.

14. Local government borrowing in the form of bonds does not exist except for a few large cities. Bond issues at the cantonal level, though possible, are not frequent.

15. In the late 1970s, the association of local bankers in the Canton of Fribourg asked the cantonal government to intervene in order that (1) the annual amortization of local debt should not only correspond to a bookkeeping operation, but also to the effective repayment of the debt; (2) the rate of amortization should be higher than the usual 1 or 2 per cent which the Canton fixed when it authorized a commune to borrow. The objective was to restore the credit position of the banks to serve private borrowers and the credit position of the regional and cantonal banks *vis-à-vis* the cantonal branches of nationwide banks.

16. For the necessity of a distinction between regular and irregular outlays and revenues in the current budget of small-size local governments, see Dafflon (1994a, pp. 209–10 and 214–15). The distinction, however, does not call into question the stricter rule of annual balance.

17. An interesting experiment has been conducted by the author when giving evening courses to local government officials in various French-speaking cantons in 1992/1993. They were asked

which would be the 'ideal medium term' (in number of years) if the requirement of pluri-annual current balanced budget should be implemented in their canton? All responses were consistent: the ideal number of years was always one or two years more than the political term; if timing was indicated, the end of term for budget purposes was always set after the end of political term. (Results not published.)

18. Excess borrowing in Fribourg is defined in the following way. It occurs if the net debt is higher than the residual value of the investments financed by borrowing, when amortization is paid strictly on a pay-as-you-use basis. Rates of annual amortization are specified in the law and vary according to the nature of the investments in terms of their economic usefulness.

19. Special mention should be made of the capital town of Fribourg and the communes in the agglomeration around Fribourg, in which the total deficit was 12.0 million SFr. and which contributed to the bulk of the negative global result.

20. Technically, a commune may undertake capital outlays without cantonal supervision as long as the new investment item is financed out of the benefit of the annual current budget, or out of capitalized benefits of successive current budgets, or a 'loan premium'. A 'loan premium' exists when $(RV-ND) > 0$, where RV is the residual value of (correctly amortized) past investments financed by debt, and ND the effective amount of net debt after repayment, in the books at the end of year.

21. See notes 4 and 12 above. One might ask if strictness in the application of the current balanced budget rule and of the debt limits has not been a substitute for the compulsory merging of excessively small communes, for which a law was passed in 1974 in the cantonal parliament but rejected through referendum.

REFERENCES

Aronson, J.R. (1971), 'A comment on the optimality in local debt limitation, *National Tax Journal*, **24** (1), 107–108.

Bennett, R.J. (1990), *Decentralization, Local Governments, and Markets: Towards a Post-Welfare Agenda,* Oxford: Clarendon Press.

Blöchliger, H. and R.L Frey (1993), 'The evolution of Swiss federalism: a model for the European Community ?', in EEC, op. cit., 213–42.

Breton, A. (1977), 'A theory of local government finance and the debt regulation of local government', *Public Finance*, **32** (1), 16–28.

Buchanan, J.M. (1958), *Public Principles of Public Debt*, Homewood: Irwin.

Buchanan, J.M. (1967), *Public Finance in Democratic Process*, Chapel Hill: University of North Carolina Press.

Buchanan, J.M. (1987a), 'The ethics of debt default', in J.M. Buchanan, C.K. Rowley and R.D. Tollison, op. cit., 361–73.

Buchanan, J.M., C.K Rowley and R.D Tollison (1987b), *Deficits,* Oxford: Basil Blackwell.

Buomberger, P. and G. Schwab (1993), 'Sind die schweizerischen Staatsdefizite eine Belastungfür unsere Zukunft', *Ischweizer Monatshefte für Politik, Wirtschaft, Kultur*, November, 1–16.

Dafflon, B. (1989), Situation financière des communes fribourgeoises 1985–1988, Institute for Economic and Social Sciences, *Working Paper No152*, Fribourg: University of Fribourg.

Dafflon, B. (1994a), *La gestion des finances publiques locales*, Paris and Genève: Economica.

Dafflon, B. (1994b), Government finance in Switzerland: institutional issues, figures and facts, Institute for Economic and Social Sciences, *revised Working Paper No 191,* Fribourg: University of Fribourg and International Centre for Ethnic Studies, Colombo, Sri Lanka.

EEC (1993), T*he Economics of Community: Public Finance;* Commission of the European Communities, European Community (ed.), Reports and Studies No. 5, Brussels: European Community.

Hand, H.J. and W.E. Mitchell (1971), 'Optimality in local debt limitation: a comment', *National Tax Journal*, **24** (1), 101–6.

King, D. (1984), *Fiscal Tiers: The Economics of Multi-Level Government,* London: Allen & Unwin.

Kirchgässner, G. and W.N. Pommerehne (1990), 'Evolution of public finance as a function of federal structure: a comparison between Switzerland and the Federal Republic of Germany', mimeograph 46th Congress, Brussels: International Institute of Public Finance.

L'Huillier, J. (1992), *Les déficits des budgets publics desservent l'économie plus qu'ils ne la servent,* Genève: Groupement des banques privées genevoises.

Maxwell, J.A. and J.R. Aronson (1967), 'The state and local capital budget in theory and practice', *National Tax Journal,* **20** (2), 165–70, and 'Reply', *National Tax Journal,* **21** (2), 213–14.

Moesen, W.A. (1993), 'Community public finance in the perspective of the EMU: assignment rules, the states of the budget constraint and young fiscal federalism in Begium', in EEC, op. cit., 167–90.

Musgrave, R.A. (1959), *The Theory of Public Finance,* New York: McGraw-Hill.

OECD (1993), *OECD Economic Surveys: Switzerland,* Paris: OECD.

Olson, M. (1969), 'The Principle 'fiscal equivalence': the division of responsibilities among different levels of government', *American Economic Review,* **49**, 479–487.

Pommerehne, W. (1978), 'Institutional approaches to public expenditures: empirical evidence from Swiss municipalities', *Journal of Public Economics***, 9**, 255–280.

Pommerehne, W.N. and F. Schneider (1978), 'Fiscal illusion, political institutions and local public spending', *Kyklos,* **31** (3), 381–408.

Rolph, E.R: (1967), 'Pay-as-you-use finance: a comment', *National Tax Journal,* **21** (2), 210–12.

Schneider, F. (1993), 'The federal and fiscal structures of representative and direct democracies as models for a European federal union: some ideas using the public choice approach', in EEC, op. cit., 191–212.

Thalmann, P. (1992), 'Des finances saines', in L. Weber (ed.), *Les Finances Publiques d'un État Fédératif: La Suisse*, Paris and Genève: Economica, 265–307.

Tollison, R.D. and R.E Wagner (1987), 'Balanced budget and beyond', in Buchanan, Rowley and Tollison, 1987, op. cit., 374–90.

Wagner, R.E. (1970), 'Optimality in local debt limitation', *National Tax Journal,* **23** (3), 297-305; 'Reply' in *National Tax Journal,* **24** (1), 1971, 109-11.

Wagner, R.E. (1987), 'Liability rules, fiscal institutions and the debt', in Buchanan, Rowley and Tollison, op. cit., 199–217.

Walsh, C. (1993), 'Fiscal federalism: an overview of issues and a discussion of their relevance to the European Community', in EEC, op. cit., 25–62.

Wiseman, J. (1989), 'The political economy of federalism: A critical appraisal', in *Cost, Choice and Political Economy,* Aldershot: Edward Elgar, 71–111.

Wittmann, W. (1992), 'Grenzen Der Öffentlichen Verschuldung Aus Sicht Der Finanzwissenschaft'*, in Emissionszentrale Der Schweizer Gemeinden,* Berne: Schuldenproblematik Der Öffentlichen Haushalte, 65–76.

Wolman, H. (1990), 'Decentralization: what it is and why we should care', in Bennett, op. cit., 29–41.

PART   IV

Fiscal Issues for Existing and Future
Federations

13. The Political Economy of State and Local Tax Structure

Howard Chernick and Andrew Reschovsky

1. INTRODUCTION

Subnational public finance in the United States is characterized by 50 different tax and expenditure systems. Not only does the level of taxation, and consequently public spending, vary tremendously among the states, but the tax structure differs dramatically across subnational units of government. For example, in seven states no revenue is collected from state and local income taxes, while in seven other states over 30 per cent of state and local government tax revenue comes from the income tax.[1] Likewise, four states have no sales tax, while three states collect over 40 per cent of their revenue from the general sales tax. The property tax, which is the dominant form of local government tax revenue in the United States, accounted for fully 70 per cent of total state and local gas revenue in New Hampshire, but only 15 per cent in Hawaii.

In part because of differences between states in the mix of taxes, and in part because for any given tax states employ a wide range of tax bases and rate structures, there is a great deal of variation among the states in the progressivity of their state–local tax systems. In a recent study of the distribution of state and local tax burdens, the Citizens for Tax Justice (1991) demonstrated that, while for the nation as a whole state and local taxes are regressive, several states, for example Delaware and Vermont, have mildly progressive tax systems. At the same time, a number of other states, for example Texas, Nevada and Florida, have tax systems that can only be described as highly regressive.

While there is a long history in state and local public finance of models of expenditure determination, until recently there has been far less attention paid to the development and testing of formal models of tax structure. We know very little about why the mix of taxes varies so much among the states, and very little about the reasons some states choose relatively progressive tax systems while other, often neighbouring, states impose quite regressive taxes. Several recent events in the US, however, have increased both academic and popular interest in gaining an understanding of the evolution of state and local tax structures. In the State of Michigan, the residential property tax was dramatically reduced as a source of school finance, being replaced in large part by the sales tax. In a number of populous states, including California, New Jersey and New York, governors have announced plans to reduce their states' progressive income taxes.

Two general approaches have been followed in the small existing literature on state and local tax structure. In the first approach, which is based on the median voter model, the government chooses a set of taxes to maximize the utility of a representative agent such as a 'decisive voter'. In these models, tax exporting, which lowers the relative cost to the representative agent of particular tax instruments, results in a hierarchy of taxes based on the proportion of each tax that can be exported (Arnott and Grieson 1981).

The second approach to modelling tax structure emphasizes the political economy of local decisionmaking by focusing on the roles of different interest groups in determining political outcomes. Such models stress the divergent incentives of fiscal interest groups, and the conflict between such groups. Tax outcomes are responsive to differences in political power of the different fiscal interest groups. Based on this approach, Hettich and Winer (1988) and Winer and Hettich (1992) argue that the cost-minimizing tax structure is characterized by complexity and differentiation, as all available fiscal instruments become political tools for the efficient matching of taxes and willingness to pay. Inman (1989) incorporates distributional objectives into a model of local taxation. Political costs are closely related to the burdens borne by each group. Chernick (1992, 1994) follows this approach in models that explain the distribution of tax burdens across income classes.

In the first part of this chapter (Sections 2 and 3), we build on the previous work of Chernick and specify a model of state and local tax incidence that builds on the premise that fiscal interest groups play an important role in determining the degree of tax progressivity chosen by state and local governments. In our empirical model, we include variables describing the distribution of income in each state as proxies for the role these fiscal interest groups play in determining state tax policy.

In the second part of this chapter (Section 4), we argue that an important factor in explaining the underlying incidence pattern of state and local tax systems is the extent to which their citizens are economically mobile over time. This argument has two parts. First is the well-known assertion that economic mobility can alter the long-run incidence of any given tax structure. Tax incidence studies based on annual income data have frequently been criticized because they fail to recognize that many people may be only temporarily poor (or rich). If most people tend to be economically mobile over time, then tax incidence analysis conducted using annual data will tend to overstate tax regressivity. This result holds whether annual incidence is regressive or progressive. If a given individual starts out poor, he or she would face a higher tax burden initially under a regressive tax system. However, as relative economic position improves over time, the relative tax burden falls. For this individual the long-term burden is less than the initial burden. The opposite holds for individuals whose relative income falls over their lifetime. Hence, the greater the extent of such mobility, the more proportional is the tax system over time.

The second part of our argument concerning the link between economic mobility and tax incidence is that economic mobility may also affect the political economy of tax choices. If tax choices reflect the power of conflicting fiscal interest groups, then the political economy model of taxation must incorporate the determinants of fiscal power. The strength of an interest group, or more generally a coalition of interests, depends on its size and cohesiveness. The hypothesis we explore in this chapter is that economic mobility weakens the fiscal power of coalitions by reducing cohesiveness. The greater the degree of economic mobility, the lower the correlation between an individual's initial economic position and his or her economic position at some point in the future. Therefore, mobility reduces the individual's incentive to lobby for a tax structure that is favourable to his or her current economic situation. In the limit, under perfect mobility, with any individual facing an equal probability of being in any given income position, individuals prefer a tax system that is proportional at all income levels.

2. A MODEL OF STATE AND LOCAL TAX INCIDENCE

In order to measure the distribution of state and local tax burdens across income classes for each state, we draw on a 50-state study of state and local tax incidence by the Citizens for Tax Justice (1991). As payments of state and local income taxes and the local property tax are deductible from gross income subject to the federal income tax (for those taxpayers who itemize their deductions), the Citizens for Tax Justice (CTJ) study estimates total state and local tax burdens both net and gross of federal deductibility. Taxes included in their study are state and local income taxes, state and local sales taxes, most excise taxes, corporate taxes and local property taxes. Local income tax rates are generally set by the state and are used only in a small number of jurisdictions in the United States. Local sales tax rates are also set by state governments. We exclude the property tax from our regression analysis because property tax rates are determined independently by thousands of independent local governments. Our analysis thus focuses on decisions about taxation made by state governments.

The dependent variable in our regressions is a measure of the degree of progressivity of each state's tax system. The measure we use is the ratio of the effective tax rate on state residents in the top quintile of the income distribution to the effective tax rate on those in the bottom quintile of the income distribution. The data confirm the result found in previous studies of the incidence of subnational taxes in the US (Pechman and Okner 1974, Phares 1980), namely, that state and local taxes are regressive. Furthermore, the data indicate that the overall incidence of the state and local system remained substantially unchanged between 1976 and 1991.[2] Underlying this stability is considerable variation over time in the progressivity of individual taxes. These patterns suggest an aggregate distributional equilibrium for state–local taxes which is relatively invariant over time, implying both a stable political cost function for taxation and stable preferences for public goods.

Our model of subnational tax incidence draws on the prior work of Chernick (1994) and is based on the assumption that the fiscal problem facing the politician is one of selecting that particular set of tax and fee changes and expenditure changes which will equate net benefits across fiscal interest groups.[3] Analogous to the minimum bundle constraint in the linear expenditure system, the politician faces a minimum revenue constraint. This revenue constraint may be thought of as the cost of a set of core public services which the government must provide. The bundle includes pure public goods, goods with substantial spillovers, and goods which the government is required to provide, either by constitutional mandate or through a legal mandate from a higher level of government.[4]

The politician will choose a set of tax instruments that achieve an optimal distribution of real after-tax income, subject to the minimum revenue requirement. Real after-tax income is defined as before-tax income minus direct taxes, such as income or payroll taxes, and also minus indirect taxes paid in the form of consumption taxes. Based on this model, we assume the incidence of subnational taxation will be a function of the distribution of income within the jurisdiction which determines the political power of the different income coalitions, tastes and political pressure factors which determine the shape of the political cost function, the ability of different income groups to export taxes, the incidence of federal taxation, and the degree of fiscal competition provided by other states. Table 13.1 provides a summary of the definitions of each variable and indicates data sources.

The detailed specification of our model begins with the political economy variables. If politicians try to use the tax system to offset inequalities in the pre-tax distribution of income, then tax progressivity should be positively related to income inequality.[5] With variable names in bold type, the measures of income distribution we use are INCDISTR, the ratio of pre-tax income of the top quintile of the income distribution to the pre-tax income of the bottom quintile, and PCTPOOR, the percentage of the population with incomes below the official national poverty standard. Both variables are expected to have a positive effect. The rationale for these variables is developed in the public choice models of Meltzer and Richard (1981) and Peltzman (1980), which predict that the greater the degree of income inequality, the greater the degree of redistribution. In these models, redistributive outcomes reflect the fiscal struggle between selfish individuals at different positions in the income distribution, each trying to maximize their net position *vis-à-vis* the fisc. The magnitude of fiscal transfers depends on the relative power of the poor and the rich, and the costs to each group of additional redistribution. For Meltzer and Richard, redistribution is a fiscal game of numbers. Hence, the greater the number of poor who vote, the higher the ratio of the mean to median income, and the greater the equilibrium demand for transfers. In Peltzman's model, the greater the economic distance between rich and the poor, the lower the cost to the poor of increasing the tax rate on higher income taxpayers to finance redistribution.

Peltzman also argues that the more equally distributed the income of those below the median, the greater will be the degree of transfers. This is because in a more equally distributed lower-income group, fewer people will face the adverse incentive effects of the higher taxation needed to finance transfers. Following Kristov et al. (1992), we include MIDPOOR, the ratio of average income of the middle quintile to the bottom quintile, as a measure of the equality of the income distribution for those below the median. We expect it to have a negative sign.

To measure tastes for altruism, we use MAX WELFARE BENEFITS, which is the maximum benefit level under the basic US cash welfare programme, known as Aid to Families with Dependent Children (AFDC). Though the financing of AFDC is shared between the states and the federal government, states are free to set benefit levels. There is in fact a wide variation across states in benefit levels, from a low of $120 for a one-parent family of three persons in Mississippi to a high of $680 in Connecticut and $923 in Alaska (US House of Representatives 1994). We also include an index of the political ideology in each state. The variable, called LIBERAL, is a weighted average of the number of Republicans and Democrats in each state legislature, where the weights are based on ideological ratings of each state's Congressional delegation, with higher ratings assigned to those with more liberal records.[6] Both variables are predicted to have a positive effect on progressivity.

Table 13.1   Variable definitions and data sources

INCDISTR: Ratio of average income, top quintile to bottom quintile, for families of four. Source: Unpublished data described in Citizens for Tax Justice (1991).

PCTPOOR: Percentage of population with incomes below the official US poverty line. Source: Christine M. Ross and Sheldon Danziger, 'Poverty Rates by States, 1979 and 1985: A Research Note', *Focus* (Newsletter of the Institute for Research on Poverty, University of Wisconsin-Madison), 10 (3) (1987), 1–8. Data for 1989 are from United States House of Representatives, Committee on Ways and Means, *Green Book; Background Material and Data on Programs Within the Jurisdiction of the Committee on Ways and Means*, 1991 edition, Appendix I, Table 7.

MIDPOOR: Ratio of average income, middle quintile to bottom quintile, for families of four. Source: Unpublished data described in Citizens for Tax Justice (1991).

MAX WELFARE BENEFITS: Maximum AFDC benefit level for a family of three. Source: United States House of Representatives, *Green Book,* 1989 edition, Table 12, p. 546 and 1991 edition, Section 7, Table 10, p. 605.

LIBERAL: Weighted average of the percentage of Republicans and Democrats in each state assembly. Source: The weights are ideological ratings of the state's Congressional delegation compiled by the Committee on Political Education of the AFL–CIO. These data were collected by Robert Plotnick of the University of Washington.

PCTITEM: Percentage of filing units who itemize their deductions for the federal income tax. Source: US Treasury Department, *Statistics of Income, Individual Tax Returns*, various years.

SALES: Retail sales in each state relative to the national average of retail sales. Source: Sales and Marketing Management Magazine, *Survey of Buying Power*, selected years.

NEIGHBORS' TAX RATE: Average of the highest marginal income tax rate in all geographically contiguous states, lagged two years. Source: See text for construction. Data from Advisory Commission Fiscal Federalism, *Significant Features of Fiscal Federalism*, selected years.

Table 13.1 (continued)

INCOME: State personal income per capita. Source: US Dept. of Commerce, *Survey of Current Business*, various years.

SHRCHARGE: Share of own-source revenues from fees and charges. Source: US Census of Governments, *State Government Finances and Government Finances*, selected years.

PCT URBAN: Percentage of the population living in urban areas. Source: US Dept. of Commerce, Bureau of the Census, *Statistical Abstract of the United States*, various years.

PCT YOUNG: Percentage of the population 5 to 17 years of age. Source: *Statistical Abstract*.

PCT OLD: Percentage of the population 65 years and older. Source: *Statistical Abstract*.

Exporting of state and local taxes occurs through two mechanisms. The first is exporting to the federal government through the deductibility provision of the federal income tax. State and local property and income taxes are deductible from federal adjusted gross income for taxpayers who itemize their deductions. Hence, for an itemizer the price of an additional dollar of state or local income or property tax is one minus his or her federal marginal tax rate.

Burdens can also be exported by taxing sales of goods and services made to out-of-state residents and firms, and imposing taxes on non-resident suppliers of factors of production. The latter include non-resident wage and income taxes, corporate income taxes, and property taxes on commercial and industrial property.

As a measure of the ability to export taxes, we include PCTITEM, the percentage of tax filing units who itemize on their federal tax returns, and SALES, an index of retail sales relative to the national average. Since deductibility is highly correlated with income, the greater the percentage itemizing, the greater the percentage of taxpayers with incomes above the median who face a reduced tax price, and the lower the resistance to a progressive state and local tax structure. Therefore, the predicted effect of PCTITEM on progressivity is positive. The variable SALES was excluded from the final specification on the grounds of statistical insignificance.

Interstate tax competition is measured by NEIGHBORS' TAX RATE, the average of the highest marginal tax rate in all geographically contiguous states. The variable is lagged two years to reduce any bias from common regional shocks or other simultaneous effects.[7] Geographic tax competition should lead to a convergence of tax systems. The more progressive are neighbours' rates, the lower the political cost to a state's politicians from increasing the progressivity of its own tax system. Thus the predicted effect of this variable on progressivity is positive.

We also include in our specification personal income per capita, INCOME, and the share of total own-source revenues derived from user charges and fees, SHRCHARGE. INCOME serves as a proxy for the demand for government spending. If the income elasticity of demand is less than unity, as most studies indicate, then under the benefits received model of state and local finance, progressivity will be a negative function of income. The predicted effect of SHRCHARGE is ambiguous because of offsetting income and preference effects.

As controls for the cost of government services and the nature of demand for government expenditures, we include a variable measuring the percentage of each state's population living in urban areas, PCT URBAN, the percentage of population less than 17 years of age, PCT YOUNG, and the percentage 65 years of age or over, PCT OLD. We also include three region dummy variables, SOUTH, WEST and NCENTRAL, to control for systematic regional differences, and a year dummy variables, YEAR91, to capture both temporal changes in tastes and changes in federal tax laws that affect all states equally. We have no sign prediction for these variables.

Studies that measure tax incidence have noted that net burdens are less progressive than gross burdens, and concluded that deductibility lessens the progressivity of state and local taxes (Phares 1980). However, under a model of tax structure such as the one developed by Inman (1989), politicians have a preferred distribution of tax burdens, measured net of federal deductibility. Implicit in Inman's model is the assumption that taxpayers actually perceive net rather than gross burdens. This means that they are aware of the impact of deductibility on their state and local tax burdens. This assumption implies that an exogenous change in the value of deductibility (referred to as the 'federal offset'), caused perhaps by an increase in federal marginal tax rates, leads state politicians to change state tax rates, with the goal of leaving the net distribution of burdens unchanged. Under this assumption, deductibility would have no effect on the distribution of net tax burdens. We test this assumption by estimating two equations, one for tax incidence net of the federal offset, and one for incidence gross of the federal offset. Under the distributional equilibrium model, we would expect that the coefficient on PCTITEM would be larger in the gross than the net equation. If the distributional equilibrium is totally exogenous to the federal offset, then the coefficient on PCTITEM in the net burden equation would be zero.

Because PCTITEM is endogenous to the progressivity of the tax structure, the model is estimated using the method of instrumental variables, with exogenous federal grants serving as the identifying instrument for PCTITEM.

3. RESULTS OF THE MODEL ESTIMATION

The regression results of the model developed in the previous section are presented in Table 13.2.

Table 13.2. Progressivity of state tax burdens (instrumental variables estimates)

Independent variables	Net incidence		Gross incidence	
INCDISTR	0.254	(0.128)**	0.345	(0.179)*
MIDPOOR	−0.649	(0.337)*	−0.823	(0.473)*
PCTPOOR	−0.007	(0.012)	−0.008	(0.017)
MAXIMUM				
WELFARE BENEFIT	0.0007	(0.0012)	0.0005	(0.0017)
LIBERAL	0.0037	(0.0019)*	0.0051	(0.0027)*
NEIGHBORS' TAX RATE	−0.026	(0.025)	−0.039	(0.035)
PCTITEM	0.034	(0.017)*	0.053	(0.025)**
INCOME	−0.0003	(0.0001)**	−0.0004	(0.0001)**
SHRCHARGE	−0.275	(0.618)	−0.264	(0.868)
PERCENT YOUNG	−0.076	(0.031)**	−0.108	(0.043)**
PERCENT URBAN	−0.0046	(0.002)**	−0.006	(0.003)**
SOUTH	−0.222	(0.141)	−0.358	(0.199)*
WEST	−0.064	(0.121)	−0.129	(0.170)
NCENTRAL	−0.017	(0.096)	−0.047	(0.135)
YEAR91	0.469	(0.207)**	0.672	(0.291)
INTERCEPT	3.497	(1.317)**	4.449	(1.850)**
ADJ R^2	0.25		0.24	
OBSERVATIONS	96		96	

Notes: Progressivity measured by the ratio of the effective tax rate on the highest income quintile of tax filing units to the lowest quintile. Taxes included in the incidence measure are state income, sales, excise taxes, and corporate income taxes, plus local income and sales taxes. Column 1 is net of the federal deductibility of state and local taxes, while column 2 is gross of federal deductibility. The sample is a pooled cross section of the 48 continental states for the years 1985 and 1991. Standard errors of coefficients are in parentheses ( ).

* Significantly different from zero at the 10 per cent level.

** Significantly different from zero at the 5 per cent level.

The estimated coefficients in the first column are for a model that explains tax progressivity net of the federal offset, while the results in the second column are from a model explaining tax progressivity measured gross of the federal offset.

The two models in Table 13.2 explain about 24 per cent of the total variation in tax progressivity. In contrast, a model using the same regressors as the distributional model is able to explain as much as 81 per cent of the variation in tax levels. This difference points to the importance of idiosyncratic and historical factors in determining tax progressivity in different states.

INCDISTR has the expected positive sign, while MIDPOOR has a negative sign. Both variables are statistically significant. However, while the signs of these two variables do not change under alternative specifications, the statistical significance of the distribution variables is sensitive to the exact specification of the incidence model. Bearing this in mind, the results are supportive of the role of fiscal interest groups in determining tax incidence. Between 1985 and 1989 the value of INCDISTR increased from 5.74 to 6.25, implying an increase in the net progressivity, or alternatively stated, a decrease in the regressivity, of the state tax system. However, about half of the increase in our measure of tax progressivity was offset by the increase in MIDPOOR from a value of 2.94 to 3.04. Thus the net effect of changes in the income distribution over the period was an increase of 0.06 in the value of our measure of net progressivity, an increase that implies a 9 per cent reduction in state tax regressivity.

These tax incidence results are consistent with several other studies of both tax and expenditure incidence. Inman (1989) shows that for large US cities, the greater the relative size of the poor population, the greater the reliance on more progressive revenue instruments. Chernick (1991) finds that state income taxation is positively related to the proportion of poor. On the expenditure side, Kristov et al. (1992) find that social affinity, as measured by the rate of growth of income, and the ratios of income of the top to the middle and the middle to the bottom of the income distribution, plays an important role in explaining cross-country differences in transfer payments.

The political ideology variable LIBERAL is significant at the 10 per cent level. This result contrasts with several studies suggesting that political party control has little effect on tax structure. This is perhaps not surprising. A state's Congressional representatives are more likely to vote along ideological grounds than representatives to state legislatures, hence changes in party control are less likely to reflect underlying changes in taste for redistribution than the direct voting pattern of a state's Congressional delegation.

The magnitude of the coefficient on YEAR91 indicates that the increase in state tax progressivity between 1985 and 1991 is not due solely to changes in the income distribution. What explains the shift? The most plausible explanation is that the federal income tax affects sub-national progressivity in two ways, through a price effect and a displacement effect. By lowering marginal tax rates and reducing the proportion of taxpayers who itemize their deductions, the federal Tax Reform Act of 1986 increased the marginal price of state income taxes, which are the most progressive of the state and local taxes. However, during the 1980s there was a cumulative reduction in average federal tax rates on the rich. The reduction eventually allowed states to capture as revenue some of the resultant increase in after-federal income tax disposable income. This inverse relationship between federal tax rates and state tax rates is known as the displacement effect. Our statistical result suggests that between 1985 and 1991 the negative impact of the increase in the price of state and local income taxes was more than offset by the reduced displacement of income, leading to an increase in progressivity.

Both PCTITEM and INCOME have a statistically significant impact on tax progressivity, though their effects are offsetting. The greater the proportion itemizing, the greater the progressivity of state and local tax systems. However, the coefficient is larger for gross than net progressivity. This suggests that when a change in deductibility reduces the net tax burden of high-income taxpayers, states offset this change by increasing gross rates. This behavior implies that states do in fact have target distributions of net tax burdens which, if disturbed, leads to offsetting adjustments.

The negative coefficient on INCOME suggests, however, that there are limits to the amount of redistribution that is possible through the state and local tax system. If tax liabilities on the rich diverge too much from the benefits they receive from public spending, high-income taxpayers will exert political pressure on state and local governments to reduce tax progressivity.

4. INTEREST GROUPS, LONG-RUN INCIDENCE, AND ECONOMIC MOBILITY

We now turn to a discussion of the role economic mobility plays in determining the incidence of state and local taxes. As outlined in Section 1, our argument has two parts. First, the incidence of any given tax system will depend in part on the economic mobility of the population over time and second, to the extent that the choice of taxes is determined by the relative power of competing interest groups, economic mobility will tend to reduce the cohesiveness and hence political power of income-based interest groups.

4.1. The Calculation of Tax Burdens

It is well recognized that economic mobility can have a substantial direct impact on tax incidence. On the basis of the permanent income hypothesis and the companion life-cycle model of consumption and savings, we expect tax burdens based on long-run or permanent income to result in less regressive tax systems than burdens calculated using annual income. Under the assumption that consumption is more responsive to changes in permanent income than to year-to-year variations in measured income, people with temporarily low incomes will face high annual burdens for consumption-based taxes, while the opposite will hold for those with temporarily high incomes. However, over the longer run, as long as most people with low (high) incomes are only temporarily poor (rich), either because of transitory fluctuations in income or life-cycle factors, consumption patterns will even out and the consumption to income ratio for most items will be closer to proportional. Although this conclusion is well known, until recently there have been few empirical efforts made to estimate the bias created by basing incidence calculations on annual rather than longer-run income.

Fullerton and Rogers (1993) and Metcalf (1993) calculate what they call 'lifetime' incidence by making an estimate of individuals' lifetime income. In ongoing research, we have addressed the issue of the 'annual income bias' in tax incidence studies by arguing that because lifetime income is not observable and extremely difficult to estimate, and because lifetime measures are not accepted by policymakers, it is preferable to calculate incidence on the basis of data for a shorter period of time. We proceed to do this by using 11 years of income and consumption data (for the period from 1976 to 1986). Our source of data is the Panel Study of Income Dynamics (PSID), a longitudinal study that has followed a random sample of over 5,000 families since 1968. By exploiting the limited consumption and tax information that is available on the PSID and imputing additional data from other sources, we have calculated 'intermediate-run' tax burdens for the gasoline excise tax, the sales tax on meals consumed at restaurants and the property tax on owner-occupied houses.

As an index of progressivity, we compute the ratio of the average burden in the top half of the distribution to the average burden in the bottom half. A value less than one indicates regressivity. Using this measure, all three of these taxes are regressive under both short-and intermediate-run measures of tax incidence. For the gas tax, the ratio using annual 1982 data is 0.68. When calculated using data for the 11-year period from 1976 to 1986, the ratio is 0.79. Similar calculations for the property tax show a rise in the ratio from 0.55 to 0.73. For the meals tax the ratio increases from 0.62 to 0.80.

These results are consistent with our expectation that the intermediate-run incidence of taxes on the uses of income is more progressive than the annual incidence. However, the results also indicate that for taxes on gasoline, owner-occupied property and meals, the reduction in regressivity is quite modest over an intermediate period of eleven years. Since these taxes weigh very heavily in the overall state and local tax burden, the implication is that those who are persistently poor over an 11-year period face significantly higher state and local tax burdens than the persistently rich.

4.2. Speculations on the Role of Income Mobility in Influencing the Choice of Taxes

In Section 2, we argued that fiscal interest groups play an important role in determining the degree of tax progressivity chosen by state and local governments. In our empirical model, we have included variables describing the distribution of income in each state as proxies for the role these fiscal interest groups play in determining state tax policy. If a given tax, let us say a sales tax, is regressive, then we would expect that low-income taxpayers will attempt to discourage use of sales taxes. We hypothesize that the degree to which they will oppose the sales tax, or lobby for the adoption of a progressive income tax, depends in part on the extent to which any given taxpayer identifies him or herself as low income. Furthermore, we assume that the extent to which individuals identify themselves as members of a coalition or interest group defined in terms of income depends crucially on their expectations concerning economic mobility. If there is a high degree of economic mobility among the poor, we expect that the political role played by the poor in influencing tax policy will be reduced. If at the same time there is less economic mobility among the rich, we expect the resulting tax system to be more regressive than it would be if a large proportion of the poor in any given year remained persistently poor over some extended period of time.[8]

As we mentioned earlier in the chapter, most states' state and local tax systems are quite regressive. Data from Phares (1980) and Citizens for Tax Justice (1991) indicate that although tax systems in individual states have undergone substantial changes over time, on average the regressivity of state and local taxes has remained largely unchanged in the 15 years between 1976 and 1991.

The distribution of tax burdens across income classes has remained stable over this period despite the fact that a large number of studies show increasing inequality of the income distribution in the United States during the 1970s and particularly during the 1980s. Danziger and Gottschalk (1993) attribute much of this growing income inequality to an increase in the inequality of wages. Research by Slemrod (1992) indicates that the increase in the number of low-income families represents more than an increase in transitory income shocks. He finds increased inequality from the early 1970s to the 1980s not only in annual incomes, but in five-year average incomes. This evidence of growing income inequality is buttressed by research by Duncan, Smeeding and Rodgers (1992), who find, based on data from the PSID, that the probability of a family falling from the middle class to the lower-income class increased, while the probability of rising to the middle class fell. At the same time, transitions from middle to high increased, while transitions from high to middle ('falling from grace' using Duncan's phrase) fell in frequency.

Our econometric results, presented in Section 3, suggest that interest groups defined over income classes plays a role in shaping state and local tax policy. This result suggests that the growing income inequality and the growth in the number of low-income households should increase the political influence of interest groups representing low-income taxpayers. However, the magnitude of the estimated effects is small, indicating that differences in the income distribution across states play only a minor role in explaining interstate variation in progressivity. Under the assumption that individuals with relatively low incomes will oppose regressive taxes and support policies that shift tax burdens to those with higher levels of income, we might expect a movement in the United States towards a less regressive tax system. However, as we have seen, despite the growing number of low-income families in the United States, state and local tax systems have not become less regressive.

One way to reconcile the stability of the incidence of the state and local tax system with the declining middle-class and the growing number of low-income individuals is to assume that income mobility at the bottom of the income distribution is sufficient to reduce the political cohesiveness and effectiveness of groups supporting the fiscal interests of the poor. In order to explore this hypothesis, we present some data on income mobility.

In Figure 13.1, we show three alternative measures of income mobility. We start by comparing 1976 annual incomes of heads and spouses in the PSID sample in 1982 to each person's average income for the five-year period between 1976 and 1980 and each person's average income for the 11-year period between 1976 and 1986. We divide our sample into income deciles based on their 1976 incomes and then we divide the people in each 1976 income decile into deciles of five-year average income and 11-year average income. In Figure 13.1 we show the proportion of individuals who are in the same or an adjacent decile of annual and average income.

As a third measure of income mobility, we compute deciles of 1986 annual income, and calculate the proportion of individuals who are in the same or

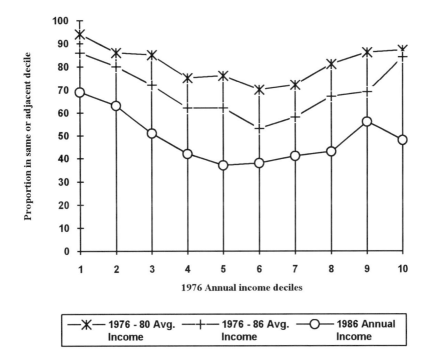

Figure 13.1   Degree of income mobility, 1976–1986 (for each 1976 annual income decile, per cent of individuals in same or adjacent average or annual income decile position)

adjacent decile of 1976 and 1986 annual income. The greater the height of each line in Figure 13.1, the lower the degree of income mobility. Each line displays the U-shaped pattern which is characteristic of a transition matrix measure of income mobility, with a higher proportion immobile in the tails of the distribution than in the middle (Atkinson et al. 1992). The top line is for five-year average income, the middle line for 11-year average income, and the bottom line for 1986 annual income deciles.

The figure indicates, not surprisingly, that income mobility increases as we extend the measurement period. Overall, 81 per cent of households are immobile (in the same or adjacent annual and average income decile) over five years, and 69 per cent over 11 years. Comparing the initial and the final year of the period (1976 deciles to 1986 deciles), 49 per cent are immobile. Nevertheless, looking at the bottom of the income distribution, almost 70 per cent of individuals in the bottom decile in 1976 were in the bottom or the second decile 11 years later.

How should we interpret the data in Figure 13.1? On the one hand, the data appear to indicate that most individuals who have low incomes in a given year, have low incomes, on average, over the next 11 years. This pattern of limited income mobility explains why consumption tax burdens, for example for the gas tax, remain regressive when burdens are calculated using 11-year average data on gasoline consumption and income. What we are finding is that over a period of years, most people's relative income position remains quite stable.

On the other hand, the data in Figure 13.1 clearly indicate that some income mobility exists, especially as we lengthen the period of observation. In an absolute sense, many people's income rises and falls from year to year, with some people experiencing quite dramatic changes in their positions in the income distribution. The question that we are unable to resolve in this chapter is whether the income mobility we actually observe over the bottom half of the income distribution is sufficient to explain the limited effectiveness of political interest groups lobbying for less regressive taxation. We speculate, however, that there is enough movement in and out of any position in the income distribution to at least dampen many people's self-identification with that income position, whether it be lower income, middle class or higher income.

The political effectiveness of income-based interest groups may be further undermined if a substantial number of people expect their current income level to change in the near future. These expectations (whether justified or not) may be sufficient to reduce the political influence of income-based interest groups, and may help explain why the progressivity of the tax system has remained unchanged despite quite marked increases in income inequality.[9]

A second reason for the apparent limited political effectiveness of groups supporting the fiscal interests of low-income households may be the fact that in the United States the participation in elections by low-income individuals is quite low. A Census survey showed that among all individuals 18 years of age and over, only 35 per cent of high school graduates and 81 per cent of college graduates voted (US Bureau of the Census 1993). Given the high correlation between income and education, the survey provides strong evidence of the low level of political participation among low-income individuals.[10] Recall that 70 per cent of the poorest individuals in a given year will still be at the bottom of the income distribution 11 years later. This might suggest the existence of a large core of people with a sustained interest in progressive taxation. However, the very low voter participation rate for the poor in the United States strongly mitigates their potential political influence. This low level of political activism by the poor may contribute to the continued regressivity of state and local tax systems in most states.

5. CONCLUSIONS

This chapter has presented a model that attempts to explain the variation in tax progressivity among state and local governments in the United States. We suggest that the tax policy of subnational governments is determined in part by the political influence exerted by various interest groups. We hypothesize that in determining the degree of progressivity of state tax systems, interest groups will be defined in terms of income class, with those near the bottom of the income distribution arguing most strongly for progressive taxes. We also argue that while economic mobility directly influences the incidence of various taxes, it may also have an impact on the choice of taxes. The strength of interest groups involved in the political struggle over progressivity depends in part on their cohesiveness. We argue that economic mobility has the potential to weaken the fiscal power of interest groups by reducing their cohesiveness.

Our econometric results are generally consistent with the interest group model of tax choice. Our suggestions concerning the impact of mobility are much more speculative. While we believe there is a link between the political influence of interest groups and economic mobility, we are unable to provide a precise quantitative measure of the strength of this link and the resultant effect on tax incidence. This is due in part to a fundamental ambiguity in the measure of economic mobility. We find that most people who have low incomes during any given year have been, and will remain, in the bottom of the income distribution for a number of years. Thus income mobility in a relative sense is low. However, there appears to be enough income movement in an absolute sense to flatten out (make more proportional) the future tax burdens of any given group of poor people. By contrast, for the rich it appears that mobility is not sufficient to have much effect on tax burdens as we extend the measurement period. Clearly, more research must be done if we are to fully understand the relationship between income mobility and the role individuals play in influencing tax policy.

NOTES

1. The data in this paragraph are for fiscal year 1991. They are calculated using data from Advisory Commission on Intergovernmental Relations (1993).
2. Although this conclusion is based on a single measure of progressivity (the ratio of the effective tax rate on those in the top quintile of the income distribution to the tax rate on those in the bottom quintile), it is likely that our conclusion concerning the temporal stability of tax incidence would hold for alternative incidence measures.

3. We assume that politicians are unable to use any other policy instruments to reward particular groups.
4. As examples of state constitutional mandates, the New York state constitution requires the government to provide care for the indigent and in New Jersey, the constitution requires that the state provide a thorough and efficient education to all children.
5. Feldstein and Vaillant (1994) argue that the causality runs the other way, that is that differences in progressivity cause differences in the pre-tax distribution of income. Chernick (1994) indirectly tests this proposition by regressing the change in state income per capita on the progressivity of the tax system. He finds no systematic effect.
6. The ratings are made by the Committee on Political Education of the AFL–CIO, (the largest organization of labour unions in the US).
7. The hypothesis implicit in this specification is that there is a recursive relationship between a state's distributional choices and those of neighbouring states, and that a state's tax burden in year *t* responds to the competitive environment with a lag. The distributional data are at an interval of six years (1985 and 1991). We assume that this interval is sufficiently long that the tax environment facing any state (that is the tax rates of its neighbours) has fully adjusted to a change in that states top marginal tax rate. Therefore this tax environment can be considered as an exogenous determinant of equilibrium. Possible simultaneity is further reduced by the fact that the interstate tax competition variable, which is specified as a nominal income tax rate, uses a different metric than the dependent variable, which is a ratio of effective tax rates. Winer and Hettich (1992), who use a similar specification, find that correcting for simultaneity in the interstate tax competition effect has no impact on the results
8. The above proposition about economic mobility should be distinguished from the concept of social affinity discussed in Kristov et al. (1992). They posit that the greater the social affinity between the middle class and the poor, the greater the degree of redistributive transfers, while the greater the social affinity between the middle class and the rich, the lower the level of transfers. Thus social affinity reflects a kind of asymmetric mobility. We concur that downward mobility, with an emptying out of the middle class towards the bottom, seems likely to promote demand for both tax and expenditure redistribution. Similarly, asymmetric upward mobility is likely to weaken redistributive demands. However, a symmetric increase in mobility will favour neither the rich nor the poor coalition and is likely to lead to more proportionality in taxation.
9. In November 1995, voters in the State of Massachusetts defeated a measure that would have increased the progressivity of the income tax. The proposal was structured so that the vast majority of households would have faced lower marginal tax rates and benefited from tax reductions. Despite this fact, it appears that one reason for its defeat was the belief among many voters that in the future their income would increase sufficiently so that they would eventually face the higher marginal rates.
10. Participation in state government elections that do not correspond with presidential elections is almost always considerably lower than participation in presidential elections.

REFERENCES

Advisory Commission on Intergovernmental Relations (1993), 'Significant features of fiscal federalism', Vol. 2, *Revenues and Expenditures*, Washington, DC: ACIR.

Arnott, R. and R.E. Grieson (1981), 'Optimal fiscal policy for a state or local government,' *Journal of Urban Economics*, **9**, 23–48.

Atkinson, A.B. et al. (1992), Empirical studies of earnings mobility No.52, in *Fundamentals of Pure and Applied Economics*, Series edited by Jacques

Lesourne and Hugo Sonnenschein, Philadelphia: Harwood Academic Publishers.

Chernick, H. (1991), 'Distributional constraints and state decisions to tax,' Paper Presented to the NBER Summer Institute on State and Local Finance, 1991.

Chernick, H. (1992), 'A model of the distributional incidence of State and local laxes,' *Public Finance Quarterly,* **20** (2), 572–85.

Chernick, H. (1994), 'Tax incidence, tax revenues, and economic performance: is Ppogressivity self-defeating?', *Working Paper No. 94–1*, Department of Economics, Hunter College.

Citizens for Tax Justice (1991) *A Far Cry From Fair: CTJ's Guide to State Tax Reform* written by R. S. Mcintyre, M. P. Ettlinger, D. P. Kelly and E. A. Fray, Washington, DC: Citizens for Tax Justice.

Danziger, S. and P. Gottschalk (1993), 'Introduction', in S.Danziger and P. Gottshalk (eds.), *Uneven Tides: Rising Inequality in America,*, New York: Russell Sage Foundation.

Duncan, G.J., T.M. Smeeding and W. Rodgers (1992), 'W(h)ither the middle class? a dynamic view,' *Policy Studies Paper* No. 1, Metropolitan Studies Program, Syracuse University, February.

Feldstein, M. and M. Vaillant (1994), 'Can state taxes redistribute income?' *Working Paper No. 4785*, Cambridge, MA: National Bureau of Economic Research, June.

Fullerton, D. and D.M. Rogers (1993), *Who Bears the Lifetime Tax Burden?* Washington, DC: The Brookings Institution.

Hettich, W. and S.L. Winer (1988), 'Economic and political foundations of tax structure,' *American Economic Review,* **78** (September), 701–12.

Inman, R.P. (1989), 'The local decision to tax: evidence from large U.S. cities,' *Regional Science and Urban Economics,* **19**, (August), 455–92.

Kristov, L., P. Lindert and R. McLelland (1992), 'Pressure groups and redistribution', *Journal of Public Economics,* **48** (July), 135–63.

Meltzer, A.H. and S.F. Richard (1981), 'A rational theory of the size of government', *Journal of Political Economy,* **89** (October), 914–27.

Metcalf, G. (1993), 'The lifetime incidence of state and local taxes: measuring changes during the 1980s,' *NBER Working Paper* No. 4252.

Moffitt, R. and P. Gottschalk (1993), 'Trends in the covariance structure of earnings in the United States: 1969–1987,' *Discussion Paper* 101–93, Institute for Research on Poverty, Madison: University of Wisconsin.

Pechman, J.A. (1985), *Who Paid the Taxes, 1966–85?* Washington, DC: The Brookings Institution.

Pechman, J.A. and B.A. Okner (1974), *Who Bears the Tax Burden?* Washington, DC: the Brookings Institution.

Peltzman, S. (1980), 'The growth of government,' *Journal of Law and Economics,* **23**, (October), 278–87.

Phares, D. (1980), *Who Pays State and Local Taxes?* Cambridge, MA: Oelgeschlager, Gunn & Hain.

Slemrod, J. (1992), 'Taxation and inequality: a time-exposure perspective', in J. Poterba (ed.) *Tax Policy and the Economy,* 6, Cambridge, MA: NBER and the MIT Press, 105–27.

United States Bureau of the Census (1993), *Voting and Registration in the Election of November 1992,* Current Population Reports, Washington, DC: US Government Printing Office, 20, 466.

United States House of Representatives, Committee on Ways and Means (1994), *1994 Green Book: Background Material and Data on Programs Within the Jurisdiction of the Committee on Ways and Means,* Washington, DC: US Government Printing Office, Table 10–11, 306

Winer, S.L. and W. Hettich (1992), 'Explaining the use of related tax instruments,' Working Paper, Sonderforschungsbereich 178, Series II, No. 189, Faculty for Economics and Statistics, Konstanz, Germany: University of Konstanz.

14. European Integration and Local Government Finance

Stephen Smith[*]

1. INTRODUCTION

This chapter considers the implications of the increasing integration of the economies of Western Europe for the structure of local government finance. In particular, it asks whether increasing economic integration will be likely to place limits on the level and type of local taxes that can be raised. If this does happen, is there a case for intervention by the EC, and what form should any such intervention take?

The chapter is in four main parts. The first (Section 2) draws out some common themes, and some contrasts, from current experience with local government and local government finance in the member states of the EC. The second part (Section 3) discusses the extent to which the steady progress towards economic integration among the EC members has placed limits on their systems of local government finance, and the extent to which the growing integration and internationalization of the European economy is likely to restrict national policy towards local government finance in the future. The third part (Section 4) sets out a conceptual framework for assessing the appropriate scope and limits of European regulation (in the form of coordination or 'harmonization') of the finance of decentralized government in EC member states. The conclusions of the chapter are set out in Section 5.

2. LOCAL GOVERNMENT FINANCE IN EUROPE

The most striking feature of local government in EC countries is the amount of diversity – in structure, functions and financing. The numbers of levels of

[*] The author wishes to acknowledge the financial support of the UK Economic and Social Research Council through the Local Governance Programme. The paper draws on joint work with Kevin Denny and Michael Ridge. The views expressed in the paper, and any errors, are those of the author alone, and not of ESRC or IFS.

sub-central government differ among member states of the EC, and the sizes of local government units differ widely. The functions allocated to subcentral government include some elements common to nearly all member states – such as, for example, the provision of local amenities – but there are also great differences, both in the extent to which major areas of public spending such as health, education, infrastructure provision and industrial/employment policies are decentralized, and in the overall level of spending of subcentral governments.

There is wide variation in the proportion of local government spending which is financed from revenue sources under local control (Figure 14.1).

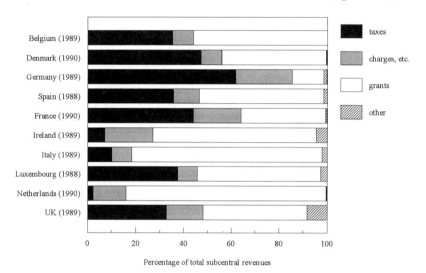

Percentage of total subcentral revenues

Note: Definition of sub-central government employed includes *Länder* in Germany, and regional and provincial governments elsewhere. Where countries have more than one level of sub-central government, fiscal transfers between subcentral levels have been omitted, to avoid double counting.

Source: Own calculations, based on IMF (1991), *Government Finance Statistics Yearbook*, Volume XV, country tables. Data for Greece and Portugal not available.

Figure 14.1.   Composition of sub-central government revenues

Transfers account for nearly all of the total resources of local governments in some member states (for example the Netherlands), but contribute less than half of total local revenues in others (for example Denmark, and municipal governments in Spain).

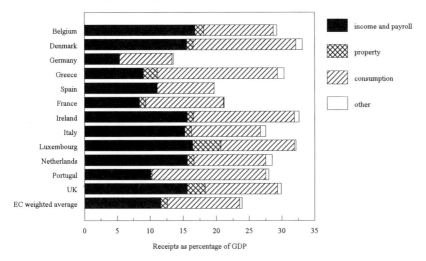

Source: Own calculations, based on OECD (1992), *Revenue Statistics of OECD Member Countries, 1965–91*, Table 123.

Figure 14.2 Structure of central government tax receipts, 1990

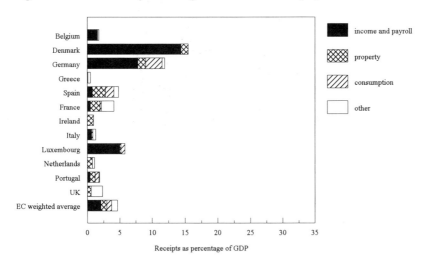

Source: Own calculations, based on OECD (1992) *Revenue Statistics of OECD Member Countries, 1965–91*, Table 123.

Figure 14.3 Structure of subcentral government tax receipts, 1990

The 'constitutional' basis on which the transfers to local government are determined varies; some member states (such as Germany) provide such transfers on a broadly automatic basis through stable tax-sharing arrangements, while others allocate grants on the basis of discretionary choices by central government.

There are some types of taxes which are frequently encountered as local taxes, such as taxes on real property (land and buildings); however, not all member states have such taxes, nor are they always allocated to local government (Figures 14.2, 14.3 and 14.4).

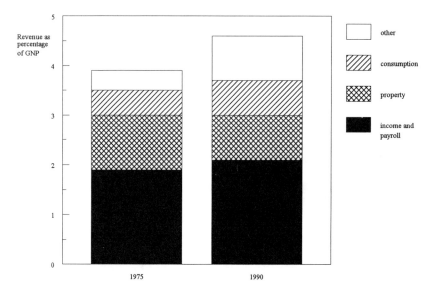

Source: Own calculations, based on OECD (1992), *Revenue Statistics of OECD Member Countries, 1965–91*, Table 123. Figures are a population-weighted average of percentages for each of the twelve member states.

Figure 14.4   Change in tax revenues of subcentral government, European Community, 1975–1990

There are wide variations in the numbers of local taxes (one each in the UK and Ireland, with larger numbers in many other member states), and in the extent to which particular tax bases are allocated to local government (for example, a large amount of local revenues is raised from local income taxes in Denmark, but not elsewhere). Nevertheless, despite this diversity, some common themes and generalizations can also be made, especially about the directions of change in local government.

There is a growing recognition of the importance of local tax-raising powers in ensuring local accountability and budgetary control. In a number of countries there has been an active debate about the need for local governments to take more responsibility for raising their own revenues, and there is a general tendency to increase the proportion of local revenues from local taxes. The UK, where the contribution from local taxes has been cut sharply in the aftermath of an unsuccessful attempt at local tax reform, appears to be an exception to this general trend.

A number of countries raise revenues from local taxes on business property or turnover, and the importance of these taxes is, if anything, growing (for example, the introduction of new taxes on local business in Italy and Spain). In countries where local business taxes have been more long-standing (for example, Germany and France) there has been an active debate about their possible distortionary effects; the UK has effectively abolished local powers of business taxation for precisely this reason.

In many countries, local powers over taxation are severely circumscribed by limits on the rates of tax that can be set. These limits, which reflect central government objectives, include examples of both upper and lower limits on tax rates; the function of the former is usually to prevent excessive disincentive effects, and the function of the latter to enforce at least a minimum degree of local fiscal accountability through taxation.

There is a growing move towards charging for specific services provided by local government, and in the importance of revenues from such charges as a revenue source for local government. The basis of such charges tends to vary widely; however, they often take the form of quasi taxes, unrelated to service consumption, and the level of charges may or may not be governed by the level of spending on the service for which the charge is levied.

There is a growing trend towards the growth of regional government, operating at a level intermediate between that of local government and the national government. Over the past two decades, systems of regional government have been set up, or given an enhanced role, in France, Italy and Spain. An equivalent layer of government in Germany is provided by the *Länder*, and only the UK of the large EC countries has no regional tier of government. In most of the countries (except for federal Germany), regional governments are financed largely through financial transfers from central government. The growing significance of regional government in member states has been given impetus by the financial flows to the regional level from the EC.

It has for some time been recognized that the diversity encountered among EC local governments may be explained, at least in part, by fundamental differences in the context and functions of local government in the different member states, reflecting the balance between the 'choice' and 'agency' roles that local government can perform.

On the one hand, local governments may be seen as a means of allowing local communities to make decisions which match their needs and preferences better than centralized decisions could. In this case, the essence of local government is that it allows local choices to be made.

Alternatively, local government may be seen as a vehicle for the implementation of policies and decisions of central government. Various tasks may be assigned to local level to administer because they are too costly (or unfeasible) for central government to implement on its own. In this case, the role for local choice may be very limited indeed; central government will wish to see a decisionmaking process which allows local discretion to be exercised only to the extent that it does not conflict with the objectives of the centre.

These two models are intended as analytical concepts, rather than as accurate and complete descriptions or categorizations of actual systems of local government. Many systems of local government combine elements of both functions. I have suggested elsewhere (Hughes and Smith 1991) that this combination of fundamentally opposed functions is one of the basic reasons for conflict and dysfunctionality in local government. Nevertheless, what is important is to recognize that in different European countries, local government tends more towards one or other of these polar extremes. In the UK, for example, it is becoming increasingly clear that the role of local government is better understood in terms of the agency model than of the choice model; in other member states, some at least of the levels of decentralized government have more genuine powers of discretionary choice over major areas of their activity. It is clear that at least some of the diversity encountered in arrangements for local government finance in different member states reflects these different basic roles being played by decentralized government.

3. PRESSURES FROM ECONOMIC INTEGRATION

What is likely to be the impact of European integration on the situation described above? The impact of economic integration within the EC on local taxation will largely take the form of a geographical 'broadening' of familiar and long-standing economic pressures and constraints on local government arising from the possible effects of local tax differences on the location decisions of individuals and businesses.

Where tax rates and structures differ between local jurisdictions, individuals and corporate taxpayers may find themselves facing different tax burdens depending on where they choose to locate. While these tax differences may in part reflect differences in the standard of local services provided, it will frequently be the case that for any individual taxpayer, the base on which they are taxed, and their interest in local services, do not exactly coincide. Taxpayers may, in other words, face non-zero 'fiscal residuals' from locating in particular areas. Consequently, the differences in taxation (and in spending benefits) could encourage some taxpayers to change their behaviour – for example, firms may relocate production in order to benefit from the lower rates of tax offered in certain areas. Where such changes in behaviour are made purely for tax reasons, the possibility arises of distortionary costs to the economies of member states – potentially productive resources may be wasted merely in the pursuit of lower taxation.

As the economic integration of the EC has developed, the mobility of businesses and individuals has increased. Consequently, the range of possible location choices which a taxpayer might wish to take into account has broadened, and may increasingly include locations in more than one member state. It is in principle possible that local tax levels in, say, the UK and France, may now affect the location choices of industry between these two countries, and not simply within each country. Nevertheless, the implications of greater integration for most of the major taxes used by local government are very limited. In general, there is no reason to believe that the existing diversity of local government and local finance will be seriously threatened by the growing internationalization and integration of the economy. While more vigorous intra-EC competition undoubtedly places limits on national tax policy, these limits are still compatible with a substantial amount of local control over taxation.

The reason for this judgement is that local governments in Europe are in general not financed from bases which are highly exposed to the impact of greater integration.

Taxes on land and fixed property, which are widely used as local taxes, are taxes on an immobile base, and consequently unlikely to be the source of major cross-country distortion. Taxes on individuals, such as the local income taxes in some member states, could potentially lead to cross-country distortion in the form of tax effects on individual residence choices; however, non-tax factors are likely to be overwhelmingly more important than tax factors in individual residence choices. Benefit taxes (i.e. taxes related to service use) could lead to movements of individuals or businesses to areas where a better 'package' of taxes and benefits was on offer; but these movements may be efficient, rather than a distortion of the internal market.

Two further types of taxation where considerable potential for distortion would arise are rarely used as sources of local revenues: taxes on goods and services, and taxes on investment incomes. If these were levied at locally varying rates, they would be prone to severe tax competition and distortion. This would also be true within member states, of course, which is the reason why the only form in which these bases tend to be used as revenue sources for local government is in the form of tax sharing, where local control over tax rates does not exist.

The local taxes where there is most concern about the possible impact of greater economic integration on taxpayer behaviour are local business taxes – such as the business assets taxes operated at a local level in a number of EC countries (*taxe professionnelle* in France, etc.). While some businesses, such as those supplying retail or other services to a local community, may have little choice about where to locate, other businesses, especially those involved in manufacturing, or wholesale distribution, may have a wider choice of possible locations, and their choices may be more liable to be distorted by local fiscal conditions. These issues arise, of course, within countries as well as between countries, and the existing debate about the role of local business taxes within countries may give some indications as to the impact of local business taxes at a wider, European, level.

Quantitative evidence on the distortionary impact of local business taxes on business location decisions is, however, very sparse in Europe, although there is a substantial US literature. In the UK, the evidence that local business tax differentials (before the abolition of local control over business tax levels in 1990) had any major effect on industrial location was inconclusive. Crawford, Fothergill and Monk (1985) found no link between business property tax ('business rates') levels and employment. On the other hand, Bennett and Krebs (1988) showed that the wide range of local tax rates on business in the UK led to appreciable differences in the cost of capital in different authorities, of a scale which might be expected to have had an effect on business investment decisions.

Part of the reason that effects on location are difficult to find is that the impact of taxation may only be felt fully in the very long term. The short-term distortionary impact of local taxes may be lower, if differences in the levels of tax between local jurisdictions are capitalized into the prices of geographically-immobile assets. Thus, for example, the differences between local jurisdictions in the taxation of business premises may be (partly) reflected in the rents or prices of business premises in different areas; where local taxes are high, the rents or prices of business real estate may be correspondingly low. Business investors who take their decisions on the basis of the cost of occupation of premises including taxes may then be indifferent between high and low tax areas, and distortions may not arise, even though tax rates differ widely. Over the longer term, however, the importance of capitalization in reducing the impact of local taxes on business and individual location decisions may well be much lower. Taxes on buildings, which may be capitalized in the short term while the supply of buildings is largely fixed, may be distorting over a longer time period when the supply of buildings in different areas is variable and can respond to differences in tax levels.

A further reason which may explain the limited impact of local business taxes on business location within countries is that other aspects of local government finance (especially central government grants) may be deployed to keep fiscal differences within acceptable bounds. The pattern of central government financial transfers to local authorities can affect the amount of economic distortion caused by local fiscal decisions. Equalizing grants, which aim to offset differences in the tax base available to authorities, can significantly reduce the dispersion of local tax rates and hence economic distortions caused by differences among the tax rates levied by local governments.

How far are the above observations about the distortionary impact of local business taxes *within* member states relevant in assessing the scope for distortion from these taxes *between* member states? There are a number of differences between the two cases, although their net impact on the balance of the argument is ambiguous.

In general, locational distortions will be greater if neighbouring jurisdictions set different tax rates than if the same tax differential exists between distant jurisdictions. Superficially this observation might suggest that if local taxes do not cause distortions within member states, then they will not cause distortions between the member states of the Community. However, this intuition is wrong, even if member states have – as would be reasonable to suppose – chosen systems of local taxation that do not cause excessive internal distortion.

Distortions may arise between member states even if they do not arise within member states. The reason is that the systems of local taxation (and more generally, the structure of local government finances, which gives rise to the level of local taxation) differ. It is then possible for some activity, asset or transaction to be subject to local taxes in some member states, while being completely untaxed in others. Although member states may have chosen local equalization grant arrangements and other provisions to keep the gap between high and low tax rates within manageable bounds, these arrangements do not prevent distortion between countries levying the local tax on a particular activity and those that do not tax that activity at all.

However, this pessimistic observation is tempered by the fact that the fiscal variable which matters for international business location decisions is not simply a comparison of local tax levels, but of the total tax burden on each given activity in the different member states of the Community – including both local and national taxes. Moreover, in principle the relevant tax burden to be compared should not simply be confined to a comparison of individual taxes (say of taxes on business assets) but should also take account of other taxes affecting the costs or remuneration of factors of production, of sales, and so on. It is not, therefore, inevitable that countries which rely on business taxes to finance *local* government are necessarily more exposed to the risks of locational distortion and the loss of business to other member states which do not levy local business taxes; only where both local business taxes and corresponding national taxes are absent will the greatest potential for cross-country distortion be encountered. Hence, for as long as national business assets taxes are sustainable, so, too, will it be possible to finance local government from locally-determined business assets taxes.

4. THE POTENTIAL ROLE OF THE EC IN LOCAL GOVERNMENT FINANCE

This section considers the extent to which a need exists for European regulation (taking the form of coordination or 'harmonization') of the financing of decentralized government in EC member states. It draws on wider analysis of the role of the Community in harmonizing and regulating tax and fiscal policies in member states.

4.1. Subsidiarity

Since the Maastricht Treaty, the demarcation and the Community's powers and responsibilities has been based on the principle of 'subsidiarity'. The principle is set out in the Treaty on European Union in the following terms:

> *In areas which do not fall within its exclusive competence, the Community shall take action, in accordance with the principle of subsidiarity, only if and insofar as the objectives of the proposed action cannot be sufficiently achieved by the member states and can therefore, by reason of the scale or effects of the proposed action, be better achieved by the Community.* (Article 3b of the Treaty on European Union)

The principle of subsidiarity thus embodies a presumption in favour of decentralization: transfer of government powers to the European level should only take place where there are good reasons for such an assignment. The Treaty definition also echoes the two possible 'good reasons' identified in the 1977 report of the MacDougall Committee for the assignment of particular policy areas to the Community – the existence of economies of scale, and the existence of cross-country spillover effects from national policy.

1. *The case for decentralization.* The general argument for decentralization in government is that it may help to ensure that the decisions taken by government adequately reflect differences in preferences and interests of different communities. Preferences and other characteristics of taxpayers play an important role in determining the optimal structure of taxation. In the area of indirect taxation, for example, the optimal structure of tax rates may tend to reflect the pattern of individual preferences for different goods and services; if different goods are necessities and luxuries in different member states, the optimal structure of indirect taxes may differ. Similarly, the optimal structure of property taxes may reflect various features specific to individual countries – the way in which property is treated elsewhere in the tax system, the structure of housing tenure, and the existence of supply constraints on new house construction, for example.

However, the case for decentralization in taxation rests on more substantial grounds than this. A key difference between tax policy assignment and the assignment of responsibility for other areas of government policy is that assignment of taxation affects the degree of autonomy in the operation of the other functions of decentralized government. Decentralized jurisdictions in the Community have different requirements for budget revenues from taxation, both because public spending choices differ, and because differences in income levels imply different rates of taxation in different jurisdictions even if all were to choose the same bundle of public services. The assignment of taxes among levels of government thus has implications for government decision-making in other areas of policy, since it affects the terms on which financial resources are available. Although fiscal imbalances between the revenue resources and spending needs of different levels of government can be handled by financial transfers between levels of government, this is rarely without a cost to the recipient tier of government in terms of reduced decision-making autonomy.

2. *The case for coordination.* The case for some form of Community coordination or harmonization of taxation mainly arises where there are significant policy externalities (policy spillovers) from national tax policies. Although administrative economies of scale might, in principle, also need to be considered in selecting the appropriate location of responsibility for tax administration and enforcement, language differences and differences in legal systems and corporate structures among member states mean that the efficient organization of tax administration will almost always be dictated by national boundaries.

The significance of policy externalities, or policy spillovers, is that where the actions of each national government have consequences which are felt outside its territory, it is unlikely that policy decisions taken by national governments will fully reflect all the costs and benefits of particular policy choices; in particular the interests of non-residents are unlikely to be given adequate weighting.

Intercountry policy spillovers in taxation potentially arise through the effects of lower-tier tax policies on the pattern of private sector decisions, the allocation of tax revenues, or the effectiveness of enforcement. The first of these forms of spillover has attracted most attention and policy interest, and can clearly be seen to relate closely to the question of whether local taxes are liable to distort the pattern of competition between member states. However, the issue of the desirability of Community involvement is not simply settled by the observation that particular taxes have a non-neutral effect on the allocation of economic activity between member states. It is also necessary to consider whether policy intervention by the Community would be liable to improve matters, and – given the concern expressed in the principle of subsidiarity for the minimum Community intervention consistent with effectiveness – the form that any Community coordination or harmonization should take.

4.2. Community Rules and Member States' Tax Rates.

Is tax competition between jurisdictions benign (or even beneficial), or does it create systematic inefficiencies in both public sector and private sector decisionmaking? There is a growing theoretical literature which sets out the circumstances in which tax competition between lower level jurisdictions is likely to be destructive, rather than a matter of indifference to higher levels of government. The literature also provides a number of useful results which indicate the types of policy intervention which are likely to improve matters.

The three examples below provide an indication of the range of ways in which tax competition may arise, the extent to which each form of tax competition has undesirable effects, and the scope for coordinated policy which would improve matters. The first example is the manipulation of the *structure* of taxes on goods to approximate the effects of tariff protection. The second is the use of low taxes on business to attract mobile businesses which might provide incomes and tax revenues or to attract cross-border shopping by individuals. The third is the case where jurisdictions set excessively high taxes in order to transfer the burden of taxation to non-residents ('tax exporting').

4.2.1. Manipulation of indirect tax structures

There is an obvious Community interest in the indirect tax *structure* of member states; excise taxes, or other non-uniform indirect taxes, can effectively operate as tariffs on goods that are predominantly imported. A country with a degree of monopoly power in international trade can improve its welfare at the expense of its trading partners by imposing taxes either on production or consumption to approximate the effects that would be obtained by an optimal tariff. Except where a country faces an infinitely price-elastic foreign demand for its exports (the small-country case), it can improve its welfare by taxing the domestic production of exportables and subsidizing the domestic production of importables, or, with a similar effect, by subsidizing the domestic consumption of exportables and taxing the domestic consumption of importables. Recognizing the potential for indirect protection through the indirect tax structure, the Community has, for example, tried to harmonize the taxes levied on alcohol in member states to prevent member states discriminating in favour of the types of alcoholic drinks produced by national producers.

4.2.2. Competition for mobile investment, or cross-border shopping

Tax competition might also arise through the use of low taxes to attract highly mobile tax bases. These could be either mobile investments, or mobile sales, in the form of cross-border shopping. A formal model of economic competition between independent jurisdictions is discussed by Oates and Schwab (1988). In this model, countries compete with each other for an internationally mobile capital stock through the corporate taxes they levy and through the standards that they set for permitted pollution levels. By levying lower rates of tax, or by setting less stringent environmental standards the country may be able to attract more investment. The advantage to countries of attracting more capital is the impact of a higher capital stock on wage levels in the country; the disadvantage is the lower tax revenue and the lower environmental quality that the country has to accept in order to attract more investment. The country thus faces a tradeoff between income on the one hand and tax revenue and environmental quality on the other.

In the simplest formulation of the model, the corporate tax revenues are not required to finance public spending (which can be financed instead through non-distorting lump-sum transfers), and all residents share the same interests regarding income and environmentally quality. In this case, the optimal policy for the country requires simple conditions on tax and environmental policy. First, the country should set a zero tax rate on mobile capital, since any positive tax rate to finance public spending has higher costs than lump-sum taxes, while any subsidy provided to business through tax rates below zero would result in a smaller increment to income than the cost of the subsidy. Second, the optimal policy would choose to set environmental standards at the point on income: environmental quality tradeoff where the marginal gain in income from more investment was just equal to the marginal willingness to pay for greater environmental quality. In other words, the simple model shows no tendency towards undesirable interjurisdictional economic competition, either in corporate taxation or in environmental quality.

However, Oates and Schwab (1988) identify circumstances in which costly interjurisdictional economic competition might arise. One would be where taxes on the internationally mobile capital were the only available financial resources to finance public expenditures. In this case, the optimal policy would seek to attract foreign investment; the value of additional foreign investment would be taken into account both in setting investment tax rates and in setting environmental standards. There would be a tendency in this case to set environmental standards which were 'too low', relative to public willingness to pay for environmental quality. A second case where costly interjurisdictional economic competition might arise would be where residents' interests differed, and where policymaking was dominated by those with greater preference for income than for environmental quality; the opposite outcome would arise where policy was dominated by those with less interest in wage levels than in environmental quality.

The simple version of the model demonstrates that the circumstances where fiscal competition may arise are narrower than sometimes thought. Where policymakers are rational and have the general public interest in mind, cutting taxes to attract business investment has a natural floor; if taxes are reduced below zero, more is spent than the income gain which results. However, the model also illustrates the complexity of the issue in other plausible contexts and, in particular, raises the possibility that fiscal distortions between independent jurisdictions may have economic effects that extend further than simply the public finance choices of individual jurisdictions.

The possibility that tax competition could arise through cross-border shopping has been discussed extensively in relation to the indirect tax systems of EC countries. Member states might, for example, be tempted to try to attract cross-border shopping, and hence extra tax revenue, by reducing the rate of indirect tax they levy in the hope that it would induce a sufficiently large increase in tax base to compensate for the reduction in the tax paid on each existing unit of cross-border shopping.

Cross-border shopping to benefit from lower taxes in other member states has economic costs like any other activity carried out purely for fiscal reasons. These economic costs include the time and travel costs of cross-border shoppers, the loss of trade suffered by businesses located on the high-tax side of the border, and the loss of tax revenue to the national exchequer. However, because these costs are predominantly borne on the high-tax side of any border, the main reason for Community action is to prevent competitive undercutting of tax rates; there is less need to prevent member states setting rates above neighbouring member states. Community policy might appropriately set a minimum 'floor' rate of tax, to counter the downward tendency arising from the process of fiscal competition.

4.2.3. Tax exporting

In contrast to this concern that interjurisdictional fiscal spillovers might lead to tax rates which are too low, relative to some defined optimum, in the local government literature there is a concern that spillovers, in the form of 'tax exporting' may lead to tax rates that are too high in relation to the optimum. This form of taxation spillover has been much less of a concern in the EC context. One important reason for this is that the monopoly advantages which are exploited in tax exporting in the local government case are frequently locational monopoly advantages, such as the convenience of a city centre location, a particular transport route and so on (It may be imagined what would be the consequences of allowing local governments to levy motorway tolls on the motorway sections passing through their territory!) There are probably rather fewer cases where significant monopoly power at the national level could be exploited through tax exporting between the member states of the EC.

4.3. Implications for EC Tax Harmonization

In many areas of regulatory policy, institutional competition, as a result of 'mutual recognition' of product standards, has allowed the Community to cut through the time-consuming business of reaching agreement on coordinated standards. Often, this process may be efficient, in the sense that competition between national standards would lead to the retention of separate national standards only where the benefit outweighs the cost. This argument can, as was recognized in the Commission's 1985 White Paper 'Completing the Internal Market', justify institutional competition in certain regulatory standards.

However, institutional competition in revenue-raising taxation is unlikely to be efficient, given the existence of significant policy externalities between member states. As the above discussion has indicated, market-driven harmonization will tend to lead to convergence on a particular pattern of taxation which may result in inefficient tax policy. To the extent that particular taxes have the potential to distort activity in the Community, *agreement* on policy intervention is required, and cannot be bypassed by relying on a process of fiscal competition between member states to harmonize the most distortionary differences between taxes.

5. CONCLUSIONS

EC policy coordination involves, at a very general level of analysis, a tradeoff between, on the one hand, the potential benefits of diversity, in the form of institutions and policies which can reflect the different conditions or requirements of individual member states, and, on the other hand, the possible costs involved when systems differ, or where member states make policy choices without regard for the impact on other member states.

As observed in Section 1, the starting point is one of considerable diversity in local government finance, reflecting, at least in part, fundamental differences in the context and functions of local government in the different member states.

This point of view naturally implies that Community policy towards local government needs to be formulated in a way which recognizes the diversity of national systems. Decentralized government structures in EC member states serve different purposes, and because of this are likely to be affected in different ways by any policy interventions from the Community level. It is relatively easy to think of hypothetical illustrations. Thus, for example, one of the ways in which some member states maintain control over local governments operating in an 'agency' mode is by maintaining a tight control over their aggregate financial resources; the availability of financial resources from the Community may have the effect of weakening this control. A second example might be drawn from the possible effects of tax policy coordination on the ability of local governments to function effectively as 'choice'-type units. The abolition of some local tax (perhaps because of its distortionary potential) could have a much more significant impact on the model of operation of 'choice'-type government units than of 'agency' units.

If, on the other hand, the EC is not to stipulate a uniform system of local government and local government finance but merely to confine its role to regulating the economic costs which may arise from a decentralized and diverse system of local government across Europe, what features of the system of local government finance should concern the Community, and what form should any Community interventions take?

Community involvement in a particular area is in general needed where the policy choices of member states have 'spillover' effects or policy externalities on other member states. In the case of tax policy, these spillovers arise mainly through the impact of member state decisions on private sector behaviour in other member states. The key question for assessing the case for Community involvement is: are member states' decisions about the system or rates of local taxation neutral in their impact in other member states or do they create cross-country distortion?

Evaluating the extent to which the current arrangements for local government finance are liable to create significant distortion between member states of the Community is complex. However, it is reasonably clear that if there are any problems, they are likely to be confined to the case of local business taxation.

Local taxes on business have the potential to cause distortions within member states as well as distortions between the member states of the Community. It might be reasonable for Community policy to proceed on the basis that member states would have chosen systems of local business taxation that do not give rise to excessive distortion internally when local government units are allowed to choose their own tax rates. None the less, there is an active debate in some member states about the economic costs of local business taxes. The potential for distortion from such taxes needs to be balanced against the potential for better accountability where local governments have adequate tax revenues.

In general, locational distortions will be greater if neighbouring jurisdictions set different tax rates, than if the same tax differential exists between distant jurisdictions. This implies that distortions between member states caused by local business tax differences are likely to arise mainly in border regions. There does not appear to be available any thorough and systematic analysis of the evidence on tax competition in local business taxes in border areas. Nevertheless, there does not appear to be evidence of much greater tax pressure in border areas than in areas away from national frontiers. Even in border areas, local business taxes may be too small, in relation to other factors, to have much effect on business location decisions.

Nevertheless, while local business tax distortions would be expected to be mainly a phenomenon affecting border areas, they could arise also between more distant locations for two reasons. One is that there may be some businesses which are highly mobile. The second is that the potential for local business taxes to be distortionary may actually be greater *between* member states than *within* member states.

The reason for the latter observation is that tax-induced distortion within member states will reflect the difference between local business tax rates in different jurisdictions. Often the range of tax rates may be comparatively small[1] and may indeed have been narrowed by provisions designed explicitly to limit the scope for internal distortion (for example through 'resource equalization' provisions in the allocation of central government transfers, or through limitations on the range of tax rates that local units may set). Between member states, however, the relevant tax differential may be wider because different member states may have different local business taxes or indeed no local business tax at all.

It is, then, possible for some activity, asset or transaction to be subject to local taxes in some member states, while being completely untaxed in others. Although member states may have chosen local equalization grant arrangements and other provisions to keep the gap between high and low tax rates within manageable bounds, these arrangements do not prevent distortion between countries levying the local tax and those that do not.

The situation may be particularly complex where member states levy taxes on similar but not identical business tax bases. The incongruence of business tax systems between member states can give rise to complex and uneven distortions which are not reflected simply in a comparison of the rates of tax which are levied. 'Gaps' in the coverage of the tax base in different member states which favour particular activities or assets may be a source of distortion even if member states levy broadly similar local business taxes at similar average levels.

What matters, of course, in competition between member states is the overall level of taxation, including both local and national business taxes of various sorts and also the impact of taxes on labour and other factors of production in influencing the costs of production in particular locations. Differences in the spending benefits which businesses receive in different areas may also need to be included in this calculation. Action to harmonize the overall level and structure of local business taxes cannot meaningfully be considered separately from the situation of other local and national taxes affecting the costs of production in particular locations.

Therefore, if the Community is to seek to reduce or eliminate the potential for cross-country distortion from local business taxes, the most feasible approach would be to seek to limit the extent to which local business taxes can differentiate or discriminate among different activities, so as to favour strongly certain activities or categories of asset. More general harmonization, on a common system or common base, would be pointless for as long as member states operate different systems of national corporate taxes.

NOTES

1. Although a narrow range of tax rates is not proof that no problem exists; indeed, extreme tax competition might often lead to convergence in tax rates, within narrow bounds. Where tax competition has this effect, it may give rise to significant economic costs, in terms of a limitation on the decisionmaking power of local governments, and, possibly, a shift in taxation away from the optimal structure to a structure less exposed to fiscal competition.

REFERENCES

Bennett, R. and G. Krebs (1988), *Local Business Taxes in Britain and Germany,* Baden-Baden: Nomos-Verlagsgesellschaft.

Crawford, A., S. Fothergill and S. Monk (1985), *The Effects of Business Rates on the Location of Employment,* Cambridge: Department of Land Economy.

Hughes, G.A. and S. Smith (1991), 'Economic aspects of decentralised government: structure, functions and finance', *Economic Policy,* **13**, 425–59.

Oates, W.E. and R.M. Schwab (1988), 'Economic competition among jurisdictions: efficiency-enhancing or distortion-inducing?', *Journal of Public Economics,* **35**, 333–54.

15. Tax Harmonization and Tax Competition at State–Local Levels: Lessons from Switzerland

Werner W. Pommerehne, Gebhard Kirchgässner and Lars P. Feld*

1. INTRODUCTION

Since the Treaty of Rome, tax harmonization, or at least tax coordination, has always ranked first on the agenda for an integrated Europe. This comes out quite clearly in various proposals by the Commission of the European Union (EU), which first aimed at maximizing rather than optimizing tax harmonization, but which was later on to follow a strategy that gave more leeway to the individual member states with respect to their tax policy. On closer inspection, however, this leeway seems to be rather narrow, or, in the words of Cnossen and Shoup (1987, p. 82), 'European Communities' policymakers appear to believe that member states should first be forced into the straitjacket of a uniform tax system'. The question whether tax competition or centralized harmonization should be favoured implies the application of concepts theoretically discussed in the literature on fiscal federalism.

After Tiebout's famous essay (1956), the main emphasis was first, for allocative reasons, on the advantages of decentralized solutions. More recently, however, allocative inefficiencies of competitive tax systems have come to figure most prominently in the discussion of the additional risk of the negative distributional consequences.

* We gratefully acknowledge support from the Federal Tax Bureau of Switzerland, especially Bernhard Stebler, in providing us with most detailed disaggregated data (so far not published) on taxpayers in different income groups, on the respective incomes, as well as on the burden of state and local income taxes. Without this help, this study would not have been possible. Astrid Bachmann, Nel Ben Yakov, Thomas Braun, Guido Gehendges, Caroline Gödde, Bodo G. Schirra, and Martina Weis provided valuable research assistance. In addition, the paper benefited from useful comments by Albert Hart, H. Henning Jank, Susanne Krebs, Georg Seeck and the participants of the Seminar on Local Government held in September 1994 in Ferrara, Italy, especially Giancarlo Pola and Andrew Reschowsky. Unexpectedly and untimely, we lost Werner W. Pommerehne in October 1994. We will greatly miss him and all that he would have taught us.

Section 2 of the chapter summarizes the main theoretical arguments in favour of and against fiscal competition. In Section 3, empirical evidence on tax competition at the state–local level in Switzerland is presented. Section 4 deals with the allocative and distributive consequences of tax competition. The final section contains some suggestions for a future European fiscal constitution based on the theoretical arguments as well as the empirical evidence.

Since the results of both the decentralization and the harmonization views rest on strong assumptions which are not reflected in the conditions of the real world, it remains theoretically open how to design a future European fiscal constitution. In order to evaluate possible influences of alternative fiscal systems, it is necessary to rely on empirical evidence. Because of its unique federal structure, Switzerland seems to be the most promising candidate for analysing the allocative as well as the distributional properties of fiscal systems.

2. MAIN THEORETICAL ARGUMENTS

Following Tiebout's (1956) arguments, we may categorize fiscal autonomy as a precondition for achieving a Pareto-efficient allocation of local public goods in a setting of diverse local communities. By 'voting by foot', citizens would choose their residence in a community which provides them with the optimal combination of fiscal burden and of public goods, according to their preferences. This migratory process forces other communities to recognize that they are operating in a competitive framework. Yet, in equilibrium, different levels in the provision of public goods will persist to the extent that there are differences in citizens' preferences.

This reasoning leads to Oates' (1972, p. 30) 'decentralization theorem' of fiscal federalism, which states that in a world of mobile individuals with different preferences, only provision and financing of public goods at the lowest level of government are compatible with economic efficiency. In this case the different demands are processed in a natural way, whereas a centralized decision system could lead to an inferior uniformity in the provision of public goods.[1]

However, quite a number of restrictive and idealized assumptions must hold for there to be an efficient supply of public goods as a result of competition between local communities or regions. For instance, if the assumption of constant, as it was employed by Tiebout, or increasing marginal costs is dropped, because public goods are characterized by increasing returns to scale with respect to the number of users, then competition does not really work. The main reason is that public goods, if produced at all, would be provided at marginal cost prices which do not cover the higher inframarginal production costs. Thus, as Sinn (1990a, 1990b) pointed out, the community would incur a loss if a competitive marginal tax price was set. As a consequence, no public goods would be provided, especially no pure public goods, which are costless in use because of non-rivalry in consumption. In the latter case, if such goods have been provided, communities will compete with each other until the tax price approaches zero. If this outcome is anticipated, no community will engage in the provision of a pure public good. Thus, given goods like these, a pessimistic assessment of the efficiency of tax competition seems inevitable.

The mobility of individuals will also jeopardize any decentralized tax policy which has set another important target, namely the distributional goal, which in this case consists in reducing income inequality by means of tax-financed transfer programmes. The theory of optimal taxation tells us that a community cannot, and should not, impose excessive taxes on goods or activities whose supply or, according to the case in question, whose demand is price elastic, because taxation will be circumvented if there is some mobility. Those who perform these activities, the rich and the mobile part of the labour force as well as the owners of capital, will have incentive to change their place of residence if they are forced to contribute more than simply the equivalent of the benefits they realize from public provision. Because of tax competition, however, there is no danger of being exploited to the advantage of less wealthy community members and, therefore, those people profit from tax competition. The victims of tax competition will be the immobile part of the work force as well as landowners, but also the poor who would benefit from a redistributional budget.

A large government sector for distribution purposes can only with difficulty be supported in a decentralized system characterized by tax competition. First, it will become difficult if not impossible for a single community to levy the necessary redistribution tax upon the rich and mobile. Second, such a policy, if undertaken in one community, will attract poor individuals from other jurisdictions and thus erode the internal redistribution policy. Therefore, no major redistributional activities are possible in a decentralized, competitive system of jurisdictions. As a consequence, those who consider redistribution as an efficiency-enhancing activity will be in favour of tax rates which are harmonized by collective arrangements among all jurisdictions or, of similar consequence in the European context, they will be in favour of a redistribution policy under the auspices of a centralized European government.[2]

There are a number of additional reasons why tax competition between decentralized government units might not produce efficient results and might be Pareto-inferior to tax harmonization or at least to tax coordination at the central level of a multijurisdictional system.

1. Allocational problems arise because of cross-border environmental pollution. Decentralized competition will maximize the respective resident's benefits. Because of migration of labour and capital induced by incentives resulting from such a policy, distortions will emerge.
2. Furthermore, tax competition with respect to commodity taxation might result in an inefficient situation similar to a prisoners' dilemma. As Keen (1989) has shown, welfare can be increased by reducing the strategic tax differences between jurisdictions.[3]
3. Similar conclusions can be drawn from the literature on tax competition between jurisdictions which finance their marginal public expenditures by burdening capital, that is the ultimately mobile factor of production (in the abuse of border controls).

The consequence will be an inefficiently low provision of public services, because of the lack of capital tax revenue which is a consequence of flight of capital to other jurisdictions. The arbitrage process may even lead to the emergence of undesirable tax havens for mobile factors, with a zero tax burden on any (non-residential and residential) capital and with the whole threat of the tax burden on the more immobile factors, namely labour and land. In order to avoid such an unfavourable outcome, it seems advisable to arrange at least some tax coordination through the central government, which determines the tax base and restricts the choice set of the subfederal governments to the determination of capital tax rates (Genser 1992, p. 212).

All these theoretical arguments cast some doubt on the reasonable working of the Tiebout mechanism. Following this line of reasoning, one inevitably arrives at tax harmonization (or, at least, tax coordination) as a desirable, efficiency-enhancing feature in an obviously non-Tiebout world. But, when considered carefully, the elegant theory of Tiebout's critics itself makes some strong assumptions which do not seem particularly realistic. Two of these assumptions are perfect mobility of skilled labour and capital which, in reality, at best holds to a limited extent. Labour, even in highly developed countries, is far from being perfectly mobile. The same is true with regard to capital: the locational choice of a firm depends on a large number of determinants of which the tax burden is but one factor, albeit an important one. However, as soon as it is assumed that mobility is restricted, differences in tax rates are possible.[4]

With respect to the provision of public goods, one has to take into account that the arguments which are brought forward in the discussion are mainly related to local public goods. It is the relation between central cities and their suburbs which is of interest. The spillovers which are relevant in this context are, at best, of minor importance to the case of European countries. With the exception of defence, which has already been 'harmonized', and global environmental quality, there are few transnational public goods which are or could be provided by a transnational government. Concerning the environment, it is obvious that uncoordinated national policies are unable to provide satisfactory solutions. But the need for coordination with respect to environmental problems does not imply that all taxes have to be coordinated or even harmonized.

Thus the discussion becomes inconclusive: fiscal autonomy with respect to taxation of the single subfederal jurisdictions could have net benefits but could also generate detrimental effects for the citizens involved. Therefore, it is important to look at some empirical evidence before giving constitutional advice. In this respect, the Swiss system can play an important role since Switzerland has by far the most decentralized fiscal system in the industrialized world.[5] A political European Union, however, if it is to be realized at all, will certainly have a more decentralized structure than most or even perhaps all of the European nations today. Therefore, for the future fiscal constitution of the European Union there is probably more to be learnt from Switzerland than from any other European country.

3. TAX COMPETITION: EMPIRICAL EVIDENCE

Summarizing the previous section, two properties of tax competition stand out: allocative inefficiency caused by underprovision of public goods and the potential collapse of the insurance state. In contrast to this theoretical pessimism, Switzerland's unique constitution features strong elements of direct democracy at all three government levels and, in addition, an established federative structure with strong competencies of the single states (cantons) and the local government units. This holds especially true for the tax structure. The main progressive taxes on personal and corporate income are state and local taxes, whose rates differ from canton to canton and – within cantons – from municipality to municipality, whereas the central government relies mainly on indirect (proportional) taxes, the general sales tax and specific consumption taxes like the mineral oil tax.[6]

Because of the small size of the country and its subfederal units, private and corporate taxpayers can easily move to places with low tax burdens. Therefore, tax competition is possible and negative consequences should, if anywhere, become obvious in Switzerland. From anecdotal evidence it is well known that there are two tax havens near or in Switzerland: the small country of Liechtenstein which is in economic union with Switzerland; and – a more important case for our analysis – the canton of Zug. Income taxes in Switzerland vary quite considerably among the different cantons. Taking the value of the (weighted) average for Switzerland as 100, in 1990 the index of burden in the form of personal income and property taxes ranked from 56.1 for the canton of Zug to 154.1 for Valais. For instance, a family with two children with a gross income of 175,000 Swiss francs (SFr.) had to pay SFr. 16,083 in cantonal and local income taxes in Zug compared with SFr. 34,475 in Berne, two cities distant less than 100 kilometres from one other.

To what extent do such differences in tax burden result in an uneven distribution of taxpayers throughout the country? There is certainly an incentive for high-income people to move to and live in (and/or pay taxes in) cantons with low tax rates. In 1990, for example, the share of taxpayers with taxable income of SFr. 100,000 or more was 9.41 per cent in the canton of Zug compared with 2.53 per cent in the canton of Jura and with an average of 5.47 per cent in Switzerland as a whole. As Figure 15.1 shows, this could be entirely because of Zug; once it is excluded, there seems to be no relation at all between the share of high-income people and the corresponding tax rates. On the other hand, if Geneva is excluded, a strong negative relation seems to exist.

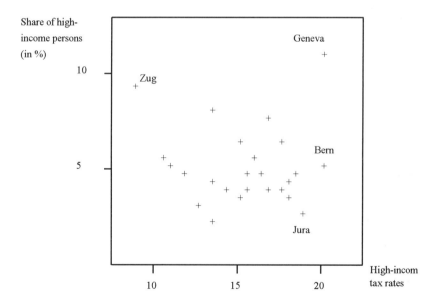

Figure 15.1 Share of high-income persons and the respective tax rates

The question is, however, which other factors influence the decision to live in a particular area. There are two principal ways of investigating this.[7]

We can examine changes in tax rates (and other variables) and the migration which results. As small changes in tax rates should not cause significant migration, a precondition for the application of this approach would be major changes in relative cantonal and local tax rates. As explained below, important changes in this regard have not occurred over the last two years.[8] A second possibility is to look at the regional spread of taxpayers and explain the dispersion. A precondition for this approach is that no significant further migration is to be expected, that is that the system is more or less in equilibrium. As no major migration between cantons and municipalities which could be related to changes of the state–local tax structure have occurred during the last few years, we shall use the second approach, that is we will try to develop a model which explains the shares of high-income people in the different Swiss cantons (Section 3.1) and in different municipalities (Section 3.2), respectively.

3.1. Results for the Swiss Cantons

For high-income (and other) people, besides cantonal and local tax rates, there are at least two other factors which influence residence decisions: (i) the attractiveness of an area; and (ii) the earning opportunities.

The attractiveness of the canton is measured by public expenditure per capita[9] and an index of the available stock of infrastructure. The index of infrastructural components is made up of several components and includes commercial (telephone density, density of motor vehicle ownership, road length per hectare, traffic and energy expenditure, assistance for courts) as well as social infrastructure (population density, housing conditions, health supply/number of hospital beds, number of physicians and dentists per capita, level of education, and expenditure for education, science, recreation, culture and sports). High-income people are assumed to prefer – *ceteris paribus* – a better infrastructural equipment. Thus, we should expect a positive sign for the coefficient of the respective variable.[10] Earning opportunities strongly depend on the economic structure of the region. To capture this influence, we included the share of the labour force in industrial production (second sector) and for services (third sector). Because of obvious multicollinearity problems (Pearson's coefficient of correlation $= 0.912$) we had to delete one of these variables from the equation. We decided to include the share of labour force in the service sector in our estimation equation, because it indicates not only earning opportunities but also the availability of services provided in the region. We expect this variable to have a positive sign, especially for high-income earners since they are usually better educated and might therefore be expected to work in the service sector. A second reason for a positive sign might be that a relatively greater availability of a whole range of different services in one canton compared to another canton increases the attraction of the former for high-income earners.

To take account of the fact that cantons serve to differing degrees as work places, the share of net 'in-commuters' (inflow minus outflow) in percentage terms of total labour force (of the respective canton) is included. Commuters usually have to pay their income taxes in the municipality and canton in which they reside. Since, as a rule, high-income earners are more mobile (in the sense that they are – *ceteris paribus* – more willing to commute) than low-income people, they may have relatively stronger incentives to live in a low tax canton, while working in another one where earning opportunities are better. In a Tiebout-like world we might therefore expect the rich to be more willing to work 'abroad' (that is, in other cantons), and, at the same time, to live in 'residential cantons' characterized by a relatively low net inflow of commuters, whereas we would expect the poor to live more often in a 'working canton' characterized by a relatively high net inflow of commuters. If this is true, we can expect a negative sign on the variable denoted as 'share of net commuters' (net inflow) in the case of high-income people. Since the cantons of Geneva and Zug may be exceptional cases, as Figure 15.1 suggests, we include dummy variables which take on the value of one for these cantons and zero elsewhere. We expect these dummies to get significant positive coefficients for high-income classes, a (probably significant) negative coefficient for low-income classes and insignificant values in between.

As the populations of the 26 cantons vary quite considerably, instead of using ordinary least squares, we perform a weighted regression, using the square root of population size as the weighting scheme; we also add a population variable. Thus, the model for explaining the shares of taxpayers in various income groups in the 26 cantons is specified: as follows:

$$S_i = f_i \ (ATR_i, \ LFS, \ INFRA, \ NINCOM, \ POP, \ DGV, \ DZG), \quad (15.1)$$

where: S_i = share of taxpayers in income group i ($i = 1,...,7$) of total taxpayers in the respective canton, in percent;

ATR_i = cantonal and average local income tax rate (on gross income) for income group i, in percent;[11]

LFS   = share of labour force in the service sector, in percent of total labour force;

INFRA   = index of infrastructural equipment;

NINCOM = net incommuters (inflow minus outflow) in percent of total labour force of the respective canton;

POP   = population in millions;

DGV   = dummy variable for the canton of Geneva;

DZG   = dummy variable for the canton of Zug.

The subscript i denotes the income group, and the group with the highest incomes contains those with a gross income of SFr. 100,000 or more. The same model was applied to the other six income groups to see if it also fits the behaviour of the people in those groups and the seven equations resulting from this specification were estimated simultaneously. Overall, the estimation of the model should produce significant results for the top- and bottom-income groups, with opposite signs respectively, and insignificant results for the groups in between. However, this does not have to hold for the tax rate.[12] If the cantons that have low tax rates for high-income people are not those with the lowest tax rates for the low-income earners, the same (negative) sign may result over the whole range of income groups.

Data on the distribution of the taxpayers according to their gross income as well as on the respective tax burden are given for a number of different incomes. The income group below SFr. 15,000 is not considered here because of specific small sample properties in this case caused by the low relative frequency (less than two per cent). The remaining data are grouped into the following gross income classes:

S_1: SFr. $15,000 \leq Y_{g,1} < $ SFr   20,000;   where $Y_{r,1}$ =   17,000
S_2: SFr. $20,000 \leq Y_{g,2} < $ SFr   30,000;   where $Y_{r,2}$ =   25,000
S_3: SFr. $30,000 \leq Y_{g,3} < $ SFr   40,000;   where $Y_{r,3}$ =   35,000
S_4: SFr. $40,000 \leq Y_{g,4} < $ SFr   50,000;   where $Y_{r,4}$ =   45,000
S_5: SFr. $50,000 \leq Y_{g,5} < $ SFr   75,000;   where $Y_{r,5}$ =   60,000
S_6: SFr. $75,000 \leq Y_{g,6} < $ SFr 100,000;   where $Y_{r,6}$ =   85,000
S_7: SFr. $100,000 \geq Y_{g\,7}$ where $Y_{r,7}$ = 175,000

with $Y_{g,i}$ being the gross income in group i and $Y_{r,i}$ denoting that income which we thought to be representative of income group i (on the basis of calculated mean income of the respective income class). The tax data are available for married taxpayers with two children, married taxpayers without children, and singles. The main results are presented for the standard case of married taxpayers with two children.[13]

It can be argued that there is a simultaneous relation between the distributions of (income) tax rates and the shares of taxpayers in different income groups. An instrumental variable estimator should be used to take this into account. However, instrumental variables are not available. In particular, there are no (consistent) time series available which would allow us to use lagged variables as instruments. The results presented below may therefore exaggerate somewhat the (causal) effect of tax rates on the distribution of income earners since high income earners will – *ceteris paribus* – vote for lower tax rates for high-incomes and the larger their share in the electorate the more successful they may be. However, as this possible additional effect – which can only occur in a situation of tax competition between different fiscal units – goes in the same direction as the influence discussed above, it will not invalidate any results as regards potential consequences of tax competition which are extrapolated from the Swiss example to the European case.

3.1.1. All taxpayers taken together

The results for the default case (all taxpayers taken together, tax rates for married taxpayers with two children) for the year 1990 are presented in Table 15.1. The model explains the share of high-income people ($Y_{g,i}$ > SFr. 100,000) quite well: more than 80 per cent of the variance can be explained statistically. The tax rate has a negative sign and is significant at the 99 per cent confidence level. The difference (= DIFF) it predicts in the shares of high-income earners between the canton with the lowest average tax rate (at a gross income of SFr. 175,000) of 9.19 per cent (Zug) and the one with the highest tax rate of 19.79 per cent (Geneva) is 3.71 percentage points. Given the mean of the dependent variable of 5.47 and its standard deviation of 1.96, the tax rate obviously has a considerable impact. The dummy variables for Zug and Geneva are significant and have the expected positive sign.

Other important factors are the share of the labour force in the service sector and the stock of infrastructure: both have a positive and, in addition, a significant impact on the share of high-income people. The share of net in-commuters as a percentage of the total labour force is significant at the 95 per cent confidence level and has the expected negative sign while the remaining variable, population, turns out to be positive and significant. With regard to the residuals of this estimation, the Jarque-Bera test applied to these as well as to all other equations for the cantons indicates that the hypothesis of a normal distribution cannot be rejected.

It can be seen from the other equations (for S_1 to S_6) that with regard to the multiple coefficient of determination (R^2) this model explains quite well the share of taxpayers in nearly all income groups with the exception of the fourth, that is, the median-income group. The coefficient of the tax rate again has a negative sign and is highly significant in the other high-income groups (five and six). In contrast to these findings, the tax rate does exert a significant positive influence on the share of taxpayers in the third income group. This may indicate that there are no systematic differences in cantons' tax schedules concerning the question whether those with low tax rates for high-income people really differ from those with low tax rates for low-income earners. Indeed, the correlation coefficient between the tax rates of the two extreme income groups considered is 0.097 (married taxpayers with

Table 15.1 Model to explain the share of all taxpayers in different income groups in 26 Swiss cantons, 1990, state/local tax rate on gross income of married taxpayers with two children[a]

Dependent variable	S_1	S_2	S_3	S_4	S_5	S_6	S_7
Income group (in 1,000)	15–20	20–30	30–40	40–50	50–75	75–100	>100
Gross income (in 1,000)	17	25	35	45	60	85	175
Constant	10.538	26.911	18.756	16.627	29.032	6.723	3.063
Cantonal/local tax rate on gross income	0.307	−0.410	0.305*	0.077	−0.477**	−0.331**	−0.350**
	(0.75)	(−1.16)	(1.68)	(0.95)	(−3.10)	(−3.82)	(−8.82)
Share of labour force in service sector (%)	0.025	0.060	0.083**	0.000	−0.182**	−0.048	0.036*
	(0.75)	(1.06)	(2.72)	(0.00)	(−3.88)	(−1.48)	(1.90)
Index of infrastructure of the canton	−0.044**	−0.103**	−0.045**	−0.011*	0.078**	0.064**	0.059**
	(−3.59)	(−4.45)	(−3.67)	(−1.75)	(4.43)	(5.34)	(8.50)
Net in-commuters (in per cent of total labour force)	0.037*	0.061*	0.034*	0.019*	−0.082**	−0.058**	−0.035**
	(2.43)	(2.31)	(2.31)	(2.27)	(−3.65)	(−3.78)	(−3.99)
Population of the canton (in millions)	−0.775*	−1.990*	−1.518**	−0.317	1.634*	1.492**	0.988**
	(−1.69)	(−2.58)	(−3.43)	(−1.38)	(2.54)	(3.36)	(3.84)
Dummy for Geneva	0.476	−1.981	−2.097**	0.163	1.289	2.201**	2.768**
	(0.60)	(−1.42)	(−2.84)	(0.39)	(1.12)	(2.66)	(5.69)
Dummy for Zug	−2.440*	−5.399*	−2.346*	−0.725	2.049	2.107	1.695*
	(−1.86)	(−2.36)	(−1.89)	(−1.01)	(1.02)	(1.52)	(2.08)
R^2	0.621	0.653	0.736	0.298	0.553	0.767	0.896
SER	0.684	1.371	0.701	0.574	1.405	0.892	0.632
J.–B.	1.206	2.372	0.912	2.121	0.152	0.319	0.343
DIFF	0.593	1.369	1.485	0.393	3.196	2.674	3.710
DIFF (per cent of mean dependent variable)	0.078	0.071	0.075	0.025	0.143	0.386	0.679
Mean of dependent variable	7.590	19.237	19.727	15.874	22.393	6.922	5.465
Std. dev. of dep. variable	1.111	2.327	1.364	0.686	2.101	1.849	1.961

Notes: [a] The numbers in parentheses contain the t-statistics of the estimated coefficients. * Statistical significance at the 95 per cent (90 per cent) – confidence level, ** Significance at the 99 per cent confidence level.

two children), which is not significantly different from zero (even at the 90 per cent confidence level).[14]

The impact of the fiscal burden on the residential decision calculus can also be seen from the computed absolute impact generated by the tax rate (DIFF). In absolute terms, this difference is very large for the three highest-income groups. In relative terms (DIFF as the percentage of the respective mean dependent variable), this impact is even more pronounced: it is at least twice as high for S_5 (0.143) as compared with S_1 to S_4 and it continuously increases up to seven to ten times the values for S_1 to S_4 when the highest-income class (0.679) is reached.

Another important factor seems to be the index of infrastructure. Its coefficient is negative for the lowest three income classes and positive for the highest three income groups, a result which is in line with the systematically divergent time preference rates of low/high-income earners with respect to the longer-run benefits of the infrastructural capital. In all these cases the influence of infrastructure is significant at the 99 per cent confidence level.

The share of the labour force in the service sector has a highly significant negative impact on the share of taxpayers in the fifth income class over and above the influence on the highest class already noted.[15] The share of net in-commuters (as a percentage of the total labour force) has a positive sign and is significant in the case of the four lower-income classes (SFr. 15,000 to 50,000 gross income), but has a highly significant negative impact on the three highest-income groups. This result partly supports the hypothesis on the differential effect of the divergent work mobility (by income level). The dummy variable for Geneva exerts a negative and significant impact in the case of the third income group and a significant positive impact in the two highest-income groups. In all other cases, it does not prove to be significant. The dummy variable for Zug is negative and significant for the three lowest-income groups but positive and significant only for the highest-income class. This confirms our a priori expectations outlined above. Finally, the Jarque-Bera test shows that the normality assumption for the residuals can never be rejected at any conventional confidence level.[16]

3.1.2. Results for subgroups of taxpayers

So far, we have analysed the relationship for all taxpayers taken together. Yet, we may argue that the degree of mobility differs in a systematic way between several subgroups such as retired people, employees and self-employed. We would expect the third group to have a significantly higher willingness to move than employees, that is, the marginal negative impact of the tax burden for high-income people should be correspondingly more pronounced in the case of the self-employed. It becomes difficult, however, to formulate a priori a hypothesis for retired persons. On the one hand, they are no longer tied to the region (canton) in which they have so far been working and living. On the other hand, they may have invested in specific human relationships for a longer period, so that they are the ones least prepared to choose another place of residence.

The estimates for the respective subgroups are presented in Tables 15A.1 to 15A.3 in the appendix, again with reference to the tax burden for the standard case of a married couple with two children, in the case of employees and self-employed, and for married retirees. All in all, these results display much the same structure as those in Table 15.1. On separation of the three subgroups the explanatory power of the estimates overall declines somewhat. However, it increases in almost all subgroups for the equations for the highest-income group with the exception of retired persons, indicating that the general conclusion still holds, that is that high-income people are especially inclined to move.

With respect to the marginal impact of the fiscal variable, we observe a low (but highly significant) coefficient in the case of retired people (-0.114 in Table 15A.1 for the highest-income group), which is even smaller than the respective coefficient in the case of employees (-0.358 in Table 15A.2). The strongest impact can be observed, as expected, for the self-employed (-0.892 in Table 15A.3). Thus, it seems obvious that retired persons have built such a stock of specific human relationships that they hesitate to move purely for fiscal reasons.

Measured in absolute terms, the tax rate differences between the cantons with the highest, respectively lowest, tax rate (for each income class) induce the corresponding sequence of impacts, with DIFF = 9.46 in the case of the self-employed (Table 15A.3), with DIFF = 3.80 for dependent workers (Table 15A.2) and DIFF = 1.62 for retired people (Table 15A.1). However, if in addition the respective income distributions are considered (with a figure as low as 2.8 per cent for all retired people in the highest-income class, 4.6 per cent in the case of dependent workers, and 17.6 per cent in that of self-employed), the sequence of the relative impacts is changed: the highest relative effect produced by differences in the tax rates can be observed for dependent high-income people (0.83 for the highest income class, cf. Table 15A.2), followed by high-income retirees (0.58 in Table 15A.1) and high-income self-employed (0.54 in Table 15A.3). Thus, while retired persons as a whole are not very sensitive to tax differentials those of them earning high incomes seem to react more strongly. Moreover, these incentives seem to be strengthened in the case that the canton in question is well equipped with infrastructure which includes health supply (number of physicians and dentists per capita as well as the number of hospital beds) as well as the provision of cultural services, the first being particularly important for the elderly.

The index of infrastructure also exhibits a significant positive effect in the equation for the higher income self-employed, although in this case it is not so much the supply of health services but rather that of cultural activities which may be relatively more important. For the remaining group of employees we observe much the same results as for all taxpayers, that is a negative and significant impact of infrastructure for below-average-income earners and a positive significant effect for the upper-income classes.

The marginal influence of net in-commuters proves to be more important with high-income earning employees than with high-income self-employed (and also, as we would expect, with high-income retirees). This result suggests that, above all, employees are much more inclined to differentiate between place of work and place of residence than the self-employed. Self-employed taxpayers lack the possibility even to make such a distinction. As a rule, they have to reside in the area where they work. For example, a physician must be able to provide rapid care to his or her patients and therefore has to live close to the practice. Failure to do so could damage his or her reputation with negative effects on income.

Interestingly enough, the dummy variable for Geneva has no role in the case of self-employed taxpayers, but has a strong impact on retired persons in the five lowest-income groups. Geneva seems to attract low income retirees but not middle- (and high-) income retirees. The impact of the dummy for the canton of Zug is almost negligible.

3.1.3. The case of the cantonal tax burden

Finally, let us consider the case where only cantonal tax rates are used instead of the combined tax burden of the state and of the (representative)[17] local levels. Table 15.2 corresponds in all respects to Table 15.1 except for the tax rates.

The overall performance of this model is inferior to that specified in Table 15.1. But the marginal impact of cantonal tax rates is higher than that of the overall tax burden. This is also true for the absolute and relative impact of the differences between the highest and the lowest cantonal tax rates (for each income class).

This result refers to the relative importance of cantonal tax rates with respect to local tax rates and their role in fiscal competition. The coefficients of the other variables remain almost unchanged which also indicates the need for differentiating between the two subfederal levels. But it could be the case that the impact of local taxation is greater than that of cantonal taxation; the theoretical explanation of this is that the costs of moving (including psychic costs) within a canton, that is in most cases to a neighbouring municipality, are obviously lower than those of moving

Table 15.2 Model to explain the share of all taxpayers in different income groups in 26 Swiss cantons, 1990, cantonal tax rate on gross income of married taxpayers with two children

Dependent variable	S_1	S_2	S_3	S_4	S_5	S_6	S_7
Income group (in 1,000)	15–20	20–30	30–40	40–50	50–75	75–100	>100
Gross income (in 1,000)	17	25	35	45	60	85	175
Constant	10.518	26.742	19.278	17.162	25.514	3.265	-2.484
Cantonal tax rate on gross income	0.561	-0.859	0.730*	0.056	-0.708**	-0.483**	-0.451**
	(0.60)	(-1.10)	(2.28)	(0.42)	(-2.8)	(-3.4)	(-6.3)
Share of labour force in service sector (in per cent)	0.027	0.060	0.075**	-0.002	-0.161**	-0.025	0.072**
	(0.82)	(1.07)	(2.64)	(-0.11)	(-3.2)	(-0.7)	(3.00)
Index of infrastructure of the canton	-0.045**	-0.102*	-0.047**	-0.013*	0.090**	0.075**	0.072**
	(-3.6)	(-4.4)	(-4.2)	(-2.0)	(5.08)	(6.01)	(7.95)
Net in-commuters (in per cent of total labour force)	0.038*	0.060**	0.042**	0.018*	-0.093**	-0.071**	-0.056**
	(2.46)	(2.27)	(2.79)	(2.06)	(-3.8)	(-4.2)	(-4.7)
Population of the canton (in millions)	-0.810*	-1.947*	-1.522**	-0.296	1.438*	1.250**	0.606
	(-1.78)	(-2.5)	(-3.7)	(-1.26)	(2.12)	(2.64)	(1.76)
Dummy for Geneva	0.485	-2.010	-2.075**	0.111	1.958	2.900**	3.701**
	(0.61)	(-1.44)	(-2.9)	(0.26)	(1.59)	(3.07)	(5.30)
Dummy for Zug	-2.443*	-5.386*	-2.279*	-0.863	2.529	2.494*	2.418*
	(-1.85)	(-2.3)	(-1.95)	(-1.20)	(1.24)	(1.76)	(2.37)
R^2	0.618	0.655	0.737	0.261	0.470	0.737	0.756
SER	0.687	1.366	0.699	0.589	1.530	0.948	0.969
J.–B.	0.901	2.518	0.791	3.259	0.092	0.108	1.708
DIFF	0.468	1.289	1.829	0.178	3.236	3.405	5.150
DIFF (per cent of mean dependent variable)	0.062	0.067	0.093	0.011	0.144	0.492	0.942
Mean of dependent variable	7.590	19.237	19.727	15.874	22.393	6.922	5.465
Std. dev. of dep. variable	1.111	2.327	1.364	0.686	2.101	1.849	1.961

Notes: See Table 15.1.

Table 15.3 Model to explain the share of all taxpayers in different income groups in the 137 largest Swiss municipalities, 1990, state/local tax rate on gross income of married taxpayers with two children

Dependent variable	S_1	S_2	S_3	S_4	S_5	S_6	S_7
Income group (in 1,000)	15–20	20–30	30–40	40–50	50–75	75–100	>100
Gross income (in 1,000)	17	25	35	45	60	85	175
Constant	12.967	33.677	22.780	14.464	27.232	5.321	1.790
Cantonal/local tax rate on gross income	0.143	−0.957**	0.043	0.199*	−0.460**	−0.438**	−0.457**
	(0.53)	(−3.52)	(0.28)	(2.15)	(−4.24)	(−6.43)	(−4.53)
Share of labour force in service sector (in per cent)	−0.060**	−0.095**	−0.020	−0.012	−0.028	0.070**	0.138**
	(−5.60)	(−4.28)	(−1.26)	(−1.09)	(−1.39)	(4.66)	(5.03)
Index of infrastructure of the canton	−0.026**	−0.084**	−0.024*	0.006	0.022*	0.031**	0.033**
	(−4.83)	(−6.40)	(−2.35)	(0.95)	(2.22)	(4.20)	(2.59)
Net in-commuters (in per cent of total labour force)	0.009**	0.017**	0.007*	0.002	−0.013**	−0.010**	−0.007
	(3.87)	(3.68)	(2.21)	(0.66)	(−3.03)	(−3.14)	(−1.24)
Population of the canton (in millions)	4.146**	3.122	1.600	2.829**	−6.386**	−5.310**	−6.924**
	(4.35)	(1.59)	(1.14)	(2.88)	(−3.59)	(−3.96)	(−2.87)
Dummy for Geneva	1.625**	0.065	−0.964*	0.662*	0.708	1.205*	0.738
	(4.60)	(0.09)	(−1.87)	(1.84)−	(1.09)	(2.29)	(0.75)
Dummy for Zug	−1.114*	−3.813**	−1.494	0.470	−0.126	−0.968	−0.874
	(−1.72)	(−2.81)	(−1.46)	(0.63)	(−0.10)	(−0.98)	(−0.48)
R^2	0.416	0.461	0.268	0.080	0.260	0.572	0.423
SER	1.145	2.332	1.598	1.179	2.098	1.520	2.862
J.–B.	1.433	0.771	17.256**	0.305	0.246	0.220	224.257*
DIFF	0.286	3.292	0.238	1.192	3.478	4.021	5.585
DIFF (per cent of mean dependent variable)	0.043	0.185	0.013	0.077	0.145	0.494	0.836
Mean of dependent variable	6.626	17.788	18.930	15.443	23.935	8.147	6.679
Std. dev. of dep. variable	1.499	3.176	1.867	1.229	2.439	2.323	3.768

Notes: See Table 15.1.

307

between cantons. Yet, this question cannot be treated using data aggregated at the cantonal level where the variation between municipalities is smoothed out by the use of a weighted average of local taxation. We shall therefore examine the question of the effects of cantonal/local tax rate differences using a large sample of municipalities.

3.2. Results for Swiss Municipalities

Table 15.3 gives the estimation results for the 137 largest municipalities in Switzerland (covering 46 per cent of total population for the year 1990). This table includes the same variables as Table 15.1 (cantonal/local tax rate for married people with two children), but the observations now relate to individual municipalities. In addition to the index of infrastructure of the canton, a number of proxies for the respective municipal infrastructure (public spending per inhabitant for health services, education, cultural service and recreation) are considered, but none of them prove to be significant. The same is true for a number of aggregates of municipal expenditures (total spending, current expenditure for compensation of public employees as well as for other current expenditure, investment expenditure).

As would be expected, when data for the individual municipalities are used the explanatory power of the estimates in Table 15.3 decreases as compared to the estimates presented in Table 15.1. Nevertheless, it can be observed that the marginal effect of the cantonal/local tax rates increases for the highest-income group and the same is true for the absolute as well as the relative impact produced by differences in the highest/lowest tax burden among municipalities (DIFF).[18] This result may be partly because of the selection bias inherent in our sample of municipalities because, in contrast to Table 15.1 which referred to all taxpayers in Switzerland (by cantons), we now consider only those living in municipalities with at least 10,000 inhabitants. The latter sample is characterized by a higher (lower) share of high- (low-) income people compared to Switzerland as a whole: high-income people prefer to live in cities.[19] The impacts of the other explanatory variables seem to be similar to those in Table 15.1, although they deviate, plausibly, from the cantonal results when a lower level of observation is chosen. For instance, the coefficients for the stock of cantonal infrastructure decrease in absolute size (and also to some extent lose statistical significance). In contrast, the coefficients for local attractiveness of work as well as the availability of local services (share of labour force in the service sector) grow in absolute size as well as in significance.

Moreover, even when we divide the taxpayers of each municipality into retired people, employees and self-employed, we obtain results that change in the same manner as in the case of all municipal taxpayers compared with all taxpayers in Switzerland (compare Tables 15A.1 to 15A.3 with Tables 15A.4 to 15A.6 in the Appendix). However, the absolute and the relative impact of the differences in the cantonal/local tax burden proves to be higher in the case of municipalities. The Jarque-Bera test in Tables 15A.4 to 15A.6 indicate clearly that the normality assumption for the residuals does not hold in many cases. Using the same method as for all taxpayers, we obtain almost the same result for employees as for all taxpayers. What is interesting is that the normality assumption of the residuals continues to hold for the four upper-income classes in the case of self-employed taxpayers.

In the case of retired persons the impact of the tax rate in the highest income classes diminishes and the impact of the cantonal/local tax rate on the share of taxpayers in different income groups is the reverse if we exclude the outliers of the residuals from the equation.[20] Apart from statistical reasons there may also be a theoretical explanation why the behaviour of retirees does not seem to exhibit a stable and consistent pattern: those who retire from working life tend to take a more comprehensive decision, that is, either to stay in the same region or to move to a different place like sunny Ticino or the shoreline of Lake Geneva. In fact, the dummy variable for the canton of Geneva exhibits a strong positive impact in the two lowest-income classes of retired persons. The strong negative impact in all other income groups may reflect the comparative advantage of competing regions.

This breakdown of municipal taxpayers allows, in addition, for a more differentiated picture regarding who among the high-income earners have a strong preference for urban life. In the case of the group with the highest income (the share of all taxpayers that this group represents is 1.2 percentage points higher in the municipalities sample than in that of all taxpayers), we observe that the respective increase in the share of self-employed taxpayers is 7.1 percentage points, while employees (1.1 percentage points) and retirees (0.9 percentage points) are now slightly underrepresented.

As suggested above, the self-employed have to reside close to their clients in the cities. This, it should be observed, is also true for the sixth income class although to a lesser extent.

In order to find out what impact the cantonal tax burden has compared to local tax rates, a distinction can be made between the respective tax rates for the standard case (see Table 15.4). The results are virtually the same as in Table 15.3, except for the fiscal burden which plays a significant role in the three highest-income classes (negative signs for both the cantonal and the local tax rates at a significant level). Although at first glance the marginal impact of local taxation makes a stronger showing than the impact of its cantonal counterpart, the absolute and relative effects of the tax rate differences ($DIFF_{cant}$, $DIFF_{mun}$) reveal that the impact of local tax rates is

Table 15.4 Model to explain the share of all taxpayers in different income groups in the 137 largest Swiss municipalities, 1990, state/local tax rate on gross income of married taxpayers with two children

Dependent variable	S_1	S_2	S_3	S_4	S_5	S_6	S_7
Income group (in 1,000)	15–20	20–30	30–40	40–50	50–75	75–100	>100
Gross income (in 1,000)	17	25	35	45	60	85	175
Constant	12.962	33.107	24.281	13.675	27.490	6.327	1.999
Cantonal tax rate on gross income	0.104	–3.167*	0.659	0.066	–0.429*	–0.339**	–0.441**
	(0.11)	(–2.18)	(1.58)	(0.37)	(–2.03)	(–2.77)	(–2.87)
Local tax rate on gross income	0.168	0.780	–0.565	0.369(*)	–0.500(*)	–0.564**	–0.476**
	(0.25)	(0.68)	(–1.37)	(1.74)	(–1.87)	(–3.90)	(–2.75)
Share of labour force in service sector (in per cent)	–0.060**	–0.085**	–0.034(*)	–0.007	–0.029	0.062**	0.137**
	(–5.54)	(–3.71)	(–1.87)	(–0.54)	(–1.30)	(3.73)	(4.53)
Index of infrastructure of the canton	–0.026**	–0.085**	–0.030**	0.009	0.021(*)	0.027**	0.032*
	(–4.60)	(–6.47)	(–2.74)	(1.27)	(1.83)	(3.24)	(2.29)
Net in-commuters (in per cent of total labour force)	0.009**	0.017**	0.007*	0.001	–0.013**	–0.010**	–0.007
	(3.83)	(3.74)	(2.23)	(0.61)	(–3.00)	(–3.09)	(–1.24)
Population of the canton (in millions)	4.143**	2.804	2.462(*)	2.455*	–6.265**	–4.724**	–6.773*
	(4.32)	(1.43)	(1.65)	(2.30)	(–3.25)	(–3.22)	(–2.53)
Dummy for Geneva	1.621**	–0.180	–1.036*	0.772*	0.617	0.680	0.605
	(4.41)	(–0.25)	(–2.02)	(–2.03)	(0.72)	(0.91)	(0.43)
Dummy for Zug	–1.116(*)	–4.058**	–1.473	0.521	–0.145	–1.004	–0.875
	(–1.71)	(–2.99)	(–1.44)	(0.70)	(–0.11)	(–1.02)	(–0.48)
R^2	0.416	0.474	0.268	0.086	0.259	0.570	0.423
SER	1.145	2.304	1.598	1.175	2.100	1.524	2.862
J.–B.	1.427	0.662	11.243**	0.400	0.292	0.196	227.100**
DIFF$_{cant}$	0.086	4.751	1.654	0.209	1.961	2.390	4.829
DIFF$_{cant}$ (per cent of mean dependant var)	0.013	0.267	0.087	0.014	0.082	0.293	0.723
DIFF$_{mun}$	0.195	1.513	1.859	1.565	2.630	3.564	4.451
DIFF$_{mun}$ (per cent of mean dependant var)	0.029	0.085	0.098	0.101	0.110	0.438	0.666
Mean of dependant variable	6.626	17.788	18.930	15.443	23.935	8.147	6.679
Std. dev. of dep. variable	1.499	3.176	1.867	1.229	2.439	2.323	3.768

310

lower in the case of the highest-income class but higher in the fifth and sixth income classes.[21]

In sum, our results strongly suggest that at least some tax competition occurs in Switzerland and that some people, especially high-income earners, choose their place of residence taking into account the amount of income (and property) taxes they have to pay. This is true for cantonal as well as for local income taxes. It becomes even more evident when the estimates refer to the municipalities in relatively large cantons (like Berne and Zurich) where there is a further increase in the absolute size and statistical significance of the coefficients for the local tax variable and for the commuting variable. (These results are available from the authors on request.) Furthermore, these results are supported by other studies such as Pommerehne and Krebs (1991) for the canton of Zurich, which suggest that residential decisions are strongly influenced by local tax rates. However, the most interesting question refers to the consequences of tax competition, namely whether or not it actually has the destructive allocational and distributional effects described above. We now consider if such effects can be detected.

4. EFFECTS OF TAX COMPETITION IN SWITZERLAND

4.1. Allocative Consequences

One popular hypothesis, first tested by Oates (1969), is that saving induced by lower tax rates is capitalized in higher rents: lower tax rates lead to higher rents and property values.[22]

To test this, we estimate a hedonic price function, where the amount of the monthly average (MDR) dwelling rent as of 1990 (per municipality, respectively per canton), net of heating costs, depends on the quality of the dwelling, its size, the attractiveness of the location area, and the willingness to pay, which itself depends on the income of the tenant.

To capture qualitative characteristics, we consider the age of the dwelling houses (AGE should be negatively related to the average dwelling rent), the length of time since the last renovation, TSLR (a negative sign is expected), the percentage of dwellings with central heating, CH (which should have a positive impact, *ceteris paribus*), and percentage of dwellings with hot water supply, HWS (positive sign). All variables are expressed in average terms. We also consider the average number of floors (NF), although no clear impact on the dwelling rent is expected a priori.[23] The average size is measured by the mean of the square metres per dwelling, SMD (alternatively we have tried to capture it by the average number of standardized rooms (NSR)), which should have a positive impact on the dwelling rent. To account for the attractiveness of location, we add a number of other variables to the model: the index of the cantonal stock of infrastructure (CSI) as it has been used so far, the amount of municipal current expenditure per capita (EXC), and an index of local income tax burden (LITB) for the standard case of married taxpayers with two children (in the latter case, a negative impact is expected, but a positive one in the other cases). In addition, we consider to what extent dwellings are owned (and partly subsidized) by the government, in which case a negative impact of the respective variable (GOVO) on the dwelling rent is expected. Demand conditions are measured by gross income per capita (GIC). Finally, since we again use a weighted regression with the square root of the number of households as a weighting scheme, the average number of households (NHH) is included in the equation. We have used various specifications. The results of estimating a log-linear model for the 137 municipalities. are as follows.

$$
\begin{aligned}
\text{LN MDR} \quad &= \quad 4.056 - 0.254^* \quad \text{LN AGE} + 0.289^{**} \quad \text{LN CH} + 0.736^{**} \quad \text{LN SMD} \\
&\qquad\qquad\quad (-4.11) \qquad\qquad\quad (2.24) \qquad\qquad\quad (3.70) \\
&\qquad + 0.082 \quad \text{LN CSI} + 0.074^* \quad \text{LN EXC} - 0.009 \quad \text{LN LITB} \\
&\qquad\quad (1.07) \qquad\qquad\quad (2.23) \qquad\qquad (-0.20) \\
&\qquad + 0.417^{**} \quad \text{LN GIC} - 0.018 \quad \text{LN GOVO} + 0.016 \quad \text{LN NHH} \\
&\qquad\quad (6.21) \qquad\qquad (-2.19) \qquad\qquad\quad (1.33)
\end{aligned}
$$

$R^2 = 0.681$; $\bar{R}^2 = 0.658$; SER $= 0.110$; DF $= 126$; J.–B. $= 9.403^{**}$; Mean (LN MDR) $= 6.686$; SD (LN MDR) $= 0.188$.

Most of the variables describing the qualitative characteristics and the size of dwellings, have the expected sign,[24] and their coefficients have – as in the case of the size variable – quite plausible values. For instance, doubling the average size of dwellings increases rent by 74 per cent, a value which coincides with other independent estimates based on individual dwelling data for the city of Basle (cf. Pommerehne 1988).[25] The income variable (GIC) has the expected positive sign and is strongly significant. Among the attractiveness variables, the index of the cantonal stock of infrastructure has a positive sign but it is not significant. Local government current expenditure per capita has the expected positive impact and is significant at the 95 per cent confidence level. Their effect does not seem to be particularly strong in absolute terms: the maximum difference caused by this variable is about SFr. 117 per month and, thus, SFr. 1,398 per year. The coefficient of the tax variable has the expected negative sign, but it is not significant according to any convention. The Jarque-Bera test indicates again that the normality assumption does not hold for the residuals.[26] Moreover, the models do not work particularly well for the municipalities in the canton of Zug with their below-average tax rates. The residual of the log-linear model for the city of Zug is SFr. −122 (for the two other cities of the canton of Zug, Baar SFr. −117 and Cham SFr. −107), indicating that the dwelling rent is systematically overestimated by the model relative to real dwelling rents.[27] All this suggests that there may be some capitalization of tax savings but this is far from being complete.

Basically the same results are derived when cantonal data instead of municipal ones are used.[28]

LN MDR	= 5.669 − 0.280(*)	LN AGE + 0.338*	LN CH + 0.177	LN SMD
	(−1.82)	(1.74)	(0.30)	
	+ 0.261*	LN CSI + 0.094	LN CEXC − 0.255*	LN CLITB
	(1.41)	(1.34)	(−1.82)	
	+ 0.273	LN GIC− 0.009	LN GOVO + 0.024	LN NHH
	(1.40)	(−0.16)	(1.05)	

$R^2 = 0.780$; $\bar{R}^2 = 0.656$; SER = 0.079; DF = 16; J.–B. = 1.537; Mean (LN MDR) = 6.641; SD (LN MDR) = 0.134.

However, the relationship between cantonal current spending per capita (CEXC) on the one hand, and monthly dwelling rent on the other hand is no longer significant if one changes from municipalities to cantons.[29] Although the cantonal/local income tax burden (CLITB) becomes significant at the 90 per cent confidence level, its impact is still rather poor when measured in absolute terms. For an apartment of about 100 square metres and a dwelling rent of about SFr. 1,300 the maximum difference caused by the tax variable is about SFr. 128 per month and SFr. 1,541 per year which, again, is not very impressive. We should add, however, that the number of regressors is large compared to the number of observations used.

As the discussion of the early results of Oates (1969) has shown, capitalization of tax savings by the increase in dwelling rents is only possible if the system is not in a perfect Tiebout equilibrium in which in all communities marginal (tax) costs are equal to marginal benefits of public activities leaving no room for the capitalization of any rent. If, however, the ideal conditions of this model are not met, as is the case even for Switzerland, tax competition could, according to the hypotheses described above, lead to a cutthroat competition producing uniformly rather low tax rates in equilibrium. As a consequence, the share of public expenditures of GNP would decline. In reality, however, there has been a rise in the share of public spending over the last 40 years in Switzerland. As is shown in Kirchgässner and Pommerehne (1995a, pp. 8ff.), total government expenditure in relation to GNP rose between 1950 and 1989 from 19.6 per cent to 25.0 per cent.[30] Of course, this is clearly below the corresponding figures for the Federal Republic of Germany, which for the same time rose from 24 per cent to 29.3 per cent.[31] Despite the fact that, as Lybeck and Henrekson (1988, p.5) indicate, Switzerland registers the lowest government share (measured as total outlays of government as a percentage of GNP) of all OECD countries, it exhibited the same pattern for growth in government during the last decades. Since the government share is lower, one might expect the level of provision of public goods also to be lower. However, compared with Germany, the share of public consumption in GNP was higher in Switzerland during the eighties and the share of public investment higher right from the seventies. Thus, tax competition does not seem to have resulted in a breakdown in the supply of public goods in Switzerland.

Although the single municipalities and cantons behave relatively independently in setting taxes, the variation and the regional structure of the tax burden remains rather stable over time. The list of standard deviations in the corresponding index is as follows: 1983 – 16.7; 1985 – 16.2; 1987 – 21.1; 1989 – 18.6; 1991 – 18.8. The (unweighted) correlation coefficient of the total tax burden indices from 1983 to 1991 is 0.822. Thus, no convergence of the tax rates in the different cantons can be observed.

4.2. Distributive Consequences

It is more difficult to derive clear-cut results for redistribution. On the one hand, government transfers in relation to GNP are lower in Switzerland than in Germany and in many other industrialized countries. However, what counts here is not the amount of money spent but the amount of redistribution achieved by these transfers. It is necessary, therefore, to look at the income distribution before and after public intervention in order to estimate its net distributional effects and to compare it with redistribution in other countries.The basic concept of inequality as used by Kirchgässner and Pommerehne (1995b) refers to the distribution of factor income (employee compensation, proprietor's income, dividends and other market payments to owners of factors of production, but not public transfers or taxes) among households. Thus, households are first classified by (main type of) factor income, and then total factor income in each class is calculated. The burden of taxation at all government levels is then subtracted, and the benefits of public expenditures are finally added to aggregate factor income in each income class under 'normal' incidence assumptions. This income concept will be referred to as 'final income'.

Conceptually, this measure presumes that all behavioural adjustments to the fisc that affect the basis for redistribution as, for example, reduced work effort caused by high marginal tax rates, are accounted for in the factor income distribution. Since the fisc affects both the final and the factor income distribution, the difference between inequality in the final and the factor income distribution can only be an approximative estimate of the 'true' but not measurable amount of redistribution. Final income is an unusually broad definition of income appropriately viewed as being generated in a simultaneous interplay of both public and private actors in a country.[32] Another important assumption made is that recipients value the benefits of public expenditures at their respective cost and hence total benefits equal public expenditures.[33] Underlying the normal income concept are conventional incidence assumptions.[34] Personal income taxes are assumed not to have been shifted, estate and gift taxes fall entirely on the highest-income class, the corporate income tax is divided equally between dividend recipients and consumers, residential property tax is paid by consumers of housing and excise as well as sales taxes are borne entirely by consumers. The incidence of public expenditure is assumed to fall entirely on those who are intended to benefit, for example on children below eighteen for elementary and secondary school expenditures. These outlays of the government for which direct beneficiaries cannot readily be identified, that is, expenditures with public good characteristics, are assigned to one half on the basis of the share of factor income and to the other half according to the distribution of households.

The results that Kirchgässner and Pommerehne derive for all government levels taken together suggest that the net incidence is 'pro poor'. Though the absolute amount of public spending per household increases with higher income classes, the absolute tax burden increases even faster, rendering a negative overall result as regards net incidence, starting from the third lowest-income class. The Gini coefficients calculated for factor income and for final income as they are derived from the conventional incidence assumptions show that ultimate inequality, with a Gini-coefficient of 226, is 108 Gini points lower than factor income inequality, with a Gini coefficient of 334.[35] This confirms that the net incidence of the public budget has a strong equalizing impact. Kirchgässner and Pommerehne also find that it is not so much the central level of government, but rather the subcentral levels of government units which influence the final income distribution. Their results further indicate that the federal government mainly uses the expenditure side for distribution purposes, whereas the cantons and the local governments predominantly apply instruments from the revenue side.

The main result that the decentralized Swiss federal system does not collapse (obviously) as a result of 'fatal' distributional effects is corroborated by other studies for individual Swiss cantons[36] which include the (regional) impact of the central government budget. They reach the same conclusion as do Kirchgässner and Pommerehne for the whole of Switzerland. The distributional impact of the public budget is approximately the same as in the US, somewhat higher than in Canada and not that much lower than in Germany. Of all four countries, Switzerland has the most equal pre-tax income distribution. For after-tax income, Switzerland still has the most equal income distribution of the four countries. Moreover, the estimates of Kirchgässner and Pommerehne do not allow for the strong 'pro poor' incidence of the mandatory part of the social security system. The main differences between these countries are not so much with the spending side of the budget, but much more with the stronger redistributional impact of the Swiss tax system. This is mostly because of the strong weight given to the progressive, individual and corporate income and wealth taxes which are mainly decided on by the subcentral units at their own discretion. It is interesting to note that in the other three federal countries considered here, not only is the respective share of the central government relatively larger, but in each of them the bulk of progressive income taxes is assigned to the central level.[37]

5. SOME CONCLUSIONS REGARDING THE FISCAL CONSTITUTION OF A EUROPE IN THE FUTURE

If the matter at hand is the question of the fiscal constitution of a Europe in the future, it seems useful to take a 'constitutional perspective' and to ask which rules rational individuals in the 'original position' would choose.[38] In this situation, individuals are ignorant with respect to their future position, but they both know as well as use all information available. This would include evidence from Switzerland. The question is, therefore, what conclusions concerning the fiscal constitutional rules of a future Europe would be drawn from this evidence.

To begin with, individuals do not know whether later on they will be members of the government (including the public bureaucracy) or private citizens. Therefore, they have to take into account the specific preferences conditional on membership in one of those two groups. This is the case especially if they use a utilitarian rule, as has been proposed, for example, by Harsanyi (1975). However, if they apply the Rawlsian difference principle, only the preferences of the least powerful group will be considered which in this case will most probably be those of private citizens. Therefore, in what follows we ask how such citizens can protect themselves against exploitation by politicians and public bureaucrats, taking for granted that the latter have such an institutional advantage that they are unlikely to find themselves in a position of disadvantage.[39]

Even from the point of view of private citizens, control of public bureaucracy is not the only and not even the dominant interest. The chief objective is rather to secure the provision of public goods and some redistribution in favour of the poor. However, as neither is possible without the existence of some public employees, once they are there, the need for controlling them arises. And the rules have to be set in a way that, even if public officials follow their selfish interests, the social outcome will be acceptable for individual citizens.

The more citizens are able to control this government, the more it will act in accordance with their preferences. An important means of control relates to the federal structure:[40] the lower the government level at which public activity is conducted, the greater the possibility for individuals to influence decisions. From this point of view, government tasks should be allocated to the lowest possible level and subcentral governments should be equipped with their own means to finance activities.[41]

Thus, it is not so much (political) competition *per se* which is called for. More relevant is the requirement that citizens enjoy enhanced possibilities of control over lower levels of government with the power to oblige them to respect their preferences. This would hold true even if there were only one such fiscal unit and, therefore, no competition at all. On the other hand, since bureaucracy has informational advantages, even in small communities, the existence of several communities at the same level does give citizens a greater possibility of comparing and, consequently, of controlling public sector activities.

One crucial question which has to be decided at the constitutional level regards assignment of taxes to different governmental levels, in particular personal and corporate income taxes and general sales (value added) and specific consumption taxes. In this respect, there exists a significant difference between progressive (yield-elastic) and proportional (yield-inelastic) taxes. If tax rates can only be changed by changing a law, which is usually the case, any increase of the relative share of government must be decided via the parliamentary process (and possibly also via a referendum). This ensures a public discussion, and governments, as recent experience in the US, Germany and other countries shows, will hesitate to increase taxes, at least as long as they wish to be re-elected. In fact, it is difficult to get a tax hike approved by a legislature, not to speak of the general public.[42] Thus, increases of indirect tax rates (or of proportional direct taxes) are comparatively rare events, even for quantity-based taxes where real yield has over time been eroded by inflation. Such proportional taxes leave relatively small leeway for Leviathan behaviour by a government.

Progressive and yield-elastic taxes, on the other hand, can lead to a larger government share of national income not only at times when private economic activity increases and, consequently, private income rises, but also when there is inflation and when there is no corresponding indexation. In such circumstances, there is really no need to change tax legislation to obtain more revenue: it arrives automatically.[43] Thus, progressive taxes offer the possibility for a government to behave in a Leviathan-like fashion.

This implies that the need for specific means of control depends on what kind of tax has been granted to the particular level of government. There is more of a need for 'controllability' with taxes where yield rises (nearly) automatically compared to taxes where it is very difficult for politicians to increase the (relative) yield. Citizens need much more external control to keep down progressive taxes than to restrict proportional ones, especially general sales taxes.

Still another problem arises with 'specific' taxes borne only by small sections of the population. At the post-constitutional level, it is relatively easy to obtain support for an increase in such taxes from the majority of people not affected. This creates additional leeway for the government. At the constitutional stage, however, the individuals will want to protect themselves from being burdened by such a tax. Therefore, they will be very hesitant to permit the use at all of such taxes.

In the light of these considerations, proportional, yield-inelastic taxes are preferable for higher levels of government, where control by citizens is difficult to implement. Progressive, yield-elastic taxes are to be assigned to low government levels where individuals exert more influence. Specific taxes as discussed above are to be ruled out as far as possible. This implies that the supranational level of the EU should be financed exclusively by proportional taxes, in particular general sales or value-added taxes, but certainly not by progressive personal income taxes. This type of tax is to be assigned exclusively to lower levels of government where there is a greater possibility for control.

These proposals take into account the Swiss experience that the assignment of progressive direct taxes to subcentral levels does not lead to fatal distributional consequences, but perhaps to even greater redistribution than under a (hypothetical) centralized system. With respect to the EU, this implies that there is no need for strong harmonization of national income taxes or even for the implementation of a supranational (progressive) income tax. Redistribution from the rich to the poor can, as is the case today, be a task of the national (or subnational) governments. Of course, redistribution will nevertheless take place on the EU level in the future, as is already occurring via regional (structural) funds. There may be some need for redistribution from rich to poor countries or regions within the EU. Yet, no direct, progressive tax system is required to achieve this. The revenue from a general sales tax or, to take other examples, from mineral oil or carbon dioxide taxes, could be used.[44]

The problem of tax havens may not be as grave as is often imagined. Even in a small country like Switzerland, the canton of Zug (and the tax paradise of Liechtenstein) do not seem to create major problems, even if many politicians and citizens would like to eliminate them as tax havens. In the EU, with its much larger member states, the possibilities and incentives for becoming a tax haven will be even less than in Switzerland. Of course, some tax havens like Monaco will always remain, if not inside then outside the EU, and they will continue to attract some wealthy people and some capital. However, this may be unavoidable and in any case at the most of little quantitative importance for development inside the EU. While the irritating existence of tax paradises has to be accepted, however, it should not dictate the tax rules of the Europe of the future.

NOTES

1. A whole number of analogous recommendations arise from the theory of clubs. For a survey, see Sandler and Tschirhart (1980).
2. See, for example Sinn (1990a), p. 503.
3. For a survey of the literature on commodity and factor taxation and the potential distortions in a multijurisdictional context, see Genser (1992).
4. Moreover, as for example Genser (1992) has shown, even with perfect mobility, equilibria with differing capital tax rates are possible if taxation of foreign capital income of residents can be enforced.
5. See, for example , Cornevin-Pfeiffer and Manzini (1992).
6. There is also a small but highly progressive federal income tax, which, however, amounts to less than 25 per cent of total federal tax revenue, while the cantons and municipalities rely on income and property taxes for more than 50 per cent of their total revenue and for more than 95 per cent of their tax revenue. See, for example, Schweizerische Bankgesellschaft (1987) pp. 120 ff., and Kirchgässner and Pommerehne (1992, 1995a).
7. For a more detailed description of these approaches, see Pommerehne (1987).
8. Moreover, even for migration within the region of Basle, Frey (1981, pp. 35ff., 48) was unable to find significant tax rate effects.
9. We first used total public expenditure but later decided to change the specification of this variable by including exhaustive expenditure, public investment expenditure and public expenditure for culture and recreation, respectively, instead of total public expenditure.
10. Taking into account the abundance of influences pooled in the index of infrastructure, the expected sign might not be obvious. The index contains a lot of agglomeration effects reflecting urbanization and localization economies and diseconomies whose expected sign is theoretically open. Nevertheless, the majority of the effects captured by the index of infrastructure exerts a clearly positive influence and, therefore, the coefficient of the whole index should be positive. In fact we assume an equal weight for all influences.
11. It should be noted that the effective tax rates refer to the burden on gross income and not taxable income, but consider the rather different tax deductions between the cantons and their different levels of tax-free income.
12. Of course, one should include the tax rates of all groups in all equations. However, because of the small number of observations this does not make sense. Therefore we included in each equation only the most relevant tax rate, that is the tax rate for the respective income group.
13. The results for all the other groups can be obtained from the authors on request.
14. This also holds for the tax burden of married taxpayers without children (the respective correlation coefficient is –0.146) and for that of singles (0.169).

15. If the share of the labour force in the industrial sector is used, we observe a negative and significant impact of this variable, especially in the case of low-income earners.
16. This is also true if a non-linear, quadratic formulation for the tax rates is employed. The overall results remain essentially the same. We also introduced the tax burden on property, but there is obvious multicollinearity between this variable and the income tax burden. If the property tax rate is used instead of the income tax rate it turns out that, again, above-average-income earners are negatively affected.
17. The representative tax rate at the local level of a canton refers to the weighted average tax rate of the major municipalities, where the number of taxpayers and their income serve as weights.
   These results seem to be somewhat called in question by the fact that, according to the Jarque-Bera test, the normality assumption does not hold for the residuals in the highest-income class. In our sample this is certainly due to outliers. Excluding the outliers from the sample and redoing the estimation the equation reads as follows:

$$S_7 = 5.266 - 0.187^{**} \quad ATR175 + 0.035^* \quad LFS + 0.008 \quad INFRA + NINCOM \quad POP$$
$$0.009^* \quad -0.935$$

$$(-2.96) \qquad\qquad 2.05 \qquad\qquad (1.03) \quad (2.33) \quad (-0.63)$$
$$+1.219 \quad DZG + 2.010^{**} \qquad DGV$$
$$(3.29)$$

$$R^2 = 0.142; \ \bar{R}^2 = 0.090; \ J.\text{-}B. = 5.526(^*).$$

The marginal impact of the cantonal/local tax rate as well as the absolute and relative impact produced by the differences in the highest and lowest tax burden among municipalities (DIFF = 2.285; DIFF% = 0.400) is then even lower than in the case of the cantonal model. On the other hand the outliers which we exclude from the estimation are the interesting cases. Since the results of the six other income groups are not altered we may conclude that the interpretation outlined in the text also holds in the case of the highest income group although the normality assumption does not hold.

19. This should not hold for high-income self-employed people. As outlined above in the cantonal case, a physician for example should reside close to his practice in order to care for his patients. The equations read as follows:

$$S_5 = 6.307 + 0.159 \ ATR60 + 0.010 \quad LFS + 0.035^* \ INFRA - \ NINCOM - \quad POP$$
$$0.005 \qquad 12873^{**}$$

$$(1.98) \qquad\qquad (0.26) \qquad (2.12) \quad (-0.59) \qquad (-4.94)$$
$$-1.388 \ DGV + 2.361 \qquad DZG$$
$$(-1.33) \qquad\qquad (1.00)$$

$$R^2 = 0.036; \bar{R}^2 = -0.018; \ J.\text{-}B. = 3.571.$$

$$S_6 = 1.778 + 0.064(^*) \ ATR \ 85 - 0.002 \quad LFS + 0.007 \quad INFRA - \quad NINCOM- \quad POP$$
$$0.001 \qquad 3.208^{**}$$

$$(1.97) \qquad\qquad (-0.13) \qquad\qquad (-0.05) \qquad (-3.99)$$
$$-0.159 \qquad DGV + 0.752 \qquad DZG$$
$$(-0.47)$$

$$R^2 = -0.058; \bar{R}^2 = -0.125; \ J.\text{-}B. = 4.440.$$

$$S_7 = 1.730 - 0.023 \ ATR175 + 0.015 \ LFS+0.004 \quad INFRA + \quad NINCOM + \quad OP$$
$$0.014^{**} \qquad 1.264$$

$$(-0.77) \qquad\qquad\qquad\qquad\qquad\qquad\qquad (1.20)$$
$$-0.828^* \ DGV + 1.274 \qquad DZG$$
$$(-2.11)$$

$$R^2 = 0.148; \bar{R}^2 = 0.096; \ J.\text{-}B. = 3.609.$$

21. This result may be a hint of the higher mobility of the highest income earners who are not so tied by local embeddedness.
22. For a critical examination of Oates' results and for a discussion of further studies see Pommerehne (1987), pp. 76 ff., or Chaudry-Shah (1988).
23. A higher number of floors coincides with a higher amount of trouble and represents more restrictive constraints on home activities of a household, but also lower complementary costs for cleaning of pavements, heating and so on.
24. Though the variables indicate the time since the last renovation, the average number of floors and the extent of the hot water supply are not statistically significant.
25. This figure already indicates a less than proportional increase of dwelling rents caused by an increase in square metres per dwelling. If we use square metres per dwelling as the only explanatory variable we obtain an elasticity of 81 per cent.
26. Using the same method as in section 3.2 does not alter the results.
27. In fact, the average dwelling rent in the city of Zug is SFr. 953 per month, SFr. 495 below that of Kusnacht (canton of Zurich) with SFr. 1,448, despite the fact that the local income tax is significantly higher in the latter municipality.
28. This is especially true with respect to the size of the dwelling. We again obtain elasticities lower than one.
29. But the *t*-values (≥ 1) indicate that this variable contributes to the overall explanatory power in the theoretically expected direction.
30. This general increase is not an overcompensation of decreasing local or cantonal expenditures by increasing the federal ones. In fact, local as well as cantonal spending, as a part of government expenditure in total, have been raised during this period, while the share of federal government spending has significantly declined.
31. To make the figures comparable, social security insurance payments are excluded.
32. To measure redistribution caused by public budgets would require data on a counterfactual state in a world with no government activity such as the Lindahl equilibrium, which could then be compared with final income. Obviously, we do not contemplate calculating the distribution of income in Switzerland in a Lindahl equilibrium.
33. For empirical evidence supporting the view that this assumption is not very misleading see Pommerehne (1977a).
34. The basic data to which they refer was taken from Borer and Schaub (1980). However, their incidence assumptions are somewhat modified in order to be able to undertake a comparison between Switzerland and other (larger) countries such as the US, Canada and the Federal Republic of Germany. A more detailed discussion of the incidence assumptions used is given in Smolensky, Pommerehne and Dalrymple (1979).
35. It is convenient to multiply the Gini coefficient by 1,000 and to speak of the differences in terms of Gini points.
36. See Pommerehne (1980) for the canton of Basle-Land and Heusler (1980) for the town of Basle.
37. For Canada in 1970 the central government realized 53 per cent of its total revenue (16.6 bn dollars) from income taxes, whereas the respective share of subcentral revenue was 20.5 per cent (17.2 bn dollars); for the US in the same year the respective figures were 65.5 per cent (193 bn dollars) and 8.2 per cent (178 bn dollars); and for the Federal Republic of Germany, also for 1970, 31.1 per cent (87.8 bn DM) and 24.4 per cent (130 bn DM). (See Pommerehne 1977b, pp. 331–3.)
38. For a further examination of the (possible) role of constitutional economics in this context see Kirchgässner (1994).
39. On the basis of this argument, one can defend the objective function used in Brennan and Buchanan (1977, 1980) against the critique of West and Corke (1979).
40. Another crucial means of control, which is not discussed here, consists in introducing direct democratic elements into a constitution. See Pommerehne (1990) as well as Kirchgässner and Frey (1994).
41. We deliberately want to leave out stabilization aspects.

42. The danger emanating from lower than optimal taxes will be left out here on purpose. For a classic discussion on how the democratic process may generate suboptimal tax levels see Downs (1960).
43. During the entire history of the 'old' Federal Republic of Germany, there has never been a permanent increase of income tax rates based on a change of the tax laws, but – on the contrary – several rate reductions took place which, however, did not even balance the effects of inflation (see Kirchgässner 1985). Such 'tax reforms' were used to present 'tax gifts' to the taxpayers in general and/or to special groups before general elections.
44. In the Federal Republic of Germany, for example, an important part of the '*Länderfinanzausgleich*' is financed by the value-added tax.

REFERENCES

Borer, M. and T. Schaub (1980), *Verteilungswirkungen der öffentlichen Haushalte von Bund, Kantonen und Gemeinden im Jahre 1977*, Basel: Institut Für Sozialwissenschaften.

Brennan, G. and J.M. Buchanan (1977), 'Towards a tax constitution for Leviathan', *Journal of Public Economics*, **8**, 255–74.

Brennan, G. and J.M. Buchanan (1980), *The Power to Tax*, Cambridge, MA: Cambridge University Press.

Chaudry-Shah, A. (1988), 'Capitalization and the theory of local public finance: an interpretative essay', *Journal of Economic Surveys*, **2**, 209–43.

Cnossen, S. and C.S Shoup (1987), 'Coordination of value-added taxes', in S. Cnossen (ed.), *Tax Coordination in the European Community*, Deventer: Kluwer, 59–84.

Cornevin-Pfeiffer, K. and M. Manzini (1992), 'La taille du secteur public', in L. Weber (ed.), *Les Finances Publiques D'un Etat Federatif: La Suisse*, Paris: Economica, 85–183.

Downs, A. (1960), 'Why the government is too small in a democracy?', *World Politics* **12**, 541–63.

Frey, R.L. (1981), 'Bestimmungsfaktoren der inter- und intraregionalen Wanderungen, eine ökonometrische Untersuchung für die Schweiz und die Region Basel', in R.L. Frey (ed.), *Von der Land- zur Stadtflucht, Bestimmungsfaktoren der Bevölkerungswanderungen in der Region Basel*, Bern/Frankfurt: Peter Lang, 13–52.

Genser, B. (1992), 'Tax competition and harmonization in federal economies', in H.-J. Vosgerau (ed.), *European Integration in the World Economy*, Heidelberg: Springer, 200–37.

Harsanyi, J.C. (1975), 'Can the maximin principle serve as a basis for morality? a critique of John Rawls's theory', *American Political Science Review*, **69**, 594–606.

Heusler, A. (1980), *Verteilungswirkungen des Staatshaushalts: personelle und räumliche Budgetinzidenz in Basel-Stadt, 1975*, Bern/Frankfurt: Peter Lang.

Keen, M. (1989), 'Pareto-improving indirect tax harmonization', *European Economic Review* **33**, 1–12.

Kirchgässner, G. (1985), 'Die Entwicklung der Einkommensteuerprogression in der Bundesrepublik Deutschland', *Finanarchiv,* **43**, 328–47.

Kirchgässner, G. (1994), 'Constitutional economics and its relevance for the evolution of rules', *Kyklos,* **47**, 321–39.

Kirchgässner, G. and B.S. Frey (1994), 'Volksabstimmung und direkte Demokratie: ein Beitrag zur Verfassungsdiskussion', in H.D. Klingemann and M. Kaase (eds), *Wahlen & Wähler, Analysen aus Anlass der Bundestagswahl 1990,* Westdeutscher Verlag: Opladen, 42–69.

Kirchgässner, G. and W.W. Pommerehne (1992), 'Zwischen Parteien- und Bundesstaat: staatshandeln in der Schweiz und in der Bundesrepublik Deutschland', in H. Abromeit and W.W. Pommerehne (eds), *Staatstätigkeit in der Schweiz,* Bern/Stuttgart/Wien: Haupt, 221–45.

Kirchgässner, G. and W.W. Pommerehne (1995a), 'Public spending in federal states: a comparative econometric study', Forthcoming in: P. Capros and D. Meulders (eds), *Modeling Budgetary Policy: Public Spending,* Routledge: London.

Kirchgässner, G. and W.W. Pommerehne (1995b), 'Tax harmonization and tax competition in the European Union: lessons from Switzerland', University of St. Gallen, Mimeo.

Lybeck, J.A. and M. Henrekson (eds) (1988), *Explaining the Growth of Government,* Amsterdam: North-Holland.

Oates, W.E. (1969), 'The effects of property taxes and local public spending on property values: an empirical study of tax capitalization and the Tiebout hypothesis', *Journal of Public Economics,* **77**, 957–71.

Oates, W.E. (1972), *Fiscal Federalism,* New York: Harcourt/Brace/Jovanovich.

Pommerehne, W.W. (1977a), 'Trasferimenti non monetari contro trasferimenti monetari: una favola di scienza finanziaria', *Rivista di Diritto Finanziario e Scienza delle Finanze,* **36**, 121–133.

Pommerehne, W.W. (1977b), 'Quantative aspects of federalism: a study of six countries', in W.E. Oates (ed.), *The Political Economy of Fiscal Federalism,* Lexington/Toronto: DC Heath, 275–355.

Pommerehne, W.W. (1980), 'Public choice approaches to explain fiscal redistribution', in K.W. Roskamp (ed.), *Public Choice and Public Finance,* Paris: Cujas, 169–90.

Pommerehne, W.W. (1987), *Präferenzen für öffentliche Güter: Ansätze zu Ihrer Erfassung,* Tübingen: Mohr (Siebeck).

Pommerehne, W.W. (1988), 'Measuring environmental benefits: a comparison of hedonic technique and contingent valuation', in D. Bös, M.

Rose and C. Seidl (eds), *Welfare and Efficiency in Public Economics*, Berlin: Springer, 363–400.

Pommerehne, W.W. (1990), 'The empirical relevance of comparative institutional analysis', *European Economic Review,* **34**, 458–69.

Pommerehne, W.W. and S. Krebs (1991), 'Fiscal interactions of central city and suburbs: the case of Zurich', *Urban Studies,* **28**, 783–801.

Sandler, T. and J.T. Tschirhart (1980), 'The economic theory of clubs: an evaluative survey', *Journal of Economic Literature,* **18**, 1481–521.

Schweizerische Bankgesellschaft (ed.) (1987), *Die Schweizer Wirtschaft 1946–1986: Daten, Fakten, Analysen* Zürich: Schweizerische Bankgesellschaft.

Sinn, H.W. (1990a), 'Tax harmonization and tax competition in Europe', *European Economic Review,* **34**, 489–504.

Sinn, H.W. (1990b), 'The limits to competition between economic regimes', *Empirica,* **17**, 3–14.

Smolensky, E., W.W. Pommerehne and E. Dalrymple (1979), 'Postfisc income inequality: a comparison of the United States and West Germany', in J.R. Moroney (ed.), *Income Inequality: trends and International Comparisons,* Lexington/Toronto: DC: Heath, 69–81.

Tiebout, C.M. (1956), 'A pure theory of local expenditures', *Journal of Political Economy,* **65**, 416–24.

West, E.G. and G. Corke, (1979), 'Tax constraints on Leviathan', *Journal of Public Economics* **13**, 395–401.

Table 15.4.1 Model to explain the share of retired persons in different income groups in 26 Swiss cantons, 1990, state/local tax rate on gross income of retired persons

Dependent variable Income group(in 1,000) Gross income (in 1,000)	S_1 15–20 17	S_2 20–30 25	S_3 30–40 35	S_4 40–50 45	S_5 50–75 60	S_6 75–00 85	S_7 >100 175
Constant	29.836	40.684	18.165	5.661	1.559	-1.026	-1.740
Cantonal/ local tax rate on gross income	0.113	0.326	-0.155	-0.125(*)	-0.080	-0.042	-0.114**
	(0.30)	(1.19)	(-1.55)	(-1.76)	(-0.76)	(-1.22)	(-2.98)
Share of labour force in service sector (in %)	-0.030	-0.069	0.036	0.040	-0.033	-0.008	0.038
	(-0.45)	(-0.93)	(0.78)	(0.94)	(-0.46)	(-0.34)	(1.21)
Index of infrastructure of the canton	-0.115**	-0.087**	0.001	0.042**	0.112**	0.046**	0.042**
	(-4.56)	(-3.21)	(0.03)	(2.69)	(4.16)	(4.90)	(3.69)
Net in-commuters (in % of total labour force)	0.028	0.034	-0.009	-0.008	-0.057*	-0.018	-0.007
	(0.92)	(1.07)	(-0.43)	(-0.44)	(-1.75)	(-1.57)	(-0.53)
Population of the canton (in millions)	0.669	0.147	-0.823	-0.513	0.585	0.652*	0.172
	(0.73)	(0.17)	(-1.45)	(-0.93)	(0.61)	(1.94)	(0.42)
Dummy for Geneva	7.458**	3.795*	-3.329**	-3.782**	-3.441*	-1.114*	-1.066
	(4.63)	(2.25)	(-2.97)	(-3.69)	(-2.02)	(-1.81)	(-1.41)
Dummy for Zug	-0.723	-1.545	-0.890	-0.317	2.023	0.786	1.247
	(-0.27)	(-0.59)	(-0.52)	(-0.19)	(0.71)	(0.77)	(0.98)
R^2	0.550	0.553	0.055	0.530	0.608	0.686	0.626
SER	1.977	1.745	1.589	1.062	1.721	0.617	0.881
J.–B.	0.980	1.677	4.690*	1.945	0.160	0.335	0.812
DIFF	0.426	1.930	1.482	1.536	0.828	0.481	1.619
DIFF (% of mean dependent variable)	0.024	0.066	0.078	0.142	0.086	0.186	0.581
Mean of dependent variable	17.750	29.297	19.054	10.784	9.580	2.581	2.788
Std. dev. of dep. variable	2.948	2.610	1.635	1.549	2.748	1.100	1.441

Notes: See Table 15.1.

Table 15A.2 Model to explain the share of dependent taxpayers in different income groups in 26 Swiss cantons, 1990, state/local tax rate on gross income of married taxpayers with two children

Dependent variable	S_1 15–20	S_2 20–30	S_3 30–40	S_4 40–50	S_5 50–75	S_6 75–100	S_7 >100
Income group (in 1,000)	15–20	20–30	30–40	40–50	50–75	75–100	>100
Gross income (in 1,000)	17	25	35	45	60	85	175
Constant	6.844	24.414	18.742	18.019	35.531	8.094	2.554
Cantonal/ local tax rate on gross income	0.484	−0.315	0.347	0.064	−0.616**	−0.388**	−0.358**
	(0.87)	(−0.69)	(1.49)	(0.55)	(−3.16)	(−3.51)	(−7.08)
Share of labour force in service sector (in %)	0.048	0.113	0.125*	0.016	−0.248**	−0.080*	0.013
	(1.11)	(1.56)	(3.22)	(0.69)	(−4.18)	(−1.94)	(0.55)
Index of infrastructure of the canton	−0.045**	−0.128**	−0.064*	−0.020*	0.099**	0.083**	0.068**
	(−2.73)	(−4.30)	(−4.08)	(−2.15)	(4.45)	(5.39)	(7.79)
Net in-commuters (in % of total labour force)	0.030	0.057*	0.045*	0.035*	−0.069*	−0.065**	−0.051**
	(1.47)	(1.66)	(2.35)	(2.99)	(−2.43)	(−3.32)	(−4.54)
Population of the canton (in millions)	−0.510	−1.902*	−1.683*	−0.696*	0.924	1.585**	1.245**
	(−0.84)	(−1.91)	(−2.99)	(−2.14)	(1.13)	(2.80)	(3.79)
Dummy for Geneva	−0.649	−2.872	−2.290*	0.571	1.795	2.985**	3.569**
	(−0.62)	(−1.60)	(−2.44)	(0.97)	(1.23)	(2.83)	(5.75)
Dummy for Zug	−1.808	−4.916*	−2.974*	−1.775*	0.473	2.214	1.921*
	(−1.04)	(−1.67)	(−1.88)	(−1.75)	(0.19)	(1.25)	(1.85)
R^2	0.542	0.646	0.717	0.370	0.545	0.740	0.885
SER	0.800	1.649	0.859	0.784	1.694	1.153	0.713
J.–B.	3.652	3.253	0.758	3.925	0.859	0.754	0.336
DIFF	0.934	1.052	1.690	0.327	4.127	3.135	3.795
DIFF (% of mean dependent variable)	0.175	0.060	0.083	0.019	0.160	0.414	0.833
Mean of dependent variable	5.352	17.592	20.379	17.257	25.749	7.566	4.554
Std. dev. of dep. variable	1.182	2.770	1.615	0.987	2.511	2.262	2.105

Note: See Table 15.1.

326

Table 15A.3: *Model to explain the share of self-employed taxpayers in different income groups in 26 Swiss cantons, 1990, state/local tax rate on gross income of married taxpayers with two children*

Dependent variable	S_1	S_2	S_3	S_4	S_5	S_6	S_7
Income group (in 1,000)	15–20	20–30	30–40	40–50	50–75	75–100	>100
Gross income (in 1,000)	17	25	35	45	60	85	175
Constant	1.894	13.404	16.324	23.609	29.077	9.803	15.613
Cantonal/local tax rate on gross income	−0.127	−0.363	0.936	0.855**	0.235	−0.453**	−0.892**
	(−0.36)	(−0.79)	(1.49)	(2.89)	(0.76)	(−2.90)	(−3.98)
Share of labour force in service sector (in %)	0.062*	0.075	0.048	−0.147*	−0.127	0.012	0.035
	(2.18)	(1.03)	(0.46)	(−2.40)	(−1.35)	(0.21)	(0.33)
Index of infrastructure of the canton	−0.018	−0.061*	−0.064	−0.041*	0.009	0.057**	0.150**
	(−1.64)	(−2.06)	(−1.49)	(−1.78)	(0.24)	(2.63)	(3.86)
Net in-commuters (in % of total labour force)	0.047**	0.099*	0.066	0.004	−0.102*	−0.063*	−0.007
	(3.58)	(2.90)	(1.28)	(0.13)	(−2.24)	(−2.30)	(−0.14)
Population of the canton (in millions)	−1.349**	−2.551*	−2.624*	0.515	2.480*	0.474	1.468
	(−3.38)	(−2.56)	(−1.72)	(0.62)	(1.91)	(0.59)	(1.01)
Dummy for Geneva	0.105	0.781	1.098	2.385	−1.049	−0.537	2.648
	(−0.15)	(0.44)	(0.43)	(1.58)	(−0.45)	(−0.36)	(0.96)
Dummy for Zug	−1.623	−6.028*	−2.003	2.642	2.762	−0.669	0.703
	(−1.42)	(−2.04)	(−0.47)	(1.01)	(0.68)	(−0.27)	(0.15)
R^2	0.386	0.326	0.421	0.539	0.191	0.446	0.712
SER	0.798	2.141	2.684	1.778	2.549	1.496	2.587
J.-B.	0.427	0.857	0.107	0.993	1.614	3.245	0.108
DIFF	0.245	1.212	4.558	4.369	1.575	3.660	9.455
DIFF (% of mean dependent variable)	0.073	0.112	0.286	0.274	0.065	0.332	0.537
Mean of dependent variable	3.351	10.827	15.935	15.953	24.406	11.012	17.593
Std. dev. of dep. variable	1.018	2.608	3.528	2.619	2.832	2.010	4.820

Notes: See Table 15.1.

Table 15.4 Model to explain the share of retired persons in different income groups in the 137 largest Swiss municipalities, 1990, state/local tax rate on gross income of retired persons

Dependent variable	S_1	S_2	S_3	S_4	S_5	S_6	S_7
Income group (in 1,000)	15–20	20–30	30–40	40–50	50–75	75–100	>100
Gross income (in 1,000)	17	25	35	45	60	85	175
Constant	35.070	39.885	19.260	5.704	-4.627	-4.374	-3.772
Cantonal/ local tax rate on gross income	0.754*	1.064**	-0.059	-0.124*	-0.045	-0.074*	-0.187*
	(2.09)	(4.72)	(-0.78)	(-1.86)	(-0.43)	(-1.69)	(-3.41)
Share of labour force in service sector (in %)	-0.206**	-0.251**	-0.006	0.064**	0.181**	0.106*	0.141*
	(-6.43)	(-7.10)	(-0.30)	(2.93)	(4.66)	(6.09)	(5.74)
Index of infrastructure of the canton	-0.069**	0.001	0.006	0.030**	0.055**	0.021*	0.016
	(-4.32)	(0.06)	(0.60)	(2.79)	(2.92)	(2.51)	(1.33)
Net in-commuters (in % of total labour force)	-0.014	-0.006	-0.001	0.012*	0.013	0.004	0.002
	(-2.05)	(-0.85)	(-0.28)	(2.54)	(1.58)	(1.09)	(0.36)
Population of the canton (in millions)	10.791**	7.471*	-0.713	-5.642**	-10.880**	-4.650*	-4.596*
	(3.83)	(2.56)	(-0.42)	(-2.96)	(-3.20)	(-3.01)	(-2.09)
Dummy for Geneva	9.287**	5.699**	-2.040*	-3.951**	-5.477**	-2.189*	-1.960*
	(9.01)	(5.12)	(-3.05)	(-5.48)	(-4.46)	(-3.75)	(-2.29)
Dummy for Zug	1.060	2.715	-0.177	-0.549	-1.370	-1.183	-0.694
	(0.55)	(1.35)	(-0.15)	(-0.41)	(-0.58)	(-1.09)	(-0.45)
R^2	0.497	0.358	-0.015	0.210	0.372	0.273	0.353
SER	2.918	3.206	1.957	2.021	3.025	1.768	2.547
J.–B.	112.715*	250.650*	0.201	41.425**	1591.739*	344.189*	352.535*
DIFF	2.926	6.097	0.590	1.242	0.500	0.927	2.822
DIFF (% of mean dependent variable)	0.185	0.222	0.031	0.106	0.043	0.260	0.772
Mean of dependent variable	15.854	27.412	19.030	11.720	11.684	3.565	3.656
Std. dev. of dep. variable	4.113	4.001	1.942	2.274	3.816	2.074	3.167

Notes: See Table 15.1.

Table 15A.5 *Model to explain the share of dependent taxpayers in different income groups in the 137 largest Swiss municipalities, 1990, state/local tax rate on gross income of married taxpayers with two children*

Dependent variable Income group (in 1,000) Gross income (in 1,000)	S_1 15–20 17	S_2 20–30 25	S_3 30–40 35	S_4 40–50 45	S_5 50–75 60	S_6 75–100 85	S_7 >100 175
Constant	7.530	31.140	24.605	16.496	34.258	6.310	1.075
Cantonal/local tax rate on gross income	0.005	−0.937*	−0.049	0.245*	−0.489*	−0.486**	−0.437*
	(0.02)	(−3.31)	(−0.27)	(2.22)	(−4.19)	(−6.39)	(−4.63)
Share of labour force in service sector (in %)	−0.022*	−0.064*	−0.014	−0.024*	−0.089*	0.065**	0.130*
	(−2.07)	(−2.74)	(−0.75)	(−1.80)	(−4.15)	(3.90)	(5.05)
Index of infrastructure of the canton	−0.016*	−0.094*	−0.037*	0.002	0.025*	0.036**	0.033*
	(−3.13)	(−6.88)	(−3.07)	(0.22)	(2.27)	(4.43)	(2.73)
Net in-commuters (in % of total labour force)	0.012*	0.022*	0.009*	0.001	−0.016*	−0.013**	−0.010*
	(5.16)	(4.42)	(2.36)	(0.36)	(−3.47)	(−3.54)	(−1.77)
Population of the canton (in millions)	−0.585	−2.347	1.727	6.465*	−1.217	−3.669*	−5.183*
	(−0.64)	(−1.15)	(1.06)	(5.51)	(−0.64)	(−2.45)	(−2.29)
Dummy for Geneva	−0.150	−1.067	−1.022*	1.567*	1.877*	1.871**	1.647*
	(−0.44)	(−1.42)	(−1.71)	(3.65)	(2.68)	(3.19)	(1.78)
Dummy for Zug	−0.955	−3.875*	−1.992*	0.354	−0.344	−0.971	−0.985
	(−1.52)	(−2.74)	(−1.67)	(0.40)	(−0.24)	(−0.88)	(−0.58)
R^2	0.208	0.451	0.298	0.157	0.273	0.543	0.446
SER	1.094	2.532	1.822	1.364	2.260	1.762	2.698
J.–B.	78.573*	1.893	32.488**	7.414*	5.166*	0.222	153.796**
DIFF	0.010	3.223	0.271	1.468	3.697	4.461	5.340
DIFF (% of mean dependent variable)	0.002	0.200	0.014	0.088	0.136	0.501	0.932
Mean of dependent variable	4.522	16.096	19.527	16.674	27.182	8.913	5.732
Std. dev. of dep. variable	1.229	3.415	2.175	1.486	2.651	2.605	3.626

Notes: See Table 15.1.

Table 15.4.6 Model to explain the share of self-employed taxpayers in different income groups in the 137 largest Swiss municipalities, 1990, state/local tax rate on gross income of married taxpayers with two children

Dependent variable Income group (in 1,000) Gross income (in 1,000)	S_1 15–20 17	S_2 20–30 25	S_3 30–40 35	S_4 40–50 45	S_5 50–75 60	S_6 75–100 85	S_7 >100 175
Constant	2.773	17.204	14.553	18.165	32.140	15.928	26.631
Cantonal/local tax rate on gross income	−0.665*	−1.336**	0.654*	0.458*	0.186	−0.476**	−1.270**
	(−2.05)	(−3.90)	(2.15)	(2.51)	(1.13)	(−5.18)	(−5.48)
Share of labour force in service sector (in %)	0.011	−0.009	−0.036	−0.090**	−0.130**	−0.016	0.190**
	(0.84)	(−0.32)	(−1.16)	(−4.12)	(−4.31)	(−0.79)	(3.00)
Index of infrastructure of the canton	−0.005	−0.062**	−0.018	−0.019	−0.007	0.031**	0.064*
	(−0.71)	(−3.73)	(−0.92)	(−1.59)	(−0.48)	(3.16)	(2.17)
Net in-commuters (in % of total labour force)	0.010**	0.015*	0.012*	−0.001	−0.008	−0.013**	0.001
	(3.53)	(2.50)	(1.88)	(−0.30)	(−1.18)	(−2.93)	(0.02)
Population of the canton (in millions)	4.195**	13.635**	5.841*	2.633	−3.543	−6.867**	−22.740**
	(3.66)	(5.51)	(2.15)	(1.35)	(−1.31)	(−3.80)	(−4.10)
Dummy for Geneva	1.409**	3.149**	3.200**	2.425**	0.013	−0.288	−2.233
	(3.32)	(3.47)	(3.21)	(3.41)	(0.01)	(−0.41)	(−0.99)
Dummy for Zug	−0.285	−5.437**	−1.417	1.079	0.929	−2.221*	−2.277
	(−0.37)	(−3.18)	(−0.71)	(0.73)	(0.47)	(−1.67)	(−0.55)
R^2	0.145	0.170	0.131	0.282	0.207	0.211	0.317
SER	1.259	2.743	2.971	2.329	3.122	2.107	6.141
J.-B.	128.390**	6.456**	17.381**	2.459	1.915	4.007	2.424
DIFF	1.330	4.596	3.617	2.743	1.406	4.370	15.519
DIFF (% of mean dependent variable)	0.450	0.518	0.290	0.212	0.058	0.342	0.629
Mean of dependent variable	2.955	8.874	12.480	12.921	24.452	12.788	24.681
Std. dev. of dep. variable	1.362	3.010	3.188	2.748	3.507	2.372	7.431

Notes: See Table 15.1.

330

Index